MARRIAGE, THE FAMILY, AND PERSONAL FULFILLMENT

MARRIAGE, THE FAMILY, AND PERSONAL FULFILLMENT

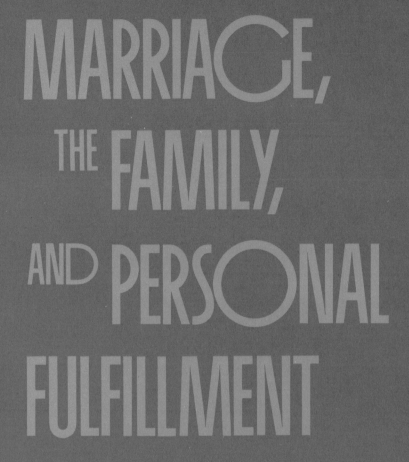

David A. Schulz
University of Delaware

Stanley F. Rodgers
Grace Cathedral, San Francisco

Prentice-Hall, Inc., Englewood Cliffs, New Jersey

Library of Congress Cataloging in Publication Data

Schulz, David A.   1933–
    Marriage, the family, and personal fulfillment.

    Bibliography: p. 393
    1. Marriage—United States.   2. Family—United
States.   3. Interpersonal relations.   4. Self-actuali-
zation (Psychology)   I. Rodgers, Stanley F., 1928–
joint author.   II. Title.
HQ728.S363   301.42'0973   74-19398
ISBN   0-13-559377-8

Printed in the United States of America

10 9 8 7 6 5 4 3 2

PRENTICE-HALL INTERNATIONAL, INC., *London*
PRENTICE-HALL OF AUSTRALIA, PTY. LTD., *Sydney*
PRENTICE-HALL OF CANADA, LTD., *Toronto*
PRENTICE-HALL OF INDIA PRIVATE LIMITED, *New Delhi*
PRENTICE-HALL OF JAPAN, INC., *Tokyo*

ACKNOWLEDGMENTS

Grateful acknowledgment is made to the following sources for permission to re-print:

Quotations on pages 17, 28–29, 38, 51, 53, 248, 249, 250, and 382, excerpted from *Becoming Partners: Marriage and Its Alternatives* by Carl R. Rogers. Copyright © 1972 by Carl R. Rogers. Used with permission of Delacorte Press.

Excerpts on pages 84–85 from *Invitation to Sociology* by Peter L. Berger. Copyright © 1963 by Peter L. Berger. Reprinted by permission of Doubleday & Company, Inc.

Illustrations on pages 115, 116, 118, and 119, from Charlotte M. Dienhart, *Basic Human Anatomy and Physiology*, 2nd ed. (Philadelphia: W. B. Saunders, 1973). Re-printed by permission of W. B. Saunders Company.

Figures 6–5 and 6–6, adapted from William H. Masters and Virginia E. Johnson, *Human Sexual Response*, page 5. Copyright © 1966 by Little, Brown and Company.

Photographs on pages 152 and 153 courtesy of Ortho Pharmaceutical Corporation, Raritan, N.J., and Youngs Drug Products Corporation, Piscataway, N.J.

CHAPTER OPENING QUOTATIONS

Chapter 1: 1 Cor. 13:1–2.

Chapter 2: Excerpted from *Becoming Partners: Marriage and Its Alternatives*, p. 220, by Carl R. Rogers. Copyright © 1972 by Carl R. Rogers. Used with permission of Delacorte Press.

Chapter 3: Martin Buber, *To Hallow This Life* (New York: Harper & Row, 1958), pp. 24–25. Reprinted by permission.

Chapter 4: Excerpted from "Why War?" Chapter XXV, of *Collected Papers of Sigmund Freud*, Volume V, edited by James Strachey. Published by Basic Books, Inc., by arrangement with The Hogarth Press, Ltd., and The Institute of Psycho-Analysis, London.

Chapter 5: Lester A. Kirkendall and Roger W. Libby, "Interpersonal Relationships—Crux of the Sexual Renaissance," *Journal of Social Issues* 22 (1966): 45. Reprinted by permission.

Chapter 6: Herant A. Katchadourian and Donald T. Lunde, *Fundamentals of Human Sexuality* (New York: Holt, Rinehart & Winston, Inc., 1972), p. 23. Copyright © 1972 by Holt, Rinehart & Winston, Inc. Reprinted by permission.

Chapter 7: Kingsley Davis and Judith Blake, "Social Structure and Fertility: An Analytic Approach," in Rose L. Coser, ed., *The Family: Its Structure and Functions* (New York: St. Martin's Press, Inc., 1964). Reprinted by permission.

Chapter 8: Quoted in Katchadourian and Lunde, *Fundamentals of Human Sexuality*, p. 23.

Chapter 9: Bronislaw Malinowski, *Sexual Life of Savages* (New York: Harcourt Brace Jovanovich, Inc., 1929), p. 24. Reprinted by permission.

Chapter 10: Reprinted by permission of William Morrow & Co., Inc. from *Coming of Age in Samoa*, p. 105, by Margaret Mead. Copyright © 1928, 1955, 1961 by Margaret Mead.

Chapter 11: R. A. Nicholson, *Rumi* (London: Allen & Unwin, Ltd., 1950), pp. 122–23. Reprinted by permission.

Chapter 12: Benjamin M. Spock, "Women and Children: Male Chauvinist Spock Recants—Almost," in Louise K. Howe, ed., *The Future of the Family* (New York: Simon and Schuster, 1972), p. 155. Copyright © 1971 by Benjamin Spock. Reprinted by permission of the Robert Lescher Literary Agency, New York.

Chapter 13: Erik Erikson, *Childhood and Society* (New York: W. W. Norton, 1963), p. 405. Reprinted by permission.

Chapter 14: Nicholas von Hoffman, commentary in the *Washington Post*, June 5, 1970. Copyright © The Washington Post. Reprinted by permission.

Chapter 15: Rosalyn Moran, "The Singles in the Seventies," in Joann Delora and Jack Delora, eds., *Intimate Life Styles* (Pacific Palisades, Calif.: Goodyear Publishing Company, 1973), p. 344. Reprinted by permission.

Chapter 16: Nathaniel Hawthorne, *The Blithedale Romance*.

Chapter 17: Sidney M. Jouard, "Reinventing Marriage: The Perspective of a Psychologist," in Herbert A. Otto, *The Family in Search of a Future: Alternate Models for Moderns*, pp. 44–45, © 1970. Reprinted by permission of Prentice-Hall, Inc., Englewood Cliffs, N.J.

To
HELENÈ
and
HELEN

CONTENTS

ix

**PART FOUR
ALTERNATIVES**

PART FIVE
THE
FUTURE
OF
MARRIAGE

PREFACE

Much is heard about the crises affecting marriage and family life in America today. This book provides a perspective on the process of change that is taking place. It examines marriage and family life and tries to assess the costs, benefits, and risks that seem to be associated with various styles of partnerships. Marriage is seen in the context of its possibilities for offering personal fulfillment to each of the partners. It is compared with other nonmarital styles of partnerships without the assumption that our traditional understanding of what is involved in marriage will (or should) satisfy everyone.

In our time marriage is becoming more of a personal contract in which we hold increasingly high expectations for personal satisfaction and fulfillment. Perhaps no other people have expected so much of marriage as a means of contributing to personal growth and fulfillment as we do. We do so in a time in which all intimate partnerships are being subjected to intense stress and strain in an antipersonal society that does not provide great rewards for the skills of intimacy.

One of the exciting things that is happening to our traditional understanding of the marriage partnership is that we are discovering that it can be more flexible than we were inclined to believe just a few years ago. Roles can be made more adaptable to individual needs, and couples can have a great deal more personal freedom to develop close friendships outside of marriage than we were inclined to think proper or possible not so long ago. Children need not "complete" a marriage, nor for that matter, need marriage complete a man's or a woman's life.

A result is the vast burgeoning of different styles of partnerships, each providing a somewhat different response to our needs for intimacy. Just what do they have to offer us? Is their promise worth their apparent risks? This book considers these questions not in terms of a theoretical model of how marriage and the family function (or should function) as social institutions, but rather in terms of how differing life styles affect the individual person and are likely to add to, or detract from, his or her chances of personal fulfillment. This assessment is made on the basis of clinical experience, case studies, personal accounts, and social criticisms. In the nature of the case, we know more at present about traditional marriage and some of its less dramatic alterations. We know less about living together outside of marriage or choosing the option of remaining single for life; we are just beginning to develop a body of reliable information about communal life styles. But we know enough to begin to assess some of the likely consequences of these choices, and this is what this book tries to do.

Particular thanks is due the following persons who attended two-day conferences in San Francisco and New York in order to provide valuable criticisms and offer useful insights: Marlene Adams, Pat Allen, John Allison, Leah Miller Clarke, John Ehle, Jr., James D. Hansen, T. Robert Moseley, Bob Tallmon, and Reginald Touchton. The authors also are deeply grateful to a number of persons who have read the manuscript in its several drafts: Carlfred B. Broderick, Helen M. Hacker, Diane Levande, John Levinson, M.D., Roy H. Rodgers, and Constantina Safilios-Rothschild.

Helene Schulz provided most of the library research that helped to broaden our base of information. Helen Rodgers typed the first draft of the manuscript under trying circumstances in San Miguel, Mexico. Both have offered valuable comments and suggestions from time to time. Phil Rosenberg greatly improved our first draft through his careful editing, and Ann Torbert made the production process run smoothly through her dedicated efforts. Finally, Ed Stanford deserves thanks for his constant encouragement and his superior managerial skills so clearly evident throughout our association with Prentice-Hall.

This book has undoubtedly been greatly improved by the efforts of all of these people. The responsibility for any shortcomings, nevertheless, must fall upon the authors who were brazen enough to feel that they had anything at all to say about marriage in a time in which so much is happening.

DAVID A. SCHULZ
STANLEY F. RODGERS

MARRIAGE, THE FAMILY, AND PERSONAL FULFILLMENT

1 INTRODUCTION

Though I speak with the tongues of men and of angels, and have not love, I am become as sounding brass, or a tinkling cymbal. And though I have the gift of prophecy, and understand all mysteries, and all knowledge, and though I have all faith, so that I could remove mountains, and have not love, I am nothing.

St. Paul

Loving partnerships such as marriage do not just happen, they must be consciously developed. Couples who have been married for many years often tell us that it takes a lot of *work* to keep a marriage going. Young people just getting married often say that they intend to make their marriage work. This sometimes means that they intend to make their partnership flexible enough to meet their personal needs even though such flexibility may change their whole idea of what marriage ought to be. Such couples are taking an experimental approach to their marriage.

Whatever the cultural climate, whatever the age, marriage has always been a venture into the unknown for the young couple about to form such a partnership. Whatever society prescribes as an ideal for their marriage, whatever the experience of marriage they may have acquired through their observation of their parents or others, *their* marriage is something unique if only in that they are two unique persons who are entering into it. Whether it works or not, whether they can change it to meet their evolving needs or not, whether they can work out together a mutually satisfying and fulfilling partnership—or not—is never pre-determined. Marriage, therefore, is always an adventure, whether it is entered into with awareness or simply accepted as a "natural" thing to do.

No book about marriage can eliminate the unknowns from such an adventure. Regardless of what we know from the experience of others about getting married or forming partnerships, such knowledge cannot be simply applied to particular cases in the way general principles in, say, geometry or physics can be applied to specific instances. Knowledge may help us reduce the uncertainty of forming partnerships but it can never eliminate it. Accordingly, this book is not intended to provide a set of guidelines about how to form loving intimate partnerships such as marriage—although some guidelines are given from time to time. It is intended to increase the reader's knowledge of some of the issues involved so that however one feels about getting married—or not getting married—she or he may shape her or his own partnerships with greater awareness. In the last analysis, the "how to do it" of partnership can be worked out only in the context of a developing partnership.

Love Is Intimate Self-Disclosure

Part of what is commonly meant when we say that love is a very personal thing is that it involves the intimate disclosure of a unique self. In intimate partnerships our personal idiosyncrasies are very important in determining whether or not the partnership develops fruitfully.

A growing partnership is one in which this self-disclosure can take place at ever deepening levels of self-awareness. The nakedness of lovers is symbolic of their history of self-disclosure. We need not assume that this nakedness demands the type of complete self-disclosure in which there can be no secrets. We need assume merely that in a loving partnership the partners feel able to reveal much more of themselves than they normally do. They feel free to "be themselves" with each other.

Love Nourishes Growth, Growth Nourishes Love

Personal growth and self-actualization are important dimensions of loving partnerships. As we conceive of them, partnerships have lost their vitality if not their love when such growth and self-actualization do not occur. To say this is to expect a great deal of partnerships such as marriage, for in our Western tradition we have not always expected marriage to play a significant role in the personal growth of those who participate in it. Indeed, many people contend that it is expecting too much of marriage or, for that matter, any other form of partnership today.

When two people grow in partnership, isn't it just as likely that they will grow apart and fall out of love as that they will grow together in increasing love? We all know of partnerships in which the partners grew apart because one partner developed faster than the other. This happens to couples before marriage as well as after, and even unmarried partners who are living together sometimes find that even their rather flexible partnership is not flexible enough to permit more rapid growth in one of the partners. What are we to do about this?

A common response is to dismiss the importance of personal growth on the grounds that a partnership should be a "team effort" and self-actualization and personal growth seem to be essentially selfish goals. Maybe it really isn't important that marriages retain the vitality that brought the partners together in the first place. Maybe the joys of growth and self-disclosure *ought* to be short-lived. After twenty-five years perhaps it's a good thing for the partners in a marriage to settle for comfort and convenience rather than going through the hassle of the perpetual adjustments that are needed when a relationship is growing. Growth, whenever it occurs, does not come about without struggle and it often brings pain.

This is a very difficult matter indeed. Life would be a lot simpler if people could grow to greater self-actualization—that is, if they could realize more and more of what they are capable of becoming—and at the same time find that their partnership was deepening and growing as a result. But this is not always possible.

It is a matter of fundamental values to assert that the personal growth of the partners should not be sacrificed for the sake of keeping them together. This can be seen as a priority to be put forth when entering into partnerships such as marriage as well as a rule of thumb to be applied—but not necessarily always followed—when it looks like the partners have to choose between their own personal fulfillment and the partnership they have entered into.

Love Requires Relationship

At the same time we also know that love, even in self-actualizing people, is not a strictly personal matter. Whatever self-love we have acquired depends upon our having been loved by others. Our parents, friends, and lovers have significantly shaped, if not totally determined, our capacity to love. Thus our experience of having been loved provides us with inner prescriptions as to how we should go about our own loving. It is not possible for us to grow and develop unless our basic human need for love and acceptance has been adequately met.[1]

So also, love requires an object for its expression. If we cannot love ourselves, it is not likely that we can love others, but if we love only ourselves we have severely diminished the stature of our love and restricted its sphere of influence. The Classical Greek philosophers devoted a great deal of analytic thought to this matter of loving, and some of their helpful distinctions are presented in Chapter 10. But love in all of its forms is as much an attribute of relationships as it is a characteristic of personalities.

In its fundamental everyday attire, love means caring for others, looking after them, seeing to their well being, ". . . for richer for poorer, in sickness and in health, . . . till death us do part."[2]

People often assume that because caring is very much related to the amount of time spent with those we care for, the longer the relationship, the more caring there will be and the more loving. Thus they ask: "Isn't it important that marriage be for life?" "Must not any partnership last a long time for it to become a deep and meaningful experience?" "After all, what do people know about love who have not had the responsibility of caring for another person over the years?" Indeed, caring *is* a significant part of what we mean by "working" at a marriage and it is an important part of any intimate partnership. For this reason this book has a lot to say about loving in partnerships. But such a conception of caring for others must be balanced by an awareness that the members of a partnership also must work for their own self-actualization. Caring for one's partner is only half of the relationship, for it is also important to care for and nurture into being one's own creative, growing self.

[1] Abraham Maslow, *Toward a Psychology of Being*, 2nd ed. (New York: Van Nostrand Reinhold Company, 1968), p. 25.
[2] *The Book of Common Prayer* (New York: Oxford University Press, 1952), p. 302.

MARRIAGE AS AN AMERICAN PARTNERSHIP

In America marriage is the social institution designed to harness for the benefit of society (as well as of the marital partners) the energy of an intimate partnership. Marriage is always a social contract, although the social functions it fulfills are more prominent in some societies than in our own.[3] This is in part because we think of it, ideally, as initiated and maintained simply for the benefit of the two people who fell in love. In our society when two adults who are able to support themselves fall in love they are expected to get married.

High Expectations

Judging by statistics, marriage is more popular today than it has ever been. In America today, 84.8 percent of the men and 84.5 percent of the women between the ages of twenty-five and fifty-four are married.[4] Because marriage is a social institution that has been with us for a long time, we have some widely accepted understandings about what a marriage ought to be. We will discuss these more specifically in Chapter 10, but here we can say that most Americans see marriage as the deepest, most vital partnership in a person's life. We tend to look to it for an experience of growth and vitality that we hope will be richly rewarding to both husband and wife. These high expectations with regard to marriage derive from the traditions of romanticism, Western Christian

[3]It is probably true that few societies place as much emphasis as ours on the personal choice of a couple who declare that they are "in love" to form the basis of a marriage. See William Stephens' assessment in *The Family in Cross-Cultural Perspective* (New York: Holt, Rinehart & Winston, Inc., 1963), pp. 190–207. Ralf Linton observes, "Most societies look upon marriage as a legal contract either between the individuals involved or between their respective families." *The Study of Man* (New York: Appleton-Century-Crofts, 1936), p. 177.

[4]U.S. Bureau of the Census, *Statistical Abstracts of the United States: 1973*, 94th ed. (Washington, D.C.: U.S. Government Printing Office, 1973), p. 38.

teachings about monogamy, concern for the preservation of private property, and the high esteem with which our culture regards personal freedom.

What seems to be happening in America today, however, is that, while we may be in some ways expecting greater things of marriage than we have in the past, we also are willing (or forced) to settle for much less. Study after study sadly suggests that marriage today typically is a quite colorless affair. These studies suggest that at least a near majority of us have settled for marriages of convenience that are at best merely comfortable because they have become routinized and demand little of the partners. If our understanding of what is happening is correct, the image that more and more young people are acquiring of marriage is not a good one. On the college campuses coeds talk of not marrying at all because of their distaste for housewifery and domestic roles. Young men and women are deferring marriage longer and longer before taking the final step.[5] Our impersonal society generates a high level of loneliness and a foreboding sense of separation. A part of our apparent eagerness to enter into marriage, therefore, may be seen not as the result of an attraction to marriage but as an attempt to escape from the loneliness and impersonality of our technologically driven society.[6] Americans thus tend to come to marriage with high expectations and great needs at a time when the institution of marriage is being subjected to enormous social pressures which make it difficult for persons to realize these expectations in marriage.

Romantic Love Complex. Particularly hard hit is the romantic young couple who fall in love and marry, only to wake up and discover that the "honeymoon is over." Their response to this realization will shape the future style of their marriage. They can pretend that it is not in fact over, simulate happiness, and live for a long time without acknowledging the lack of a deep intimate partnership. They can cease to expect very much of their marriage and settle for a more or less comfortable routine characterized by lifelessness rather than vitality. They can persist in a peaceful coexistence, "for the sake of the children," or because there is nothing better in sight. Another alternative, however, is that they can begin to face their disillusionment and fashion new expectations. Inherent within this alternative is a demand that they utilize the skills of creative interaction—which are not easily acquired in our society—and, perhaps, that they consider the possibility of a totally new kind of partnership.

[5]Even the median age of first marriage has begun to increase since 1950. *Statistical Abstract*, p. 65.
[6]See Jules Henry's critique in *Culture Against Man* (New York: Random House, 1963), pp. 22ff.

In any event, a part of the satisfaction that is to be derived from any of these alternatives results from the expectations that have been realized. The higher the expectation, the greater the difficulty of realizing it. High expectations are easy to hold when it is not necessary to face the problems of living together. This issue is resolved only in part by college students who choose to live together before marriage, as we shall see in Chapter 5. Very few societies expect marriage to depend as heavily upon the personal choice and skills of the partners as we do. In many societies of the world today marriages are arranged. In such societies couples are not expected to be in love before they get married —though they may come to love each other after they have been married for a number of years. Marriage, in these societies, is primarily a social contract uniting kinship groups. The couple is expected to work out a reasonable way of managing their household, raising their children, and fulfilling their other social obligations, but even in these endeavors, they are greatly assisted by their kin. In contrast, we expect marriage not only to meet many social needs (such as the bearing and raising of children and the establishment of a fundamental economic partnership that is the major consumer unit in our economy) but also to fulfill the personal needs of the partners. Furthermore, the partners are expected to work these matters out as best they can with comparatively little assistance from others. Thus our romantic young couple faced with the decision to marry or not to marry must make that decision largely alone. They are then expected to realize a much higher set of expectations in regard to what this marriage will accomplish for them than is true in most societies—also largely on their own.

If the couple should decide to have children—as most do in our society—they are likely to experience further difficulties. In the view of some experts on the family, parenthood has been even more romanticized than marriage in our culture.[7] Children are idealized as natural assets and the considerable impact they have upon the partnership is often ignored or minimized in discussions of the subject. Although it is often pointed out that children offer their parents an opportunity for a fuller life, young parents or prospective parents are not often warned that they also sap the energy and the attention of the marital partners, who are more totally responsible for their upbringing in our culture than is true in most societies. These matters will be discussed more fully in Chapter 12.

Two results of our placing high and unrealistic expectations on partnerships such as marriage at the same time that they are subjected to enormous social stress are the increasing divorce rate and the search for alternative kinds of partnership demanding new and different life styles.

[7]See E. E. LeMasters, *Parents in Modern America*, rev. ed. (Homewood, Ill.: The Dorsey Press, 1974), pp. 18–32.

The understanding of what a marriage ought to be thus seems to be changing for many people today.

Marriage Is Changing

Our newspapers and magazines are full of glimpses into different life styles. The middle-class suburban family with its two children, ranch house, two cars, cat, and dog is placed alongside of quite different styles in our advertisements and news items. Catchphrases like "the sexual revolution," "the generation gap," and "women's liberation" point to aspects of our traditional understanding of marriage and the relationship between the sexes that seem to be crying out for changes. The middle-class model of what a marriage ought to be is contested by swingers, communards, sexual libertarians, and famous actresses who announce the birth of twins while disclaiming any intention to marry. A twenty-six-year-old woman remarks, "I really would like to have a baby. No, I don't want to get married, but I really would like to have a baby to care for. I think I am the kind of person who really could give a lot to a child."[8] Most of these people come from respectable middle-class families and have found middle-class marriage lacking in some respects. The whole matter was brought home to middle America in a most dramatic way in the spring of 1973 when a sports page headline announced that two pitchers for the New York Yankees had decided to exchange families.

The gay liberation front has been active in most of our cities and on our campuses, and homosexuals are today petitioning our courts to legalize their marriages. A thirty-six-year-old man remarks, "Bill and I have lived together for nine years, both here and in Chicago. Our relationship is better than most of the marriages of our friends and the people I work with. We think it is criminal that we can't be legally married and that the church will not bless our relationship."

Living together without benefit of clergy is becoming increasingly common on campus as well as off. "We plan to get married in about a year. We're living together to see what it is like. I think if my mom and dad had lived together before they were married they would have found out that they weren't going to make it and would have avoided twelve years of misery," says a twenty-five-year-old woman. As we shall see in Chapter 5, living together does not seem to be primarily a kind of trial marriage; there are many reasons why persons choose to live together. Because premarital intercourse is no longer considered unacceptable, at least among the college educated young, sexual relationships assume a validity of their own. "You don't have to love someone to go

[8]This quotation and the others so generally identified in this chapter are taken from the clinical experience of Stanley F. Rodgers.

Bonnie Freer, Rapho Guillumette

to bed with him," remarks an eighteen-year-old coed. Living together for some means little more than an extended weekend; for others it amounts to a kind of relationship that differs little from traditional marriage.

A Conflict of Attitudes

A recent Gallup poll confirms a marked difference of opinion between young people and their elders on the matter of premarital intercourse and experimental partnerships. "Seven out of ten persons twenty-one and older believe premarital sex relations are 'wrong.' One does not need a survey, therefore, to be sure that a large percentage would also be likely to disapprove of the idea of trial marriages and communal living." Students, on the other hand, approve of premarital sex by a ratio of two to one.[9]

In general, those most likely to favor greater sexual freedom and experimentation in marital life styles are under thirty-five, college-educated, middle-class, of "liberal" persuasion politically, and less likely than the average American to say that religion is an important part of their lives. Those opposed are likely to be over thirty-five, non-college-educated, working-class "conservative" who find religion important.[10] Thus, as we shall see in Chapter 10, the term "generation gap" does not adequately describe the confrontation of life styles that is a significant factor in the American scene today. Indeed, in some ways those

[9]George Gallup, "Is there Really a Sexual Revolution?" *The Critic* (New York: The Thomas Moore Association, 1972), p. 23.
[10]Gallup, "Is There Really a Sexual Revolution?" p. 26.

over thirty-five are more radical in their experimentation than those under this arbitrary age, because they are experimenting with alternatives to traditional monogamous marriage whereas it is likely that the majority of college undergraduates still hold lifelong monogamy with exclusive rights in the spouse to be the ideal form of marriage. Much will depend on how successful the current experimentation in alternative styles of partnerships seems to be to the young people who are watching.

Finally, a small percentage of our population seems to be experimenting in a new style of partnership, the distinctive feature of which is that the individuals involved get married several times over the course of their lives. About one divorce occurs each year for every three marriages in the nation as a whole. Most of these divorced persons will remarry only once, but a small number will marry three or more times, tempting some observers to claim that we are beginning to practice "serial monogamy"—that is, a system in which a person has several spouses, but only one at a time. A nine-year-old girl observes, "It's good at Christmas. We have eight grandparents and they all send us presents. But I miss my real dad." And a fifty-two-year-old man reminisces, "My first wife was good with the children and life was fairly comfortable. My second wife was always bothered by the children and she and that damned interior decorator were always doing something to the house. My present wife and I do a lot of traveling since I don't have to work so hard these days."

The increasing rate of divorce and the more overt experimentation with alternative styles of partnerships lead us to ask an important question: How typical is traditional marriage?

How Typical Is Traditional Marriage?

It is difficult to answer this question precisely. We do not have reliable studies upon which to determine the extent to which people are experimenting. We do not have the detailed studies that will help us determine if a deviation from the traditional pattern is the result of voluntary experimentation or of circumstances beyond the control of one or both partners. Census data can tell us something about the kinds of partnerships that are common, but they do not tell us much about the quality of the partnerships. Furthermore, these data will tell us nothing about partnerships that are illegal, since most persons would not report such partnerships even if the Census Bureau were asking about them.

Nevertheless, we can determine that about 42 million adults over the age of eighteen either are not married, are not living with their spouse, or have been married more than once.[11] We do not know how many of

---

[11]*Statistical Abstracts*, p. 38.

the single persons will never marry or how many intend to marry but just haven't gotten around to it yet. Of the unmarried, only those who intend to marry can be said to be following the traditional pattern. These are probably a small portion of the 42 million. A rough estimate, then, of those adults who do not live in a style of partnership that has the traditional structure would be around 40 million.[12]

Approaching the matter from another perspective, we know that extramarital sexual relationships are common. To the extent that they are, this is evidence of a violation of our traditional norm regarding exclusive sexual rights in the spouse. Kinsey's studies in the 1950s are still the best source of data on this matter, and they report that about half of the married men and about a third of the married women had engaged in extramarital sexual intercourse at least once.[13] Studies such as Cuber and Harroff's suggest that the percentage is higher if we limit our sample to the upper middle-class professional person.[14]

Perhaps the most disturbing findings—from the point of view of those who tend to see the changes that are coming about in our intimate life styles as a crisis—come from clinical sources and small intensive studies. These sources help us understand something about the *quality* of American marriages, though they do not help us determine how representative their findings are. Masters and Johnson believe that at least half of the married couples in America are unable to use sexual intercourse as a means of intimate communication.[15] Cuber and Harrof tell us that only a very small percentage of the couples in their study of professional persons had "good" relationships—by the couple's own understanding of what constitutes a good relationship—and most of these were to be found among the unmarried.[16]

Taking a broad overview of American marriages, marriage counselors estimate that the total marriage failure rate is between 50 and 55 percent. This includes 32 percent legal termination, 15 to 20 percent who would rate their marriage as "very unhappy," and 3 percent who have a permanent separation.[17] The remaining 45 to 50 percent are rated as

[12]The term "structure" here refers to a set of traditionally interrelated roles, such as father-child, husband-wife, mother-child. These roles make up the structure of the nuclear family and entail relatively well understood expectations of appropriate behavior associated with them. See Chapter 11 for some further discussion of their content.

[13]Alfred C. Kinsey et al., *Sexual Behavior in the Human Female* (Philadelphia: Saunders, 1963).

[14]John F. Cuber and Peggy B. Harroff, *Sex and the Significant Americans* (Baltimore: Penguin Books, 1968).

[15]William E. Masters and Virginia E. Johnson, *Human Sexual Inadequacy* (Boston: Little Brown, 1970).

[16]Cuber and Harroff, *Sex and the Significant Americans.*

[17]Lloyd Saxton, *The Individual, Marriage, and the Family* (Belmont, Calif.: Wadsworth Publishing Company, Inc., 1972), p. 267.

"average" to "very happily married." To the extent that satisfaction with marriage is a part of our normal expectation, those who report that they are not satisfied with their marriage could be said not to be living up to the expectations we place on marriage. Thus a probably conservative "guesstimate" would say that perhaps about 30 to 35 percent of our marriages can be said to be meeting in practice both the structural and the qualitative expectations associated with our beliefs about what marriage should be. Although it is not unusual for behavior to fall short of the norms expected, in the case of marriage it seems that the behavior of almost two-thirds of us falls far short of our ideals.

These findings may help to explain why some people are directly challenging the ideals. The number of persons who are intentionally experimenting with alternative kinds of partnerships is at present probably quite small, but as dissatisfaction with traditional marriage increases and the social pressures likely to create stress for the traditionally married couple continue to mount, the number who intentionally try another life style will probably increase. At least this is what seems reasonable to expect given the information available to us in the middle of the 1970s. This experimentation need not be seen as indicative of a "crisis," although it undoubtedly will create some problems for persons who cannot adjust either their own behavior or their expectations of others. It is a basic assumption of this book that such experimentation can—and we hope will—bring about some viable creative alternatives to marriage as we have traditionally tended to define it. If these alternatives can create loving intimate partnerships in which partners can develop their potentials and fulfill their needs for intimacy, then they should be acceptable regardless of the extent to which they depart from conventional marriage.

SUMMARY

We cannot love others if we do not love ourselves and we are not able to love ourselves unless we have been loved. In much condensed form, these seem to be the lessons of love we have discovered from our experience of loving. Americans expect marriage to fulfill much more of the personal needs of the partners for love and acceptance than most societies of the world have typically expected. When we talk about marriage as a self-actualizing partnership, we are expecting even more. Without doubt marriage, in its traditional form, cannot meet these expectations for everyone, given the tremendous needs we bring to it and the enormous stress social forces place upon it. As a result, while more and more of us are getting married than ever before in our history, we are also getting out of marriage at an increasing rate. Many of us seem to be experimenting with modifications of traditional marriage and some few of us are intentionally experimenting with alternative kinds of partnerships and quite different life styles. Rather than see these changes in norms and behavior as symptoms of a "crisis," this book chooses to view them as having at least the potential for leading to creative alternative forms of partnership.

Marriage and what we expect of it are indeed changing in our time, perhaps at a faster pace than we have experienced before. Precisely because it is changing it can continue to offer the possibility for growth and development in our changing world. It is not likely that a return to pre-World War II norms and life styles—even if this were possible—would help us avoid the conflict and solve the problem of the quest for intimacy and community we are presently experiencing in our society. A greater cultural civility, a greater tolerance for alternative life styles in others, will help us to discover creative ways of living together in intimate partnerships and restore new vitality to old life styles intentionally chosen because they meet our personal needs, not lived up to because we are simply expected to live up to them.

PART

ONE

ON BECOMING PARTNERS

2

ON
PARTNERSHIPS

I want to add that the concept of partnerships—married or not—as a vast and promising laboratory has been forced on me by my learnings from [my case studies]. I did not start with this idea at all. I tried to choose reasonably representative people. They did not—and do not—seem to me to be unusual couples or unusual persons, except for their surprising willingness to tell of their life as it is. Only gradually did I see that there is an enormous, exploring experiment going on all about us. What will be our stance toward it?

Carl Rogers

INTRODUCTION

Two people enter into a partnership when they discover that they share an understanding of what each one expects to get out of their relationship. They may largely accept a widely held set of expectations about what it means to be a "good husband" or a "good wife" when they decide to get married, or they may emphasize their own unique understanding of marriage by writing out their own marriage contract—and perhaps publishing it in one of our popular magazines.[1] They may not have a formal agreement at all, they may simply have "an understand-

[1] For examples see the contract of Harriet Mary Cody and Harvey Joseph Sadis in *Ms.* (June 1973), pp. 63–67 (reprinted in this volume, pp. 260–65); and that of Joyce Winslow and Jack Richards in Robert H. Rimmer, ed., *Adventures in Loving* (New York: New American Library, 1973), pp. 132–35.

17

ing." The point is that a partnership is more than a relationship, because the partners make explicit in some way what they expect of each other in their continuing relationship. They develop a kind of "contract" that binds each to the other whether that contract has legal status or not.

This chapter assumes that whatever else a partnership such as marriage has going for it, it should have the kind of understanding or "contract" that helps the partners to grow into richer fuller human beings. In Abraham Maslow's words, it should help them in the process of "self-actualization."[2]

Self-actualization is a basic human need in Maslow's view. Every human being has the need to become what he or she is capable of becoming. But this need cannot be met, according to Maslow, until certain other needs are reasonably well met. The need for safety and security is at the base of his heirarchy of human needs and self-actuali-

[2]A discussion of the meaning of this term is found in Abraham H. Maslow, *Toward a Psychology of Being*, 2nd ed. (New York: Van Nostrand Reinhold Company, 1968), pp. 97ff. See also Abraham H. Maslow, *The Farthest Reaches of Human Nature* (New York: The Viking Press, 1971), pp. 41–56.

zation is at the top. When the lower needs—which Maslow calls deprivation needs—have been met, the individual is free to take steps to meet the higher need for self-actualization. We posit, in this chapter, that human beings can best meet this need for self-actualization in creative, life-giving partnerships.

The profile of partnership that is developed in this chapter focuses on what goes on between persons in partnerships. The dimensions of intimacy, love and romance, commitment, dependability, vitality, separateness and togetherness, openness and self-disclosure point to important aspects of this process and can help us to understand that self-actualization can take place within a wide variety of life styles. When we are so bold as to ask "What are the costs, the risks, and the benefits of this particular style of partnership?" our profile can help us look more thoughtfully at what is going on between the partners in their struggle for self-actualization. It is important to avoid letting ourselves become overly concerned about the particular form their partnership may take.

BASIC HUMAN NEEDS

Whether or not there are such things as basic human needs has been the subject of a continuing debate in the social sciences.[3] Obviously, food, air, water, shelter, and sex are essential for the survival of the individual and the species, and thus these needs may be considered "basic," in the sense that they are common to all human beings.

Are there other basic human needs? Some social scientists contend that there are not, for they feel that, except for the fundamental biological needs mentioned above, the other needs people commonly experience are shaped by the culture to which they belong rather than by their basic human nature. For example, we often hear it said that a young child needs a certain amount of privacy—"a room of his own"—if he is to grow into a healthy adult. In our society, given its emphasis on self-reliance, this may well be true, but in other societies with different priorities hundreds of millions of children have grown to be normal, healthy adults even though the idea of privacy for young people was

[3]Gerhard Lenski provides one discussion of this debate in his *Power and Privilege* (New York: Basic Books, 1966), pp. 25–31; another is found in Amatai Etzioni, *The Active Society* (New York: Basic Books, 1968), pp. 622–30.

unheard of. In other words, there may be a need for privacy in contemporary American culture, but this is not a basic human need. It is a need only in a specific sociocultural context.

Recently, however, a number of social scientists have begun to feel that limiting the list of basic human needs to the elementary biological needs for food, air, water, shelter, and sex does not do justice to our sense of what it means to be a human being. Because human nature is a complex phenomenon which requires more than mere survival for its full development, these social scientists reason, there must be needs that are higher than the simple biological needs and yet still qualify as basic human needs in that they are shared by all people regardless of their specific cultures. Among the social scientists who rediscovered and re-emphasized the concept of basic human needs, one of the most important was Abraham Maslow.

As Maslow sees it, human beings have many needs in addition to the elementary biological needs. The most productive way to think of these needs is to imagine them arranged in a hierarchical order. The lower ones must be satisfied before the higher ones can be adequately realized, but all of them are important for full human development.[4] Maslow divides his hierarchy of needs into four levels:

1. safety and security needs
2. needs for belongingness, love, and acceptance
3. needs for self-respect and self-esteem
4. the need for self-actualization.

Shortly we shall be discussing the specific needs Maslow assigns to each level of this hierarchy, but first let us consider why Maslow considers needs to be arranged hierarchically. According to Maslow, the mistake made by those social scientists who would reduce the list of human needs to simple biological needs is that they fail to recognize that human beings everywhere find it essentially important to feel that they belong to some entity larger than themselves, feel a need to love and be loved, feel a need to be accepted in their community—if not the larger community that makes up the majority of their society, then at least some smaller community with which they can identify, such as a political movement, a religious sect, or even the subculture of a criminal underworld. Even the bohemian artist who imagines himself to be a total "loner" identifies himself with some community of great artists to which he feels he belongs.

On the other hand, if we accept the idea that the needs to belong, to love and be loved, to be accepted are basic human needs, we must also recognize that they are needs of a different sort than the need for, say,

[4]Abraham Maslow, *Toward a Psychology of Being*, p. 155.

air or food. A human being could survive indefinitely if he were placed in total isolation from all other human beings, but he could not survive for more than a few days without food or more than a few minutes without air. In an important sense the isolated individual would not be living a fully human life, for he would be completely cut off from a wide range of the experiences that we think of as distinctively human. Just as a human being deprived of food or air cannot exist at all, so a human being deprived of a community to which he can feel he belongs, in which he can find love and acceptance, cannot exist as a fully realized human being. Thus, according to Maslow, the need for love is as much a basic human need as is the need for food, although satisfying the latter is obviously a prerequisite for satisfying the former.

Now that we have seen how Maslow justifies expanding the list of basic human needs and why he feels these needs form a hierarchy in which each level is a prerequisite to the next, let us consider his hierarchy of needs in greater detail.

Safety and Security

Our existence as living organisms depends upon our satisfying those needs that Maslow groups together as *safety and security needs*. Our well-being, and indeed our survival, depend upon our success in obtaining sufficient food, shelter, clothing, air, water, and defense. Modern industrialized society has more than provided for these needs for most people, although even in the most affluent countries there are large numbers of desperately poor people who are still struggling to meet their safety and security needs.

Because most Americans do not have to spend most of their energy in the struggle to meet these needs, they are able to turn a good deal of their attention to their higher-level needs. People who are reasonably confident that they will be able to provide food, clothing, and lodging for themselves and their families can afford to give their attention to such things as satisfying their need to be accepted, their need for self-esteem, their need to earn the respect of their peers.

The poor, however, are constantly preoccupied with the starker dimension of the struggle to satisfy the lower-level needs. Repeated frustration, continued deprivation of the basic essentials of our society, the derived sense of hopelessness and powerlessness associated with poverty go a long way toward making a person feel worthless, just as wealth and social status contribute to the feeling of self-respect, the feeling of "being somebody."

It takes a considerable amount of courage to be poor and yet still to retain a positive attitude toward one's inner self. Because the higher-level needs are, as we shall see, so intimately related to the ability to form and preserve successful human partnerships, it is no wonder that

partnerships are difficult to maintain among those whose lower-level needs are not adequately satisfied. Thus marriages tend to break up more frequently in the lower classes than among the better off segments of our society.[5] The continuing blows to the sense of self-esteem are but one of many factors that make it difficult to develop and maintain partnerships in the midst of poverty. In general, we must have a sense of repeated gratification and an expectation of continued reward before we are able to maintain a positive attitude toward ourselves. We must achieve an adequate sense of protection and security before we can risk growth in interpersonal relationships. Before we can venture forth on the journey toward what Maslow calls self-actualization we must have all of our lower-level needs more or less adequately met.

Belonging, Love, and Acceptance

The need for belonging, love, and acceptance cannot be met adequately until the need for safety and security has been satisfied. Our need for

[5]The effects of deprivation upon partnerships such as marriage is well illustrated in such works as Lee Rainwater, "Crucible of Identity," *Dadaelus* (Winter 1965), pp. 172–216; Joyce Ann Ladner, *Tomorrow's Tomorrow* (Garden City, N.Y.: Double-day & Company, Inc., 1971); and David A. Schulz, *Coming Up Black: Patterns of Ghetto Socialization* (Englewood Cliffs, N.J.: Prentice-Hall, Inc., 1969).

belonging, love, and acceptance derives from our nature as social creatures; it is what brings us into the human community. We achieve a
sense of belonging by participating, along with other members of our
society, in a common way of life that includes at least a common language, a more or less common view of the world, and a more or less
established social structure.

In the normal course of development, acceptance or belongingness
is first discovered in the context of family life, where affection and love
are less contingent upon an individual's accomplishments than is generally true in society at large. This is especially true in advanced industrial societies, where the emphasis is on high achievement and is to a
large extent contingent upon performance. People who do not do the
"right" things, who are not adequately productive, or who do not sufficiently conform to the expectations of others in our society are quickly
made to feel left out. Indeed, sociological studies of our society suggest
that large numbers of us do in fact feel left out.[6]

Today the problems of belonging, love, and acceptance are compounded by the rapid rate of change in our society. Traditions are
upset before the generation that spawned them has died. New techniques, new faces, new expectations are the very stuff of our lives, making it increasingly difficult for modern men and women to feel they "belong" to a community that is changing almost from day to day.[7] Less
than a hundred years ago a young person learned the values of his or her
parents and then moved easily into the adult community. Today the
values of one's parents may seem archaic to one's peers, and so countless
thousands of young men and women are caught in a conflict between
the values of two communities, to neither of which they fully belong.

In a complex, rapidly changing, pluralistic society such as ours, one
must be very selective of the values, ideals, and ideas that one encounters. It is not possible to merely "mirror" a culture as complex as ours.
It is unlikely that anyone can manage to develop consistent, wholly
integrated world views that adequately encompass the whole of our cultural heritage. Because we find many people each day who differ from
us in basic values and commitments, who hold different truths to be
self-evident, the development of a consistent and satisfying set of values
and beliefs becomes a difficult task. Yet it is a necessary task, for the

[6]See especially the collection of studies in Eric Josephson and Mary Josephson,
Man Alone (New York: Dell Publishing Co., Inc., 1962); Philip Slater, *The Pursuit
of Loneliness: American Culture at the Breaking Point* (Boston: Beacon Press,
1970); Jules Henry, *Culture Against Man* (New York: Random House, 1963); Erich
Fromm, *The Art of Loving* (New York: Bantam Books, 1970).
[7]The effect of rapid social change upon human relationships is particularly well
described in Warren G. Bennis and Philip E. Slater, *The Temporary Society* (New
York: Harper & Row, 1968), and Alvin Toffler, *Future Shock* (New York: Bantam
Books, 1970).

F. B. Grunzweig, Photo Researchers

things that we value and the way in which we look at ourselves and our world determine, to a considerable extent, what we are able to see in the world around us, how we feel about ourselves, and what we will do with our time and talents.[8]

Self-Respect and Self-Esteem

In achieving a sense of self-respect and self-esteem the individual begins to differentiate himself from his community. He comes to value himself both because of the applause of others and in spite of their con-

[8]In Chapter 10 we attempt to show how ideas and attitudes arising out of our Western heritage have shaped our understanding of love, sex, and marriage and suggest how this understanding has affected our behavior.

demnation. Self-respect and self-esteem thus raise the issue of conformity. If our sense of being somebody is supported *only* by our community, then our self-respect and self-esteem are dependent solely upon the rewards that others can provide. If, however, our sense of self-respect and self-esteem is rooted in a deeper understanding of ourselves, we have the freedom to stand over and against the community whenever something in our value system tells us it is necessary to do so. We can feel free to participate or not to participate. We can feel free to judge the community as we are judged by it.

Obviously, the need for belongingness, love, and acceptance and the need for self-esteem and self-respect are intertwined in complex ways. In the first place, it is virtually impossible to develop a healthy sense of self-respect and self-esteem—a healthy sense of one's own worth—without the aid, especially in one's formative years, of some powerful supportive agency such as a family or group of peers. For example, the young girl who does not feel fully accepted by her parents because they wanted a boy often finds it extremely difficult to develop a high sense of her own worth as an adult. Similarly, the child of either sex who for some reason is rejected by his or her peers may come to feel that there is something wrong with him or her, and unless something happens to change the situation he or she may well suffer in adulthood from a low sense of self-esteem. This is why Maslow ranks the belongingness needs lower on his hierarchy than the self-esteem needs: because the feeling of belonging, of being loved and accepted, is a prerequisite for the sense of self-esteem and self-respect.

Ideally, one's feelings of acceptance and belongingness and one's feelings of self-esteem and self-respect should be complementary, but in many cases they tend to split off and become reciprocal. Many individuals put all their eggs in the basket of belongingness; instead of moving on to develop a sense of their own value on the basis of the strength they derive from feeling accepted, these compulsive "joiners" let the group's acceptance of them replace their own acceptance of themselves. Conversely, compulsive "individualists" are people who can feel secure in their sense of themselves only when they oppose the group. Both of these extreme types represent unhealthy adjustments; the one sacrifices the possibility of self-respect for the security that comes from being accepted while the other cuts himself or herself off from the community in order to preserve a tenuous sort of self-respect. Neither type can enjoy the secure sense of self-esteem that derives from a sure sense of belongingness, of being loved and accepted.

Self-Actualization

Maslow groups the three levels of needs we have been discussing to this point under the general heading of "deprivation needs." A person cannot develop fully as a human being if she or he is deprived of satisfaction on any of these three levels. Maslow also points out, however, that there is a step beyond these needs which can give us more life, more humanness. He calls this level the need for self-actualization. In describing self-actualization, he uses the following words to suggest more fully what he means: "self-fulfillment, emotional maturity, individuation, productiveness, authenticity, full humanness."[9] The term *self-actualization* and its synonyms describe for Maslow the psychological health of the adult.

Maslow describes the healthy human being as a "self-actualizing" individual because he believes that self-actualization is basically a process through which a person develops his or her own inner nature. In sharp contrast both to traditional Christian thought, which tends on the whole to see our inner nature as essentially sinful, and to modern psychoanalytic theory, which tends to see our inner nature as essentially amoral and instinctual, Maslow sees this inner core or self as essentially good; it is a positive potential that must be developed if we are to live happy lives.[10] As we shall see, many of our problems in this regard derive from the fact that our social institutions—including the institution of marriage—often tend to work against and frustrate the development of this self.

Indeed, it is no accident that our social institutions work in this way, for in important respects they were designed to do so. Modern society

[9]Abraham Maslow, *Toward a Psychology of Being*, p. 197.

[10]Sigmund Freud saw the inner man as a trilogy of instinctive and acquired forces or drives (the ego, superego, and the id), the most primitive of which is the id. The id is instinctive, animalistic impulse that must be directed and socialized by the ego and the superego, both of which develop in the process of growing up in a family. Thus for Freud, the inner man is essentially antisocial insofar as he is id. Other social scientists besides Maslow, however, have seen man's inner nature as essentially good. C. G. Jung, for example, saw the unconscious as a deep well or reservoir from which integration or wholeness springs. Charles Horton Cooley, a sociologist, saw "human nature" as the capacity to empathize with another person. Without this capacity it is impossible to take the role of another, or to put oneself in another's place. Thus socialization would be impossible. Some social psychologists such as George Herbert Mead, in *Mind, Self and Society*, saw the "I" or inner self as little more than a point from which the social self (or "me") is observed. The important thing for Mead was not the instinctive (or, for that matter, the personally distinctive) aspects of the self, but the socially determined behavior that is appropriate to particular social situations. Finally, many behaviorists, such as B. F. Skinner, have no need whatsoever for the concept of an inner man or self. For them what is important is observable behavior and the techniques by which it can be changed. For references see Sigmund Freud, *An Outline of Psychoanalysis* (New York: W. W. Norton & Company, Inc., 1949), pp. 13–18; C. G. Jung, *Modern Man in Search of a Soul* (New York: Harcourt, Brace & Co., 1933), pp. 115–24; Charles Horton Cooley, *Human Nature and Social Organization* (Glencoe, Ill.: Free Press, 1922); and B. F. Skinner, *Science and Human Behavior* (New York: Free Press, 1953), pp. 11–22.

has been shaped to a considerable extent by the Judaeo-Christian tradition, which is profoundly ambivalent about the nature of our inner core or self. On the one hand, the creation of man is recorded in the Bible in such a way as to affirm his goodness: he was created after the image of God to have dominion over the earth.[11] On the other hand, the dramatic story of the fall overshadows the essential goodness of man for many Christians.[12] The doctrine of original sin emphasizes our total depravity in such a way that the net effect of the Judaeo-Christian tradition seems to be an excessive concentration upon our depravity rather than an affirmation of our essential goodness. As a result, it becomes difficult for us to talk about ourselves in a positive way without feeling either guilty or self-righteous. To be sure, there is another way of looking at the doctrine of the fall. The fall can be seen as the occasion of our becoming human. It can be read as the myth of our falling into existence—the story about the moment of the birth of our awareness of ourselves and others. But in point of fact, this view has been far from dominant in Christian thinking, which has tended largely toward the negative interpretation. As a result, most of the institutions we have created have been created under the assumption that we are essentially bad and, therefore, must be rigidly controlled if we are to become fully human. Thus, self-actualization as Maslow sees it is a very rare phenomenon, for it is the process by which an essentially good inner core is permitted to develop into its full potential.

A PROFILE OF PARTNERSHIP

The foregoing discussion of basic human needs has led us to observe that we become human in community. When we find love, acceptance, and a sense of belongingness we enter the human community as social creatures. We must now, therefore, talk of human relationships and partnerships. The focus in this book is upon marriage, a particular kind of partnership that should be seen as existing in the midst of a number of other relationships. Marriage is much more highly institutionalized than other forms of partnership. It has associated with it a relatively fixed set of social expectations about what is appropriate behavior in the relationship and what society and the marital partners should expect to get out of it. The following profile describes the set of personal expectations that most of us bring to partnerships such as marriage.[13]

[11]Genesis 1:26.
[12]Genesis 2:7–3:24.
[13]These personal expectations are expectations that can be fulfilled in many kinds of partnerships; marriage is only one of these, although, to be sure, it is by far the dominant one in our culture. But sometimes marriages become stifling because the partners settle for the social expectations (described in Chapter 10) and do not work to achieve the personal goals outlined here. Irene describes the moment of her awareness of the discrepancy between these sets of expectation on page 28.

Intimacy

Intimacy involves touching and being touched, in both the physical and the psychological senses. An intimate partnership is one in which both partners are able to be open to each other. To be open is to be able to share feelings both good and bad—particularly about ourselves—to be able to "let our hair down" and reveal who we really are as far as we are able to understand ourselves. We cannot do this in a relationship unless we are confident of being accepted by our partner. The extent to which we can expect acceptance of even those things that we would hide from others determines the degree of intimacy in the relationship.

Intimacy depends to a large extent on trust. In William Golding's novel *Lord of the Flies* a group of young boys is marooned on a deserted island. Two of them meet for the first time on the beach and after they talk for a while one of them confesses to the other, first making him promise never to tell anyone, that back home his nickname was "Piggy." A few minutes later other boys arrive and the new friend soon betrays the confidence by calling his companion Piggy. Everyone has had painful or embarrassing experiences of this nature, and as a result we learn that it is best to be open and intimate only gradually, as our trust in our partner grows. It may be true that people can fall in love "at first sight," and what is commonly called "physical intimacy" can be achieved by two people who are virtually strangers, but true intimacy is the result of a gradual process in which the partners learn to trust each other enough to open up to the other and learn to open up to each other as they find that their trust is justified.

Richard Frieman, Photo Researchers

Love and Romance

Love and romance are an important part of the expectations most young people bring to marriage. You expect to share the emotion of love as expressed in gestures such as holding hands in the moonlight, you believe in the validity of exclusive sexual rights in your partner, you picture a man, a woman, and their child nested together against the world. You expect to sit down with your partner and plan for the future. Above all, you expect to be cared for.

These expectations are essentially romantic in their origin. They make for a very pretty picture, but in a real sense they have little to do with love, which is often quite different from our romantic preconceptions about what a loving relationship should be like. When young people think that an ideal marriage should be all romance, that the honeymoon should never be over, they are forgetting that a honeymoon is not "real life." Those two weeks in Hawaii may have been idyllic but you can't live in Hawaii forever—unless you are a Hawaiian, and even then one of you will probably have to start going to work five days a week. Thus, when the husband stops bringing flowers home all the time and the wife fails to put candles on the dinner table, inexperienced outsiders may assume that the romance has gone out of their marriage when in fact all that has happened is that the couple no longer finds certain conventional gestures of affection necessary.

This is well illustrated in the following narrative. Irene, the subject of a case study published by Carl Rogers, had been married three times and was living with a fourth partner, Joe. In this passage she describes the moment of awareness that became the turning point in her relationship with Joe:

We'd been living together for close to a year, which seems unbelievable to me. How that ever worked in that neighborhood I don't know, but it did. At any rate, Joe was out of town—he was away on business and I was home—the kids were asleep, and I was sitting in the living room watching television, which was across the room from me, and next to the television set was a window, a big picture window. Normally, I had the curtains closed, but I didn't this night, and so when I looked across at the TV I could see my reflection in the window. And I kind of had a conversation with myself. It was very important to me, and I don't know if you can hear what I'm saying, but it was sort of like this: "Hello. Here you are, thirty-four years old, and how *differently* life has turned out from what you expected." I had always had a very unreal picture of life. I thought I wanted to get married, settle down, have six children, God forbid, raise the family and live happily ever after. It seemed like such a simple, reasonable dream. And it really hadn't worked that way at all. I'd found a man, I'd love him, I thought, I thought I was straight and open and honest, whatever that meant, and it really hadn't worked. There had been so much unhappiness. I'd had a lot of illness, I'd had so many problems with my children, I hadn't been able really to cope with life. I didn't know anything about it at all, it was really a devastating thing. Life had been pretty much hell.

I kind of talked to myself and listed all the things that had gone wrong. And then I began to wonder about some of the things that might be right. And one of the questions that came up—and you know, these are questions from me to me—was, "What is it you really want? What is it that you're looking for?" And the answer turned out not to be a marriage, not to have six children, not to live happily ever after at all. It turned out to be that I wanted to learn how to love someone, just one person, and to be loved, and that's all. I didn't need the house, I didn't need anything else, but just really to know how to do that. To know how to experience that—both ways.

And my reflection in the window said, "Well, you jackass, what do you think you've got now?" And I sat there and thought, "Well, for crying out loud, you know, I really have a man I'm learning to love, and that means sharing myself. If that is my goal, to love and to be loved, I have it. Joe loves me, I love him, he loves the children. What do I want that I don't have?"[14]

Commitment

A minimal definition of commitment involves the simple acceptance of socially defined roles. Thus someone might say, "I am really committed to being a good wife, husband, fiancé," meaning that he or she subscribes to the socially accepted expectations appropriate to these roles. This often can be done without reflecting or thinking about the quality of one's unique interaction with others in these relationships. For example, I can be a good husband without asking if my being a good husband really meets the needs of my wife or provides us with an occasion for growth or development. Many marriages have ended with, say, the wife wretchedly unhappy while the husband explains to one of his friends, "Look, it wasn't my fault. What did she expect. I was a good husband. If that wasn't good enough for her, you can't blame me."

Carl Rogers offers a more creative way of defining commitment. As Rogers see it, commitment should be directed to the relationship itself and not to some set of social expectations or roles:

We commit ourselves to working together on the changing process of our present relationship because that relationship is currently enriching our love and our life and we wish it to grow.[15]

Commitment in this sense places a high value on a voluntary relationship that is personally satisfying. This redefinition is clearly in line with the change that has taken place in our common normative definition of a marriage contract. Marriage, for most people under thirty-five, is no longer thought of as a sacrament of the church that can never be terminated, or as a social contract that must be fulfilled in spite of our personal lack of fulfillment. We tend to think of it as a voluntary relationship wherein the needs of the spouses should receive primary consideration.

[14]Carl Rogers, *Becoming Partners*, pp. 92–93.
[15]Carl Rogers, *Becoming Partners*, p. 201.

Such an understanding of commitment is on the one hand creative, and on the other risky. We are committing ourselves to interaction in a process that is continually changing and whose outcome cannot be guaranteed. What is more, if we commit ourselves to another in this way we assume personal responsibility for working out a partnership without the supports that we typically rely upon in other areas of our lives. That is, we deny ourselves the luxury of being able to say, "It wasn't my fault; don't blame me." We can find evidence of commitment in deep and heavy encounters or in simple ongoing daily personal exchanges. Commitment is a necessary ingredient of true humanness. We are not fully human without it.

Dependability

Dependability is a much abused concept. Too often when people say that a husband is dependable they mean merely that he has a good and steady income and doesn't stay out drinking all night with the boys. Dependability in a wife often means no more than that she is sexually faithful and gets dinner on the table every night.

Dependability in a partnership should mean more than these things. It is one's sense that one knows in what circumstances and in what ways the other can be counted upon. This does not imply that the other will always do what we expect, but merely that we know each other well enough so that there will not be needless disruptions in the communication process.

Another way to describe dependability is in terms of something we can feel as "presence." Presence is simply the capacity to convey to another person that one is "there," listening and attentive. Presence, then, is the feeling that one can be depended upon to be there in the dialogue rather than drifting away thinking about other things. More will be said of this aspect of dependability in Chapter 3.

Vitality

A vital partnership is one that is intrinsically rewarding and satisfying to the partners. They enjoy each other, not merely the things that they do or do not do together. Vitality conjures up words like joy, spontaneity, freedom, humor, surprise. It suggests to us that routines have been transcended, that we have, for the moment, done something new.

We do not ordinarily associate vitality with dependable relationships because dependability suggests routine whereas vitality suggests spontaneity. But this need not be so. Partnerships become routinized when dependability becomes an end in itself. Conversely, vitality as an end in itself tends to disrupt lasting relationships because of its constant emphasis upon the new and the different. The proper balance is like a good jazz musician improvising on a song. The spontaneity of improvisation provides the vitality within the context of the basic melodic and harmonic structure of the song. When Miles Davis plays *Moonlight in Vermont* it's never the same thing twice but it's always *Moonlight in Vermont*. In a partnership, too, such a combination of vitality and dependability is possible.

Vitality, in the context of a lasting partnership, is the acknowledgement of the many facets of our personalities. It rejoices in the fact that we are not merely those aspects of ourselves that are called forth by our daily routine, but are also far more. Vitality is the capacity to call forth something new in the other and to reveal something new in the self. For most of us, vitality is associated with our emotions, because it is our emotions that we are trained to control more than other aspects of ourselves. The realization of self-actualization is an experience of vitality.

Separateness and Togetherness

When you enter a partnership it is important that you preserve your own uniqueness. It should not be expected that you give up being yourself in order to melt into your partner.

The issue of separateness and togetherness most frequently focuses upon expectations about what is to be shared in the relationship and what is not. The emphasis upon togetherness that was so characteristic of our expectations of marriage in the 1950s stressed sharing as much as possible. Indeed, couples who read diligently in the magazines of the day were likely to end up feeling they had a bad marriage if she didn't develop a passion for football and he didn't cultivate an interest in gardening. It was better for a couple to do nothing at all, the apostles of togetherness preached, than for them to do things separately.

Trying to fulfill these expectations very often leads to unhappy compromises, one partner feeling that for the sake of the marriage she must give up what she really wants to do while the other feels obliged to participate in activities that don't interest him. Such a marriage can get to be little more than an encumbrance. Thus one fifty-five-year-old unmarried man with a son remarks:

Marriage is simply an institutional arrangement for the immature—for people who can't stand the strain of regulating their lives themselves—who need laws and public opinion and the Church to tell them what to do and what not to do. So, I'm all for marriage for the country and for most people, but not for me. . . . To do my best work I need to be unencumbered—and even with the most ideal marriage I've seen, there is a lot of simple encumbrance.[16]

Any relationship must have "psychological space" in it. Some of us need more room than others. Some of us are more afraid of this free-

[16]Arlene and Jerome Skolnick, *The Family in Transition* (Boston: Little, Brown, 1968), p. 158.

dom than others, but all of us must be able to work out a satisfactory solution to the problem of how much autonomy and how much togetherness we are going to experience in each relationship.

Openness and Self-Disclosure

The hazards of a developing relationship, be it a courtship or otherwise, derive from the fact that in a given situation it is sometimes impossible to determine the intention of the other from the cues he or she gives off. The partner may not be aware of his or her true intentions, may be intentionally and skillfully deceiving, or may in fact be "open and aboveboard." Self-disclosure usually is ventured incrementally, in proportion to the amount of trust the relationship has established. We enter into various types of partnerships, in part, in order to reduce this uncertainty. Without self-disclosure at some depth there is little true intimacy, but on the other hand even an intimate relationship is not a confessional in which it is a sin to keep any secrets.

COSTS AND BENEFITS

On the preceding pages we have discussed some of the needs and expectations that we bring to partnerships. They may be conscious or unconscious; they may be only partially fulfilled in any one of our relationships. But all of them are important issues for vital, self-actualizing partnerships. These dimensions may be in tension with each other. For example, as we have seen, sometimes we have to pay a price for achieving dependability in terms of losing touch, to a certain extent, with the possibility of spontaneous vitality. Similarly, in striving for separateness we may lose the opportunity for an intimate discovery of another.

Some of these ingredients of partnerships are more closely associated with simple duration of time than others. We can describe a brief encounter as a vital or even an intimate affair, but we normally do not think of it as involving much of a commitment. Love at first sight would not be recognized as such if the couple who fell in love at first sight had not continued their relationship. The emotions they experienced in the single encounter are likely to be given some other label than love if that single encounter proves not to be the first of many encounters.

Finally, these ingredients of relationships are valued differently by each of us. In general, most of us would say that a valuable relationship should be dependable, vital, intimate, and committed, and should involve a considerable degree of togetherness. However, the precise weight we give to each of these elements will vary and the extent to which we are willing to trade one for the other will differ. For some of us dependability will be the most important aspect of a relationship, for others it will be vitality or intimacy. In fact, most people value these ingredients differently in different relationships, desiring to be intimate with some people and not with others.

Any choice of one against the other has within it the possibility of losing another. In this, as in any situation, there is always a cost and a risk, as well as a benefit. By benefit we mean the realization of something we desire, value, or need. Cost refers to what we have to pay in order to get what we desire, value, or need. Risk takes place when there may not be a relationship between the costs and the benefits. Indeed, all choices are made with some degree of risk. The choice to enter into and maintain a relationship is no different than other choices in this regard. Because it is easy to miscalculate the benefits and the costs of entering into a relationship, the risks in human interaction are greater than in most other situations of choice. Creative partnerships require risk-taking to a greater extent than less creative ones.

SUMMARY

This chapter has begun our discussion of marriage as a particular kind of partnership by noting that a partnership is more than a simple relationship such as a casual date or an affair. Partners have an understanding or "contract" between them as to what they each expect to get out of their partnership. In creative partnerships a prime ingredient of this contract is the expectation of self-actualization.

Abraham Maslow describes self-actualization as the highest of our basic human needs. It can be achieved only after the lower (or deprivation) needs have been reasonably well met. Men and women must be able to find safety and security; must feel belonging, love, and acceptance; and must achieve a reasonable degree of self-esteem before they can give themselves to the process of self-actualization.

Historically, the social expectations we commonly associate with marriage—including conventionally established conceptions of the roles of husbands and wives, common residence, children, and lifelong monogamy—arose at a time when most persons were much more involved in meeting their deprivation needs than they are today. It is no wonder, then, that the notion of marriage as a self-actualizing partnership is a very new one indeed.

The profile of partnership we have sketched in this chapter gives some of the personal expectations that we associate with self-actualizing partnerships. We will look at a number of differing forms of partnerships in this book, in addition to marriage. Self-actualization *can* occur in most. There are simply different costs, risks, and benefits that are associated with different life styles.

Marriage—and any other type of partnership—should be assessed in terms of the extent to which what goes on between the partners encourages self-actualization. By looking at the dimensions of intimacy; love and romance; commitment; dependability and vitality; separateness and togetherness; and openness and self-disclosure we focus on the *process* of partnerships rather than their form or style. We ask of each, "To what extent is self-actualization possible under these conditions?" This is simply another way of trying to assess the costs, risks, and benefits of each.

> The basis of man's life with man is twofold and it is one—the wish of every man to be confirmed as what he is, even as what he can become, by men; and the innate capacity in man to confirm his fellow man in this way. That this capacity lies so immeasurably fallow constitutes the real weakness and questionableness of the human race: actual humanity exists only where this capacity unfolds.
>
> *Martin Buber*

3 CONFIRMATION AND COMMUNICA-TION

INTRODUCTION

The great theologian and philosopher Martin Buber used the word "confirmation" to signify the process whereby a person can become more fully who he or she is, can realize his or her human potential. Whether we realize it or not, the longing for confirmation in this sense is, perhaps, the greatest expectation we bring to loving partnerships. Why, then, does it appear that we give it so little attention and that it lies, as Buber says, "fallow"?

One answer is, quite simply, that nobody ever told us that we really can help others realize their human potential. We have been told, of course, that we can help our children develop their skills by providing them with the best teachers and equipment, with the time and encouragement needed if they are to succeed in our competitive society. But nobody ever told us that we could or should do anything in particular to help our children achieve greater authenticity, autonomy, or integrity in their personal lives. Thus, it is a national scandal when we discover that Johnnie can't read, but no one seems to devote any systematic effort to discovering why an alarmingly large number of Johnnies and Janies have troubled, unsatisfactory marriages that fail to give them a sense of fulfillment.

Furthermore, if we think at all about helping another to realize his or her potential—to become "authentic"—we tend to think of it as a process that has greater costs than benefits to ourselves. This is because we are not really thinking about authenticity, or human potential, in Buber's sense of these terms, but rather we are thinking merely in terms of the acquisition of skills. Thus, when we deal with the situation of a wife who wants to develop her professional career, we tend to think readily of the costs in terms of the services and attention she will be unable to provide her family, and we assess the benefits in terms of the added income she will be able to provide. But how do we assess the benefits that might derive from

her greater authenticity as a person? It is easy to imagine that she might benefit personally by being happier, more fulfilled as a person, but our normal way of analyzing this situation all too often leaves such factors out of the picture. Thus, we are likely to conclude that the husband who helps his wife in a case like this is simply her altruistic benefactor rather than her partner in a joint process of growth.

This chapter will discuss some of the aspects of human communication as they enhance the establishment, maintenance, and deepening of loving, caring partnerships. It will sketch some of the basic skills that can help us confirm our partner's greater authenticity. It assumes that it is a good thing to grow in partnerships. It acknowledges that there are real costs involved in any growth, but concludes that in most instances the joy and vitality of growing relationships and the increasing capacity to call each other forth into greater authenticity are real benefits that far outweigh these costs.

GETTING IN TOUCH WITH ONESELF

It has been said that the degree to which we are capable of knowing another person is directly related to the degree to which we know ourselves. The more I know about myself and my own feelings, the more receptive I can be when another person reveals something about herself or himself. For example, if in the quietness of my own existence I have known, tasted, and experienced loneliness, I then can recognize loneliness when another hints of it.

The problem is that in many cases we do not know what is going on inside ourselves. To some extent this is unavoidable, for we do not want to be so self-involved, so constantly preoccupied with taking our own mental temperatures that we lose sight of other things; inevitably we must fall short of full understanding of ourselves, and there will always be thoughts we think without knowing why and feelings we feel without acknowledging them to ourselves. For most people, though, the danger is not one of too much self-involvement but one of too little self-awareness. To a considerable extent this problem results from the way we are trained, for we are all taught as we grow up that certain emotions and feelings are bad and wrong. If not at home then at school, and more probably both, children learn that it is "wrong" to express anger and hostility, for example. So we learn to hide these emotions, in many cases to hide them even from ourselves. Consider the following story.

36

Marge spent the afternoon with an old boyfriend from her college days while her husband Bill stayed home and babysat with their children. When she got home, Bill greeted her curtly and quickly took off for his office.

Later that evening Marge, sensing a certain coolness in his behavior, asked if anything was wrong. "Not a thing, honey. Did you have a good time this afternoon?" Bill answered.

"Yes, we did, but why didn't you ask when I got home?"

"I was in a hurry and I had other things on my mind," Bill said.

Marge felt that he wasn't telling her the whole story. "Are you angry about something?" she asked.

"No, but you know that I do have a lot to do at the office and you were a little late."

"But you said that you thought that it would be great for me to go and now you are angry," Marge protested. "I don't understand."

"I am not angry!"

Bill himself doesn't understand. He behaves from a level of feeling that is real for him, but he doesn't know what those feelings are, and as a result he has lost control of his feelings and has also lost the ability to communicate with Marge. Later he confessed to a counselor that he was indeed angry, that he really had nothing to do at the office, and that what he was mad about was the fact that his wife had had a good time while he had stayed home and struggled with the children. Because he was unaware of how he really felt when he first confronted Marge, Bill confused her and they were unable to resolve the conflict that emerged. Bill did not know he was angry because for him anger was an inappropriate emotion in this situation.

In a sense he was right: his anger *was* inappropriate. But dealing with an inappropriate emotion by hiding it from oneself usually serves only to make things worse. Consider what would have happened if Bill had acknowledged what he was feeling. If Bill had said, "Yes, I'm angry. I had to stay home all afternoon while you went out and enjoyed yourself," the situation would have been out in the open and the two of them could have talked about it. Perhaps Marge would have pointed out that she often helped him out in similar ways. In the end, if they were open and candid with each other, Bill might well have come to realize that indeed he had been angry but there was in fact "nothing to be angry about." Inappropriate emotions often dissipate when we recognize their inappropriateness, but we can't do this until we first recognize the emotion.

The Visceral Quality of Feelings

The feelings, thoughts, and emotions that fill our inner world are very important to us. We are these things and more, and not to share them is to isolate ourselves from others and from ourselves. To make believe that they do not exist leads to disaster. When we no longer know how we truly feel about the world and ourselves we no longer know ourselves and we confuse others as to who we are. The poet T. S. Eliot used the term "hollow men" to describe people thus cut off from their own inner natures. When hollow men are angry they do not know that they are angry, and of course they do not know why they are angry.

Getting in touch with ourselves is a tantalizing task. We know that emotions are real in a way that ideas are not, for they have a visceral origin that we can feel whenever we let ourselves. Although there are powerful forces in our culture telling us to "control" our emotions, to keep them in check, we all have had moments of intense emotion when we can actually taste the authenticity of our feelings. Perhaps this accounts for our sense of being beckoned toward our inner feelings while at the same time being threatened by them. Nevertheless, the fact that getting in touch with our deepest feelings is in some ways a frightening thing should not blind us to the fact that savoring these feelings is also an exciting possibility.

Some of this excitement is reflected in the following passage from Carl Rogers:

Perhaps I can discover and come closer to more of what I really am deep inside— feeling sometimes angry or terrified, sometimes loving and caring, occasionally beautiful and strong or wild and awful—without hiding these feelings from myself. Perhaps I can come to prize myself as the richly varied person I am. Perhaps I can openly be more of this person. If so, I can live by my own experienced values, even though I am aware of all of society's codes. Then I can let myself be all this complexity of feelings and meanings and values with my partner—be free enough to give of love and anger and tenderness as they exist in me. Possibly then I can be a *real* member of a partnership, because I am on the road to being a real person. I am hopeful that I can encourage my partner to follow his or her own road to a unique personhood, which I would love to share.[1]

Just as the possibility for confirmation very often lies fallow within us, so also the ability to get in touch with who we are deep inside often eludes us. If it is true, as we observed earlier, that getting in touch with others is a function of getting in touch with ourselves, it is no less true that getting in touch with ourselves is in important ways a function of getting in touch with others. We discover ourselves in interaction as well as in reflection. But because interaction with others has so many variables, it seems at first glance to be a most difficult arena for self-discovery.

Difficult it may be, but the difficulty must be met if we are to meet the dual challenges of being most fully ourselves both in the privacy

[1] Carl Rogers, *Becoming Partners: Marriage and Its Alternatives* (New York: Delacorte Press, 1972), p. 209.

of our inner lives and in our lives as loving, caring partners. For this reason, as the structure of the present chapter makes clear, the problems and rewards of getting in touch with oneself cannot be discussed apart from the equally complex challenges and possibilities of getting in touch with others. Our examination of the former leads us naturally to the latter, for as we saw in Chapter 2, fully developed human beings function both as individuals and as social creatures.

Congruence

Carl Rogers uses the term "congruence" to describe successful functioning in both modes of our being—that is, both as private individuals and as members of partnerships with other human beings. For Rogers a person is congruent who is aware of the feelings that he or she has and is able to communicate them accurately to another. A person who is congruent creates the sense of authenticity and presence which tends to foster in another an inclination to respond authentically. Thus the concept of congruence bridges the gap between getting in touch with ourselves and getting in touch with others. As Rogers sees it, congruence is the basis of good, healthy partner relationships, which depend upon self-awareness and open communication.

**GETTING
IN TOUCH
WITH OTHERS:
MODES**

"Words, words, words," Hamlet complained, well aware that we rely on words to communicate our feelings and that often they are inadequate. Their inadequacy arises both out of our inability to use them with utmost accuracy and out of the inadequacies of language itself. In addition to being symbols with common meanings that are universally accepted within a language community, words also have more or less private meanings arising out of the experiences we associate with them. Because each of us has a unique history or biography, the words that we use tend to have unique meanings for us and, for similar reasons, for those listening to us. These private meanings generally do not interfere with the transaction of everyday affairs but they can be quite troublesome when we try to use words to say something important about who we are or how we feel about another.

One of the more obvious problems with language is the fact that the same words mean different things to different people. This is true both on the private level and on the social level. Privately, I may have personal and idiosyncratic associations with certain words that affect me whenever I hear these words used. If, for example, I was brought up in a family where squabbling was constant and often vicious and painful, the term "argument" may have meanings for me that it will not have for someone else. Indeed, it may well be that if a class of fifteen or twenty students were to discuss the role of arguments in family life, no two of them would be talking about the same thing; for one an argument would be a healthy airing of differences while for another it might be a deadly battle of wills that should be avoided at all costs.

In addition to the differences of meaning words have on the private level, there are also socially determined differences. On this level the associations I have with certain words are shared by others in my social group but not by people in different groups. For example, words like "rich," "poor," and even "work" obviously mean different things to different social classes; words like "masculine," "feminine," and so forth undoubtedly mean different things to members of the two sexes; words like "liberal," "radical," and "conservative" mean different things to people with different political outlooks. A mother might tell her friends that the young man her daughter is going out with is "a nice boy," but perhaps the daughter wouldn't understand those words in the same way or, if she understood them, might use other words entirely.

Perhaps even more important than the fact that words have different meanings to different groups and different individuals is the fact that, even when such communications problems do not exist, language is often inadequate for conveying our deepest emotions. We all have had the experience of wanting to say something and not knowing how. Indeed, it is a sad fact that it is often the tenderest, warmest, most human emotions that are most difficult to express in words. Greeting card companies thrive on the fact that people find it so difficult to say things like "I care about you and am really sorry to hear that you are sick" that they must fall back, in desperation, on prefabricated expressions of emotions like concern, love, and gratitude. How many of us could find the words to adequately convey to a friend our genuine appreciation of some strikingly pleasing act of consideration?

Because of these inadequacies of language, intimate caring partnerships tend to develop their own language in which common words have very private meanings. Consider the following telephone conversation.

Caller: Hello, Beth, am I disturbing you?
 Beth: Oh no, we were in the meadow. (Giggles.)
Caller: The meadow?
 Beth: We were getting up.

Over the years of their marriage, Beth and her husband had come to call their bed "the meadow." Once the association between "bed" and "meadow" is made, however, even an outsider can understand the warmth, the beauty, and the carefreeness which they must have associated with their lovemaking. By the use of one word in their private language, Beth and her husband can convey to each other a rich heritage of experience which is uniquely theirs. This private language enables them to express easily a wide range of feelings and emotions and to recall events in which they have been able to move closer to one another in the past.

Most of us have used words with others in this way to one degree or another. Friends develop a common language. Groups of people who live together for any length of time tend to develop a set of words to express important aspects of their lives together. Indeed, for most of us, the type of relationship commonly known as courtship is to a large extent involved with the cultivation of just such a private vocabulary.

Of course, many people are not particularly verbal in their behavior. These people may not invent words or radically change the meanings of common words, but they may rely on nonverbal signs and gestures to supplement their associations with common everyday words like "I love you." For most people, in fact, the language of relationship goes far beyond words. It involves the whole being. We communicate by our tone of voice, by our facial expression, by the use of our eyes. Our whole body is a medium of communication. If we are congruent—that is, if we know how we think and feel about ourselves and our world and can express this to others—the signals that we give off are apt to be clear. If we are not in touch with ourselves or cannot bring ourselves to express what we feel, then we are likely to confuse others by what we communicate.

"It's good to see you," he said with his eyes glued steadfastly to the floor.

In this simple example the lack of eye contact seems to contradict what is said. We wonder if the speaker is just shy or if he really is not very pleased to see us. Even such a simple discrepancy can hinder our ability to understand what is communicated. We have to wait for further information in order to be sure of what is being "said." All of us give off discrepant signals like this from time to time. It is when such behavior becomes a persistent part of a relationship that the relationship itself may be unable to grow and develop.

Making Contact

To communicate with another person is to make contact with him or her. In intimate partnerships, actual physical touching is an important part of the way the couple communicates, but in a sense any two people who try to communicate with each other are trying to touch.

Communication is a process that involves our whole beings. Not only are what we say and how we say it important, but so is the "language" we speak with our hands, our bodies, and our eyes. In the incident described above, for example, the lack of eye contact seemed to contradict what was said. Often we make contact with another with our eyes before we speak to them, and so the expression that accompanies the glance and the length of time it persists tell us a great deal about the person looking at us.

Because Americans in general are not a people who take looking into each other's eyes seriously, we tend to reserve eye contact for intimate relationships and to limit its use in public interaction. Nevertheless, our eyes can readily convey our feelings even in public contexts. This is why people who want to conceal something about themselves often cover their eyes with dark glasses. These people intuitively sense the communication potential of the eyes, and they are right. Our eyes are a part of our equipment for communicating that we all too often ignore.[2]

Touching is also an important part of any complete communication process—so important that psychologist Bruno Bettelheim claims that "the ability to experience touch as pleasant must precede any human relationship."[3] Again, Americans as a people tend to minimize the use they make of touch in communication. As Sydney Jourard observed:

[2]Leonard Zunin, *Contact: The First Four Minutes* (Los Angeles: Nash Publishing Co., 1972), pp. 74–88.
[3]Quoted in Zunin, *Contact*, p. 84.

In Paris the average couple came into physical contact 110 times during an hour (and they were just having a conversation!) In San Juan, Puerto Rico, couples patted, tickled and caressed 180 times during the same interval; but the typical London couple never touched at all, and Americans studied patted once or twice in an hour's conversation.[4]

Touching another on the arm or shoulder readily conveys warmth, just as the withdrawal from touch conveys distaste. Most people respond positively to being touched, although there is a large number of individuals who typically find touching unpleasant or threatening.

To a large extent, the use of touch as a means of communication is governed by socially accepted conventions of what is permissible. As Sydney Jourad's observation confirms, among Americans touching tends to be considered inappropriate for casual social occasions; thus the use of touch tends to be confined to our intimate and sexual behavior. This is unfortunate, because it produces a sort of vicious circle that severely inhibits our communications resources. The more touching is seen as exclusively a sexual mode of communication, the more rigorously it is avoided by people who are not on intimate terms with each other, and the more it is avoided, the more exclusively sexual it becomes.

In our society a man who habitually did such things as reaching across a table to put his hand on a woman's hand or forearm to get her attention or to indicate some response to something she said would run the risk of having her think he was "coming on" with her, making sexual advances. Indeed, the inhibition about touching is not confined to relations between the sexes; in other societies, for instance, it is not at all unusual for men to embrace and touch each other. In America, however, such contact is largely forbidden, for our predisposition to see touching as sexual immediately makes us suspect that any touching between members of the same sex must be homosexual. We have, however, all seen football players patting, slapping, and hugging their teammates as a way of communicating, and many of us are familiar with the sight of two prizefighters embracing in the center of the ring after the final bell as a way of communicating without words the feelings of respect and closeness that their intense struggle has generated.

One cannot help feeling, when one sees such demonstrations, a bit sorry that all of us are not free to make more use of this means of communication. Of course, it would not be reasonable to advise anyone simply to ignore the social conventions of his or her culture and to engage freely in types of touching that our society disapproves, for the result probably would not be an increase in communication. Because of the socially conditioned responses of the person being touched, excessive departures from the norms in this area might well end in misunderstanding. But this doesn't mean that we can't make small and gradual changes in our attitudes toward touching and being touched. Any effort

[4]Quoted in Zunin, *Contact*, p. 85.

Hella Hammid, Rapho Guillumette

to be a bit more free, a bit less inhibited, in our use of touch is bound to have beneficial effects on our ability to communicate with others with whom we come in contact. It is possible for us to broaden our communications repertoire even though we live in a society which tends to be relatively restrictive in this regard.

Body Language

We communicate with others by many means. Just as we are often unaware of the richness within ourselves, so also are we unaware of the richness of interpersonal communication. The subtleties of our communication cover a wide range that includes not only our use of words, eye contact, and touching, as discussed above, but also a whole gamut of almost imperceptible things we "say" with our bodies. Indeed, a few years ago a widely read book was devoted to the subject of "Body Language," and we will confine ourselves here to merely suggesting some of the richness of this communications resource.

Undoubtedly, we are all aware that a person's posture often betrays feelings not expressed in words. The position of someone's body as she or he sits in a chair and listens to someone else speaking readily be-

44

trays interest or noninterest. By the same token, it is difficult to say convincingly that you are not tired when your whole body betrays the fact that you are.

These two examples make clear that body language is not something we can either use or not use as we choose. We are using it all the time, whether we know it or not. Thus, if our communication is to be as full as possible, it is important for us to realize what we are saying with our bodies. Consider the following incident.

Your roommate says, "I've got to meet my date in about ten minutes and I don't know what time the movie starts. Do me a favor and call the theater." You don't really want to do it—you're reading and don't want to be interrupted, your roommate should have taken care of these things without depending on you—but on the other hand you don't think it would be right to refuse. So you decide to do it but unconsciously you want your roommate to know how you feel. You say "Okay," but you get up very slowly from your chair, like it's a real problem for you to move, and slouch over to the telephone.

Your roommate sees the way you are moving and gets the point. Perhaps she says, "Oh, don't bother. You don't feel like doing it and it'll only take me a minute. I'll do it myself." Or perhaps she merely makes a mental note that she owes you a favor. In any case, the discrepancy between the way your body acted and what you said communicated a complex message: that you would do this thing but that you didn't really like doing it. There's nothing wrong with such a discrepancy in this case, for the two parts of the communication accurately conveyed the two things you were thinking and feeling.

Where problems might arise, however, is where one does not pay attention to one's body language, so that one is out of touch with one's own feelings. We probably all have been in situations like the one just described, and at some time or other we probably have reacted by not being open about our communications. The following dialogue is what might result in such a situation:

Betty: Do me a favor and call the theater.
Suzanne: Okay. (Moves laboriously toward the phone.)
Betty: Oh, never mind. You don't want to do it, so I'll do it myself.
Suzanne: I *said* I'll do it.
Betty: I know, but you don't feel like it, and it's no trouble for me.
Suzanne: I didn't say I didn't feel like it. I said I'd do it.

The result is a kind of double bind. Betty correctly interpreted Suzanne's reluctance to make the call and dropped her request. But Suzanne, who probably felt it was wrong not to want to do this favor and so refused to admit that she felt that way, denied having communicated what her body language clearly said and then got annoyed with Betty for responding to it. The result was one of those little squabbles that almost invariably result from a failure to communicate. Both parties were made unnecessarily uncomfortable.

Our bodies, in short, are almost always communicating our feelings to other people. A large part of this communication is unconscious, but it is important that we try to make ourselves aware of as much of it as possible. Only in this way can we get in touch with our own feelings and be aware of the messages we are sending to other people.

**GETTING
IN TOUCH
WITH OTHERS:
MEANS**

In the context of this chapter, communication with others is a means to help others (and ourselves) become more authentic, to become more fully all that we are capable of being. The modes of communicating with others discussed above offer us the possibility of touching each other deeply. The extent to which we feel comfortable in using these modes is a measure of the extent to which we have come to grips with our own inner feelings and have tasted some degree of our own authenticity.

Attentiveness

One of the marks of authenticity in a person is his or her ability to be attentive to others.[5] Attentiveness means a whole range of things, and perhaps the best way to clarify what we mean by the term is to recall some instances in which we have felt another being attentive to us. The attentive waiter notices the slight movement of the hand toward the empty coffee cup and fills it almost before the diner has become aware of his own wishes and his own movement. The host who is there with an ashtray when you light a cigarette at a party is being attentive. Of course, the fact that we expect persons in these roles to be attentive does not diminish our feeling of pleasant surprise when they are in fact so.

One of the factors that tends to make a person attentive is an awareness of what the relationship means to him or her. The host, for example, is attentive to his guests for a number of reasons having to do with such things as his regard for them as friends and associates, his conception of himself in the socially determined role as host, and so forth; the waiter is attentive because his relationship to his customers can mean financial reward if it is a pleasant one and because he may take pride in fulfilling his role in the relationship well. That is to say, both the host and the waiter are eager to succeed in their roles and their attentiveness is a result of the amount of meaningfulness they attach to the relationships in which they act out these roles.

[5]Zunin, *Contact*, pp. 13–14.

The same is true of the roles of husband, wife, lover, parent, or friend. All relationships have some value to us, or we would not be in them. Unfortunately, sometimes we either are not aware of or cannot acknowledge what our stake in a particular relationship really is. Whenever this happens, the result is likely to be a failure of attentiveness on our part. When being in a relationship to a particular person doesn't seem to matter to us, we cease relating to that person, we stop *attending* to what he or she is saying. Consider the following dialogue:

Sally: Gosh, I had a great time in New York yesterday.
 Ben: Yeah, New York is great. I went to New York two weeks ago.
Sally: I spent two hours at the Guggenheim Museum. What a fantastic place!
 Ben: Yeah, well I went to the Museum of Modern Art. They have some really beautiful things there. Like . . .
Sally: I particularly liked David Smith's sculpture . . .
 Ben: Oh, sure, Smith is good, but you should have seen . . .

Ben is obviously more interested in telling his story than in hearing what Sally has to say. Although she initiated the conversation, he never picks up on what she is saying in such a way as to encourage her to say more. Instead, he uses each of her observations as though its only purpose was to provide him with an opportunity to tell his thoughts and experiences.

This is a fairly typical kind of conversation. It could take place between casual acquaintances, a guy and his girlfriend, or a married couple. Regardless of the level of intimacy in the relationship, this kind of conversation can be damaging. If Ben and Sally are just strangers striking up a conversation, they are missing the possibility of a good conversation and are likely to end up as much strangers to each other as when they began talking. If they are going together and are looking forward to a developing partnership, their chances are not very good because Ben is signaling Sally that he doesn't really care about her thoughts and feelings. He may say he cares about her, but his inattentiveness says otherwise. And if this kind of conversation is a persistent feature of a long-term partnership such as marriage, then it is clear that the partnership has lost an important part of its capacity to grow.

Of course, we should recognize that any particular example of inattentiveness may not be decisive for the relationship as a whole. It is perfectly normal for there to be areas in a person's life that simply may not be of much interest to his or her partner. Imagine for a moment that Ben is an art major while Sally is majoring in economics. He is going through a stage in which he is trying to find his bearings in the world of art, and so, when she brings up the subject it is for him an occasion to talk about his thoughts on art, which for the time being are far more important to him than her thoughts. The point is that countless husbands and wives have noticed that their partners are inattentive *in certain areas* and it does their relationship no harm. But when inattentiveness spreads beyond certain well-defined, limited areas, to characterize the relationship as a whole, it is safe to say that the relationship has become one in which the partners do not relate.

One of the things that helps us to be attentive in general is our genuine interest in others. This means having some appreciation for another person simply as a person, and also some recognition of the value of that other person's experience. It involves a recognition that we enjoy being with these other persons and an acceptance of the possibility that we can learn from them.

Inquisitiveness

Inquisitiveness or interest is not simply listening to Sally tell her story. It involves recognizing in her story those things that are of value to her and the possibility of pursuing them because they may be of interest to Ben also. This, in effect, changes the conversation from one in which the partners are simply exchanging information to a conversation which may have intrinsic value for both because both are really "turned on" by what is happening.

Learning to Transfer Skills

There are no easy ways to teach people the skills that are involved in being an attentive and inquisitive partner. On the other hand, many of us already have these skills well developed but we do not readily transfer them to our intimate partnerships. For example, a good salesman must be an attentive and inquisitive listener. In his job he has developed the capacity to intervene creatively in conversations for his own purposes. If he didn't have these skills he wouldn't be a good salesman. But, even though he has skills and knowledge about developing relationships, he frequently fails to utilize them in his personal life. It may not dawn on him that if he listened to his wife as attentively as he listens to prospective buyers, the result would be payoffs in terms of their personal relationship as surely as there are payoffs for his attentiveness in his business dealings.

All of us need to become more aware of the fact that it is appropriate to use such highly prized skills in our intimate partnerships. Of course, the skills of the salesman need some adjustment when they are applied to personal partnerships. The aim should be cooperation rather than manipulation, and the growth of the partnership must be more important than the advancement of one party's personal objectives. Sensitivity plays an important role here. Increased awareness of the expressed and unexpressed needs of each partner helps redirect the skills that are used on the job simply to sell a product.

CONFIRMATION

The modes of communication and the means of managing within relationships have most value for us when they help us to confirm each other as authentic persons. This means that we must at least have some feeling for the reality of the message our partner is giving us. Our responses must be to the total message our partner is sending us. Whether we say "yes" or "no" to the person, we must respond to all that he or she is telling us about himself or herself.

In any partnership, what our partner is telling us must be heard in the context of a history of many past self-disclosures. This past history of self-disclosure and confirmation bears directly upon our response in the present because it provides us with another reference by means of which we can infer what is most valuable to the partner. If a couple has a relatively full history of self-disclosures in which they were able to give of themselves in their relationship, then they can build upon this in the present. Conversely, if they have been unable to give much of themselves in the past, they must clear up the ambiguities in their communication process before they can progress.

For example, say a woman has for years harbored a vague feeling that her role as wife and homemaker is not fully satisfying, and she would like to resume her education or find some sort of work in which she can find satisfaction. Every once in a while she mentions these aspirations to her husband, but he refuses to confirm them. He doesn't say that she must not do any such thing, but he generally gives her no encouragement and brushes her remarks aside with a casual statement such as, "Well, I don't see any need for it, but if that's what you want to do, go ahead."

Finding no encouragement, she puts her desires to the side. Finally, however, she reaches the point at which she decides that having some sort of career outside the home is of considerable importance to her. She enrolls in courses at a local university, but her husband treats her new career as a student lightly. Because he was not attentive to what she was saying all these years, he cannot imagine that it is important to her and he tends to regard her studies as little more than a way to "get out of the house" for a few afternoons a week. Even when she tells him this is not the case, he is skeptical because, from where he stands, behind a wall produced by years of inattentiveness, her decision looks like just a spur-of-the-moment notion she is following up on. Had he been listening to what she was saying all along, he could have saved her years of frustration and, what is more, could now be sharing, as an interested and confirming partner, in her new experiences.

Obviously, the power and capacity for confirmation is greater in an ongoing relationship than in a relationship of short duration, but this does not mean that we cannot find and give confirmation and support even in short-term or non-intimate relationships. Confirmation depends upon moments of touching deeply, regardless of who does the touching. The following example might help us understand some of the dimensions of confirmation.

Jim is a vice-president of Continental Packaging Corporation. He has made a radical suggestion to improve sales and production that will involve a major shakeup in the final status of the company and a reassignment of personnel. The plan is basically acceptable and desirable by the majority of the board, but because of the radical shift it entails, the board is leery and anxious. Jim has reason to believe that the board meeting he is about to attend will be explosive and that he will be challenged at every turn. As he prepares to leave his office for the board meeting his secretary touches him on the arm and says, "You'll make it. I know it. The plan is great. Good luck!"

Although this seems like a simple kind of exchange, Jim reported later that these words and the touch allowed him to go through this grueling experience with much more self-confidence than he would have imagined possible. As Jim thought about this afternoon, he saw in this simple exchange a power of confirmation that goes much beyond what appears on the surface. He heard an expression of genuine concern for himself, a concern that revealed an inner knowledge of him that he had not expected. His secretary not only had confidence in his plan but also seemed to know just what he was thinking at that moment, and her words said more than just her opinion of the plan. They said that she was with him just then. Although in his past experience women had not been able to share his feelings about his job, in this instance he felt that she was doing so. He reported that this was a truly supportive experience.

The exchange between Jim and his secretary is an example of confirmation. What is important in this event is an attentiveness that carried within it care, concern, and a genuine knowledge of the other and what the other was experiencing. The encounter was an insight, a support, and a warmth which transcended what Jim thought of as the normally defined masculine and feminine roles. In its small way it was a life-giving moment for Jim.

Confirmation may involve a calling forth of a side of the partner that the partner did not recognize in herself or himself before the relationship began. Sometimes this can result in a very dramatic change in self-image and behavior, as Irene, the subject of one of Carl Rogers' case studies, discovered. Joe, the man with whom she was living, had the capacity to confirm in Irene aspects of her personality that had gone unawakened in her previous partnerships:

Joe came into my life, and he's a man who has always been loved, knows it, accepts it without question, and I still feel in awe of that. He knows he has worth —that's something that is never questioned—and yet at the same time, he could look at me, who had an almost exact opposite opinion of myself, and not be bothered by that, or be put aside by that, and not encourage it either. He never confirmed my negative feelings about myself. He would hear them and accept them, and then, in his own way, say that they were kind of nonsense. "I realize you feel that way, but that's not the way you are."

And I began to try to look at myself. It was as if, just maybe, the way he sees me is closer to the way I am than the way I see me, and I began to sort of try that on a little bit.[6]

Joe's ability to accept Irene's negative feelings without confirming them, while at the same time presenting to her another image of herself that was more positive and self-fulfilling, lies at the basis of many growing partnerships in which the partners help each other experience growth and self-actualization. In Irene's case, because she had been deeply troubled by self-doubts, such growth was experienced as a kind of therapy. Joe enabled her to realize much more of her potential by his sensitive confirmation.

Whether because of or in spite of its importance, confirmation is not an easy thing to engage in. This is particularly true when we are involved in a relationship with someone who is quite different from us.

People differ from one another in values or world view, in physical stamina, in sex drive, in gregariousness, and in a host of other ways. Because of these differences, we aspire to different things, handle the world around us and ourselves in different ways, and place differing values on our relationships. In growing partnerships—that is, partnerships in which each partner is becoming more authentic—differences have a positive value because an important part of becoming authentic lies in discovering the uniqueness of each partner. Unfortunately, however, people tend not to like to discover significant differences between themselves and those with whom they enter into relationships. These differences tend to create a feeling of loneliness (because one feels that the partner cannot possibly understand), to invite comparison ("my way is better"), and thus are likely to generate tensions. Instead of confirming what is unique in one's partner, there is a tendency to try to disconfirm it, to discourage the partner from developing those sides of himself and herself that are different.

In *Sanity, Madness, and the Family*, psychologists R. D. Laing and A. Esterson tell of a patient, Claire, whose mother felt threatened by any apparent differences between Claire's views and her own. Far from confirming Claire's own existence as an autonomous individual with feelings and thoughts of her own, her mother met every sign of Claire's

[6]Rogers, *Becoming Partners*, p. 90.

difference from herself with one form of repudiation or another. "A constantly repeated sequence," Laing and Esterson write, "is that Claire makes a statement, and her mother invalidates it by saying:

(i) she does not really mean what she says, or
(ii) she is saying this because she is ill, or
(iii) she cannot remember or know what she feels or felt, or
(iv) she is not justified in saying this."[7]

In Claire's case the result of these repeated disconfirmations of her thoughts and feelings was an intense insecurity about her own autonomous existence as a unique individual with ideas and opinions of her own.

Although most people do not carry their intolerance for difference as far as Claire's mother did, the tendency to refuse confirmation to our partners when they differ from us is a common one, and it is one we should try to eliminate in ourselves as much as possible. Every disconfirmation of your partner's assertions of his or her own unique selfhood thwarts the development of that uniqueness and is in fact an obstacle to the growth of the partnership.

There can be a real joy in discovering that your partner is a unique and different person. Indeed, a large part of the excitement of courtship lies in two people discovering each other—both in their similarities and their differences. This exciting process of revelation and discovery can be continued in an ongoing partnership if we do not let ourselves forget that both parties are richly varied persons with a complexity of feelings, meanings, and values. If we continue to meet signs of difference by honestly accepting them, by confirming our partner's unique individuality, the relationship is free to change and grow and the process of discovery can continue indefinitely.

[7] R. D. Laing and A. Esterson, *Sanity, Madness and the Family*, Vol. I, *Families of Schizophrenics* (New York: Basic Books, 1965), p. 74.

SUMMARY

Human relationships are complex. The capacity of human beings to create situations and develop relationships is very great. For this reason it is not possible or desirable to try to describe *a* good relationship. To do so would be a travesty on each person's capacity to develop his or her own unique relationships. It is better to ask what kind of general guidelines seem to be helpful in most relationships. Carl Rogers has provided a set of four such guidelines in the conclusion to his *Becoming Partners.*

1. Redefine the nature of our commitment to one another, focusing on what is happening between us rather than upon the "oughts" that we have been taught about how partners should behave toward one another. Rogers says, "We commit ourselves to working together on the changing

process of our present relationship because that relationship is currently enriching our love and our life, and we wish it to grow."[8] The emphasis here is upon the partnership itself, which is maintained because it is personally fulfilling to the partners.[9]

2. Keep the channel of communication open. Rogers says:

I will risk myself by endeavoring to communicate *any persisting feeling*, positive or negative, to my partner—to the full depth that I understand it in myself—as a living, present part of *me*. Then I will risk further by trying to understand, with all the empathy I can bring to bear, his or her response, whether it is accusatory and critical or sharing and self-revealing.[10]

As we have seen in this chapter, the communication of feelings is critical to vital relationships. Rogers points out that it is particularly important to communicate persisting feelings because these are the ones that are likely to tell us what parts of our relationship are working well and what parts need adjustment.

3. "We will live by our own choices, the deepest organismic sensings of which we are capable, but we will not be shaped by the wishes, the rules, the roles which others are all too eager to thrust upon us."[11] This guideline is also known as "role transcendence," meaning that it is possible for persons to transcend socially prescribed roles and in that transcendence to discover more personhood. Open communication is especially important in this area.

4. Try to keep in touch with your inner self.[12] Rogers believes that it is only through a deep awareness of our inner natures that we can find authenticity, and only by becoming more authentic ourselves can we participate fully in a growing partnership.

[8]Rogers, *Becoming Partners*, p. 201.

[9]Implicit here is a belief that relationships that are not rewarding should be terminated. This will be discussed more fully in Chapter 14.

[10]Rogers, *Becoming Partners*, p. 204.

[11]Rogers, *Becoming Partners*, p. 206.

[12]See page 38 for the appropriate rule. A very useful perspective on the popular movement to increase our capacity to communicate with one another is found in Kurt W. Back, *Beyond Words: The Story of Sensitivity Training and the Encounter Group Movement* (New York: Russell Sage Foundation, 1972).

4

CONFLICT IN INTIMATE PARTNERSHIPS

According to our hypothesis, human instincts are only of two kinds—those which seek to preserve and unite, which we call erotic, and those which seek to destroy and kill, which we class together as the aggressive or destructive instinct. The phenomena of life arise from the operation of both together, whether acting in concert or in opposition. An instinct of one sort can scarcely ever operate in isolation—it is always accompanied (or, as we say, allocated) with an element from the other side which modified its aim. Thus, for instance, the instinct of self preservation is certainly of an erotic kind; but it must have aggressiveness at its disposal if it is to fulfill its purpose. . . . It is rarely that a given action is the work of a single instinctual impulse which must in itself be compounded of Eros and Destructiveness.

Sigmund Freud

INTRODUCTION

Thus far in this book we have scarcely touched on the subject of conflict in intimate relations. This does not mean that we accept the myth of the happy marriage, which would have us believe that the successful partnership is conflict-free. On the contrary, we feel that conflict is an intrinsic part of any developing relationship. This chapter will explain how this is so. The question that arises about conflict is not whether it exists or does not exist in any given relationship, but how it is expressed, lived with, and managed.

55

The word "conflict" brings to mind a host of related associations. It is not possible to live in this world without encountering numerous examples of conflicts that take the form of violence; this is especially true in the context of the social and political struggles going on throughout the world. Newspaper references to "conflict" in the Middle East, or in Ireland, invariably mean violent conflict. In addition, we also use the word "conflict" to describe various *crises* that arise in our social scene and in our personal lives. Both of these types of conflict occur sporadically, and in both of them we tend to assume that where there is conflict there is someone who is "right" and someone who is "wrong." If this is so, it is natural to assume that the conflict should be "resolved" with the "right" person vindicated and the "wrong" person condemned.

Thus, conflict is generally seen as something that should be done away with—and as quickly as possible. Generally speaking, this is the strategy we follow in our superficial encounters. Where people have little at stake in an encounter, it is quite possible for them to avoid conflict. If the laundry can't be convinced to leave the starch out of your shirts, it may be simpler to find another laundry than to have a "scene" with the overzealous starcher; if the person sitting next to you in your English class won't stop tapping his pencil on the desk all the time, you can try to sit elsewhere or you can learn to ignore the tapping. Casual acquaintances can be annoying, and every once in a while you may feel an overwhelming desire to "have it out" with them, but for the most part "having it out" in such situations simply isn't worth it. Instead, you deal with these potential conflicts by avoiding them.

In ongoing relationships, however, it may be impossible to avoid conflict in this simple way. Indeed, even if it were possible it would probably be detrimental, for conflict is inherent in all relationships and is essential to autonomous growth and development. With every increase in the amount of time we spend with one another, the number of decisions we have to make together, the number of things we do together in an intimate partnership, we increase the possibility for conflict. This is not "good" or "bad," it is simply the way things are.

Because conflict is a part of all relationships, it must be appropriately managed. Managing it, however, does not mean doing away with it. It means, first, recognizing its existence, accepting its reality, and discovering a way to live with it creatively. It means anticipating it, even in its occasionally destructive aspects, in partnerships such as marriage. Recognizing conflict as an intricate part of the growth process will lessen our surprise when we discover it in intimate relationships, will make us prepared for it, and thus will increase our chances of being able to use it as a means of deepening intimacy.

This chapter will explore some of the dimensions of conflict as it appears in intimate relationships. The dynamics of conflict in ongoing relationships will be examined, with the focus initially on some of the major sources of conflict between partners in intimate relationships. We will then turn to a discussion of the creative aspects of conflict, after which we will examine the two extreme forms of the inability to manage conflict creatively. One of these, which we call "pseudomutuality," represents the attempt to eliminate all conflict from a relationship; the other, which we call "total war," is a situation which arises when conflict gets out of hand and swamps all other types of communication. A growing relationship cannot afford to be dominated by conflict, but neither can it survive in the sterile atmosphere of conflict-free intimacy. Conflict is, thus, both unavoidable and necessary.

TROUBLE SPOTS

No one can predict in advance what areas will prove to be troublesome in an intimate partnership. Each pair of partners is unique, and one couple may find that it slides blissfully through areas where other couples bog down in squabbling and contention. The following discussion, therefore, attempts merely to describe in an approximate way those places where partners most frequently run into difficulties. Our assumption is that before we can begin to discuss conflict in general terms it is useful to have some ideas of the specific types of conflict that commonly arise.

We have chosen—somewhat arbitrarily to be sure—four areas for preliminary examination. These are sex, money, in-laws, and conflicting expectations. It is not our intention here to tell you how to avoid conflict in these areas. Rather, by raising the question of why conflict so easily arises in these areas we hope to come to some understanding of the dynamics of conflict in intimate partnerships—what kinds of things cause it, what kinds of effects it has. Then we can move onto a more general discussion of the sources of conflict and the creative and destructive aspects of it.

Sex

Sexual relations are not only the most intimate aspect of an intimate partnership, they are probably also, for a great many people, the most potentially troublesome. Nor is it difficult to see why this should be so. Whatever the sexual feelings, desires, attitudes, and behaviors of oneself and one's partners, it is important to realize that they have been developed over a lifetime and are not likely to change overnight. While some partners may come to their marriage or partnership relatively well matched in these feelings and attitudes, others may be so mismatched and "incompatible" that a great deal of patience is required in order to achieve a mutually satisfying sexual relationship.

Obviously, the couple that finds their sexual attitudes and desires mismatched is going to run into some difficulties—difficulties that can, with patience, love, and cooperation, be dealt with in a way that contributes to the growth of both members of the partnership and of the partnership itself. But even once we have recognized that this is so, we have barely begun to scratch the surface of the potentially troublesome dimensions of sexual relations. For the simple fact is that trouble in this area is by no means confined to couples who are sexually "incompatible."

Think for a moment about what your "ideal" sexual partner would be like. If sex is to be an important aspect of the communication process within your partnership, he or she undoubtedly would be a person with complex and varied sexual tastes which match your own complex and varied feelings. At some times you want your physical intimacies to communicate the tender, loving, and gentle aspects of your relationship; at other times your lovemaking will be more passionate. In Chapter 8 we will be discussing the art of sexual intimacy in more detail, and there you will get a fuller sense of the rich potential of sex as a communication tool. Here it is enough to observe that sex can and should mean different things at different times to the same partners.

From this it follows that your "ideal" sexual partner will be someone capable of expressing, through sex, all the things you want expressed. This is where the snag comes in, because unless your partner is a sexual robot you can program to be tender when you want tenderness, passionate when you want passion, seductive when you want to be seduced, submissive when you want to be dominant, and dominant when you want to be submissive, you undoubtedly are going to find that your needs and desires are not always going to be met in the way you want them met. Precisely because sex is such a complex part of any intimate relationship, even an "ideally" matched couple is not going to find that their desires are perfectly synchronized throughout the life of their relationship.

Unless you, your partner, and your relationship become static, you will never outgrow the necessity to sit down and openly discuss your feelings, desires, attitudes, and behaviors. This is an ongoing and important part of achieving a better understanding of yourself, your partner, and your relationship. As Richard Klemer observed in *Marriage and Family Relations*, "For the great majority of young marrieds, though, the sex adjustment process itself is both necessary and rewarding. After all, there is no other adjustment in which just trying can be so satisfying and so love enriching."[1]

Money

We don't know whether Aristotle and Jackie Onassis have a perfect marriage, but we can be reasonably sure that, whatever their marriage is like, money is not one of the trouble spots they have to deal with. Except among a handful of inordinately rich people, however, money is a subject likely to be associated with some form of conflict in most partnerships. In Chapter 13 we will be discussing income management in some detail, so here let us confine ourselves to a few general observations about the nature of money conflicts in a partnership.

Money is what economists call a scarce resource; but the desires you and your partner have for things that cost money are not scarce. In a sense, the whole problem is no more complex than this one sentence. Even wealthy people must make decisions about how to spend their money, and these decisions must be shaped by some hierarchy of priorities. In some families the choice is between lamb chops for dinner and staying home or macaroni and cheese for dinner and going to a movie; in others a decision must be made about whether to get a new

[1]Richard Klemer, *Marriage and Family Relationships* (New York: Harper & Row, Publishers, 1970).

television set or to have the dents taken out of the car; and in still others it is a choice between the yacht that sleeps twelve or that lovely old fourteen-room house in Bucks County. Except among the fabulously rich, lines have to be drawn somewhere, and the drawing of these lines is a task that most partners will find some degree of difficulty negotiating.

Money conflicts provide an excellent example of the fact that mutual awareness of each other's habits and attitudes is probably the most effective factor in reducing conflict of all sorts. In any new partnership there is a tendency for the partners to look askance at the way their mates spend money simply because the mate's habits are unfamiliar. A young wife, for example, may be shocked when her husband spends three hundred dollars for stereo equipment. She has to admit that they can afford the expense, but it seems to her like a lot of money to throw away on something trivial. It seems that way to her because music wasn't as important to her parents as it was to her husband; her father once spent fifty dollars for a portable phonograph but that was the extent of his spending in this area. On the other hand, her father drove a car as big as a houseboat and traded it in every two years. So if her husband had announced that he wanted to invest four thousand dollars in an automobile she probably wouldn't have batted an eyelash, but when he lays out a fraction of that for his stereo system she complains about his financial irresponsibility. In time, though, she will learn that it is not a matter of irresponsibility; it is simply that her husband has priorities that are different from those she is familiar with.

Of course, familiarity does not eliminate conflict entirely in this area. In a sense, each change in a couple's financial situation—the birth of a baby, a significant increase in his or her salary, the gain of income when she starts working again once the children are all in school—presents a new situation which they must learn to handle afresh. But if the partners have had conflicts over these matters before, if they have learned to tell each other what they think and to listen to what the other has to say, if each has learned to respect the other's judgment and to have confidence in his or her own judgment, conflict over money matters can take the form of a clear presentation of grievances, a fair assessment of the situation by both individuals and a sensible resolution.

In-Laws

Jokes about mothers-in-law are about as old as the institution of marriage, and it is only because of the sexual biases of our society, which tend to make the female partner in a marriage and her female parent especially appropriate targets for humor, that jokes about fathers-in-law aren't as common. We joke about in-laws for one simple reason: they make us nervous. While we have pretty clear expectations about what it means to be a good husband or a good wife, we do not know with anything like the same assurance what it means to be a good in-law. Some societies go to great lengths to define precisely how one should behave with every conceivable in-law.[2] Ours does not. This means in practice that an in-law is someone whom we should feel close to somehow—especially if the in-law is a parent-in-law—but we are not quite sure how to express this closeness. It is a very rare mother-in-law or father-in-law who can fully accept being treated like a parent and a very rare person who is able to treat them as such.

Not the least part of conflict where in-laws are concerned boils down down to a simple matter of jealousy. Before marriage, your parents and siblings are your family; after marriage your spouse is. In most cases this change isn't traumatic; rather, it is a subtle shifting of loyalties that may go almost unnoticed but is very real nevertheless. It is not easy to assess just what this change entails, but it is probably safe to generalize and say that for most people becoming married is a gradual process. In a marriage your primary commitments are to each other and to your relationship, but these commitments are not born overnight. While they are in their gestation phase, it would not be unusual if you were to experience some doubts about whether your mate really was fully committed to you and, conversely, about whether you are fully committed to your mate. Often these doubts center on your in-laws, who are the chief rivals for the loyalties you expect. "Why do we have to go over to your parents' house so often?" a young bride may complain. "Don't tell me your sister's coming to visit again. Don't you two get enough of each other?" a new husband may lament. "Can't you find someone else to go shopping with besides your mother?" "If you think Consolidated Asbestos is a good investment, go ahead and buy it. I don't see why you have to ask your father's advice." All these are the statements of mates' jealousy of their partners' involvement with their families. But if you are or have ever been married, you probably have had the experience of heading home with your spouse after a visit to your parents' house and saying or feeling something like, "You know, it's funny, but while we were sitting there in the living room this afternoon it suddenly struck me that I don't live there any more."

What we are saying, in short, is that any individual's relations to his or her parents are among the most complex in his or her life. And one's relations with one's partner are every bit as complex—probably more so. Put the two sets of relationships together and you have six people connected with each other in an extremely intricate web of emotions.

[2]Typically, these societies are unilinear societies in which descent, inheritance, and succession to office are traced through either the mother's side or the father's side of the family. For a detailed description of how kinship controls interpersonal behavior in such societies, see William N. Stephens, *The Family in Cross-Cultural Perspective* (New York: Holt, Rinehart & Winston, Inc., 1963).

Expectations

A final trouble spot can be described as a difference in expectations about what the partnership is all about. Marriage means different things to each one of us, depending upon our experiences with married persons and our evaluations of those experiences. Most often, when we feel ourselves in conflict with our partner over the way he or she behaves sexually, handles the family finances, or relates to his or her own family and ours, the conflict can be traced to the fact that our partner is not behaving in the way we expect. Many of the examples given in our discussion of sexual, financial, and in-law conflicts make this clear. To take just one instance, if we have come to expect that an important part of a spouse's role is to satisfy our sexual desires in a certain way, the fact that our spouse occasionally fails to do so may be a source of conflict. To the extent that we can avoid bringing expectations like these to our partnership, we will be less likely to find ourselves in conflict with our mates.

Each individual has a unique frame of reference, which Lloyd Saxton has succinctly defined as a "cluster of values, expectations and factual assumptions which underlie most of a person's adult perception" of the world.[3] It is almost inevitable in most partnerships that the frame of reference of the partners will be different. This has been illustrated briefly in the example of the wife who disapproved when her husband bought a new stereo. Because two individuals do not share the same frame of reference they do not interpret their "common" world in precisely the same way. A certain amount of misunderstanding and conflict is therefore inevitable and the major tactic in coping with conflict from this source is to try to understand the frame of reference which the partner brings to the situation under dispute. At the very minimum, it involves a recognition that this different frame of reference is legitimate and need not be compromised in order to work out a satisfactory way of managing the conflict. But because, in many instances, the frame of reference will not change—even in regard to simple matters like buying clothes and stereo equipment—conflict must be managed, not resolved once and for all.

SOURCES OF CONFLICT

In order better to understand conflict in partnerships, let us examine four common sources of conflict. These are defensiveness, differences in background and outlooks, inadequate feedback, and frustration.

[3]Lloyd Saxton, *The Individual, Marriage and the Family*, 2nd ed. (Belmont, Calif.: Wadsworth Publishing Company, Inc., 1972), p. 232.

Defensiveness

Defensive behavior generally is directed not toward satisfying a need, but rather toward alleviating the tension and self-depreciation associated with the *failure* to meet the need in question. In this sense, defense-oriented behavior differs from what we may call reality-oriented behavior in that it is aimed at achieving some substitute goal that will reduce tension rather than at overcoming the barrier that inhibits the attainment of the basic goal. Among the most common defense mechanisms are: withdrawal, conversion of tension into physical illness, substitution, rationalization, excessive sleeping, and fantasizing.

For example, in *Communes U.S.A.*, Dick Fairfield reports a dramatic form of withdrawal. One of the members of Harrad West was so torn by the tensions within the group marriage that he hid himself in a closet for several days.[4] His behavior was, of course, an extreme version of a type of defense we all use from time to time. When you avoid calling a friend because you lost the book you borrowed from him you are using withdrawal as a defense. So is the young man who avoids sexual conflict with his girlfriend by scheduling all their dates so that they are never alone together until he has to take her home.

Rationalization is probably the most commonly used defense mechanism. The student who attributes his failure to bias on the part of teachers is engaging in a rather transparent form of rationalization. There is an old adage that advises, "When confronted with failure, redefine success." In some cases this may be sound advice. If you always wanted to be a jockey but didn't stop growing until you were six foot three, you would be well advised to reassess your goals. The trouble with the adage is that it is difficult to tell if you have tried "hard enough" before redefining success. If the slightest obstacle leads you to abandon your objectives, you are not being realistic so much as you are engaging in a form of rationalization.

Reality-oriented behavior in a partnership involves trying to understand the issues and coming to some sort of workable resolution of the problem. Lloyd Saxton sums up the difference between reality-oriented behavior and defense-oriented behavior with the following example:

When a husband comes home late and his wife is angry because of it, and when she says that she is angry, and when they both agree that coming home late creates a problem which they must try to solve—this is reality oriented behavior. But if she refuses to speak (withdrawal), shows no interest in his comings and goings (apathy), gets a headache (psychosomatic ailment), or punishes the children (substitution); or if he explains that he "couldn't reach a phone" (rationalization), dozes in front of the television set or goes to bed early when they are finally

[4]Richard Fairfield, *Communes U.S.A.: A Personal Tour* (Baltimore: Penguin Books, 1972), p. 300.

together (escapist sleep), or imagines that "next time" he will arrive home early bearing an expensive gift (fantasy)—this is defense-oriented behavior.[5]

One of the main reasons why people engage in defense-oriented behavior is because reality, when it is especially unpleasant, threatens their image of themselves. If an important part of your self-image is your belief that you are a great lover, you may respond to sexual problems in your partnership by such strategies as avoiding sexual situations or attributing the problem to your partner. Similarly, the man who shouts at his wife, "I am not shouting!" when she tells him to stop shouting and be reasonable probably does so because he is trying to preserve his image of himself as a reasonable man who handles conflict in a reasonable way.

These strategies, of course, do not solve the problem at hand; all they can do is save you the pain of recognizing that your own image of yourself does not correspond to reality. The man with the sexual problem cannot begin to deal with it until he admits to himself that he is not an accomplished lover; the angry husband cannot contribute to a resolution of the situation that has made him angry until he acknowledges his anger.

What is more, the problem with defense-oriented strategies is not merely the fact that they fail to contribute to a resolution of conflict. Often, in fact, they intensify conflict. The woman who refuses to speak to her husband after he comes home late not only does nothing to avoid a repetition of the incident but also provides a new source of tension between them. The man who avoids confronting his sexual problem by avoiding intimate situations with his wife is adding to their marital difficulties by making her feel rejected. Defensiveness, in short, is not only an inadequate means of coping with conflict but also an important source of conflict in its own right.

Differences in Background and Outlook

In our discussion of some of the common trouble spots in partnerships we observed that holding inappropriate expectations about your partner's behavior and attitudes was a major source of conflict. Obviously, therefore, differences in background and outlook between the partners provide a rich storehouse of potential problems. Here such factors as differences in social class, economic position, family structure, religion, and race may come into play.

Such differences are far more significant in our modern, highly mobile society than they used to be in the past. Until quite recently, the range of people available for mate selection tended to be quite narrow. Marrying the boy or girl "next door" was not at all uncommon. If for

[5]Saxton, *The Individual, Marriage and the Family.* p. 234.

no other reason than the lack of geographical mobility—before the pro-
liferation of automobiles travel was extremely restricted by modern-day
standards—the circle of an individual's acquaintance was likely to cover
very little territory. This made it more likely than not that the mate an
individual selected would share many of the individual's socially determined attitudes and beliefs.

Today all this is changed. Especially in urban settings, public schools
draw their students from a wide variety of backgrounds and colleges
intensify this trend. The people you meet in your college classes come
from just about every segment of our society and, indeed, from all over
the country. Sociologically speaking, the range of potential mates available is much wider than was formerly the case, and with this change
comes an increase in the likelihood that any partnership you form will
contain a greater divergence in background and outlook.

We do not mean to suggest that it would be wiser or safer to limit
yourself to partners who share your background. On the contrary, differences in background and outlook can contribute immensely to the
growth potential of a partnership, for there are few things more helpful
in opening a person's mind to new experiences than an intimate association with someone whose view of the world differs markedly from his
or her own. We might almost speculate that there may be something
seriously wrong with anyone who failed to grow and develop in such
a situation. But on the other hand, it would be unrealistic to imagine
that major differences in background and outlook do not produce significant problems which partners must confront.

A marriage in which, say, the husband is the son of a corporation
vice-president and the wife is the daughter of an assembly-line worker
is going to have problems which would not have arisen if the two partners had each married individuals whose backgrounds were more like
their own. These problems are going to include not only obvious differences in their attitudes toward money but also differences in their
feelings about entertaining friends, leisure activities, personal habits,
domestic roles, and even sexual preferences. Each of these differences
is a potential source of conflict—just as each is a potential source of
growth. It is, to use a popular term, a liberating experience to learn
that the way you, your family, and friends have always done things is
not the only way. As you learn this, you find that you have more options, a richer variety of responses to a given situation. But it also can
be a painful process, for the discovery of new options can be profoundly
unsettling inasmuch as it forces you to give up the comfortable assumption that your way is the only way.

Another type of conflict involving the individual outlooks of the
partners arises from what sociologists call "discontinuity of role conditioning." Adult roles in our society are discontinuous from childhood
roles. That is to say, the role of a mother is not at all like the role of

daughter; the role of father is not at all like the role of son. A man who wants his partner to treat him as his mother once did is likely to have trouble in his partnerships. Nor is it reasonable for him to want to treat his partner as though she were his mother. Yet when two people form an intimate partnership, especially for the first time, they have little or no experience in the new roles they are expected to fulfill. To a certain extent the wife may expect her husband to relate to her in many of the ways her father did, just as the husband may expect his wife to "mother" him to some degree.

Fortunately, this sort of conflict tends to diminish as the partners "grow up" and learn both what is expected of them in their new roles and what they can reasonably expect from their partners. Of course, if one or both of the partners does not grow up in the relationship, destructive conflict is likely to be pervasive. Various aspects of this matter of role discontinuity will be discussed more fully in Chapter 11.

Inadequate Feedback

The term "feedback" is used by sociologists to describe the signals given off by our environment (personal or impersonal) in response to our behavior. We can use this feedback to adjust or modify our behavior in order to realize our objectives. Sometimes this adjustment takes place consciously, as when an associate tells you you look good in brightly colored clothes and you take this response into account the next time you are shopping for something to wear. Sometimes it occurs unconsciously. For example, if you are a salesperson who tends to "come on strong" with your customers, you may instinctively adopt a softer approach with customers who seem unresponsive to your usual method and you may not even realize you are doing it. Problems tend to arise when people are unaware, both consciously and unconsciously, of the feedback they are receiving and when the feedback they are receiving is not adequate for allowing them to assess the situation and to make the proper adjustments.

When we think of feedback, a number of examples from the non-personal environment come readily to mind. Thermostats and computers are well-known devices employing feedback; when you tune an engine or a musical instrument, the sound you hear after each adjustment is the feedback that tells you what to do next. But to describe feedback in human interaction is a much more complicated process, because so much more is involved. In the first place, the environment gives off many cues, not just a single stimulus such as a change in the amount of heat, as in the case of the thermostat. We are able to respond to many stimuli simultaneously, although we may not be consciously aware of all of them. Furthermore, our behavior is not in reality a discreet act, it is a process. Thus it is sometimes difficult, if not actually impossible, to relate the feedback we are receiving to a specific act. Finally, before we can use the feedback we receive we must interpret it in terms of our own capacities and self-images. Our interaction with our environment is a complex process with multiple messages being communicated in many directions at the same time. For example, consider this incident in a training group:

Don: John, it seems to me that every time Eric tries to say something, you interrupt him.
John: Oh, I don't think that's true.
Eric: I think you do.
Sue: I don't think John interrupts Eric. I feel that every time Eric makes a contribution, John seems to add to and build upon what Eric said. Don't you feel that way, Eric?
Eric: No! Sue, you always seem to be supporting John. As far as you're concerned, John can do nothing wrong in this group.
Mary: I agree with Don. I think John does interrupt Eric, and I'm annoyed that Sue always stands up for John.

This is a classic example of a whole lot of feedback being given in a group setting. John, of course, is getting conflicting feedback about his behavior in this group. There is a discrepancy between the signals he is getting from Don, Eric, and Mary, and the signals he is getting from Sue. How is he to evaluate what he hears? What is he to make of this discrepancy. What changes should he make in his behavior as a result? Can he assume that Don, Eric, and Mary must be right simply because they constitute the majority of the group? Probably not. The point is that in real-life situations, responding to the feedback you receive from your environment is not an easy task because the feedback is often complex and even contradictory. What is more, as we can see in the preceding example, the other members of the group also are getting feedback on their behavior. The communication of feedback is an ongoing and complicated process.

Couples in partnerships can grow only if they receive adequate feedback. If the relationship is to be a vital one, both partners must give and receive feedback that enables them to grow. The feedback you give and receive can be classified in a number of ways. It may be either divergent or convergent. *Divergent feedback* tells us that our behavior is not bringing us a result we desire; *convergent feedback* tells us that our behavior is appropriate to our objectives. In a partnership or marriage, divergent feedback moves the partners away from one another and engenders frustration. A sensible response to divergent feedback would be to make an attempt to clarify the issues so that appropriate adjustments of behavior become possible. Often, however, people respond to divergent feedback by pouting, becoming miffed and angry, and by try-

Philip Teuscher

ing to make their partners feel uncomfortable also. There is a tendency to answer divergent feedback by responding with more divergent feedback, and so the downward spiral of disengagement accelerates. Often a "cooling off" period is necessary before this pattern can be broken. Sometimes the partners may push each other away for weeks or months, perhaps even bringing about the end of the partnership.

Feedback also can be classed as limited or free, immediate or delayed. In the nonpersonal world of inanimate objects, feedback is typically free and immediate. In the world of interpersonal relations it is typically limited and delayed. As Lloyd Saxton writes:

For example, the husband who perceives himself as the life of the party, a belief which his wife's smiles seem to support, may find after the two of them leave that (1) he was not really getting convergent feedback from her but was misinterpreting the limited feedback she was providing and (2) the only reason that she was providing limited rather than divergent feedback was that she was trying to conform to the cultural expectations of emotional control in a public place and of harmony between a married couple. Only with the delayed and now free feedback of her explosion of anger on the drive home is the husband able accurately to process the information which may modify his behavior at future parties.[6]

Because feedback in partnerships is likely to be limited and delayed in many situations, and because it is almost always ambiguous (inasmuch as it reflects a multitude of needs), couples must work hard at trying to interpret correctly the feedback they receive from their partners and strive to reduce the ambiguity in the feedback they give off. If they cannot do this, their partnership is in for a world of trouble. Conflict will be inevitable and, inevitably, it will be destructive as well.

[6]Saxton, *The Individual, Marriage and the Family*, p. 225.

One of the reasons why feedback is so important is tied to the fact that the feedback a person receives has a lot to do with the formation and maintenance of her or his self-image. Our conception of who we are is derived from the feedback we have received throughout our life—particularly the early portion of it. Convergent feedback makes us feel comfortable, adequate, and at ease with ourselves. Indeed, a person who has benefitted from consistent convergent feedback in one area of life may well tend to feel relaxed and competent in many or all areas.

Just as convergent feedback is an essential part of the process by which the self-image is maintained, so divergent feedback is an essential part of the process by which the self-image is modified. Because we are always to some extent a mystery to ourselves, we are constantly listening for who others say we are. Statements or behaviors that make emphatic judgments about us are not easily dismissed. This is a common experience in training sessions. Kurt Back reports having had conversations with two of five men who were on special assignment during the first year of the National Training Laboratory in Bethel. Because of the special tasks, they received intensive divergent feedback and criticism. Both reported the pain of the experience ten years later and vowed never to expose themselves again so openly to the criticism of others.[7]

The destructive potentiality of divergent feedback has important implications for intimate partnerships. In a partnership we are apt to be open enough to lower many of the normal defenses, and in this sense we are most vulnerable in our most intimate relationship. When our partner attacks who we are at this deep level, we are apt to see this as disloyalty and betrayal, for it is very difficult to withstand attacks directed against our self-image at a very deep level.

On the other hand, the fact that partners can and should reinforce each other's self-image presupposes a willingness on their part to accept the differences between them. If one partner lacks this willingness, the other may feel that he or she is being pressured to become the person his or her partner wants him or her to become. Unfortunately, there is a common tendency to limit the convergent feedback we give to those areas where we are not aware of differences and to feel, when we cannot confirm a partner, that this is somehow the partner's "fault." In fact, however, those areas where convergent feedback and confirmation are not possible may well be the areas of the other's greatest growth and potential.

For example, imagine a situation in which a wife was overly dependent on her husband's judgment in most of the major decisions that confronted her. As she grows to be less dependent, however, her husband may find himself incapable of supporting and confirming her new-found independence. The feedback she gets from him may be mostly negative. What is progress and growth from her point of view may be

[7]Kurt Back, *Beyond Words* (New York: Russell Sage Foundation, 1972), pp. 52–53.

threatening to his self-image, and thus conflict may result. The conflict, though, may accelerate her growth toward independence and the negative feedback he receives from her may open his eyes to the fact that his image of himself as a decisive man does not need to depend on her indecisiveness. This example reminds us once again that conflict is an integral part of any relationship and that, in some mysterious way, it can be a life-giving and growth-enhancing force.

Frustration

Frustration, which often manifests itself in feelings of depression, anger, or indifference, derives from our inability to realize our objectives, to meet our needs or expectations. When we cannot live into our self-image or fulfill our dreams, frustration is a likely response. Often it is difficult for a person to identify the sources of his or her frustration. Although sexual frustration readily comes to mind as an example, it is by no means the only, or even the major source of frustration in partnerships. The inability to get the job done around the home, the pressures from work that overlap into the partnership, the unmatched needs and expectations of the partners all can prove to be sources of frustration.

One possible response to frustration is aggression. When things do not go as expected, we often give vent to an angry outburst at the supposed culprit. Frustration also can be turned inward, so that the frustrated person feels deeply depressed, often without knowing why. A third response to frustration is projection, an unconscious process in which responsibility for the frustrating situation is "projected" onto some "innocent" party or object. Thus, for example, a man who has been frustrated by the inefficiency of his staff on the job may project his anger onto his wife, scolding her when he gets home for not having dinner ready on time. The wife is thus unwittingly brought into the conflict generated by the frustrations of the job. If it is not clear to the husband or the wife that his real reason for scolding her is his anger at his staff, they are likely to get involved in a fight that seemingly has no purpose—or at least its purpose has no reality at the moment.

No one reacts to frustration the same way all of the time. We probably can call to mind examples in our own behavior of each of the three ways of responding to frustration. Nevertheless, most people tend to favor one type of response over the others, so that it becomes identified as their typical way of handling frustrating situations. The fact that this is so can be of some help to one's partner. If you are able to recognize that certain behaviors by your partner are his or her usual response to frustration, you may be able to cope with the situation far better than you could if you had to take the response at face value. There is, of course, no reason why a wife should be expected to tolerate outbursts of anger directed at her simply because she knows it is really something that happened at work that has got her husband upset. But she will be able to deal with the situation in a far more appropriate way if she recognizes its real source. So long as she misunderstands the situation, her response to his anger is likely to be merely defensive—perhaps by offering excuses for why dinner was late—but once she understands the real cause of his anger, she can take the offensive, attempting to show him the real root of the problem.

It is not uncommon to find that couples who know each other well have learned to tell when what they are fighting about is "really" what they are fighting about and when it is not. This knowledge can be of tremendous help because it makes it easier to keep conflict in perspective. The partners know when real issues are at stake and respond accordingly; they also know when an apparent conflict is simply a result of the fact that one of the partners is responding to frustration by "letting off steam," and so they don't let this sort of inessential conflict get out of hand. As we shall see when we discuss learning how to fight, an important part of the successful management of conflict involves knowing what is worth fighting over and what isn't. Partners who do not know this are likely to find their relationship degenerating into the situation we describe as "total war."

THE CREATIVE DIMENSIONS OF CONFLICT

Conflict that is creative—or at least that has the potential for being so—is conflict that recognizes the personhood of the partner with whom one is in conflict. This means essentially that neither partner in the conflict attempts to reduce the other to the status of a nonperson through labeling or abusive language or denial; rather, each person sees the other as a "worthy adversary" with ideas, dreams, and thoughts which have validity and must be taken into account. It takes an intense openness to appreciate and respect the ideas of another which may be in direct conflict with our own ideas, but this is in fact the only way that conflict can have a creative dimension. Only equals are worthy adversaries.

If equals engage in conflict and if their communication is of significance, what emerges is a complicated process which enables each to define and clarify—both for himself or herself and for the other–the issue around which their conflict is focused. This does not mean that the contestants simply accept the various statements their partners may make, but it does mean that they take advantage of the intensity of the debate, with its defining and redefining of the issues, so that the conflict provides an opportunity to deepen their understanding of what is at stake.

If the issues are drawn with clarity, the conflict almost inevitably serves to broaden the base of contact which two persons make with each other. Things that simply would have been accepted or rejected had there been no conflict are explored, examined, and defended. The

Drawing by Dana Fradon; © *1974 The New Yorker Magazine, Inc.*

result is an expanded picture of reality, which allows each partner to live more deeply into the situation and provides an occasion for a more intimate glimpse of each other as each grapples with the new reality. Thus intimacy is facilitated.

Respecting Feelings

As we have pointed out earlier, one of the major sources of conflict in intimate relationships is the fact that two partners are quite likely to feel quite differently about the same thing. The conflict thus serves to bring these different feelings out into the open, but in many cases it will not do anything to change these feelings. You may be tempted to assume that this means the conflict is pointless. If a husband and wife have different feelings about something, argue about it, and still have different feelings, what, you may well ask, is gained by the conflict?

To answer this question we must first understand that changing your partner's attitudes and feelings should not be the primary goal of conflict. A person feels what he or she feels, and being told (or telling yourself) that it is wrong to feel that way doesn't do much to change it. The feelings remain, and added to them are feelings of guilt for feeling that way in the first place. If either partner were to be pressured into renouncing his or her feelings as a result of conflict, he or she would be surrendering an authentic part of himself or herself. (On the other hand, we do not mean to suggest that people do not sometimes genuinely learn, as a result of conflict, that their feelings were wrong. Most people have had the experience of getting into an argument with someone and realizing, in the course of it, "Gee, you know you're right; I don't know why I let myself get so worked up about that. I guess I wasn't thinking straight; I just got carried away.")

Well, then, if we cannot reasonably expect one of the partners to renounce his or her feelings in most cases of conflict, what does the conflict accomplish? If we recognize that conflict often arises from the fact that an ongoing relationship has numerous goals and sometimes some of them are mutually exclusive, we can see that conflict can help to bridge this gap so long as each partner realizes that it is important to respect the other's feelings. If the two of them simply denounce each other for being selfish, they will only make the situation worse. But if they come, as a result of the conflict, to a fuller appreciation of each other's feelings, they will be better able to navigate through the difficult periods in their relationship. Many situations of conflict persist through the whole length of a relationship. The important thing is not to make conflicts go away. It is to appreciate and respect each other's feelings so that you and your partner can approach your problems as something you are struggling through together rather than as something that drives you apart.

Avoiding Win-Lose Battles

There is an old sporting adage that says how you play the game is more important than whether you win or lose. It is probably safe to say that in our intensely competitive society not many people take this adage seriously; it seems old-fashioned, naive, and unrealistic. Twentieth-century America is unmistakably a meritocracy in which "nothing succeeds like success"; in such a society it matters quite a bit whether you win or lose. How you play the game also matters, but perhaps not quite as much.

One could argue at great length about whether the American success ethic, with its emphasis on winning, is good or bad, healthy or unhealthy. We are going to avoid the temptation to take a side in this argument. Instead, we will simply point out that in most situations of conflict between intimate partners, who wins and who loses is not very important at all. Regardless of how you feel about the importance of winning in business, sports, or life in general, an intimate partnership simply is not a competitive situation.

Conflict situations in which one partner can win only at the expense of the other's loss tend to be destructive for both parties. When conflict in a partnership is conducted on the winner-take-all principle, there is little possibility that the conflict will produce mutual growth, for one can "grow" only at the expense of the other. In a win-lose situation, someone is always going to get hurt, regardless of how socially acceptable or appropriate the loss may be.

Unless there is something seriously wrong with your partnership, you probably do not engage in conflict with your partner in order to score points. Rather, you come into conflict when one or both of you feel some sense of grievance, some sense that something is wrong that must be corrected. Usually, too, the aggrieved party feels that his or her partner is responsible for the situation. If the television isn't working right, that is a situation that needs correcting but it is not an occasion for conflict. But if the television isn't working and you think your partner should have fixed it—that is, if you hold your partner responsible for the problem—then it is a situation that could lead to conflict. But your point in initiating the conflict was not to force the other party to confess, "I was wrong, you were right"; it was to get the television fixed—that is, to do something about the problem that caused the conflict in the first place.

The adoption of a win-lose approach to conflict is often unfair. In many partnerships, the individuals are not equally matched in their ability to fight. Often it will be the woman who is at a disadvantage for the simple reason that our society tends to encourage aggressiveness in males and to discourage it in females. In many partnerships, therefore, the husband will find that if he pushes a fight far enough and hard enough his wife will surrender. This discovery can be the undoing of a partnership, for there is no denying that winning is a tempting prospect.

Closely related to the win-lose approach to conflict is the type of conflict that arises out of competition between the partners. Some people are highly competitive; they try to turn almost any kind of activity in which they engage into a competitive game. Such people may carry this tendency over into their partnership. They compete with their partners for other people's attention, they compete with each other to see who can do more chores or who can manage the affairs of the partnership better. This sort of behavior easily can become a source of endless conflict, and it quickly degenerates into one continuous win-lose battle. When you compete with someone else, you are attempting to demonstrate that you are better than they are. This also means you are attempting to demonstrate that they are "worse" than you. Insofar as this is the case, competition is a denial of your partner's personhood. The fact that our society places a high premium on competition in the job, in the school, and in the marketplace indicates that this is one area in which the interpersonal skills rewarded by our society may in fact be destructive to interpersonal relationships.[8]

Of course, it is easy enough for us to advise our readers to avoid win-lose confrontations, but it is not so easy for people in the heat of conflict to follow this advice. Creative conflict involves accepting the anger and hostility in oneself and in one's partner as real and legitimate. But feelings can be accepted and experienced without being acted upon either by letting it all hang out in a violent fistfight or by an uncontrolled avalanche of abusive language intended to exterminate the partner. The ability to allow the partner to "save face" even in the heat of an argument is a skill that can be learned. It takes time and patience and, we

[8]See particularly the critique of the anti-personal, anti-intimate society in Jules Henry, *Culture Against Man* (New York: Random House, 1965), and Erich Fromm, *The Art of Loving* (New York: Bantam Books, Inc., 1970).

think, begins with cultivating an ability to accept feelings we commonly find unacceptable.

Learning to Fight

The Intimate Enemy by George Bach and Peter Wyden provides a rich repertoire of skills necessary for creative fighting in intimate partnerships.[9] Their book is highly recommended for anyone who wishes to further explore this fascinating and important aspect of intimate relationships. It should be read along with Suzanne K. Steinmetz and Murray A. Strauss, *Violence in the Family*, which demonstrates on the basis of a study of 385 couples that certain kinds of verbal "ventilation" of aggressive feelings can be quite destructive.[10] Because the subject is too complex to be dealt with fully here we will confine ourselves to a few central observations.

For some people learning to fight means starting out with the fundamentals of self-defense. That is to say, some people come to a partnership without having learned how to stand up for themselves. It may be that in their parents' home conflict was always hidden from the children; or it may be that the parent who was the young person's role model was chronically submissive in any conflict. Whatever the reason, you cannot realistically expect your partner to be able to see things from your point of view if you are not able to stand up for your point of view and defend it.

For others, learning to fight means learning to fight fair. Boxing and wrestling both have sets of rules that dictate what is fair and what is unfair; even war is subject to internationally accepted standards. Unfortunately, no one has yet codified the laws that govern intimate conflict. Nevertheless, it is important that couples work out their own standards. What these are will vary from couple to couple, but it is not hard to figure out the sort of thing that would constitute a "low blow" in any partnership.

The important thing to bear in mind in fighting with your partner is to keep the conflict in perspective. You will want to drive home your points, but you don't want to inflict permanent damage. Say a husband and wife have gotten into an argument about sex; she initiated it by

[9]George R. Bach and Peter Wyden, *The Intimate Enemy: How to Fight Fair in Love and Marriage* (New York: William Morrow & Company, Inc., 1969).
[10]Suzanne K. Steinmetz and Murray A. Strauss, *Violence in the Family* (New York: Dodd Mead and Company, 1974). See also Murray A. Strauss, "Leveling, Civility, and Violence in the Family," *Journal of Marriage and the Family* 36 (February 1974), 13–29. In this article Strauss examines the factual basis for therapy and family advice urging "leveling in the sense of giving free expression to aggressive feelings" in a study of 385 couples. "The study tested the hypothesis that verbal aggression is a substitute for physical aggression." His conclusion was that the hypothesis was wrong: he found that partnerships with more verbal aggression also had more physical aggression. The results were particularly pronounced for working-class couples.

complaining to him that he rushes the sex act too much. After a few minutes of quiet discussion the situation escalated into an argument. For the first ten minutes, though, it was kept in bounds. Then he hit her with a low blow, angrily shouting, "Don't blame me for the fact that you're terrible in bed! I had plenty of women before we were married and I never got any complaints." Or say a husband and wife have gotten into an argument on how much she spends for clothes, food, or anything else. Tempers flare over whether or not she budgets carefully enough, but then she floors him with a rabbit punch, ending the fight by saying, "If you made a decent living we wouldn't be having this problem. I'm sorry if I haven't adjusted to the fact that you'll never amount to anything!"

Finally, learning to fight means learning when to stop. For many people this isn't a problem; indeed, their most passionate moments of closeness may come after their bitterest fights. Such couples, however, are probably far more rare than the folklore on marriage would have us believe. In real life, calling off a fight is a difficult art to master. In part this is because the desire to win dies hard and it is not easy to recognize when you have made your feelings clear to your partner and your partner has made his or her feelings clear to you. One couple we know of hit upon a deceptively simple strategy for stopping fights. One of them —we won't say which—would recognize that they had made their feelings as clear as they were going to make them and would say, "If I was wrong, which I tend to doubt, I'm sorry." And the other would say, "And if I was wrong, which I tend to doubt, I'm sorry."

The strategy worked because it provided a convenient way out of conflict when both parties recognized that there was nothing to be gained by pursuing it. The formula, though, isn't magic. Even after they discovered the formula they still pushed some of their fights too far simply because neither one of them was willing to invoke it. There is, in fact, no strategy that can guarantee that you and your partner will be able to stop your conflicts before they reach the point of being counterproductive, but experienced couples generally find that it helps to work out some mutually intelligible signal for letting your partner know when you think it is time for a truce.

Leveling

Psychologist Carl Rogers claims that one of the keys to a successful relationship is a commitment by both partners to expressing any persistent feeling about the partnership that they may have. This also entails a commitment to listen to the partner's reaction. In short, the partners promise to "level" with each other.[11]

Leveling is difficult to do because of a natural fear of hurting or offending one's partner, or of being hurt or offended by his or her re-

[11]See Chapter 3, p. 39

sponse. When we are afraid to level with our partner, we tend to run away from the potential fight. Sometimes flight is an appropriate reaction to a looming conflict but it should not be allowed to become a habitual response to tension. Postponing a fight to avoid conflict in an unsuitable setting is generally a good idea, but if a couple makes these postponements permanent they are not leveling with each other. Although no conflict may be apparent between them, this is in fact only because communication has broken down.

EXTREMES OF CONFLICT

Our discussion so far in this chapter has concerned itself with situations in which conflict often arises and with some of the more common sources of conflict in intimate relationships. All along, we have tried to emphasize the importance of controlling conflict and using it as a creative and constructive part of our communication network. In this section we are going to look at conflict from a different perspective. We are going to examine two distinct types of relationship, which are polar opposites as far as their handling of conflict is concerned. One results when the partners make an effort to ban conflict from their relationship on the mistaken assumption that any manifestation of conflict in a partnership represents a failure on the part of the partners. The other arises when conflict gets out of hand and becomes the whole of the relation between the two individuals instead of merely one form of communication within the partnership.

Pseudomutuality

Pseudomutuality is basically an attempt to avoid conflict and give the appearance of happy mutuality and cooperation. It is likely to occur when two very insecure persons enter into a partnership. This insecurity usually focuses around the "positively valued identity" of either the husband or the wife.[12] The man may think little of himself because he is not handsome, because he is not as successful as he thinks he should be in his career, or because he experienced—probably in adolescence—a series of painful relationships with the girls he dated. As a result he does not value himself highly and looks at it as a sort of miracle that his wife agreed to marry him. As he sees it, she is the repository of everything good in their partnership, and he is afraid to jeopardize her inexplicable toleration of him by entering into conflict with her. Conversely, the woman may harbor serious questions about her beauty or her ability as a housewife, homemaker, or sexual partner. But she is relieved to be married and wouldn't want to do anything that might endanger their partnership.

These two insecure people bring a tremendous emotional investment

[12]Lynn C. Wynne et al., "Psuedo-Mutality to the Family Relations of Schizophrenics," *Psychiatry* 2 (May 1958), 206–207.

to their relationship. Their relationship becomes, in some distorted way, their bulwark against their insecurity. The problem is that this bulwark is also a barrier that prevents genuine intimacy. It must be preserved at all costs, and so the partners are willing to pay a high price for it in terms of disguising their true feelings from themselves and their mates.

In such a partnership the partners tell each other only what they think the other wants to hear. They are constantly dealing with their impressions of each other's wishes and needs for they are never willing to risk having those impressions confirmed or denied. Thus, they never really communicate. As Lynn C. Wynne observed in an article on pseudomutuality that appeared in a psychiatric journal a number of years ago:

Psuedo-Mutuality refers to a quality of relatedness with several ingredients. Each person brings into the relation a primary investment in maintaining a sense of relation. His need and wish for this particular relation is especially strong for one or more of a variety of possible reasons. . . . The past experience of each person and the current circumstances of the relation lead to an effort to maintain the idea or feeling, even though this may be illusory, that one's own behavior and expectations mesh with the behavior and the expectations of the other persons in the relation.[13]

Ironically, an outsider observing a pseudomutual couple sees what looks like a pretty happy pair. To their friends they may be the ideal couple, but in fact they are so preoccupied with keeping their relationship going that they never really get around to having much of a relationship. They are afraid to be intimate.

One common characteristic of a pseudomutual partnership is a compulsion to do things together. Neither partner shows an interest in developing his or her own interests and needs. They dare not stand out as different from one another. Things that they may have enjoyed prior to their partnership are given up for the sake of the partnership. Thus the remnants of a career in interior decorating are neglected and the fishing rods lie unused in the garage. Or, conversely, he forces himself to develop an interest in wallpaper and furniture while she convinces herself that she enjoys wading in cold trout streams at dawn.

A number of years ago something called "togetherness" was all the rage among the people who dispense advice to married couples. To a considerable extent, togetherness is simply another word for pseudomutuality. Fortunately, the height of this fashion has now passed, but traces of it still can be found. Only a few years ago a college offered courses in football for wives whose husbands were glued to the television set every Sunday afternoon from August through January. Apparently the wives who felt the need to sign up for such courses had enjoyed a pseudomutual relationship with their husbands until the husbands became hooked on football. Since this unilateral addiction upset the pseu-

[12]Wynne et al., "Pseudo-Mutuality . . .," p. 207.

domutuality, and since the addiction seemed to be incurable, the wives tried to reestablish the relationship on its old footing by becoming addicts themselves. It is too bad no one was there to tell them to go home and find something to do themselves on Sunday. From the standpoint of a healthy relationship between two unique individuals, the husband's passion for football should have been seen as a golden opportunity for the couple to break out of the trap of togetherness and start establishing autonomous lives.

Another common trait in pseudomutual partnerships is the fact that the partners tend to play very carefully defined roles. They see themselves exclusively as husbands and wives rather than as unique persons who happen to be married. Any deviation from these roles is felt as a threat to the partnership. As Gail Fullerton notes, "Someone who is certain that he or she has no imagination, no sense of humor, no playfulness and cannot do anything but follow a detailed set of instructions, has to live by the book."[14] Living by the book is easier than striking out on your own; it can be more comfortable. Often, however, such relationships begin to decompose the moment children are born. The entrance of a child on the scene places conflicting role demands on any couple, for the woman must learn to be a mother while continuing to function in the role of wife just as the man must be both husband and father. The pseudomutual couple, however, has no experience with role flexibility. In extreme cases the results can be disastrous for the child, who simply does not fit in the stiflingly cozy atmosphere his parents have created. Thus Israel Charny has written of his deep sense of inappropriateness when he watched a pseudomutual couple walking happily arm in arm, her head upon his shoulder, toward the hospital with their psychotic child in tow.[15] Indeed, the concept of the pseudomutual relationship arose as a result of one psychologist's attempt to explain the appearance of certain patterns of psychotic behavior in children.

Total War

When conflict becomes an end in itself, the result is almost invariably terribly destructive for both members of the partnership. We all know people who, it seems, are never happy unless they are complaining about something. When two such people form a union we have what John Cuber and Peggy Harroff call a "conflict habituated" relationship.[16] In such a relationship, the partners find the basis of their life together in the expression and management of conflict. Although others cannot understand how such a couple can stand the constant hassle, the

[14]Gail Fullerton, *Survival in Marriage: Introduction to Family Interaction, Conflicts, and Alternatives* (New York: Holt, Rinehart & Winston, Inc., 1972), p. 383.
[15]Israel Charny, *Marital Love and Hate* (New York: The Macmillan Company, 1973), p. 383.
[16]John F. Cuber and Peggy B. Harroff, *Sex and the Significant Americans* (Baltimore: Penguin Books, 1965), pp. 44ff.

partners do not feel any desire to end the relationship, in part because they do not have any better prospects in sight, but more importantly because they find a kind of appropriate "happiness" in their squabbling, which is the cement that holds them together. One such couple has described their relationship in the following terms:

Now these fights get pretty damned colorful. You called them arguments a little while ago—I have to correct you—they're brawls. There's never a bit of physical violence—at least not directed to each other—but the verbal gunfire gets pretty thick. Why, we've said things to each other that neither of us would think of saying in the hearing of anybody else. . . .[17]

In such situations, conflict seems to have replaced intimacy. Curiously enough, these relationships can be surprisingly durable. They may last a lifetime. But if one or the other partner tires of such interactions and seeks deeper involvement or a different mode of communication, the partnership is likely to fall apart. A conflict habituated relationship seems to have severe limits and does not readily lend itself to development or growth in the partners.

[17]Cuber and Harroff, *Sex and the Significant Americans*, pp. 45–46.

SUMMARY

This chapter has explored some of the dimensions of conflict in intimate relations. We have seen that it can be either a creative or a destructive force in partnerships. Conflict is a necessary ingredient if an intimate partnership is to grow and develop. The acceptance and recognition of it is the first step toward its creative use. As long as conflict is seen as a means to an end—the growth and development of each partner—it can be a creative mode of communication.

When conflict becomes an end in itself, however, it is usually destructive. When it becomes a win-lose proposition for the partners, it tends to create a situation in which one partner gains at the other's expense. By losing, a partner can suffer a diminution of his or her personhood that is not easy to regain.

This chapter has also described pseudomutuality, a carefully programmed arrangement to avoid conflict. Pseudomutual couples adjust their life styles to avoid conflict to such an extent that individual growth and development become impossible. Clinical studies have identified this behavior as a source of psychosis in children.

We have explored four major sources of conflict—defensiveness, differences in background and outlook, inadequate feedback, and frustration. In addition, we have looked at some of the most common trouble spots in intimate partnerships—sexual relations, money, relations with in-laws, and divergent expectations.

Conflict can be creative when it respects the personhood of the partner with whom one is in conflict. It can provide an occasion for honest and open interpersonal communication that allows a couple to ventilate their feelings and clarify and define the issues in their partnership. Thus it can contribute to the freedom and autonomy of the individual partners.

5

DEVELOPING PARTNERSHIPS

Many influential people are moving away from the view that sexual morality is defined by abstinence from nonmarital intercourse toward one in which morality is expressed through responsible sexual behavior and a sincere regard for the rights of others. . . . In other words, the shift is from emphasis upon an act to emphasis upon the quality of interpersonal relationships.

Lester Kirkendall

INTRODUCTION

Dating in America has gone through a number of changes in the fifty or so years since it first became recognized as the acceptable way for young people of the opposite sex to get to know one another. A young girl in the 1970s will smile at her mother's account of dating when she was a teenager. Drive-in movies, rock concerts, and school sponsored ski weekends are all phenomena that point to the immense changes in the circumstances under which high school dating occurs. What is more, dating generally begins earlier in a young person's life today than it did a generation ago. These changes are so pervasive and so significant that we may well wonder to what extent they actually imply changes in the meaning of dating as a social phenomenon. Whether or not dating is still the same thing and still serves the same function now as it did then is one of the questions we shall be examining in this chapter.

Like so many other aspects of relations between the two sexes, dating has become the subject of a large body of stereotyped beliefs. Whether or not these clichés are true—or rather, to what extent they are true —is also a topic we will be exploring here. These clichés can be summed up briefly as follows: dating is fun; it provides young people with an opportunity to try on for size the adult conceptions of masculinity and femininity; it provides them with a context within which to develop social skills; and it is the area within which they come to grips with their developing sexual desires. Dating is also a means by which young people eventually discover their future mates.

College offers the middle-class young person an environment within which to form partnerships that is in many respects markedly different from the high school environment in which dating flourishes. "Living together"—that is, simply cohabitating with a person of the opposite sex—undeniably is becoming an increasingly popular option. By some estimates as much as 30 percent of the undergraduate population in a typical large American university has experienced some period of living with a roommate of the opposite sex during their college years.[1] For this reason our discussion of developing partnerships would be incomplete without a thoughtful examination of this major new option.

Another development that carries great significance for the formation of partnerships between young men and women is the emergence of the commune as a distinct and common type of social environment. In a commune a couple may develop their own unique partnership and share their own private living space, or they may renounce a considerable amount of their privacy in order to share their experiences with other members of the commune. Thus becoming partners in a commune environment is distinct from becoming partners by simple cohabitation if for no other reason than that the couple chooses to develop their partnership while living closely with others.[2] The members of the commune may share little more than the common residence, or they may hold all things in common, as did the early Christians.[3] In either case, the commune offers a unique environment within which to become partners. This chapter will look at the process of becoming partners in these three distinctively different environments.

[1]This figure represents the highest estimate taken from a group of working papers presented to the Groves Conference on Marriage and the Family at Myrtle Beach, North Carolina, May 1973.
[2]Participants at the Groves Conference tended to report that persons who are living together generally reject the idea of communal intimacy in favor of dyadic relationships.
[3]Acts 2:45.

DATING
PATTERNS

In America in the middle of the twentieth century dating is still the most socially acceptable means of establishing relationships with persons of the opposite sex. Normally, it is the first step that a young person takes on the way to marriage. Because we no longer expect parents to choose mates for their children, as they did for centuries and still do today in many parts of the world, dating has arisen as a means of providing young people with opportunities to develop social skills and to acquire information about themselves and persons of the opposite sex that will help them make this choice for themselves. To be sure, marriage generally is far from the minds of young teenagers asking for or accepting dates. Nevertheless, asking a girl out and accepting a date with a boy—or the reverse, which is becoming increasingly common—are minor versions of the mate selection process and, as such, they have an undeniable connection to the choice of a partner in later life.

Anthropologist Margaret Mead points out a number of distinctive characteristics of the dating pattern as it appears in our society. (1) A young man does not have to be introduced to a young woman by a member of her family. (2) The young couple does not have to be chaperoned. (3) Beyond the time of the date itself there is no obligation on the part of either the male or the female to continue the relationship. (4) Elders do not plan the date; it is planned by the young people themselves. (5) Sexual intimacies are expected rather than forbidden, but the degree is dependent upon a number of variables, including the socially announced state of the relationship.[4] These distinctive characteristics appear to give the young couple a great deal of freedom in developing their relationship.[5]

Dating arose in the 1920s, in part in response to the efforts of women to achieve greater political and sexual equality. As Lloyd Saxton has noted:

The "ideal girl" of the Roaring Twenties was the Flapper, a thoroughly urbanized and industrialized product. In keeping with her emancipated place in society, she wore her skirts above the knee (they had been ankle-length for centuries); she shingled, bobbed and marceled her hair (which had once reached her waist); and she replaced the old whalebone corset with brief panties. Moreover, she became acquainted with young men outside the family circle and felt free to "go out" with them. Commercial establishments soon arose in response to a developing need; and within one generation, age-old rituals of courtship had been abandoned and the pattern of dating had emerged.[6]

Other changes taking place in our society at the time combined with the movement for sexual equality to free women to participate more fully in dating. New jobs opened up for young women, putting increasing numbers of them into close contact with young men outside the home for the first time. The growing availability of automobiles and telephones also facilitated greater personal contact between the sexes at the same time as new inventions to facilitate housework came on the market, freeing many young women from household chores. In response to these changes, magazines such as *Prom* and *Seventeen* grew to popularity by propagandizing a romantic view of what you ought to do to have fun on a date.

In the field of psychiatry, the popularization of the views on human

---

[4]Margaret Mead, "The Life Cycle and its Variations: The Division of Roles," in Daniel Bell, ed. *Toward the Year 2000: Work in Progress* (Boston: Beacon Press, 1969).

[5]To some extent this freedom of choice is illusory. Many social factors intervene to reduce the parents' anxiety that their children will not make the "right" choice of mate. Unwritten social expectations about who is or is not a proper choice of mate define a "pool of eligibles" that have characteristics generally acceptable to the parents—particularly middle- or upper-class parents. This social prescription of proper mate choice will be discussed in a later section of this chapter.

[6]Lloyd Saxton, *The Individual, Marriage and the Family* (Belmont, Calif.: Wadsworth Publishing Co., Inc., 1972), p. 139.

sexuality developed by Sigmund Freud turned Freudianism into a proclamation of the "naturalness" of the sex drive (even infants had it) and
even an endorsement of greater sexual experimentation (after all, repression was bad). What is more, the development of increasingly effective
contraception reduced some of the risk of the experimentation. Thus,
young people were given more time to spend together, more options as
to how they should spend that time, and a changing perspective on
sexuality. The result was the dating pattern that emerged in the twenties
and has continued to evolve and change ever since.

Even though the circumstances under which dating takes place have
changed noticeably since the 1920s, many of the expectations that we
bring to dating have ancient roots. Sociologist Peter Berger, perhaps
overstating the case, puts dating in its historical perspective:

Let us imagine a scene in which a pair of lovers are sitting in the moonlight. Let
us further imagine that this moonlight session turns out to be the decisive one, in
which a proposal of marriage is made and accepted. Now, we know that contemporary society imposes considerable limitations on such a choice, greatly
facilitating it among couples that fit into the same socioeconomic categories and
putting heavy obstacles in the way of such as do not. But it is equally clear that
even where "they" who are still alive had made no conscious attempts to limit
the choice of the participants in this particular drama, "they" who are dead have
long ago written the script for almost every move that is made. The notion that
sexual attraction can be translated into romantic emotion was cooked up by
misty-voiced minstrels titillating the imagination of aristocratic ladies about the
twelfth century or thereabouts. The idea that a man should fixate his sexual drive
permanently and exclusively on one single woman with whom he is to share bed,
bathroom and the boredom of a thousand bleary-eyed breakfasts was produced
by misanthropic theologians some time before that. And the assumption that the
initiative in the establishment of this wondrous arrangement should be in the hands
of the male, with the female graciously succumbing to the impetuous onslaught
of his wooing, goes back right to prehistoric times when savage warriors first
descended on some peaceful matriarchal hamlet and dragged away its screaming
daughters to their marital cots.

Just as all these hoary ancients have decided the basic framework within which
the passions of our exemplary couple will develop, so each step in their courtship
has been predefined, prefabricated—if you like, "fixed." It is not only that they are
supposed to fall in love and to enter into a monogamous marriage in which she
gives up her name and he his solvency, that this love must be manufactured at
all cost or the marriage will seem insincere to all concerned, and that the state
and church will watch over the menage with anxious attention once it is established
—all of which are fundamental assumptions concocted centuries before the
protagonists were born. Each step in their courtship is laid down in social ritual
also and, although there is always some leeway for improvisations, too much
adlibbing is likely to risk the success of the whole operation. In this way, our
couple progresses predictably (with what a lawyer would call "due deliberate
speed") from movie dates to meeting the family dates, from holding hands to
tentative explorations to what they originally planned to save for afterward, from
planning their evening to planning their suburban ranch house—with the scene
in the moonlight put in its proper place in the ceremonial sequence. Neither of
them has invented this game or any part of it. They have only decided that it is

with each other, rather than with other possible partners, they will play it. Nor do they have an awful lot of choice as to what is to happen after the necessary ritual exchange of question and answer. Family, friends, clergy, salesmen of jewelry and of life insurance, florists and interior decorators ensure that the remainder of the game will also be played by the established rules. Nor, indeed, do all these guardians of tradition have to exert much pressure on the principal players, since the expectations of their social world have long ago been built into their own projections of the future—they want precisely that which society expects of them.[7]

Written slightly over a decade ago, Berger's picture of course does not take into account the significant changes in dating patterns that appeared in the 1960s—changes which we shall be examining later in this chapter. Nevertheless, it does contain an undeniable core of truth. Berger is not arguing that individual communication is fixed or determined by our culture in such a fashion that improvisations do not occur. Rather, he is insisting on something we all know intuitively—that our culture defines the rules within which personal relationship of whatever sort must occur. In this case what is happening is a sequence of events that is shaped by commonly held cultural expectations. Even those who depart from culturally prescribed norms do so—unless they are self-consciously rebellious—within a range that is largely determined by those norms.

Dating Sequence

Dating begins about the age of fourteen for both boys and girls. Boys and girls from happy homes tend to begin dating somewhat earlier—perhaps at about the age of twelve—whereas young people from "broken" or unhappy homes do not typically begin to date until they are sixteen. In any event, dating does not last long. It is typically ended at about the age of twenty or twenty-one. Most American boys and girls date.[8]

When a boy and girl date, they may experience a relationship that progresses in a clearly discernible way. Over time, we have come to give names to the stages of this development. Landis and Landis report the following sequence:

. . . The students distinguished five categories of dating: *Casual dating*, the purpose of which is to get acquainted; conversation is general; a goodnight kiss is acceptable depending on individual choice. Dates may be double. *Steadily dating*, which involves going out with one person more than with others but with no special agreement and with both free to date others. The boy asks. The code

[7]Peter Berger, *Invitation to Sociology* (Garden City, N.Y.: Doubleday & Company, Inc., 1963), pp. 85–87.
[8]Judson T. Landis and Mary G. Landis, *Building a Successful Marriage*, 5th ed. (Englewood Cliffs, N.J.: Prentice-Hall, Inc., 1973), pp. 34–35.

permits "necking." *Going steady*, in which two go out only with each other. Companionship is important; they see each other informally and formally. The dating is now two-way, rather than having only the boy ask the girl. The behavior code permits "heavy petting." Some gift may be given as a symbol of a couple's going steady. *Engaged to be engaged*, which these students called "an extreme form of going steady." Here there may be discussion of marriage and of educational or occupational goals. This is in a sense a trial period of engagement. "Increased physical intimacy" is involved. *Engagement*. This stage is more a preparation for marriage than for the purpose of "having a good time." There is increasing physical intimacy. The two may consult professionals, such as medical doctors or marriage counselors, and make financial and other specific plans for marriage.[9]

Not all of these stages are recognized in all parts of the country, but the assumption that a sex code of some sort is linked to a more or less explicitly acknowledged state in a relationship remains fairly constant. The specific strictures dictated by the sex code vary greatly, so that one finds different norms prevailing in different parts of the country, in different social classes, and even in different "sets" or cliques within the same school. Generally, young people know what the guidelines are for each stage in a relationship in their particular community of peers. This knowledge serves to ease some of the pressure on individual decision making.

By the same token, the availability in many communities of different sets with different norms makes it possible, to some extent, for a young person to choose a group of peers who subscribe to a sexual ethic with which he or she can be comfortable. Especially in large urban or suburban high schools and colleges, it is possible for the young man or woman who is sexually adventurous to find a social milieu in which his or her preferences will not lead to being stigmatized as a playboy or a promiscuous girl. Conversely, the young person who wants to take his or her sexual development more slowly often can find a congenial set of peers who will not insist that reluctance to engage in sexual activity is a symptom of frigidity, impotence, or even latent homosexuality.

In one sense, the emergence of different groups with markedly different sexual standards is nothing new. The parents of any college age person today probably can remember that there was a clearly identifiable "fast set" in the high school or college they attended. What does seem to be new, however, is the extent to which such differences are coming to be seen as differences in taste, in choice of life style, rather than as moral differences. There has been a tendency for hard-and-fast distinctions between "normal" kids, "fast" kids, and "wallflowers" to break down. Indeed, sociologists today are finding it increasingly difficult, if not impossible, to say what constitutes "normal" sexual behavior for adolescents. Instead of there being one standard ethic, with

---

[9]Landis and Landis, *Building a Successful Marriage*, 5th ed., p. 36. © 1973. Reprinted by permission of Prentice-Hall, Inc., Englewood Cliffs, New Jersey.

clearly delineated deviations on both sides of it, there seems to be a genuine plurality of ethics, none of which can be clearly identified as dominant.[10]

Developmental Tasks of Dating

In our society, preadolescent young people generally associate with members of their own sex. Indeed, they often have difficulty relating to members of the opposite sex. Dating provides them with an opportunity to overcome some of these difficulties. As interest in the opposite sex increases with the onset of puberty, young people gain experience through dating that often helps them overcome their initial feeling of being uncomfortable with the opposite sex. The context of dating provides many young people with an opportunity to develop the skills necessary for successfully relating to the opposite sex.

Of course, in many cases the opposite is true. For countless young people of both sexes, the dating ages are a period of almost unrelieved trauma. It would be easy to assume that dating is a problem only for "unpopular" individuals, but this would be an oversimplification that simply is not justified. Consider for a moment what is meant by "popularity" in this context. When we say that a young person is "popular," generally we mean simply that she or he is successful at relating to the opposite sex in dating situations; she or he has the social graces, whatever they are, that make her or him a desirable partner on a date. The folklore is rich with examples of high school girls and boys who have many friends but few dates. Any young man in college probably can remember a female classmate from his high school days with whom he could enjoy spending an afternoon, who was a stimulating colleague on the school paper or the student government, who was the sort of bright and intelligent person one liked to get together with to prepare for an exam, but whom he would never have dreamed of "asking out." Young women probably can come up with analogous examples of high school boys.

[10]Ira Reiss, one well-known student of college sex codes, contends that there is a trend toward reliance upon situation ethics which tolerates a wide variety of ethical attitudes and behaviors that are contingent upon the factors of the specific situation in which partners find themselves and the overarching commandment to love one another. See his "Premarital Sexuality: Past, Present and Future" in Ira L. Reiss, *Readings on the Family System* (New York: Holt, Rinehart & Winston, Inc., 1972). In an earlier article, Reiss contended that there are four basic sexual codes on the college campus: abstinence, permissiveness, permissiveness with affection, and the double standard in which the male is granted much more permissiveness than the female. In this article he contends that "permissiveness with affection" is the emergent norm while the double standard remains the dominant norm. See his article, "How and Why America's Sex Standards are Changing," in Joann S. and Jack R. Delora, *Intimate Life Styles* (Pacific Palisades, Calif.: Goodyear, 1972).

Hella Hammid, Rapho Guillumette

Such people, we can see quite clearly, may have been extremely "popular" in all contexts except dating; obviously, then, unpopularity does not explain anything when we are trying to understand why some individuals have trouble with the dating process. But it does explain why the dating years can be so traumatic. The fact is that dating is simply one of many types of social interaction young people engage in, but it is often mistakenly taken to be the alpha and omega of social competence. We can imagine a boy saying, "Yeah, she's terrific to work with on the yearbook committee, but I wouldn't want to go out with her." We tend to take this as a serious criticism. On the other hand, if he were to say, "Betty's great to take to a movie or a concert or a dance, but if you ever had to spend two afternoons with her trying to work out arrangements for a class picnic you'd never want to do it again," we might tend to assume that he wasn't criticizing her in any fundamental way. That is to say, we take success in one type of inter-personal relationship as a sign of overall popularity and assume that success in other types of relationship doesn't count for much. The fact that even the young people who suffer from the application of such standards may accept the validity of the criteria being used means that problems with dating can be far more damaging to the self-image than is really warranted.

In this connection, it is important to recognize that dating is a highly artificial social situation. When two young people of the opposite sex spend an afternoon together working on some school project, notice that it has gotten to be six o'clock and that they are both hungry, adjourn the conference for dinner together, continue it at his house or her house until they are finished, and then spend the rest of the evening together, their social contact flows naturally out of the things they are doing together. Similarly, a group of young people may get together for a pizza after school and then spend the afternoon just "hanging around"; maybe one of them will say, "I feel like seeing that movie that just opened downtown—anyone wanna go?" and an ad hoc group ends up agreeing to see the movie together. This type of social situation also evolves naturally from the larger social context in which these young people operate. But when a young man says to himself, "I gotta get a date for Friday night. Who should I call?" he is attempting to fabricate a social context where none in fact existed before.

It is precisely this artificial quality of the dating experience that has led to its decline in some quarters in recent years. Thus, for example, in many suburban communities it is no longer necessary for one to have a date in order to attend a party. Word will spread at school that so-and-so is having a party on Friday night, and on Friday night young people will arrive—sometimes in couples, sometimes singly, and sometimes in miscellaneous carloads of boys and girls. They are all there together and, except for established couples, no one has any clear sense of who is whose date.

This is not to say that the couple is becoming defunct as a socio-sexual unit. But in some circles being one half of a couple is becoming less and less of a prerequisite for engaging in extracurricular social activity. You may come *out* of a party or movie with a girlfriend or boyfriend, but it is not necessary to have a girlfriend or boyfriend in order to go to a party or to the movies. In other words, with this type of arrangement social occasions provide the context in which couples may form, whereas in traditional dating two people who do not in any meaningful sense constitute a couple are expected to agree to act like a couple for the purpose of entering into the social context.

Another aspect of the dating process is significant here. For many young people dating provides the occasion in which conventionally accepted adult masculine and feminine roles are rehearsed for the first time.[11] From their earliest days boys have been taught to be aggressive, but they have never before had an opportunity to learn what it means to be dominant in regard to females. Heretofore, it is likely that all of the women in their lives—mainly their mothers and teachers—have been dominant over them. The context of dating thus provides the boy

[11] These roles will be discussed more fully in Chapter 9.

with an opportunity to develop the socially expected skill of being dominant over the female. He is expected to make the date, to decide where they should go, to initiate whatever sexual advances are to be made. Eventually he may learn to do these things with some style.

Conversely, in the dating process girls learn to be submissive to boys. The skills they are encouraged to master are the purely passive skills of seduction. That is to say, girls do not learn how to initiate social contact, but how to get someone else to initiate it—i.e., how to get asked out by the boy you want to go out with, rather than how to ask him out. Similarly, in the sexual relations of the couple the girl is expected to play a passive role. To be sure, she is permitted to actively encourage sexual experimentation, but only under the condition that her encouragement is manifested in subtle and almost imperceptible ways. She may make herself as sexually alluring as the bounds of propriety permit, but the code dictates that she is not to openly initiate sexual advances. If a couple is to get together sexually, in other words, it is the boy's job to express desire and the girl's job simply to make herself desirable. The girl who gives evidence of sexual desire runs the risk of being stigmatized as "aggressive"—clearly a gross distortion of the English language, inasmuch as a loving desire for intimate contact with another person is about as far from an act of aggression as it is possible to get.

Paradoxically, there is one area of the dating situation in which the girl is expected to be in control. To the extent that the couple is to refrain from sexual activity, it is the girl who is expected to "draw the line." If sexual play is to begin, it is his job to initiate it; if it is to stop short of consummation, it is her job to call a halt. Inevitably, these norms of sex role behavior lead to conflict between the sexes. For boys especially, the conflict that arises may not necessarily be damaging. A young boy who experiences some success in being the initiator may gain a degree of self-assurance. He also may fail occasionally, and this may lead him to discover that he can live with that too. As long as there is some balance between his success and his failure he may see this conflict as positive—at least in terms of his development as a self-confident male. On the other hand, many people feel—undoubtedly with some justice—that this sort of sexual contest is damaging to the young men who engage in it insofar as it encourages them to see sex as a competitive game. Even if they emerge from it with their egos intact, they will tend to look on women as friendly adversaries, much as professional athletes regard players on rival teams, but not as partners in a joint endeavor. The use of the slang term "scoring" to describe sexual success indicates how pervasive these attitudes are.

But the most pernicious effects of the dating system undoubtedly are felt by the young women who engage in it. The fact that they are limited to a passive role in dating relationships does nothing to further their development as autonomous individuals. This is why the women's movement has been especially severe in its denunciations of traditional American dating patterns, and its success in raising the level of consciousness among young people may be responsible to a considerable extent for some of the changes in dating patterns that have emerged in recent years. In those parts of the country where the traditional dating pattern is being replaced by a freer and more spontaneous type of social intercourse, as described above, the emphasis on male dominance is much less apparent. When a young girl, for example, can attend a party without having to depend upon an invitation by a boy, her position with regard to the boys at the party is much more nearly one of equality. Even where traditional dating is still the dominant pattern, it is no longer unheard of for a girl to telephone a boy and ask him for a date. To be sure, girls who do ask boys out, like girls who initiate sexual activities, are running the risk of scaring away potential boyfriends, who may tend to see such conduct as threatening to their own conception of their roles. Apparently a fair number of young women are willing to run this risk, however, and as their numbers increase the risk should diminish simply because the boys will be forced to adjust to this new balance of power in sexual relationships.

Dating, in sum, is a type of social interaction between young people of the opposite sex; its principal purpose, from the point of view of society at large, is to socialize young men and women into their adult sexual roles. To a large extent these roles involve an acceptance of the principle of male dominance, and insofar as one subscribes to this principle, one may conclude that on the whole our traditional dating pattern succeeds in accomplishing its developmental task for most people. In those communities—primarily middle-class and upper middle-class suburbs—where this principle has been called into question, however, traditional dating patterns have been altered in certain ways that make it possible for young people of the opposite sex to socialize with each other more nearly as equals.

The Game of Romance

The social expectation that the boy establish his ability to be dominant over girls, the romantic understanding of love as a sexual contest, the double standard under which boys are supposed to be sexually knowledgeable and experienced and girls are not, all combine to produce some of the common tactics in what we can call the "game of romance." For most young people, learning the rules of this game is at least a minimum requirement of growing up. Unfortunately, developing skill in playing it can often become an impediment to genuine intimacy in mature, growing relationships.

In our society, romance is largely a game played under the assumption that the man must pursue the woman, who is nevertheless free to adopt various tactics that will facilitate her capture. Men commonly initiate relationships in order to derive the personal satisfaction that comes from sexual fulfillment, the demonstration of dominance or competence, and so forth; when they fall in love the game is over and the players begin the next stage of their relationship. Thus the game of romance is an intentional display of the competence of the man in managing the aggressive arts of pursuit. The woman demonstrates her competence in coquetry, the strategy by which she conveys the notion that she is receptive to his advances. The stereotype, therefore, is of the dominant, competent male who is persistent in his pursuit of the helpless female in flight. Her competence, that is to say, must be hidden, whereas his should be an overt part of the strategy of the game.

The game of romance can have many subtle objectives, but, as we have seen, one of the most common is the establishment of one partner's dominance over the other. In the lower socioeconomic classes, the man who is skilled at playing the game is known as a hustler. He is the man who has learned to "play it cool." That is, he has mastered an admirable control of his emotions so that they can be employed when needed in the strategy of the game.[12] An important element of the game is the program, or "line," he gives the girl, or "chick." He tells her how much she "turns him on" and how he cannot live without her. He tells her in graphic terms how her charms are superior to those of any other woman he has seen. Love is a common word on the street. But he convinces her (or she pretends he does) that she is truly unique, the only person for him. The middle-class version of the game differs from the lower-class model essentially in the fact that normally a greater amount of time is required to play it and the sexual advances are generally more hidden, less explicit.

One of the main problems with the game of romance is the fact that it is often difficult for the players to determine the objectives of the game, which may range from a serious desire to establish an intimate partnership to a fleeting desire for a temporary sexual liaison. The formalized rules of the game, however, make it difficult for the partners to declare their intentions or to be believed if they do. The rules permit either partner, but especially the males, to indicate a desire for a more or less long-term partnership when no such desire in fact exists. This convention of permissible dishonesty allows the partners to "hedge their bets" on the relationship and gives them an "out" to cover their disappointment should they be tricked or rejected. By such tactics one gains a certain competence in manipulating interpersonal relationships

[12]Boone Hammond, "The Contest System" unpublished Masters Thesis, Washington University, St. Louis, Missouri, 1966. For an excellent discussion of the art of courtship as strategy or game, see Alex Blumensteil's "The Sociology of Good Times" in George Paathas, ed., *Phenomenological Sociology: Issues and Applications* (New York: John Wiley & Sons, 1973), pp. 187–218.

but hardly gains in the objective of achieving greater intimacy. Competence in the game lies in mastering the art of controlled self-disclosure and in creating a well managed environment, but not in learning to determine how you and your partner really feel in the relationship and how to express it honestly.

CLASS VARIATIONS IN DATING PATTERNS

As we shall see in Chapter 9, the sexual behavior of Americans differs with socioeconomic class. These differences are reflected in differences in dating patterns that appear to be class based.

Because upper-class families have a vested interest in preserving the family fortune, they often attempt to retain a considerable degree of control over the mate selection process by sequestering their homes and sending their children to private schools, clubs, and chaperoned social activities. Upper-class families commonly express concern over who is dating whom, and such expressions of concern can be effective in enforcing the family's norms because of the threat of disinheritance. Another unique characteristic of the social activities of upper-class young people is the great amount of formality and ritual involved, especially as expressed in the "coming out" parties of debutantes. This ritual is the formal announcement of a daughter's introduction to the prescribed social world. Daughters usually "come out" at the age of eighteen, although ordinarily they have had dating experience prior to that time.

In certain lower-class urban communities dating has a quite different pattern because it occurs under quite different conditions. For example, sexual intercourse may be something that has been played with since a very early age and may have been fully experienced before adolescence in the case of boys. Girls, too, often engage in sexual intercourse for "fun" when they are still quite young and as "a form of exchange" when they are older. As Ladner and Hammond report in a study of an urban ghetto: "Thus, girls have been known to engage in sexual intercourse in exchange for a movie date, a ride in a car, food, and other things that will take them out of the family life. The male in turn offers these things because he knows the girl is desirous of them and can offer what he wants in exchange."[13]

In such contexts dating generally is not something that the family regulates or participates in. Indeed, it is in a sense inappropriate to use the term "dating" to describe heterosexual relationships in this environment inasmuch as social encounters between the sexes usually are not planned in advance by the boy or the girl. Rather, boys and girls hang

[13]Joyce Ladner and Boone Hammond, "Socialization into Sexual Behavior," paper presented to the Society for the Study of Social Problems, San Francisco, 1967, pp. 12–13. See also their article in Carlfred Broderick and Jessie Bernard, *The Individual, Sex and Society* (Baltimore: The Johns Hopkins Press, 1969), p. 49.

around public places and couples may "single out" for a part of the evening, but there is no decision required to participate in dating. As we have seen already, this casual approach to heterosexual socializing is becoming increasingly popular in some middle-class and upper middle-class suburbs.

In middle-class communities dating often emerges in response to intense expectations of its emergence on the part of parents and peers. Middle-class mores place a heavy emphasis on the value of the social skills. This is understandable in light of the fact that in many middle-class occupations success depends to a considerable extent on being "liked" by one's business associates. Popularity thus counts heavily in the middle-class ethic, and as a result parents encourage their children to get early training, through dating, in the social graces that are necessary for popularity. Fortunately, because middle-class children often have a great range of social activities available to them, through the school, clubs, churches, and a variety of coeducational interest groups, they are often able to respond positively to the pressure to date early.

The preceding outline of three major class variants in the dating pattern is, of course, only a crude sketch. A detailed study of the phenomenon would show countless variations between the extremes of intense parental involvement in the dating process and absolute parental ignorance of the dating behavior of one's children, between the highly stylized and formal dating situation of a debutante ball and the almost completely unstructured ambience of streetcorner contact. What is more, there is considerable variation in the way different communities—and different families in the same community—subscribe to the norms we have associated here with particular socioeconomic classes. The reader is cautioned, therefore, against taking any of the foregoing description as normative for any particular social class. Our point in offering this outline was simply to demonstrate that dating patterns vary considerably and that these variations can be correlated, in at least an approximate way, with the socioeconomic position of the people involved.

ENGAGEMENT

Engagement is the final stage in premarriage for the typical middle-class couple. It takes on quite a different character from all previous dating because by the time a couple becomes engaged they have already begun to ask serious questions about each other that can help them to determine if they would make desirable marriage partners. It is a time for confessing secrets and for self-disclosure; it is a time for deeper self-knowledge. At least this is what it is supposed to be. It is also the time during which they may consult professional marriage counselors, take physical examinations, and make concrete plans for their marriage. Engagement involves a great deal more work and self-conscious commitment than any previous stages in the couple's developing relationship. Landis estimates that one-half to two-thirds of all engagements end in marriage.[14]

Because engagement is thought of as a much more binding relationship than any of the other stages, it is not rapidly rushed into. For 54 percent of the couples in one study engagement came at least nine months after their first date. In the early part of this century short engagements were encouraged because engagement was primarily a period of preparing for marriage—making wedding arrangements and domestic arrangements for after the wedding—but not a period for testing the relationship. Today, marriage counselors often urge couples to seek longer engagements—from six months to two years—so that they have an opportunity to discover each other before marriage. The classic correlation between reported good marital adjustment and long engagement seems to support their argument. Nevertheless, the extent to which engagement actually functions as a means of testing partners in marriage remains somewhat questionable inasmuch as the conditions of engagement are quite different from the conditions of marriage.

Various things need to be cleared up during the engagement period. Some professionals provide a checklist of individual characteristics that each partner should complete as a test of their suitability for marriage to each other. Some feel that it is important that engaged couples begin to try to answer some of the important questions they will have in marriage, such as whether or not they should have children. Such steps may or may not be beneficial, but they can be distracting from the real tasks of engagement if they lead us to view marriage as a static situation and to assume that engagement is quite like it. A young couple should not forget that engagement should be a time in which two partners begin to develop their own style of coping with the common problems of everyday life. For example, if a basically neat and tidy woman is engaged to a sloppy man the couple has potential trouble on their hands. Sometimes couples come to engagement without really realizing that they differ in even such an obvious way. Each has seen how the other lives, but neither has given any thought to the fact that their blatantly different styles could be a source of conflict when they come to live together. An engaged couple needs to know this kind of thing about each other, needs to have the capacity to talk about it, and enough skill in give and take so that a reasonable resolution can be reached. (This resolution, as

[14]Landis and Landis, *Building a Successful Marriage*, pp. 191ff. When asked why their engagement was broken off, the most common reply (39 percent of the men, 40 percent of the women) was that they "lost interest in the relationship." Although about 10 percent of the students in one study reported that they got over the emotional involvement of engagement by the end of the final date with their former fiancé(e)s, 50 percent of the women and 46 percent of the men took at least three months to recover.

we saw in our discussion of conflict in Chapter 4, need not change either partner's basic habits.) Engagement, in other words, is the period when work should be done in the area of developing their skills and their style of handling these kinds of basic differences. An engaged couple should be working on what they know about each other with regard to the potentially creative and destructive aspects of their relationship. In short, they need to become adept at communicating their feelings about their partnership.

MATE SELECTION

When we look at the problems of engagement, we are looking at the problems associated with making a personal choice of a mate. This choice is always made in the context of norms more or less explicitly defined by society and more or less rigidly enforced. Thus social factors which, in modern American society, are normally below the level of consciousness of the young couple in love affect their choice of a mate. In the next few pages we will examine some of the ways in which society intervenes to affect the selection of a partner.

Lynn McLaren, Rapho Guillumette

In our society, couples are supposed to fall in love before they get married. By world standards this is an odd assumption. In many societies, marriages are arranged and the field of eligible mates is severely restricted by explicit, formal norms. In some traditional societies, such as Japan, love is expected to develop after marriage, not before it. Most of us find it very difficult to understand the young Japanese girl who is apparently satisfied to let her parents make the choice of her mate:

We girls don't have to worry at all. We know we'll get married. When we are old enough, our parents will find a suitable boy and everything will be arranged. We don't have to go into competition with each other. . . . Besides how would we be able to judge the character of a boy? . . . We are young and inexperienced. Our parents are older and wiser, and they aren't deceived as easily as we would be. I'd far rather have my parents choose for me. It's so important that the man I marry should be the right one. I could so easily make a mistake if I had to find him for myself.[15]

Falling in love in our society implies freedom of choice in a relatively open marriage market. Theoretically, any two people should be able to marry if they fall in love, but of course we know that this is not the case. To be sure, our social system places very few formal restrictions on the choice of a mate; rather, it tends to rely upon informal but quite effective controls to insure that children marry the "right" person. For example, in any given year, approximately 4 percent of all blacks who marry, marry whites. Obviously, a much smaller percentage of all whites who marry, marry blacks.[16] Likewise, if we break down religious denominations into the gross categories of Protestant, Catholic, and Jew, we discover that most marriages tend to take place within these groups (endogamy) rather than between them (exogamy). Studies vary, but one report based on a large sample of 35,000 households in 1960 indicated that 91 percent of the Protestants, 78 percent of the Catholics, and 93 percent of the Jewish population made homogamous (like marries like) choices.[17] Sociologist Paul H. Besancency, S.J., cautions, how-

[15]David and Vera Mace, *Marriage East and West* (Garden City, N.Y.: Doubleday & Company, Inc., 1960), p. 131. © 1960 by Doubleday & Company, Inc.
[16]An excellent review of the empirical literature on the subject of interracial marriage is found in James D. Bruce and Hyman Rodman, "Black-White Marriages in the United States: A Review of the Empirical Literature," in Irving R. Stuart and Lawrence E. Abt, eds., *Interracial Marriage: Expectations and Realities* (New York: Grossman Publishers, 1973), pp. 147–61. This report notes that a study in Los Angeles showed that only 0.1 percent of all black marriages involved a white partner, while in Hawaii 16.9 percent of all black marriages involved a white partner. These two cases represented the range. In the nation as a whole the percentage of marriages involving one black partner, as a percentage of all marriages, ranged from a low in Michigan of 0.03 percent to a high in Washington, D.C., of 0.77 percent. See page 151 of Stuart and Abt for a summary table.
[17]Paul C. Glick, "Intermarriage and Fertility Patterns Among Persons in Major Religious Groups," *Eugenics Quarterly* 1 (1960), 31–38. Robert O. Blood, Jr. *Mar-*

ever, that these figures tend to underrepresent the actual rate of mixed marriage inasmuch as many individuals convert to the religion of their spouse in order to have a more harmonious household.[18]

Additional restrictions on mate selection seem to be in effect with regard to age and socioeconomic status. Statistics show that Americans tend to choose mates who are within two and a half years of their own age. In 1972 the average age at first marriage of the bride was 20.9 years and that of the groom 23.3 years.[19] There is also a tendency to marry persons within one's own socioeconomic class. Although there is some indication that exogamy is increasing in all these dimensions, the trend in this direction is moving quite slowly. However free we may perceive our choice of mates to be, the fact remains that we are most likely to marry someone with the same ethnic, religious, and class background, someone who is nearly of the same age, and someone who most likely lives in the same city if not the same neighborhood.

Bernard Murstein has developed an interesting theory of how young people in our culture go about the business of choosing their mates.[20] As he sees it, there are three basic stages to this process. First comes the "stimulus" stage in which physical attractiveness is of considerable importance, particularly in the open field setting where continuing interaction is unlikely to occur as a matter of course. This is followed by a "value" stage wherein couples explore each other's attitudes toward life, politics, religion, sex, the role of men and women, and their general style of viewing the world. In Murstein's view, the fact that people who are alike in terms of their socioeconomic backgrounds will tend to have similar values and life styles is one of the major factors leading to endogamous mate selection. This is because endogamous selection increases the likelihood of finding a partner who will support one's own value system. This is important, Murstein points out, because many values an individual holds are so personal that their rejection is experienced as a rejection of the self who holds them.

In the final stage, which Murstein calls the "role" stage, the prospective partners experiment in compatibility. At this stage, couples can be

---

riage (New York: The Free Press, 1962), p. 81, shows how this percentage varies for Catholics depending upon the percentage of the population that is Catholic in Canadian provinces. Thus 2 percent of Quebec's Catholics marry non-Catholics, while 46 percent of British Columbia's Catholics do likewise. Eighty-eight percent of Quebec's population is Catholic, while only 14 percent of British Columbia is.
[18]Paul H. Besancency, S. J., *Interfaith Marriages: Who and Why* (New Haven: College and University Press, 1970), pp. 48–74.
[19]U.S. Bureau of the Census, *Statistical Abstract of the United States: 1973* (Washington, D.C.: U.S. Government Printing Office, 1973), p. 65.
[20]Bernard Murstein, "Stimulus-Value-Role: A Theory of Marital Choice," in *Journal of Marriage and the Family* 32 (1970), 465–81.

said to be making good progress in the courtship process to the extent that they are able to satisfy each other's role expectations.[21]

Of course, the fact that homogamous mate selection offers certain payoffs in terms of increased likelihood of compatible values does not mean that heterogamous choices should not be made. We all know that couples can and do make choices in their selection of a mate that go against social expectations. Couples marry in spite of racial, class, religious, ethnic, and regional differences. It would be naive to deny that such couples must pay a certain price for their choice. They may experience greater stress in their partnership than homogamous couples, and they may find that family, friends, and outsiders are willing to give them less support in coping with their problems than they would give to a homogamous couple. How important these factors are will vary greatly from case to case. On the one hand, it is safe to say that many potentially successful heterogamous marriages have run aground under the constant onslaught of family and peer group pressures. On the other hand, it is no secret that two autonomous individuals with widely different backgrounds can bring to their union a rich diversity in outlooks that helps each of them to grow and strengthens their partnership.

COST AND BENEFITS OF THE TRADITIONAL STEPS TO MARRIAGE

Looked at as one social environment in which partnerships develop, the traditional courtship patterns from dating to marriage has some apparent costs as well as some easily recognizable benefits. The three major benefits of this social environment are: (1) *Respectability*. Because this sequence is the generally accepted way by which heterosexual relationships develop, persons who follow it meet with general social acceptance. They need not hide from anyone or feel guilty about their relationship so long as it conforms to the norm. This respectability thus serves as an affirmation of themselves and their relationship. (2) *Well-defined expectations*. Couples generally know the stage of sexual intimacy appropriate to a given stage of relationship in a given social context. They also have some idea about what is traditionally expected

---

[21]There are several other factors that affect the rate at which a partnership is able to develop depth in Murstein's model. Among the most important of these is a similarity in sex drive. Couples who have dissimilar sex drives—particularly those in which the woman has a much greater sex drive than the man, or in which the man's sexuality involves greater neurosis—will have greater difficulty making good courtship progress than couples whose sex drives are more nearly matched or those whose sex drive dissimilarity is in line with the traditional notions of male dominance. This latter point is not an argument for male dominance, but rather an indication of the extent to which this cultural trait has played a role in the socialization of most of us to the present time.

of them as men and women. Most couples know something about how long it should take for them to move through each stage of their relationship. All these things provide standards by which they can evaluate themselves and their relationship. (3) *Greater access to professional advice and consultation.* Because the orientation of the professional world is largely toward the traditional trajectory, a couple following the standard path can more readily turn to professionals if they experience any problems they cannot handle or if they desire advice.

Three of the most significant costs of the traditional approach to developing relationships are (1) *Inclinations toward role conformity.* Because the traditional approach provides clearly defined roles, there is a temptation to conform to these role expectations rather than to discover one's own uniqueness—and one's partner's—in a relationship. (2) *Sexual inequality.* The so-called "double standard" is still the dominant sex code within the traditional courtship environment. The cost to the woman's development as an autonomous individual may be considerable. What is more, the double standard, as a sex code, entails a built-in tendency toward deception. (3) *The railroad toward marriage.* Couples following the traditional path may well feel themselves propelled toward marriage. It is possible that someone who would really like to get out of a developing relationship may find himself or herself unable to get off the train.

Living Together: Costs and Benefits

In addition to the traditional dating sequences, from steady dating through engagement to marriage, living together is becoming an increasingly viable alternative environment within which partnerships can develop in our society. It is rather new on the scene, not having come into prominence until the 1960s. Precisely because of this newness, it offers considerable possibility for experimentation and flexibility in defining role expectations within the developing relationship. Where this environment is available, it will have its effect upon the kinds of choices people make in becoming partners. It shapes the experience they will have and influences the character of the information they will be able to obtain about each other.

The fact that young unmarried heterosexual couples live together has attracted a good deal of attention in the popular press in recent years. Ever since 1968, when Linda LeClair, a Barnard College sophomore, asserted before the college's Judicial Council that she felt Barnard's regulations governing the living arrangements of single students were unjust, newspapers and magazines have been filled with articles on the subject. There are, however, few serious studies of the issue and we really know very little about it in a systematic way. Nevertheless, some of the characteristics of this life style are beginning to emerge.

One survey, for example, reports that 71 percent of the men and 43 percent of the women thought that they would like to try "living with" someone.[22] By "living with" these researchers meant "eating, sleeping and socializing at the same residence with someone of the opposite sex." If we accept as a definition of "living together" something like "Two single persons of the opposite sex living together in a common residence," then a rough estimate of the number of college students who have lived with someone of the opposite sex at some time in their college career is about 30 percent.

Contrary to what might be supposed from popular coverage, students who live with roommates of the opposite sex do not generally think of themselves as revolutionary. Thus, in a study conducted at Penn State, although a significant number of students who were living together thought that unmarried cohabitation was the most desirable post-college choice, very few thought they would prefer to live in communes.[23] This

[22]John W. Hudson and Lura F. Henze, "Personal and Family Characteristics of Cohabiting College Students: Whose Kids are Living Together?" unpublished working paper.
[23]Dan J. Peterman and Carl Ridley, "A Comparison of Background, Personal and Interpersonal Characteristics of Cohabiting and Noncohabiting College Students," unpublished working paper.

Margot Granitsas, Photo Researchers

finding suggests that cohabiters are not radical experimenters in alternative family styles. They remain strongly attached to the norms of dyadic partnerships and marriage. In most cases, they are not outspoken advocates of innovative life styles. Rather, they seem often to have gradually worked their way into their arrangements, as the following statement from a student at Columbia University suggests:

"We began studying together," she says. "Then I made his dinner before we studied. Then we came back and I made him coffee. At first, I let him out. Then he let himself out. Then he stayed and I made him coffee in the morning. Then he went shopping for groceries and in a week he was here all the time."[24]

Such an arrangement, it should be clear, is easy to enter into. Unlike marriage, which requires blood tests, licenses, and some sort of ceremony at a minimum, partners who want simply to live together can just move in—and out. In this latter connection, rough estimates suggest that perhaps no more than a third of the relationships between unmarried couples living together last more than six months. At Cornell, the average length of time seems to be about four and a half months, and most such arrangements apparently last only a few days or weeks.[25]

From these statistics it is easy to jump to the conclusion that such relationships have a high rate of failure. This conclusion, however, would be unjustified, for it is based on the erroneous assumption that living together can be judged by the same criterion we use in judging marital stability. Couples often move in together without either partner making the assumption that the relationship is to be permanent; indeed, it is often precisely because they either do not want or do not expect permanence that they refrain from getting married. Thus, the dissolution of their arrangement should not be taken as evidence of a failure in the partnership, which may well have satisfied all the goals both participants set for their relationship.

What kind of student is likely to choose this form of partnership? The answer is far from clear in most details. As far as parentage is concerned, he or she could be anybody's child. There is no evidence at present to suggest that children from "broken" or unhappy homes are more likely to choose this option than children from happy homes. Cohabiters do seem to share a different life style among themselves, however. They see themselves as politically liberal, are more likely than the average college student to smoke marijuana, and most often consider themselves to be agnostic or atheistic.[26]

[24]*Time Magazine* (May 1973).
[25]See J. L. Lyness et al., "Living Together: An Alternative to Marriage," *Journal of Marriage and the Family* 34 (1972), 305–11.
[26]Hudson and Henze, "Personal and Family Characteristics . . ."

There is great diversity among cohabiting students with regard to what their partnership means to them:

"Do you consider yourselves engaged or going steady or . . . ?" a couple at Florida State University in Tallahassee was asked. "We don't consider ourselves anything," the nonmate said. "We've never tried to pin it down." In Iowa City, Iowa, a girl says, "I guess he came and never left." At L.S.U., Dale says brightly that her arrangement with Tom "is the first time I've gone steady."[27]

With such diversity of opinion, it is no wonder that the researchers are confused about what "living together" means. The major question most raise is, "What does it have to do with marriage?" Is "living together" a more honest form of courtship? Is it an alternative life style that is someday going to replace marriage? The answers to these questions are ambiguous. Most couples, it seems, do not consider their premarital cohabitation to be a trial marriage, while they are experiencing it. That is to say, if we define a trial marriage as an arrangement in which two people who intend to marry each other decide to live together in order to assess their compatibility before formalizing the relationship, the evidence seems to indicate that trial marriage is not often the motive for cohabiting. On the other hand, many couples who live together ultimately marry each other, and insofar as they may not have married had they not lived with each other, we can conclude that in retrospect their cohabitation functioned very much like a trial marriage. What is more, most cohabiting partners report that marriage is one of their eventual objectives, although they do not intend to marry the partner with whom they are living. For such people, cohabitation is equivalent to trial marriage only in the limited sense that it is a test of how well they adapt to marriage as an institution—that is, a test of their ability to share living conditions with a partner of the opposite sex.

Sex is not a big issue for most cohabiters, although the Penn State study cited earlier suggests that cohabiters will be more likely than the average student to report that they have a "heterosexual relationship of very high quality."[28] But very few will contend that they are living with their mates because of the greater pleasures they can derive from sexual intercourse. Indeed, sexual relations were not mentioned in our definition of "living together" because several researchers contend that many students do not see sex as an essential dimension of their arrangement. There seems to be a wide variation in the kinds of sexual relationship that can be found among cohabiting couples. Some such couples apparently have no sexual relationship at all; their cohabitation is for economic, social, or emotional reasons and explicitly excludes sex. To be

---

[27]*Time Magazine* (May 1973).
[28]Peterman and Ridley, "A Comparison of Background . . ."

sure, nonsexual cohabitation is probably the exception rather than the rule. On this score about the only thing that can be said is that data presently available do not permit us to generalize with any confidence about the sexual behavior of unmarried cohabiting couples.

Because we know so little about living together, it is difficult to assess accurately the costs and benefits of such an experience. Nevertheless, the following generalizations seem appropriate based on what we do know. Three major benefits seem possible:

1. The couple has greater freedom than they would have in the traditional premarriage trajectory to set their own role expectations and to define the character of their relationship. They can decide if sex is to be a part of their relationship or if it is not; they can decide whether they are going to share most of their expenses or keep their own monies; and they can decide whether their relationship is to be exclusive or whether they will be free to seek sexual partners outside their relationship.

2. Compared to the couple who chooses to become engaged and to postpone cohabitation until marriage, the unmarried cohabitors enjoy the possibility of getting to know each other in a wide variety of situations, including the running of the household. They are therefore likely to have a much less idealized image of each other than a couple who enters marriage with no such experience.

2. Compared to the couple who chooses to become engaged and to postcompulsion to marry. We reach this conclusion from the fact that the percentage of cohabiting people who choose not to marry their roommates is higher than the percentage of engaged people who choose not to marry their fiancé(e)s. This suggests that engagement is a measurably more irrevocable step toward marriage than is cohabitation. In other words, it is far easier to end a "living in" arrangement than to end an engagement. In either case, of course, there is the possibility of hurt feelings.

Three major costs of living together also seem evident on the basis of our present knowledge:

1. Living together creates the danger of greater exploitation, particularly of the woman, than does the traditional sequence of engagement and marriage. This danger arises from the fact that the woman, as in marriage, may assume the responsibility for keeping house and may give up her job or career in order to fulfill this responsibility. Unlike the married woman, however, the cohabiting woman has no legal safeguards to protect her in case the union dissolves. She thus may find herself with no claim to support by her former mate and little chance of earning the

living she could have earned if she had not interrupted her career to become a homemaker.

2. To some degree the couple who chooses to "live together" may be cut off from their parents and some of their old friends. This means that they must provide their own authentication of their relationship and may not be able to rely on those around them for support. In this connection, however, it should be noted that mores are changing rapidly and parental acceptance of unmarried cohabitation is far more common than it was even a decade ago. Consider the fact that in the 1940s, when film star Ingrid Bergman bore a child by a man who was not her husband, the expressed outrage was so vociferous that Ms. Bergman was unable to continue her career. A few years ago, however, actress Mia Farrow bore twins by a man to whom she was not married and the event was reported in the social columns of newspapers and magazines with scarcely a twitch of the editorial eyebrow; indeed, the birth announcement was often accompanied with a laconic note to the effect that "Mr. Previn and Ms. Farrow announce that they have no intention to marry at present." Given this social climate, it is not at all unheard of for parents to accept the fact that their child is living with his or her partner and to treat the partner much as they would a son-in-law or daughter-in-law. In such circumstances cohabitation becomes, in the eyes of concerned onlookers, a sort of de facto marriage. Nevertheless, although such acceptance is far from unheard of, it is also far from universal—indeed, it is probably still less common than rejection.

3. "Living together" can prematurely narrow the range of the dating experience for some students who come to college. Although the data suggest that in the typical case students who choose cohabitation already have dated about twenty-five persons and, therefore, can be said to be fairly experienced in heterosexual relationships at the dating level, some students move in with a partner without having reached this performance level. Cohabitation thus shuts them off from the widening experience the social life of the college community offers.

YOUTH COMMUNES: COSTS AND BENEFITS

A third social environment in which partnerships can develop is the commune. The commune differs from the "living together" environment primarily in the fact that much less emphasis is placed upon the partnership. It is also socially less acceptable to the average American. Couples who develop partnerships in the communal environment must be willing to accept a much greater burden of social criticism than couples who take either the traditional path of dating-engagement-marriage or the untraditional step of living together. The generally critical stance adopted by those outside the commune, however, is in part compensated by the fact that the commune itself, as a mini-society in its own right, provides its members with a supportive social environment.

Communes come in a wide variety of styles. As Richard Fairfield says:

There are many possible ways—none of them are very accurate—of categorizing the types of communes that exist. Most communes defy definition because they are constantly changing and growing. Nevertheless, over-simplification can be valid when introducing unfamiliar material to a reader. I've [classified] . . . communes as religious, ideological, hip, group marriage, service and youth.

. . . Youth communes, which do not fall into hip or ideological categories, are those which are usually composed of college graduates or dropouts who wish simply to share the advantages of group living.[29]

No information is available on how many young people are living in youth communes, although it has been estimated that between 100,000 and 250,000 Americans of all ages have lived in between two thousand and three thousand communes of all sorts at one time or another.[30] Some unknown percentage of these persons falls within the age group with which we are concerned. Coming at the problem from another perspective, it has been estimated that about 500,000 young Americans take to the road each year, cutting family ties at least temporarily.[31] Some unknown percentage of these persons live in youth communes. Although the number of persons who live in youth communes is, therefore, probably not large, every large city has a number of youth communes that house students from the local universities along with nonuniversity people.

A frequent setting for these communes is on the border between an urban university and the poor neighborhoods that ring it. In such a setting houses are often large and rents cheap. This is important because one of the major motivations for establishing a commune is simply to cut the cost of living for all concerned. Such youth communes often are either open to anyone or have very flexible requirements for establishing residence. They are not concerned primarily with working out a new form of family or community living, although this goal may emerge as the commune ages. In this connection the following comments, in which a girl who is living in a commune recalls her earlier experience, are relevant:

[29]Richard Fairfield, *Communes USA: A Personal Tour* (Baltimore: Penguin Books, 1972), p. 2.

[30]Fairfield, *Communes USA*, p. 3.

[31]See Jane O'Reilly, "Notes on the New Paralysis," *New York Magazine* (October 1970), for a vivid picture of these suburban nomads. See also a report *Families of Sand: A Report Concerning the Flight of Adolescents from Their Families* (Columbus, Ohio: The School of Social Work, The Ohio State University, 1974).

The community scene two years ago was a little weird because like people were living in communities but they were all on individual trips. In other words, they were just a bunch of individuals living in one area, one house or one building, but everybody was solely, completely—you know, if they wanted a dish they had to go wash it or if they wanted some food they would have to go down to the store and buy it and more than likely would try to eat it all before they got back to the house. Like I've seen some "communes" that even had separate cupboards.

A boy responded to her remarks:

That's pretty much everybody's first experience, if all the people there are trying a commune for the first time. It seems like the first commune you move into was a completely open one, at least this was my trip and most of the people I know, this was their scene. And progressively, the communes you live in are more and more selected in the sense that it is a more unified thing, more positive, and it ends up where you are all living together and like it's the sort of scene you couldn't handle living with that many people if you weren't on this kind of unifying trip, you'd have to go live by yourself or with one other person.[32]

Gale Fullerton sees these youth communes as having an important socializing function for their members: "Living with a group of other young persons . . . provides an opportunity for the young American to develop role behavior, role expectations and a self-image within the shelter of a group that is neither family nor larger society, and is in fact a kind of half way house."[33] She also points out that communes provide their members with the advantage of what she calls "status through ascription." That is to say, especially in open communes, people are accepted simply because they are of about the same age. Thus the commune provides a setting within which a young person can learn responsibility as an adult member of a social unit rather than as a child in a family.

Youth communes do not foster the development of partnerships of any depth. If we accept Fullerton's description, their major role is to provide a sheltered environment within which youth may try on adult roles. Intensive involvement in heterosexual relationships tends to detract from the life of the commune, as Richard Fairfield observes in connection with a commune called the Yellow Submarine located in an Oregon suburb:

In fact, many of the group's interpersonal and recreational activities took place outside the commune. As the male-female ratio was about 3:1 and as each female was involved in conventional monogamous pairing, most guys had to seek female companionship elsewhere. This kind of arrangement tends to make the membership in a commune more transitory; it also reduced depth interaction and interdependence—characteristics that, if present, can create a more satisfying and permanent community.

[32]Gail Fullerton, *Survival in Marriage.* pp. 244–45.
[33]Fullerton, *Survival in Marriage*, p. 242.

But should every member of every commune be intent solely upon the purpose of developing depth interaction and interdependence? There are now many people, especially the young, who are content with a Yellow Submarine type of situation.

These people are not ready to make a permanent commitment to any one endeavor while there is still a whole world of alternatives out there for them to explore—a universal wall chart to choose from. Only after a broad and satisfying experience of many diverse possibilities can a person really hope to find the place where he really wants to be—the place he can grow with, rather than beyond.[34]

This kind of transitory environment is, nevertheless, a setting in which partnerships develop. At the very least it provides a situation in which persons of the opposite sex get to know one another at the "value" and "role" stages of courtship who might not have found each other attractive in an open field setting.[35] Such pairing off from youth communes probably contributes to the population of young people living together off campus. To what extent this is so is not known. If Murstein's theory of stimulus-value-role mate selection is correct, we could predict that couples who are living together after a communal experience are much more psychologically compatible as partners than those who do not have this communal preparation.

As a social environment in which people can grow (or fail to grow), the commune has costs and benefits just as do traditional dating and living together. Because youth communes are new on the scene, any assessment of the costs and benefits must be offered tentatively. It would appear safe to say at this stage that the three major benefits are as follows: (1) *Acceptance by age.* In the open commune and "crash pad" type commune there are few restrictions on membership other than age. In an achievement-oriented society such as ours, this sort of ready acceptance is a great boon for many. (2) *Family substitute.* The commune is an environment in which one learns such things as adult responsibility in an environment which is more flexible and more tolerant than the world at large. (3) *Economic benefits.* The economic benefits are two-fold: living in a shared dwelling place enables young people to survive with very little income, and this in turn permits young people who could not otherwise afford it to achieve independence from parental control—certainly a major step toward adulthood.

Four factors come readily to mind as apparent costs of communal living: (1) *Social rejection.* Many parents cannot understand what their children are doing living in communes and, indeed, American society as a whole tends to be somewhat hostile to the idea of communalism. (2) *Exploitation.* Communes provide an environment in which the exploitation of the female may flourish; indeed, individuals of either sex

[24]Fairfield, *Communes USA*, p. 351.
[35]See the discussion of Bernard Murstein's findings earlier in this chapter, pp. 98–99.

run considerable risk of being exploited. Someone's got to get the bread, someone's got to keep the house clean, and in large groups it is easy to keep passing the buck. Getting stuck with responsibility for a disproportionate share of the chores is a common complaint of people, especially women, who have tried living in open communes. (3) *Difficulty of re-entry.* A number of observers have remarked on the problem middle-class young people find in trying to get back on the beaten path of middle-class life after living in a commune. (4) *Constant moving.* It is a tossup as to whether this is a cost or a benefit. Many participants in communal living report that the need to relocate frequently induces them to feel themselves to be part of a large community of people rather than simply part of a limited local environment. On the other hand, others experience this as a sense of rootlessness that gives them little opportunity to develop deep and significant relationships with others.

SUMMARY

This chapter has explored three social environments within which partnerships may develop: the traditional path toward marriage, "living together," and youth communes. Of the three, the traditional courtship pattern has the greatest built-in expectation that couples will eventually marry. Couples who live together or who live in youth communes may eventually marry, but to a considerable extent they are experimenting with life styles that may provide alternatives to marriage for them.

Each of these social environments entails certain costs and benefits. The traditional pattern may be the most comfortable inasmuch as the guidelines it offers are fairly clear. The other two social environments, in contrast, are still largely undefined. As alternatives to the traditional pattern, they undeniably offer benefits not readily available to those who follow the path from dating through engagement to marriage. On the other hand, precisely because they are new they may present many new problems and few guidelines for coping with them.

PART

TWO

HUMAN
SEXUALITY

6
THE BIOLOGY OF SEX AND REPRODUCTION

The human body has no other parts as fascinating as the sexual organs. Venerated and vilified, concealed and exhibited, the human genitals have elicited a multitude of varied responses. They have been portrayed in every art form, praised and damned in poetry and prose, mutilated with religious fervor, and amputated in insane frenzy.

Many of us combine a lively interest in the sex organs with an equally compelling tendency either to deny such interest or to be ashamed of it. There are [people] who have been married for years, who have engaged in sexual intercourse countless times, but who never looked frankly and searchingly at each other's genitals. Nor is this aversion merely a matter of prudishness. To many people the sex organs appear neither beautiful nor sexy when viewed directly. Unfortunately, although concealment may promote desire, it also perpetuates ignorance.

Herant A. Katchadourian
and Donald T. Lunde

INTRODUCTION

Our scientific understanding of human sexuality is largely confined to anatomy and the reproductive process. Very little is known about sexual response outside of reproduction. More than twenty centuries ago Aristotle observed that the testes were raised inside the scrotum during sexual intercourse; not until the 1950s did Masters and Johnson confirm this observation in the laboratory. It seems incredible, giving the universality of sex, that we should know so little about it.

113

Even in our day when we are inundated with pornographic movies, subjected to constant debates about sex education in the public schools, exposed to a wide array of books and articles about human sexuality, many of us still have to confess profound ignorance about even rudimentary facets of our sexual nature. Despite the fact that the mass media assure us we have gone through a "sexual revolution," many people still find it difficult to look at their own bodies. Some sex therapists, therefore, prescribe as a first stage in their therapy that persons who come to them for help become acquainted with their own bodies by examining themselves in a mirror.

Masters and Johnson cite a case of a thirty-five-year-old man and a thirty-four-year-old woman who had been married nine years without consummating their marriage. The woman was suffering from a severe case of vaginismus—an involuntary contraction of the vagina—which prevented her husband from entering her. "When vaginismus was described and then directly demonstrated to both husband and wife, it was the first time Mr. A. had ever seen his wife unclothed and also the first time she had submitted to a medical examination," Masters and Johnson report.[1]

Some simple straightforward knowledge of our anatomy is necessary for an adequate understanding of human sexuality. Our growing knowledge about the nature of erotic response can help us understand our own sexual arousal, thus enabling us to become better sexual partners. Thus, although we remain largely in ignorance about many aspects of human sexual response and human sexual behavior, there have recently appeared several excellent texts which make very good use of the little that is known about our sexuality.[2]

[1]William H. Masters and Virginia Johnson, *Human Sexual Inadequacy* (Boston: Little, Brown, 1970), p. 233.
[2]We are particularly indebted to Katchadourian and Lunde, *Fundamentals of Human Sexuality*, and James Leslie McCary, *Human Sexuality: A Brief Edition* (New York: D. Van Nostrand and Company, 1973).

HUMAN ANATOMY

Although it is certainly not necessary to have a detailed understanding of sexual anatomy in order to perform adequately sexually, knowledge in this area helps dispel some of the numerous myths and fallacies that have adhered to our understanding of human sexuality. Understanding our bodies helps us to feel comfortable with them, and this is an important part of developing good relationships.

External Genitalia

Male Anatomy. The reproductive system of the human male—and of the human female—is an integrated and complex system, parts of which are housed in the body and parts of which are located outside of the body. Naturally, we are more familiar with the external portions of these systems. The internal portions are, more often than not, as much a mystery to us as the function of any other highly complex internal organ. Just as we are aware of the ears as external organs but remain largely ignorant of the workings of the inner ear, so the external sexual organs have very obvious sexual significance for us while the internal "plumbing" that makes them work is more or less a mystery to us.

The *penis* and the *scrotum* are the external reproductive organs of the male. (The testes, which are carried in the scrotum, are not technically considered external organs.) The penis serves not only as the organ of copulation but also as the organ through which the male urinates. "The average penis is three to four inches long when flaccid, and somewhat more than six inches in erection. Its diameter in a relaxed state is about one and one quarter inches and increases another quarter inch in erection. Penises can, however, be considerably smaller or larger."[3] The size of the penis bears little relationship to its physiological capacity to stimulate the female in sexual arousal.

The foreskin of the penis, or *prepuce*, has been the object of ritual mutilation ever since the earliest times in recorded human history. Removal of this skin, or circumcision, often is performed early in a boy's life for both religious and hygienic reasons. After circumcision smegma, a cheesy substance with a distinctive smell which is secreted by glands in the penis, cannot accumulate under the prepuce. Biologist Alex Comfort contends that the uncircumcised male can enjoy more erotic pleasure than the circumcised male because of the greater variety of manipulations of the penis that are possible with the prepuce present.[4] Many

[3]Katchadourian and Lunde, *Fundamentals of Human Sexuality*, p. 28.
[4]Alex Comfort, *The Joy of Sex* (New York: Crown Publishing Company, 1972), p. 67.

FIGURE 6–1

External male genitalia.

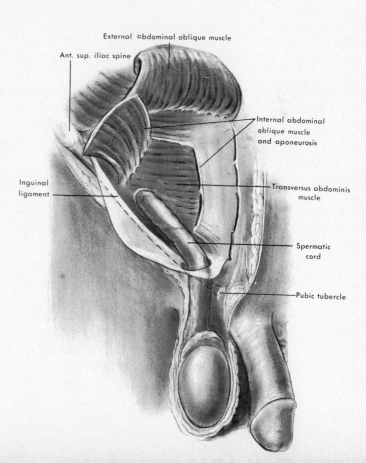

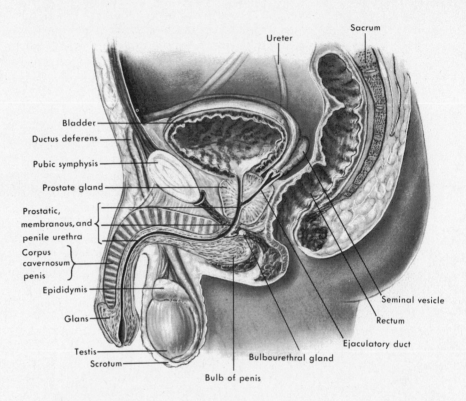

Ureter

Sacrum

Bladder

Ductus deferens

Pubic symphysis

Prostate gland

Prostatic, membranous, and penile urethra

Corpus cavernosum penis

Epididymis

Glans

Seminal vesicle

Rectum

Ejaculatory duct

Testis

Scrotum

Bulbourethral gland

Bulb of penis

FIGURE 6–2

The male reproductive system.

authorities, however, do not support this contention; on the contrary, they maintain that circumcision, by exposing the sensitive tip of the penis, heightens sexual sensation. Perhaps research will settle this controversy soon; at present it is a glaring example of our ignorance about some very fundamental facets of sexual experience.

The scrotum is a sac of skin, darker in color than the rest of the body, lying directly behind the penis. It retains the testes outside of the body cavity because the production of sperm inside the testes will not occur at body temperature. Sperm are continuously produced in the testes. They are generated in the *seminiferous tubules* of the testes and mature in the *epididymis*. If ejaculation does not occur within thirty to sixty days, the sperm die and are replaced by new ones.

Because a change in temperature of even two to three degrees centigrade will adversely affect sperm production, the scrotum regulates the temperature of the testes by drawing them closer to the body on cold days and allowing them to hang further away on hot days. The fact that sperm production is inhibited by increases in temperature has led to the widely held belief that taking a hot shower before sexual intercourse can serve as a contraceptive technique. Although it is true that a hot shower will kill some sperm, the effect will be negligible as far as contraception is concerned. The hot shower method may reduce the chances of impregnating the woman by some small fraction of a percent, but any sensible person would have to regard it as a highly unreliable means of contraception.

The penis is attached to the pelvis at its root. The body of the penis, the pendulous portion, is made up of three channels. These three separate channels of spongelike tissue are served by a network of blood vessels and nerves. During erection they become engorged with blood, thus creating the characteristic stiffness of the erect penis. The *glans penis* is the smooth round head of the penis. It is the most sensitive part of the penis and contributes greatly to the pleasure of sexual arousal when stimulated. The neck of the penis is also rich with nerve endings but the shaft itself is relatively insensitive. The *urethra* runs through the middle of the penis. It is the passageway through which urine is emitted. It also serves as a channel for the emission of semen during sexual intercourse.

Female Anatomy. The term that is applied to the entire external female genitalia is "vulva." The *mons pubis* is the most visible portion of the female genitalia, being the elevation of fatty tissue over the pubic bone. In a woman who has reached puberty it is normally covered with pubic hair.

The *clitoris* is the female homologue of the penis.[5] It does not hang free from the body, however, and only its upper portion, or *glans clitoris*, is visible. It is one of the few organs of the body—if not the only one—whose sole purpose is to provide pleasure. Being essentially a bundle of nerve endings, it seems to have no other function. The discovery of the pleasure-providing role of the clitoris and the techniques by which it may be stimulated are an essential component of the sexual revolution. Like the penis, the clitoris has suffered ritual mutilation in various societies.

The clitoris is located near the upper joining of the *labia majora*, or major lips. The shaft of the clitoris may be located by tracing the finger upward between these lips until their juncture is reached. The glans is about one inch below this juncture at the joining of the *labia minora*, or minor lips. Typically, the clitoris is slightly under an inch in length, including its buried portion, and in diameter it measures about four to five millimeters.

[5]The term "homologue" refers to the fact that two apparently different organs have emerged from the same anatomical tissues. Thus the penis and clitoris have a common embryological background.

The labia majora are the homologue of the scrotal sac. They cover the minor lips and the clitoris. The appearance of these lips varies, sometimes being heavy and bulging, sometimes small. They almost always hang together, thus closing the vaginal orifice. In front, the major lips are ridgelike and pronounced, but toward the anus they recede into the surrounding tissue.

The labia minora, like the labia majora, are two vertical folds of skin. But unlike the major lips, which are partially covered with pubic hair on the outside, the minor lips are pink and hairless. They form the vestibule to the vaginal opening and are very sensitive to the touch. The urethral opening is found above the vaginal orifice and is protected by the labia minora.

The vaginal orifice varies in appearance, depending upon the condition of the *hymen*. Much folk custom has been associated with the hymen, or maidenhead, a membrane located inside the vaginal opening. It has traditionally been regarded as the seal of the virgin under the fallacious assumption that the presence of an unbroken hymen was proof of virginity while its absence was proof of prior sexual intercourse. It is true that the hymen normally remains intact unless it is forcefully ruptured by some penetration of the vagina. But it is also true that the hymen can be ruptured in other ways and that it is possible

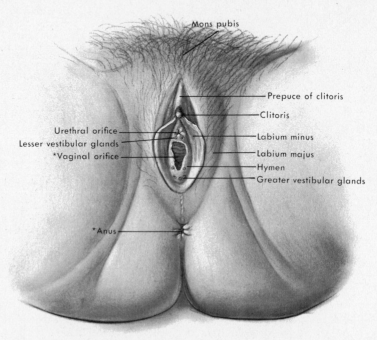

FIGURE 6–3

External female genitalia.

*The clinical perineum lies between these two openings.

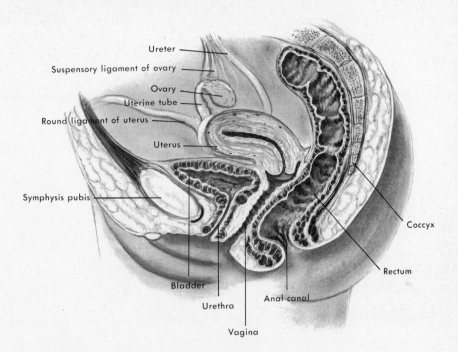

Ureter
Suspensory ligament of ovary
Ovary
Uterine tube
Round ligament of uterus
Uterus
Symphysis pubis
Coccyx
Rectum
Bladder
Anal canal
Urethra
Vagina

FIGURE 6–4
Internal female reproductive system.

to engage in sexual intercourse without damaging this sturdy membrane. Be that as it may, the fact that the rupture of the hymen is often accompanied by bleeding led to the practice in some countries of displaying the sheets of the wedding night with their bloodstains signifying that the hymen had been broken.

Strictly speaking, the female breasts are not a part of the reproductive system inasmuch as they do not play a determinative role in the process of conception. But they are, of course, closely linked to the reproductive system. They undergo changes in size and sensitivity in response to hormonal signals that are part of the menstrual and reproductive cycles; lactation, which occurs during pregnancy, is also a hormonally triggered response. What is more, the breasts play an important part in sexual arousal. The nipples are the most sensitive portion of the breast. This sensitivity is totally unrelated to the size or shape of the breasts.

HUMAN SEXUAL RESPONSE

Until the precedent shattering research of Masters and Johnson only a few years ago, scientifically verified knowledge about human sexual response was abysmally meager.[6] Even today our ignorance far exceeds our knowledge in this area. Nevertheless, it is now possible to offer some account of the process of sexual response, and in the following few pages we shall do so.

It is important to bear in mind that this is an area in which psychological passions run deep—deep enough, in fact, to have profound effects on the physiological processes we will be describing. For example, a vociferous debate has been raging for a number of years about

[6]This research is reported in numerous articles and two major books: *Human Sexual Response* (Boston: Little, Brown, 1966) and *Human Sexual Inadequancy.*

Joel Gordon

whether women experience orgasm in the vagina or in the clitoris. Seemingly the simplest way to settle this debate—by asking women—has not proved satisfactory; some women report experiencing vaginal orgasms and some report clitoral orgasms. This may indicate that both types of orgasm are physiologically possible, but it also may indicate that women who feel a strong psychological need to experience vaginal orgasms will experience orgasm as though it occurred in the vagina regardless of the fact that it was in actuality a clitoral orgasm. And vice versa. In short, role expectations may lead us to believe we are having experiences which are in fact physiologically impossible and, conversely, they may make it impossible for us to experience sensations which our physiological equipment can provide.

Thus, any account of the physiology of sexual response must be read with an awareness of the fact that people differ not only physiologically but also psychologically in the extent to which they conform to the response pattern outlined here.

Sexual Response in the Male

The external genitalia and the breasts of the female have been objects of sexual arousal for the male from time immemorial. In some cultures the exposure of the vulva by the female constitutes an invitation to sexual intercourse. In our own tradition there seems to be a preference for covering the sexually stimulating body parts and letting the suggestion of their presence produce the desired erotic effect.

Although there is considerable debate over the matter, it seems that, within our experience, men respond to visual stimuli differently than do women. It is common knowledge that men experience erection in response to visual stimulation and it is often maintained that women do not commonly manifest such signs of sexual arousal as lubrication of the vagina in response to purely visual phenomena. This difference —if in fact it exists—may well be a result of cultural conditioning rather than of physiological differences in the response mechanisms of the two sexes.

Masters and Johnson have completed the most thorough study of human sexual response ever conducted, and they describe both the male and the female response in terms of four phases. Consider first the four phases of male response.

Excitement Phase. The sources of excitement or arousal need not be specified at this point. Suffice it to say that different men are "turned on" in different ways and that visual stimuli are frequently effective in this regard. The first response to effective stimulation is an erection of the penis, which occurs involuntarily. The penis becomes engorged with blood and achieves varying degrees of stiffness depending upon the state of arousal. One cannot will an erection, one can only relax and remove the distractions that may impair its occurrence. Nor can one will an erection away, although one can, by deliberately distracting oneself, effectively eliminate the source of stimulation from one's perceptual field, after which the erection will subside spontaneously.

Men are capable of maintaining an erection in the excitement stage for many minutes. Various kinds of diversions, such as loud noises, obvious changes in lighting, or conversation on an extraneous subject, may cause partial or total loss of the erection.[7]

During the excitement phase the scrotum contracts and the testes are pulled toward the body cavity. The folds disappear. During prolonged copulation the scrotum may relax without loss of erection.[8]

Plateau Phase. The plateau phase is reached when the fully erect penis undergoes a slight involuntary enlargement of the cap and a small amount of mucoid fluid is secreted from the *Cowper's gland*, located on the urethra just below the prostate gland. This secretion generally is clear or slightly clouded in color. Researchers are not certain of its function. It may serve to lubricate the urethra for the easier passage of the forthcoming semen, or it may serve to reduce the acidity of the urethra, which is essential if conception is to occur because sperm cannot survive in an acidic environment. In any case, this secretion may contain a small amount of semen, thus making it possible for conception to occur without ejaculation. For this reason the practice of *coitus interruptus*—withdrawing the penis from the vagina before ejaculation—may prove ineffective as a contraceptive technique.

There are no further changes in the scrotum in either the plateau or the orgasmic phase of sexual response. A reddening of the skin (sex flush) occurs infrequently in the plateau stage.

Internally, the testes enlarge to about one and a half times their normal size and are pressed against the body. This pressing of the testes against the body is necessary for orgasm and anticipates it occurrence.[9]

Orgasmic Phase. Orgasm is a highly pleasurable involuntary response to sexual stimulation. In the male it normally lasts from two to ten seconds, after which the male must undergo a period of relaxation (refractory period) lasting a few minutes to several hours.

Orgasm in the male is experienced as an involuntary contraction of the urethra and the muscles around the base of the penis and the anus. These contractions involve the entire length of the urethra and are re-

[7]Masters and Johnson, *Human Sexual Response*, p. 183.
[8]*Human Sexual Response*, p. 205.
[9]Katchadourian, *Fundamentals of Human Sexuality*, p. 67.

sponsible for the ejaculation of the seminal fluid, which occurs at about 0.8-second intervals for the first three or four contractions. These initial contractions are followed by others at gradually lengthening intervals and with weakening intensity.

Orgasm is normally a very intense physiological response, as evidenced in the changes in heartbeat, blood pressure, and breathing. Heartbeat increases from a norm of about 70 to 80 beats per minute to a high of 110 to 180 beats per minute. Blood pressure may double. Respiratory rates increase from the normal 18 per minute to as high as 40 per minute, although if the orgasm is mild or of short duration there may be no increase in the rate of breathing at all. Many people experience a sense of loss of oxygen and respond by gasping for air, or hyperventilating.

The internal organs participate in the orgasmic response. The sperm which have been maturing in the epididymis are forced upward through the *vas deferens* by the contraction of its walls. Before entering the urethra they are enveloped in milky liquid produced in the seminal vesicle and the prostate gland to form the semen. The passage of the semen through the urethra is furthered by the contraction of the urethral walls. The contractions of these internal organs as they pour their secretions into the urethra are responsible for the feeling of the "inevitability of orgasm."

The ejaculate emerges from the erect penis in a series of spurts. Semen may be ejected from the penis with a force capable of propelling it a distance of three or four feet, or it may simply ooze from the urethra. Once ejected, the sperm will die unless they reach the Fallopian tubes of the female, where they typically survive for two or three days. In rare instances they can survive in the Fallopian tubes for five days or longer.[10]

The more effective the sexual stimulation, the more completely the entire body is involved in the release of tensions in orgasm. About 25 percent of the male population in Masters and Johnson's study experienced a well developed sex flush or reddening of the skin during orgasm.[11]

Orgasm is almost always marked in the male by the ejaculation of semen. Semen is characteristically white. Its substance varies from a thick almost gelatin-like fluid to a thin watery substance. "Frequent ejaculation generally results in a thinner fluid."[12] The amount of semen ejaculated is normally about 3 to 4 cubic centimeters, weighing about

[10]Lloyd Saxton, *The Individual, Marriage and the Family*, 2nd ed. (Belmont, Calif: Wadsworth Publishing Company, Inc., 1972), p. 56.
[11]Masters and Johnson, *Human Sexual Response*, p. 290.
[12]McCary, *Human Sexuality*, p. 33.

4 grams. McCary estimates that the caloric value of the ejaculate is around 36 calories and concludes, "The evidence is therefore convincing that a normal discharge of semen cannot in any way 'weaken' a man."[13] This evidence contradicts the folk notion that a man must conserve his semen in order to conserve his strength. The amount of semen in the ejaculation is positively correlated to the pleasure experienced by the male in orgasm, particularly after long periods of abstinence.[14]

Resolution Phase. Masters and Johnson observe that a basic rule of male response to sexual stimuli is that there is "psychophysiologic resistance to sexual stimuli immediately after an ejaculatory experience."[15] This period of time during which males are unresponsive to sexual stimuli is called the refractory stage. Its length varies greatly. Masters and Johnson cite an example of a male subject who was able to "ejaculate three times within ten minutes of the onset of stimulative activity,"[16] but with most men stimulation following within a few minutes after ejaculation will fail to produce a second erection and ejaculation, let alone a third.

After ejaculation, the penis typically shrinks to about twice its flaccid size during the first stage of resolution. During the second stage of the resolution phase the penis returns to its normal prestimulated size. This stage may be prolonged or shortened, depending upon the effectiveness of sexual stimulation experienced. It is likely to be prolonged if the penis is kept in the vagina and the couple continue to hold each other close and to caress. The penis will rapidly lose its erection in both stages if the couple disengage and the male's attention is directed to nonstimulating activities such as urinating or smoking.

The testes return to normal size during resolution. This may occur rapidly or slowly, depending upon the length of the plateau phase.[17] The scrotum loses its tenseness and returns to its prestimulated state.

Sexual Response in the Female

The female, of course, may receive semen from the male without being sexually aroused. She may be penetrated with the assistance of artificial lubricants—or by sheer force, as generally happens in cases of rape—and thus may conceive a child without ever experiencing sexual pleasure. Indeed, in puritanical cultures the female is not expected to enjoy sexual intercourse and many women, in fact, do not. Masters and John-

---

[13]*Human Sexuality*, p. 33.
[14]Masters and Johnson, *Human Sexual Response*, p. 216.
[15]*Human Sexual Response*, p. 214.
[16]*Human Sexual Response*, p. 214.
[17]*Human Sexual Response*, p. 293.

son, however, have clearly demonstrated that the female capacity to enjoy sexual stimulation is far greater than that of the male.[18] Women, in fact, are physiologically capable of experiencing a fairly large number of orgasms in rapid succession, whereas men, as we have seen, generally cannot experience a second orgasm until a considerable period of time has elapsed after the first. Conclusions reached by Kinsey and Freud to the effect that women are not as excitable by sexual stimuli as men and do not have an adequate body image because of the supposed "penis envy" have reinforced common folk notions about the sexual inferiority of women. These notions, it is now becoming clear, have absolutely no basis in fact. Indeed, Dr. Seymour Fischer contends:

The woman can more easily integrate her body meaningfully into the pattern of her life than can the man. It is the man, rather than the woman, who is more likely to feel insecure from his body and alien from it.

The material presented [in Fischer's study, *The Female Orgasm*] indicates with clarity that there is no factual basis for regarding women as psychologically less sexually secure or able than men. To continue to promulgate ideas about such alleged inferiority would seem to be an expression of antifeminine prejudice.[19]

Excitement Phase. During the excitement phase, the clitoral shaft increases in diameter and length. The major lips of women who have not had children flatten and separate. The lips of the vulva begin to expose the vaginal opening. In women who have had children there is a thickening of the major lips and a slight opening. The minor lips thicken and expand toward the vaginal vault. Within ten to thirty seconds after effective sexual stimulation, lubrication appears in the vagina and the vaginal vault lengthens and expands.

In both sexes the nipples of the breast become erect and increase in size. The breasts of the female enlarge and develop a pronounced veinous engorgement. A sex flush typically appears first on the abdomen and then spreads to the breasts during the late stage of excitement. The entire uterus elevates at the onset of sexual stimulation. The cervix slowly retracts upward from the vaginal vault.[20]

The production of the egg in the female's ovary and its migration down the Fallopian tube ordinarily is unrelated to the presence of sexual stimulation. However, the frequency with which the so-called "safe period" in the woman's menstrual cycle proves not to be safe at all may well be attributed to the fact that females sometimes ovulate in response to sexual arousal. The ovaries are generally almond shaped and measure

[18]*Human Sexual Response*, p. 65.
[19]Seymour Fischer, *The Female Orgasm: Psychology, Physiology, Fantasy* (New York: Basic Books, Inc., 1973), p. 393. By permission.
[20]Masters and Johnson, *Human Sexual Response*, p. 112.

1½ by ¾ by 1 inch. They normally weigh about a quarter of an ounce and are, therefore, somewhat lighter than the testes. Unlike the male, who must continuously produce new sperm, the female is born with about 400,000 eggs imperfectly developed. The typical pattern of maturation is one in which one egg develops on an alternate ovary each month. However, an ovary may produce two eggs at a time or may produce more than once during a month if the woman experiences intense sexual stimulation.[21]

The ovaries are detached from the Fallopian tubes and the ripened or matured egg breaks the surface of the ovary and, by some process as yet unknown, "seeks" the opening of the Fallopian tube. Normally, fertilization by the sperm occurs at the opening of the Fallopian tube.

The Plateau Phase. In the plateau phase the clitoris draws back and is positioned directly above the pelvic bone. The labia majora of women who have never given birth to children may become enlarged. In women who have borne children, they continue to become engorged with blood at this phase of arousal. The outer third of the vagina further increases in length and depth, swelling into what Masters and Johnson have called an orgasmic platform. The *Bartholin gland* excretes a mucoid liquid which aids in the lubrication of the vaginal outlet. The major source of lubrication, however, is simple perspiration.

The nipples become further enlarged and distended, breast size increases, and the engorgement of the *areola*—the pigmented area surrounding the nipple—increases. There is further voluntary and involuntary tension in the face and abdominal musculature.

The uterus becomes fully elevated as the cervix's continued retraction further increases the sensitivity of the vaginal vault.

The Orgasmic Phase. During orgasm the clitoris and the major and minor lips do not change their structure. Contractions in the vagina occur at about 0.8-second intervals (as in the male pattern), and reoccur from five to twelve times. After the first three to six contractions, the intervals lengthen and the intensity diminishes. The breasts do not undergo any noticeable change. The sex flush parallels the orgasmic experience in about 75 percent of females. There is a momentary loss of voluntary control of muscle groups and involuntary contractions are experienced.

As the involuntary contractions of the orgasmic platform take place in the vagina, there are also involuntary contractions of the anal sphincter. The experience of hyperventilation and increase in blood pressure and heartbeat generally are similar to the pattern experienced by the

[21]McCary, *Human Sexuality*, p. 39.

male. Because the female has a greater variation of orgasmic intensity than the male, she may experience heartbeat rates above 180 per minute.

Just as a male's anxiety over his sexual prowess focuses on his ability to achieve and maintain an erection, so the female's fear centers on her ability to experience orgasm. All women register the physiological responses of orgasm, but many do not experience the sensations that accompany these responses. That is to say, they *have* orgasms but are inhibited—most often for psychological reasons—from *feeling* orgasms. These fears and inhibitions that men and women bring to their sexual behavior in our society are to a large extent the products of cultural conditioning.

Resolution Phase. Unlike the male, the female does not have a physiologically determined refractory period. She is capable of experiencing another orgasm immediately if stimulation is resumed. If unstimulated, the clitoris returns to normal size and position within five to ten seconds. The major and minor lips return to normal thickness and midline position within ten to fifteen seconds. The relaxation of the vaginal wall may take as long as ten to fifteen minutes. The cervical orifice remains open for twenty to thirty minutes.

There is a rapid diminution of the areolae and an involution of the

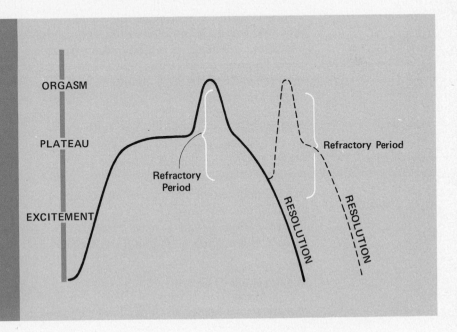

FIGURE 6–5

The male sexual response cycle.

FIGURE 6–6

The female sexual response cycle.

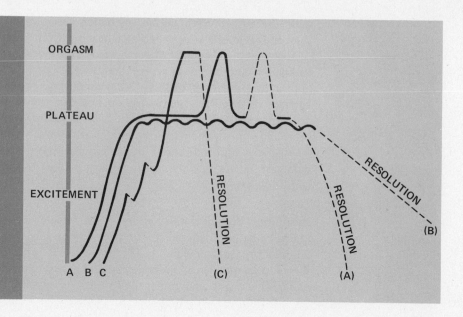

nipples. The sex flush disappears. Muscle tensions rarely are carried more than five to ten minutes into the resolution phase.

In the resolution phase of the female's sexual response, the appearance of a widespread film of perspiration not related to the degree of physical activity is noticeable. In the male, this sweating reaction, when it occurs, is usually confined to the soles of the feet and the palms of the hands, but in females it is often more pervasive.

As Figure 6–5 indicates, there is considerable similarity in the sexual response cycle of the male and the female, especially through the plateau stage. The typical female pattern A closely approximates the typical male pattern except that there is no refractory period so that a second orgasm can occur within seconds of the first. (Some men also are capable of experiencing a second orgasm within a few seconds if their refractory period is short.) In Figure 6–6 B and C represents less typical feminine response patterns. In B, the excitement mounts rapidly and immediately bursts into a series of sustained orgasms, which are experienced as one sustained climax. In such cases, the resolution phase lasts longer. Pattern C shows more abrupt moments of excitement followed by an intense climax and a rapid resolution.

The Reactions of Older People

We are sexual beings all of our lives. Some of us, indeed, may not come to experience the full pleasures of sexual intercourse until we have reached what is commonly regarded as old age.[22] This is an unusual pattern but one that should cause us to think twice before assuming that older persons are asexual. The more common course is to bring the pattern of sexual behavior experienced in middle age into old age.

As with other parts of the body, the process of aging causes changes in the sexual organs. These changes modify, but need not radically alter, sexual performance. Most men and women over sixty-five are capable of experiencing orgasm, although our cultural conditioning often makes them embarrassed about this sexual capacity.

The older male requires a longer period of time to achieve an erection regardless of how exciting the sexual stimulation may be. In many instances, manual stimulation of the penis is necessary where formerly visual stimulation was sufficient to achieve an erection. In the elderly male, the penis typically does not achieve its full erection until just before orgasm. If he should lose his erection in lovemaking, it is more difficult for him to recover it. However, he is also typically capable of maintaining an erection for longer periods than in his youth. Ejaculation declines in vigor, and in very old age the semen simply flows from the penis but is not forcefully ejected.[23]

The internal organs may be affected by the aging process. Typically, the scrotum does not change in appearance or structure, but the testes may cease to expand in size during sexual intercourse. The resolution stage is much more abrupt and the refractory period is likely to last longer. Thus older men generally do not seek multiple orgasms, although some are quite capable of doing so.

The aging female has greater physiological changes to undergo. After *menopause*, the vaginal walls decrease in thickness and lose their color, their texture, and their elasticity. Lubrication of the vagina is slower to occur and less complete. The swelling of the first third of the vagina, associated with the plateau stage, becomes less noticeable, but this change is partially compensated for by the increased tightness in the *introitus*.[24] As with the aging male, orgasmic responses are fewer in number, less intense, and shorter in duration.

The uterus undergoes dramatic changes after menopause. When the reproductive period has passed, the uterus diminishes in size until it is no larger than the cervix. Although neither the elevation nor the contraction of the uterus occurs in the typical aging female, some women report unpleasant spasms of the uterus which disincline them to engage in sexual intercourse. This phenomenon, however, is far from universal; the majority of women, like the majority of men, can continue to enjoy

[22]Isadore Rubin, *Sexual Life After Sixty* (New York: Basic Books, 1965).
[23]Katchadourian, *Fundamentals of Human Sexuality*, p. 76.
[24]*Fundamentals of Human Sexuality*, p. 77.

sexual intercourse into old age. The external genitalia also undergo a reduction in size. The minor lips, however, continue to swell upon excitation, and the clitoris remains largely unchanged in its sexual sensitivity even into very old age. The nongenital physiological response to orgasm in old age is generally less intense.

In sum, despite the stereotyped belief that sexual pleasure is reserved for the young, elderly people are in fact quite capable of leading full and rich sex lives. As Herant Katchadourian observes, "Time takes its toll, but need not quench sexual desires nor cripple its fulfillment."[25]

CONCEPTION AND PREGNANCY

Conception

The fertilization of the egg normally occurs in one of the Fallopian tubes. As the fertilized egg moves down the Fallopian tube, it begins the process of cell division that eventually will produce a full-term fetus. There is little change in the overall mass of the fertilized egg as it moves down the Fallopian tube, but it continues to divide into cells which form a shell around a liquid core. Between five to seven days after ovulation, the fertilized egg makes its way to the uterine wall and, with the assistance of enzymes that dissolve the lining of the uterus, it links itself up with the blood supply beneath the tissue. By the tenth to twelfth day it becomes firmly attached to the uterine wall and has established a continuing supply of nutrient. There is no overt sign of pregnancy at this time, however, because menstruation is not due to occur for several days.

Pregnancy

The normal term of pregnancy in the human female is 266 days, or approximately nine calendar months. For convenience in understanding it, this period of gestation is conventionally divided into three trimesters. These trimesters will be described on the basis of what is happening to the pregnant woman. Those interested in fetal development and embryology can find much more adequate coverage of these topics in standard texts devoted to these subjects.[26]

[25]*Fundamentals of Human Sexuality*, p. 79.
[26]For some excellent texts on human embryology, see the following: R. Rugh and L. B. Shettles, *From Conception to Birth* (New York: Harper & Row, 1971); K. L. Moore, *The Developing Human* (Philadelphia: W.B. Saunders Co., 1973); and H. Tuchmann-Duplessis and P. Haegel, *Illustrated Human Embryology*, trans. L.S. Hurley (New York: Springer Verlag, 1973).

First Trimester. One of the first signs of pregnancy is the failure to menstruate. Although not a reliable sign, it certainly is a sign that most women recognize. The reaction to missing a period will be varied, depending upon whether a child is expected or not. A woman may, however, fail to menstruate for many reasons other than pregnancy. Emotional upsets, illnesses, age, conditions associated with nursing a child, and so forth also may cause a woman to miss a period.[27] To complicate the matter further, some women can be pregnant but still emit a smaller menstrual flow. This diminished menstrual flow is called "spotting." Spotting can be an early sign of miscarriage, but it normally occurs in about 20 percent of all pregnancies and is not necessarily ominous.

Other symptoms of pregnancy include the enlargement and tenderness of the breasts. The nipples become more sensitive to tactile stimulation. Many women experience "morning sickness"—a general feeling of nausea occurring shortly after getting out of bed—during the first six to eight weeks (four to six weeks after missed period). This can be accompanied by vomiting and aversion to food. Fatigue, drowsiness, and a desire for more sleep very often are signs of pregnancy during this period. There is an increase in the need to urinate because of the swelling of the uterus and the pressure on the bladder. But even if a woman has all of these symptoms, the earliest time that a physician can determine with complete certainty that she is pregnant is after nine to twelve weeks (seventh to tenth week after missed period), although modern techniques makes it possible for physicians to diagnose pregnancy with 95 percent reliability after only two weeks.[28] A pelvic examination and various laboratory tests can be performed that will greatly assist in the determination of pregnancy.

Once pregnancy has been established, the most likely date of delivery can be determined within five days in most instances by the use of the following formula: Add one week to the first day of the last menstrual period, subtract three months, then add one year. Sixty percent of all deliveries will be made within five days of the projected date.

In the first trimester there is no reason why pregnancy or the suspicion of pregnancy should inhibit sexual activities. It is not likely to harm the developing fetus. There may be some practical considerations, however. Morning sickness may inhibit the desire for sexual activity in the early part of the day, just as fatigue and sleepiness may limit sexual

[27]*Fundamentals of Human Sexuality*, p. 109.
[28]*Fundamentals of Human Sexuality*, p. 110. This issue raises the argument between physicians about the reliability of diagnosing pregnancy. Because of the heated controversy over abortion, the public debate goes on. The figure cited here—two weeks—seems generally supportable, although Katchadourian prefers a more conservative figure.

activity in the evening. Because of the physiological changes described above, the already tender breasts may become painful during stimulation. Nevertheless, most couples can find mutually satisfactory occasions for continuing sexual relations.

During the first trimester, the *placenta* begins to develop. This is the organ through which the growing fetus exchanges nutrients and waste products with the mother. It also serves as the endocrine gland producing hormones essential to the maintenance of pregnancy. Complications to pregnancy during this period are transmitted through the placenta. Many drugs have been known to have an effect upon the development of the embryo—for example, thalidomide, a sedative which was banned from the market in the 1950s after its horrible effects on unborn babies became known. The drug caused abnormal development of the arms and legs. Regular users of addictive drugs such as heroin and morphine have produced babies who were born addicted to the drugs. When such children are born, they suffer withdrawal symptoms if further doses of the drug are not given. Synthetic hormone drugs resembling progesterone administered during the first trimester to women who show signs of possible miscarriage sometimes have resulted in the masculinization of the female fetus (see Chapter 9). Diseases such as rubella, or German measles, are quite likely to produce serious disorders in the fetus if the mother contracts them during the early part of the first trimester. As a result, many argue that women who contract German measles during the first two months of their pregnancy should be allowed to have abortions. During the third month of their pregnancy, the risk that German measles will produce abnormalities in the fetus decreases to 10 percent.

Second Trimester. By the time the second trimester begins—i.e., the fourth month of pregnancy—it is possible to detect fetal heartbeat and movement. An x-ray of the mother's abdomen will show a fetal outline. Danger from radiation, however, limits the use of x-rays to extreme situations.

During the second trimester the nausea and drowsiness experienced in the first trimester tend to disappear. Concern about miscarriage should diminish now, and the pregnant woman can continue her normal activities. She will experience the sensation of the movement of the fetus and will notice an increase in her waistline. Her abdomen will begin to protrude.

With the decrease of nausea, drowsiness, and breast tenderness, sexual intercourse can be enjoyed more fully now. Women often report an increase in interest in sexual activities and greater satisfaction from them during this period. Indeed, many women report that they find sexual intercourse to be more satisfying at this time than at any other time in their lives. During sexual stimulation there is a significant increase in vaginal lubrication. Late in the second trimester, however, certain coital positions (e.g., the man on top) become too tiring or painful for the woman.

At the end of six months the developing fetus weighs about two pounds and is about fourteen inches long. The fetus moves its arms and legs spontaneously and can open its eyes. Should the fetus be delivered at this time, there is a 95 percent chance of death. However, "the smallest infant known to have survived weighed less than one pound at birth. (It weighed 400 grams; one pound = 455 grams.) The fetus was estimated to be twenty weeks old at the time of delivery."[29]

Third Trimester. During this period—the seventh to ninth months of pregnancy—the fetus becomes more active. In her swelling abdomen, the woman experiences what seems to be perpetual kicking, tossing, and turning, which are sometimes severe enough to keep her awake all night. During this trimester physicians often become concerned about the weight of their patients. A weight gain of about twenty pounds is considered by most physicians as ideal. Of this twenty pounds, the average infant makes up about 7.5 pounds at birth. The remaining 12.5 pounds consist of the placenta, the amniotic fluid, the increase in uterine size, the enlargement of the breasts, and fluid and fat accumulated by the mother. Controlling weight is often difficult for the mother, for she may have to struggle against an increased appetite which is caused in part by the hormonal changes of pregnancy. Women who gain weight excessively experience difficulty in movement and subject themselves to the possibility of medical complications such as strain on the heart and high blood pressure.

Women in the third trimester commonly are anxious to be delivered. They begin to count the days and wonder about the character of their about-to-be-born infant. What will be its sex? Will it be a healthy, normal child? They begin to make concrete plans for the nursery and bringing the baby home.

Although sexual activity need not be discontinued during the third trimester if the woman is in good health, it does tend to decrease during this period. Many women feel uncomfortable, complaining of backaches and fatigue which tend to decrease their sexual interest. Yet many women are surprised by their responsiveness during late pregnancy. Many people fear that intercourse during the third trimester will induce premature labor, but there is no evidence to support this if the woman is in good health. Although fear of infecting the fetus leads some phy-

[29] *Fundamentals of Human Sexuality*, p. 119.

FIGURE 6–7
Development of fetus,
by weeks.

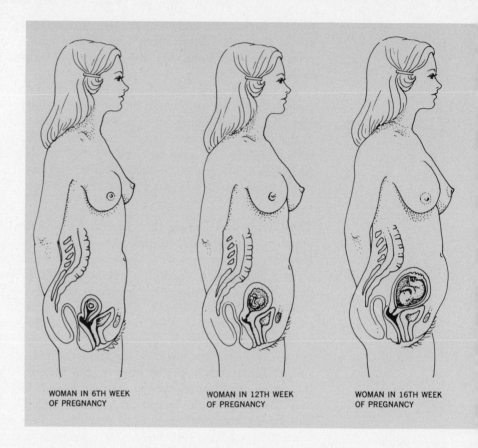

WOMAN IN 6TH WEEK
OF PREGNANCY

WOMAN IN 12TH WEEK
OF PREGNANCY

WOMAN IN 16TH WEEK
OF PREGNANCY

sicians to advise their patients to abstain from sexual intercourse during
the last four to six weeks of pregnancy, sexual relationships need not be
disrupted. "Some couples practice intracrural—between the thighs—intercourse or mutual masturbation during the last month of pregnancy."[30]

The fetus continues to mature and has developed all of the essential
organ systems by the seventh month. By this time the fetus normally
has assumed the head down position, with only about 12 percent remaining upright beyond this point. By full term only about 3 percent
are still in the upright (breech) position.[31] At birth the average infant
weighs 7.5 pounds and is 20 inches long. "Ninety-nine percent of full
term babies born alive in the United States survive, a figure that could
be improved even further if all expectant mothers and newborn babies
received proper medical care."[32] In our inner cities, where medical care

[30]*Fundamentals of Human Sexuality*, p. 120.
[31]*Fundamentals of Human Sexuality*, p. 121.
[32]*Fundamentals of Human Sexuality*, p. 121.

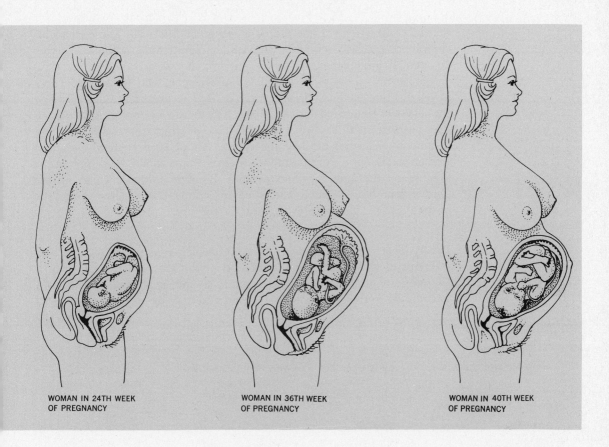

WOMAN IN 24TH WEEK OF PREGNANCY

WOMAN IN 36TH WEEK OF PREGNANCY

WOMAN IN 40TH WEEK OF PREGNANCY

is often terribly inadequate, the infant mortality rate is high. It is not uncommon for 40 out of every 1,000 live births to die within the first year of their lives.[33]

About 7 percent of the live births in the United States are premature.[34] Mothers who have high blood pressure, heart disease, syphilis, or are experiencing multiple pregnancy are especially prone to giving birth prematurely. In about 50 percent of the cases, the cause of premature delivery is not clearly known.

Childbirth

As the end of pregnancy approaches, some women, particularly those who have not previously had any children, may experience false labor—

[33]U.S. Bureau of the Census, *Statistical Abstract of the United States*: 1972 (Washington, D.C.: U.S. Government Printing Office, 1973), p. 59.
[34]*Fundamentals of Human Sexuality*, p. 120.

that is, contractions of the uterus at irregular intervals. These irregular contractions, which resemble the regular contractions of labor, in fact do not signal impending delivery.

We do not know what finally initiates labor. The fetus drops to a lower position in the abdomen three or four weeks before delivery and the cervix begins to soften and dilate. Just before labor begins, a woman may notice a small slightly bloody discharge which represents the plug of mucus which has blocked the cervix. About 10 percent of pregnant women experience a dramatic bursting of water as the fetal membrane breaks and the amniotic fluid escapes. If labor does not ensue within twenty-four hours, there is risk of infection. The mother should be hospitalized for observation after such a rupture.

Labor. There are three stages to *labor*, which consists of regular contractions of the uterus and the dilation of the cervix. The first stage is the longest, and during it the woman, if she is hospitalized, usually is confined to the labor room. Her husband may or may not be present,

FIGURE 6-8 Stages of childbirth.

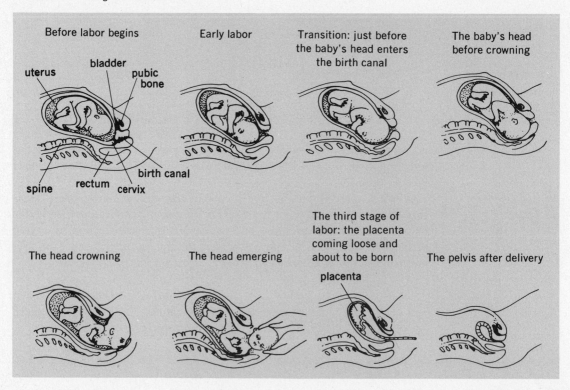

depending on hospital rules. (If a couple is interested in having the husband present during labor, they should check out hospital policy beforehand so that they can plan to have the baby delivered in a hospital where the husband's presence in the labor room is permitted.) The contractions during this period of labor can start at fifteen-minute intervals and increase to four- or five-minute intervals. This stage can last from eight to fifteen hours. The stage is marked by the beginning of these contractions and ends with the complete dilation of the cervix to about 10 centimeters in diameter.

The second stage may last from a few minutes to a few hours. This stage is marked at the beginning by the complete dilation of the cervix and ends when the baby is delivered. At most hospitals it takes place in the delivery room, which is similar to a surgical operating room. The husband may or may not witness delivery, depending upon local laws, hospital regulations, the discretion of the physician, and the wishes of the couple. (Again, this is an area the couple would do well to investigate beforehand if they are interested in having him present at delivery.)

In the third stage, the placenta and the fetal membranes separate from the uterine wall and are discharged as the *afterbirth*. The uterus contracts to a significantly smaller size during this stage, which lasts about an hour. During this time the physician examines the baby and mother carefully and, if there have been any tears in the perineum, may repair them at this time.

If the baby is too large to be delivered through the mother's pelvis, it is delivered by means of a *Caesarean section*—an operation in which the infant is surgically removed through the abdominal wall.

Natural childbirth is a label given to several techniques aimed at conditioning the mother to disassociate pain, fear, and tension from the experience of childbirth. The two major techniques are the Lamaze Method and the Dick-Read Method.[35] The Lamaze Method originated in Russia and was popularized by a French physician, Bernard Lamaze. This method is based on Pavlov's conditioned reflex responses. The Dick-Read Method, introduced by the English physician Grantley Dick-Read in the early 1930s, involves eliminating fear through education about the birth process before delivery.

Post Partum. Today it is common practice for women to return home three to four days after a normal delivery. Bringing a child home can often be a chaotic experience as the couple must learn the techniques of

[35]L. Chertok, "Psychosomatic Methods for Preparation for Child Birth," *American Journal of Obstetrics and Gynecology*; also, refer to *Fundamentals of Human Sexuality*, p. 123.

feeding the child (sometimes at all hours of the day and night), bathing him or her, changing diapers, and countless other details of infant care. What is more, the process can be complicated by anxious fathers and a host of curious, intrusive, but well-meaning friends. A new mother experiencing these new pressures may well be fatigued and perhaps will feel "let down." Many women go through a period of depression at this time, experiencing moments of sadness and fits of crying during the first ten days after delivery. This phenomenon is called "post partum blues." As Herant Katchadourian observes, "Doubts about their competence as mothers, fatigue, feelings of rejection or neglect by their husbands and the drastic hormonal changes that occur at this time are some factors involved."[36] Husbands are well advised to be prepared for manifestations of these feelings, which they should recognize as a normal and usually transitory phase through which new mothers often pass.

Sexual Activity. There is great variation in the period of time that elapses before the first menstrual period after childbirth. Mothers who are nursing may go as long as eighteen months before having a period. However, because ovulation can occur while a mother is nursing and because, in any event, ovulation occurs before the first period, it is possible for a woman to become pregnant without having experienced her first period after childbirth.

For the most part, physicians advise women to refrain from intercourse during the first six weeks after delivery, although the only medical reason for this advice is the fear of possible infection. Of course the recommended period of abstinence from vaginal intercourse need not be a period of abstinence from sexual activity. Manual stimulation of the genitalia, crural intercourse, and other forms of nonvaginal intercourse can safely provide sexual enjoyment for both partners if they so desire. In many cases, however, factors such as fatigue and physical discomfort may decrease the desire for sexual activity.

Sex and Conception in the Year 2100

The impact of our scientific understanding of the process of human conception has not only made it safer for women to give birth to healthy babies in our day than was formerly the case, but has also given us insights and instruments that make it possible to alter the entire process of procreation. Among the many possible alternatives that are now at the threshold of discovery for human procreation, none is more widely

---

[36] *Fundamentals of Human Sexuality*, p. 124.

anticipated—albeit with greatly mixed emotions—than the "test tube baby." As early as 1959, an Italian researcher named Daniel Petrucci claimed to have grown a human embryo in a container filled with amniotic fluid. He terminated this first experiment after twenty-nine days but reports that one of his embryos survived for fifty-nine days.[37] A few years ago it would have been thought impossible to get even this far in the artificial development of a human embryo outside the womb. Now the possibility of full term development of such embryos is considered quite likely.

Whether it will be considered desirable is another matter. There seem to be costs as well as benefits to raising children *in vitro*—that is, in an artificial environment. Among the benefits would probably be the fact that many women would be freed from the burden of pregnancy—to the extent that they found pregnancy to be a burden. What is more, the embryo would be available for constant surveillance and corrective microsurgery should that be necessary. This might eliminate many birth defects, but it might also create others.

On the other hand, it is obvious that changes of so fundamental a nature in so fundamental an area of human life raise profound ethical questions. For example, what about the problem of terminating such an experiment? Would we tend to define the fetus as a human being from the moment of fertilization because we could now observe the entire course of its development? Would termination therefore constitute murder? Or would the detachment of the fetus from the mother also detach the parent or designated "overseer," so that the decision to abort could be made on more "objective" grounds? The impact of test tube babies upon family life is difficult to forecast. Clearly, women would be freer to pursue their careers if they were not required to carry their children, but couldn't this objective be achieved more easily by enforcing more enlightened policies about maternity leaves for working women? And what about the problem of preparing the family for the coming event? Even adoptive parents must go through a prolonged period of waiting, involving much effort and preparation on their part before the adopted child arrives. Mightn't the test tube baby arrive too easily, entering a family that is psychologically unprepared to welcome a new member?

Another significant step in controlling the process of procreation is much closer to realization. Dr. Paul Erhlich estimates that within twenty years it will be possible to predetermine definitely the sex of a baby.[38] Various techniques already make it possible to partially separate sperms

[37]Albert Rosenfeld, *The Second Genesis: The Coming Control of Life* (Englewood Cliffs, N.J.: Prentice-Hall, Inc., 1969), p. 103.
[38]*The Second Genesis*, p. 115.

carrying the X chromosome from the lighter, speedier sperm carrying the Y (male) chromosome. In studies involving animals, the partially segregated semen significantly increases the occurrence of the desired sex in the offspring. It is not yet possible to segregate the sperm perfectly, but this seems to be but a small obstacle that should soon be resolved. One benefit that could derive from such a capability would be the elimination of many sex-linked defects such as hemophilia. For example, if all hemophiliacs (males) and hemophilia carriers (females) refrained from having female children for one generation the disease would disappear. In this regard, the social engineering aspect of the task is probably much further beyond our present capability than is the ability to predetermine the sex of the child.

The discovery of the genetic proteins DNA and RNA and the possibility of their synthesis increases the likelihood that we can alter the characteristics of the human species through genetic surgery. For example, the size of the human brain could be doubled if, in the process of development, the 9 billion cells of the brain could be induced to divide for a thirty-fourth time.[39] The control of such cell division lies within the chromosomal heritage of each individual and, as our knowledge of these basic molecules increases, our capacity to change them to suit our tastes increases as well. Presumably, an individual with a brain twice normal size would have increased intelligence and ability to act. Such a baby could not be delivered by normal methods, but the size of the brain would make little difference in a test tube baby. It need not follow, however, that larger brains would make a better world. They would merely provide equipment with which to work toward whatever goal they deemed desirable.

Infertility

About 10 to 15 percent of all couples in the United States are involuntarily childless. Sometimes their childlessness can be overcome by minor adjustments in their lovemaking techniques or by hormonal treatment. For others the "cure" may involve surgery or extended treatment. For some it is a permanent condition called "sterility." About 40 percent of infertile marriages are a result of a sterile male partner.[40] When a couple wishes to have a child, a year of unsuccessful results should alert them to the need of seeing a physician.

The physician normally will take complete medical histories. Each partner will have a complete physical examination with particular attention given to the reproductive organs. A series of laboratory tests will

[39] *The Second Genesis*, pp. 119–20.
[40] Masters and Johnson, *Fundamentals of Human Sexuality*, p. 107.

be made to rule out infections, anemia, and hormonal deficiencies. The husband will be tested more thoroughly in the early stages because his infertility is more easily determined. He will be instructed to bring a complete ejaculation for a sperm count. Such a count should contain between 60 million and 100 million sperms per cubic centimeter, 60 percent of which should be active.[41] In this connection, it is important for us to be clear about the distinction between infertility (or sterility) and low fertility. As the figures just cited indicate, a normal ejaculate contains an immense number of sperm, but only one sperm is needed to fertilize an egg. If a man's ejaculate contains a significantly smaller number of sperm, or if the sperm are significantly less active than normal, the chances of his impregnating a woman are reduced. But fertilization is, of course, possible. Such a man is not sterile, but unless steps are taken to increase the odds in his favor, he may not succeed in impregnating his mate. Various techniques are available for enriching the sperm—i.e., increasing the sperm count. Artificial insemination with the husband's sperm is also a possibility when the problem is one of low mobility of the sperm.

If tests of the husband indicate that the failure to conceive cannot be traced to a low sperm count or low sperm activity, the wife will be instructed to keep a temperature chart during her menstrual cycles in order to help determine when and if she ovulates. If it is determined that the female is ovulating and that the male is producing adequate sperm, further tests will be necessary. These tests will focus on the female.

"Rubin's Test" will be performed to see if the Fallopian tubes are obstructed. This test consists in forcing carbon dioxide into the uterus. If the pressure diminishes, the tubes are clear. If the tubes prove to be open, the cervix is examined. Normally, the mucus of the cervix impedes the progress of the sperm to a considerable degree, except during ovulation when it becomes thinner and more penetrable. Thus abnormality in the composition and visosity of this mucus is a possible cause of infertility.[42]

There are many more tests that can be performed to help diagnose the causes of infertility. Considerable assistance can be provided to most couples who seek help in having children. Many can be helped to conceive with a minimum of tests. In a few cases a woman has conceived after she and her husband sought help from a clinic but before anything had been done for them—an indication that the couple's infertility

[41]Lawrence Crawley, James L. Malfetti, Ernest I. Stewart, Jr., Nini Vas Deas, *Reproduction, Sex, and Preparation for Marriage*, 2nd ed. (Englewood Cliffs, N.J.: Prentice-Hall, Inc., 1973), p. 218.
[42]*Reproduction, Sex, and Preparation for Marriage*, p. 219.

may well have had a psychological cause. About half of the infertile couples who come to clinics can be helped to have children.

Artificial Insemination

In those instances in which the wife has been shown to be fertile while her husband has been diagnosed sterile, the couple may wish to conceive through artificial insemination. This is not a totally successful procedure, but many women have become pregnant by this means and it is now widely available. In artifiical insemination, the sperm from a fertile male is mechanically inserted into the vagina by a physician at a time when the woman is ovulating. Impregnation takes place in the normal way. Because so many considerations impinge on a decision to use artificial insemination—including religious, legal, moral, psychological, and physiological questions—it is important that any couple considering this approach learn all the dimensions to the problem before reaching a decision.

Many people, especially men, react to the idea of artificial insemination with a spontaneous feeling of aversion. The initial reaction of many husbands is one of repugnance, and they often express the feeling that a child produced by the sperm of an anonymous donor would not really be "their" child. In a sense, of course, this is true, but often husbands who feel this way are quite willing to adopt a child once they are convinced they are sterile—a clear indication that such husbands are not in fact unwilling to accept responsibility for the rearing of children who are not their biological offspring. Perhaps one way to look at artificial insemination is as a sort of semi-adoption in which the husband agrees to raise what is in effect for him an adopted child while the wife, who is capable of conception, can enjoy the personal satisfactions that come from carrying and giving birth to a baby.

In many cases artificial insemination is conducted using the sperm of the husband. As mentioned previously, this procedure is recommended when either a low sperm count or low sperm mobility makes it extremely unlikely that the woman will conceive by her husband's sperm unless it is "enriched"—that is, concentrated—artificially and delivered directly to the egg it is to fertilize.

SUMMARY

Understanding something of the biology of human sexuality can help us feel more at ease with ourselves. This is an important part of developing intimate partnerships such as marriage. This chapter has presented the fundamentals of the biology of sex and reproduction, including a brief description of the external genitalia, a discussion of human sexual response, and a short account of conception and pregnancy from the point of view of the pregnant woman. Some of the technically possible contributions to these processes were listed in a speculation on what sex and reproduction might be like in the arbitrarily selected year 2100. We stand at the threshold of a biological revolution in the extent to which we will be able to control these processes. This revolution should have an enormous impact upon the future of intimate partnerships.

Whatever the extent to which our sexual behavior is determined by our biology, as we come to understand our biology more and more we find it increasingly possible to shape that biology after our own desires. What is more, an understanding of the biology of human sexuality can help dispel the numerous folk myths which have clouded our self-awareness and can free us to be more fully open to others.

7

ON BIRTH CONTROL

Underdeveloped societies . . . practice little contraception and virtually no sterilization. Consequently, the tendency is to *postpone* the issue of controlling pregnancy until a later point in the reproductive process, which means that when a couple wishes to avoid children, those methods nearest the point of parturition—abortion and infanticide—are employed.

Industrial societies, on the other hand . . . [use] readily available institutional mechanisms with respect to marriage and [employ] the possibilities of their advanced technology for conception control. Gradually, in the late stages of industrial development, contraception has gained such predominance that it has made [other approaches] unnecessary.

Kingsley Davis and Judith Blake

INTRODUCTION

Many societies of the world prescribe or permit sexual intercourse outside of marriage, but none prescribes conception outside of marriage. Although it is true that placing and caring for an "outside" child constitute more of a problem in primitive societies than they do in advanced societies such as contemporary America, the fact remains that most unmarried couples who engage in sexual intercourse do not wish to conceive a child. Further, many married couples also wish to retain control over the size of their families. The day is long past when pregnancy could be regarded as a natural accident, and all over the world increasing numbers are turning to contraception in order to make the birth of a baby the result of conscious decision. It has been estimated that if a couple continues intercourse for at least a year without the use of a contraceptive, the normally fecund female has a 90 percent chance of becoming pregnant. This is the factual base from which any discussion of birth control must begin.

Birth control is not limited to contraception, although it is frequently assumed that the two terms are synonymous. This chapter discusses four techniques of birth control: contraception, sterilization, abstinence, and abortion. Each technique has its own costs as well as benefits and the decision to control conception by means of a particular technique must take these factors into consideration. A final section raises the issue of venereal disease, which has reached pandemic proportions in the United States.

The reality of venereal disease should affect the choice of contraceptive method as well as the style of sexual behavior.

We are well aware that controlling conception by "artificial" means is at odds with the official position of the Roman Catholic Church and counter to the inclinations of some individuals. Thus, when we describe the pros and cons of any particular technique, we assume that it goes without saying that for some people a religious prohibition far outweighs any of the "pros" we list. It is not part of our intention to quarrel with the religious or ethical convictions of any individual; rather, we want simply to present a factual account of a subject that is of considerable interest to large numbers of people who are presently involved in heterosexual partnerships or who intend to become involved in them.

CONTRACEPTION

Techniques to prevent conception are part of the folk wisdom of most peoples. The practice of *coitus interruptus* (withdrawal of the male before orgasm) is thought to be forbidden in the Bible.[1] The oldest records on the subject come from Egypt and date from between 1900 and 1100 B.C. Man's early attempts to control fertility frequently involved magic, superstition, and religious beliefs. The methods employed were related to the understanding of the reproductive process and the traditional beliefs of the culture in question. The ancient Chinese, for example, believed that a woman would not become pregnant if she remained completely passive during intercourse.;[2] the Egyptians are responsible for the oldest known medical prescription for a contraceptive—a vaginal suppository concocted of crocodile dung and honey.[3] Various other unbelievable birth preventive substances have been advised, including mouse dung, amulets, and induced sneezing. The Greeks believed that oil impeded the movement of the sperm and advised inserting oil-permeated material such as paper into the vagina to cover the cervix. James McCary gives the following account of a primitive contraceptive technique:

Casanova, the eighteenth century Italian adventurer, is alleged to have used a gold ball as a contraceptive by placing it in the woman's vagina to block the pas-

[1] Paul Blanchard, "Christianity and Sex," *The Humanist* (March–April 1974), pp. 27–32.
[2] James Leslie McCary, *Human Sexuality: A Brief Edition* (New York: D. Van Nostrand Company, 1973), p. 87.
[3] *Human Sexuality*, p. 87.

sage of his sperm. He is also credited with using a hollowed-out lemon as a diaphragm to cover the woman's cervix. Perhaps the lemon shell did serve as an effective contraceptive, for citric acid can immobilize sperm. However, if Casanova deserved his reputation for prodigious sexual activity, and if his claims of never impregnating any of his lovers were true, the logical explanation is that frequent ejaculations kept his sperm count so low that he was sterile in effect if not in actuality.[4]

Ancient peoples are not alone in having folk methods for handling the task of preventing conception. Even today, various folk ideas persist, many of which are unsupported by evidence of their effectiveness. For example, some people believe that having intercourse while standing will prevent pregnancy, or that if the woman urinates immediately after intercourse she will avoid becoming pregnant. We also tend to cloud the issue when we assert that certain periods of the month are "safe" periods; Masters and Johnson have shown this to be largely wishful thinking.

Arguments For and Against Birth Control

The major argument against the use of artificial methods of birth control is made by the Roman Catholic papacy in the Encyclical *Humanae Vitae*. The Roman Catholic Church is still struggling with the idea of contraception. It holds that the so-called "rhythm method" is the only acceptable form of contraception because it does not interfere with "natural" processes. The rhythm method, of course, is designed to frustrate these natural processes, but it does so without any artificial interference—by confining sexual intercourse to those times within the woman's monthly cycle when it is believed that conception will not occur. The Roman Catholic Church also insists that sterilization in any form, whether by chemical, surgical, or other means, is immoral.[5]

In a sense, there is not much we can say here about the arguments against birth control—insofar as these arguments are based upon religious prescriptions, as for the most part they are. In the final analysis, such arguments boil down to a belief that birth control simply is morally wrong. Whether or not one accepts such arguments is largely a matter of faith; they are convincing to those who accept them and unconvincing to those who do not. We do not mean to disparage such beliefs by giving them such scant attention here; on the contrary, we are well aware of what an important role they play in the lives of those who hold them. Indeed, when all is said and done, it appears clear that all

[4]From *Human Sexuality: A Brief Edition*, p. 88, by James McCary © 1973. Reprinted by permission of D. Van Nostrand Company.
[5]Herant A. Katchadourian, *Fundamentals of Human Sexuality* (New York: Holt, Rinehart & Winston, Inc., 1972), p. 472.

the arguments in favor of birth control—to which we shall now turn—pale into insignificance for many religious people when they are set against the overriding injunction against birth control which is an important tenet of their faith.

Turning to the arguments in favor of birth control, there are many reasons why we may wish to control the reproductive process. We may wish to postpone children until we can afford to care for them; we may want to space them so that they can receive more parental attention when they are very young; or we may want to maintain a family size that we can afford or that we feel is appropriate in light of the world-wide population "explosion." Some couples may not wish to have children because they have reason to believe either that the mother may suffer illness as a result of pregnancy or that the child is quite likely to be handicapped or diseased in some way. A woman cannot reasonably be expected to want to give birth to a child if she must risk her life or her health in the process. Still other couples simply may prefer to have no children at all.[6] These motivations and others are involved in the decision to use contraceptives and should affect the choice of the appropriate method.

The argument for birth control in terms of the world population problem has been the subject of considerable discussion in recent years. Indeed, it seems that this argument has had a considerable effect on women in this country under thirty-five years of age, for we are already approaching zero population growth. Because our population does seem to be coming under control, many people have begun to wonder if it is still necessary to be concerned about population problems. A few points must be made in this connection.

1. In order to achieve zero population growth it is not necessary that couples cease to have children; it is only necessary that most couples have only two children while a few have three. That is to say, the plea for zero population growth is a plea for limiting the size of the average family, not for eliminating parenthood.

2. Population is related directly to a host of other critical problems. Although these problems will not necessarily be solved if population is controlled, they will be easier to solve with lower population figures.

---

[6]Joseph Fletcher sums up the situational ethics approach to this matter when he writes: "(1) Making babies is a good thing, but making love is, too, and we can and should make love even if no baby is intended. There ought to be no unintended or unwanted babies. (2) The best way to make love without making babies is to prevent their conception; the next best way is to prevent fertility itself; and the least desirable way is to end a pregnancy already begun. But any of these methods is good if the good to be gained is great enough to justify the means." Joseph Fletcher, *Moral Responsibility: Situation Ethics at Work* (Philadelphia: Westminister Press, 1967), p. 123.

Among these problems are pollution, energy conservation, and food production.

3. Our population problem is perhaps best described as a problem of distribution of population (overconcentration in the major metropolitan areas) rather than simply a problem of too many people. At first glance it may seem that excess population is a problem only in the underdeveloped parts of the world, for surely America, with all its affluence, is able to provide for its population—or at least more nearly able to do so than are the poorer nations of the world. In a sense, however, precisely the opposite is true. Because the average American consumes so much more of the world's resources and contributes so much more heavily to its pollution than does the average citizen of an underdeveloped country, the control of our population is more critical from a worldwide perspective than is the control of the population of many other countries.

4. Although the family planning approach is popular in our society as a valuable means of birth control, it is not an effective population control measure because the average American woman still wants more children (three to four) than are necessary to achieve zero population growth.[7] Achieving zero population growth is not simply a matter of reducing the number of unwanted children who are born; it is also a matter of reducing the number of children who are wanted.

Even after a decision to use some method of birth control has been made, there may be many reasons why a particular person should not use a particular method. It might cause undesirable side effects, it might be too expensive or too troublesome, or it might offend the user's sense of propriety. But these are, in the last analysis, simply arguments against a particular form of contraception. They are not arguments against birth control itself. There are at least eight effective contraceptive methods available today, and the choice of the best one for a particular person can best be made in consultation with a physician or planned parenthood counselor.

Contraceptive Techniques

Modern interest in contraceptive technology has produced a host of contraceptives which vary greatly in terms of effectiveness, cost, and convenience. Some have no side effects, some have considerable side effects. The choice of which contraceptive to use depends upon many factors in a person's life, not the least of which is his or her motivation for using contraceptives. If a couple already has the number of children

---

[7]Judith Blake, "Population Policy for Americans: Is the Government Being Misled?" *Science*, 164 (May 2, 1968), 524.

they desire, sterilization might be the best option for them. The following is a survey of contraceptive alternatives.

Contraceptives Available Only with a Doctor's Prescription. Prior to the introduction of the birth control pill and the intrauterine device (IUD), the diaphragm and other mechanical devices were the most commonly used contraceptives. These mechanical devices designed for use by the woman operate by covering the cervix, thus preventing entry of the sperm into the uterus.

The Diaphragm. The diaphragm is a thin rubber dome-shaped cup attached to a flexible rubber-covered metal ring about three inches in diameter. The diaphragm must be fitted by a physician; if it is not the correct size and shape for a particular woman, it will be highly ineffective. Before a woman can be fitted for a diaphragm, the hymen must be broken. After childbirth a woman should not resume use of the diaphragm she was using before she decided to become pregnant; changes in the size or shape of her cervix may well cause it to be ineffective, so she should be fitted with a new one. If properly inserted, the diaphragm should not interfere with the conduct or pleasure of sexual intercourse.

The diaphragm must be used with contraceptive cream or jelly which is designed to kill sperm. A common error is the mistaken assumption that a diaphragm itself is an adequate means of contraception. The spermicidal cream or jelly, by the way, has the added benefit of providing lubrication. In order to insure the effectiveness of the jelly, the diaphragm should be inserted no more than four to six hours before intercourse. If a woman does not know in advance that she is going to have intercourse, she will have to stop during lovemaking to insert the diaphragm. (An unwillingness to interrupt sex play in order to insert a diaphragm is one common reason for the failure of the diaphragm method.) After intercourse, the diaphragm should remain in place for at least six hours, although it may be left in for as long as twenty-four hours.[8] The diaphragm should be removed and washed, and additional jelly should be applied, before reinsertion.

The diaphragm-plus-spermicide method fails for any one of a number of reasons between 4 and 10 percent of the time; the failure rate of diaphragms used without spermicidal substances jumps to 5 to 20 percent.[9] The diaphragm fails because it is not used when it should be, because it is incorrectly inserted, because it cannot be absolutely per-

---

[8]*Human Sexuality*, p. 89.
[9]*Human Sexuality*, p. 90, and Garret Hardin, *Birth Control* (New York: Pegasus, 1970), p. 129.

fectly fitted to all changes that occur in the vagina during lovemaking, and because vigorous lovemaking involving multiple insertions of the penis sometimes dislodges it.[10] It is more likely to fail when the woman is on top of the man than when the man is on top of the woman.[11]

The Cervical Cap. Another mechanical device similar to the diaphragm is the cervical cap. It is smaller than the diaphragm, shaped like a large thimble, and is made of rubber, plastic, or metal. It is also known as a pessary cap (as is the diaphragm). This device is much more popular in Europe than in America. In contrast to the diaphragm, which covers the cervix and a portion of the end of the vagina, the cervical cap fits only over the end of the uterus, or cervix. Because of the differing sizes and shapes of cervixes, not all women can use these caps. It takes more skill to insert a cervical cap properly than to insert a diaphragm, but once inserted it can be left in place for days or weeks. As with the diaphragm, it may become dislodged during intercourse, but this is less common. The failure rate for cervical caps is about 8 percent.[12]

The IUD. There are a large number of intrauterine devices (IUDs) on the market and a wide variation in size, shape, effectiveness, and side effects. The use of intrauterine devices goes back to the time of Hippocrates, and a version of the device still used on animals in the Sudan and Tunisia goes back for centuries. Arab camel drivers insert a round stone in the uterus of the female camel before a long journey across the desert. During the nineteenth century a variety of intrauterine devices were used for gynecological disorders and for contraception, but in the early twentieth century these devices fell into disrepute. Many early models suffered from high rates of expulsion and often required surgical removal because they damaged the uterine wall, often causing hemorrhaging.

In the 1930s a German physician, E. Geafenberg, developed a coiled silver ring that in his studies produced a failure rate of 1.6 pregnancies per hundred women. Nevertheless, there was strong opposition to his device and IUDs remained unpopular until 1959. In that year two reports, one by an Israeli who had worked with Geafenberg and one by a Japanese physician, triggered new enthusiasm for the IUD. Failure rates were 2.4 and 2.3 per hundred and no serious complications were reported. These studies involved a total of 21,500 women. In spite of

[10]Ruth and Edward Brecher, eds., *An Analysis of Human Sexual Response* (New York: Signet Books, 1966), p. 102.
[11]Mary S. Calderone, ed., *Manual of Family Planning and Contraceptive Practice*, 2nd ed. (Baltimore: The William and Wilkin Company, 1970), p. 234.
[12]*Fundamentals of Human Sexuality*, p. 141.

TABLE 7-1   COMPARISON OF VARIOUS METHODS OF BIRTH CONTROL

	Sterilization	The Pill	Intrauterine Device (IUD)	Diaphragm with Chemical
How it works	Permanently blocks egg or sperm passages	Prevents ovulation	Uncertain; may stop implantation of egg	Barrier to sperm
Possible side effects	Psychological only	Initial weight gain and nausea; long-term effects not known	Initial discomfort and irregular bleeding; long-term effects not known	Chemical may cause irritation
Physician's assistance required	Operation performed by physician	Must be prescribed by doctor; periodic checkups required	Must be inserted by doctor; periodic checkups required	Must be fitted by physician
Cost	Vasectomy: $100 to $250; salpingectomy: $200 to $300	Approximately $2.50 per month	From $15 to $75	From $15 to $25
Average pregnancy rate per 100 women per year	0.003	2–5 (minidose) 0.5 (sequential) 0.1 (combination)	2–3	4–10

Source: Data from *Life and Health* (Del Mar, Calif: CRM Books, 1972) pages 256–57, by permission. © 1972 by Ziff-Davis Publishing Co.

Rhythm	Condom	Withdrawal	Foams and Jellies	Douche
Abstinence during fertile period	Prevents sperm from entering vagina	Ejaculation occurs outside the vagina	Barrier to sperm; spermicidal	Rinses sperm from vagina
Psychological only	Loss of sensation	Psychological only	May cause irritation	None
Possibly for consultation	None	None	None	None
Approximately $10 for calculator and $4.50 for basal thermometer	Approximately 3 for $.75	None	$1 to $3 per month	Approximately $2.50
14–35	10–11	8–40	20–22	30–36

153

the fact that physicians still do not know why the IUD works, its demonstrated effectiveness and ease of use has made it popular in the United States since 1959. The total number of IUD users is unknown, but informed estimates suggest that about 5 million women in the world were using the IUD in 1968—about 1 to 2 million of them in the United States.[13]

IUDs are made of various materials and come in many sizes and shapes. The Lippes Loop (see Table 7–1) is made of plastic. Its size ranges from 22.5 to 30 millimeters in diameter. A physician inserts this device by stretching the loop into a linear form and pushing it through a plastic tube into the uterus. This procedure is performed through the cervical opening. All IUDs have tiny nylon threads attached to them which hang down through the cervical opening into the vagina. The wearer or a clinician is thus able to determine if they are properly in place by checking for the presence of these threads. Some of the new models are treated with barium so that they will be readily visible on x-rays. The IUD in no way affects the fertility of the woman or the health of the children she might bear when it is removed. If a woman wishes to become pregnant, the IUD must be removed by a physician. After birth it may be repositioned in the uterus until another pregnancy is desired.

The current failure rate for the most popular IUD is on the order of 2 to 3 pregnancies per 100 women during the first year of use, with slightly lower rates thereafter. About 10 percent of the women using IUDs expel them during the first year of use, usually during the early months of use and frequently during menstruation. Because the IUD can be expelled without the user's notice, frequent checks to make sure it is in position are important.

A small percentage of women (0.4 percent in one study) experience side effects from the use of the IUD. The most common of these effects are bleeding, cervical pain, and uterine cramps. In the same survey 0.1 percent of the women showed infection of the pelvic organs (uterus and tubes); on the other hand, half of these women had had previous histories of such infections. Another possible danger of IUDs which should be taken into account is perforation of the uterus. Perforation occurs in only about one case in 10,000, but it can be fatal.

The Pill. The most common types of oral contraceptives are various combinations of synthetic progesterone-estrogen. The pill prevents ovulation by creating the hormonal balance found in pregnancy. In 1934 progesterone was isolated and purified in the laboratory. At the same

[13]C. Tietze, "Oral and Intrauterine Contraception: Effectiveness and Safety," *International Journal of Fertility*, 13 (October-December 1968), 377–84.

time estrogen was isolated chemically. By 1940, estrogen was being used clinically in the treatment of menstrual disorders. In 1954 Carl Djerassi synthesized in the laboratory a group of steroid chemicals called progestagens. These compounds induced pseudopregnancy in females.

The first large-scale testing of the pill was done in 1956 in Puerto Rico. On the basis of the success of these trials Enovid, the first pill for public consumption, appeared on the market in the United States in 1960. By 1970, an estimated 9 million women had used the pill in one of its forms.[14] In the last fifteen years about twenty different types of pills have been produced by five or six pharmaceutical companies. Each has its own effectiveness and side effects. The proper matching of a particular pill to a particular female requires a physician and continuing evaluation. Most commonly, women are advised to change prescription from time to time in order to reduce the adverse side effects.

The pill in whatever form is a powerful agent in the human body. It can have both physiological and psychological effects. Therefore, to give clear indicators of who should not use the pill is a very difficult task. Apparently women who have very irregular menstrual cycles are likely to experience more complications—particularly in regard to having more children after they have stopped taking the pill—than those with more regular cycles.[15] Also, women who have histories of cardiovascular troubles may experience complications from the use of the pill.[16] The adverse psychological effects of the pill are more difficult to detect. An excellent discussion of the clinical aspects of oral contraceptives can be found in L. P. D. Tunnadine, *Contraception and Sexual Life.*[17]

Most oral contraceptives are taken over a twenty-one day cycle, beginning on the fifth day after the start of the woman's period. Menstruation usually begins three to four days after the pills have been stopped. The first day of this menstruation is considered the first day of the next cycle and pills are resumed five days afterward. Enovid, Ortho-Novum, Ovulen, Provest, and Norinyl are examples of the progesterone-estrogen "combination" type pill. C-quens, Oracon, and Norquen are examples of a second major type of oral contraceptive called the "sequential type." These differ from the combination type in that the first fifteen pills in a fixed-sequence dispenser contain only estrogen while the last five contain a combination of estrogen and progesterone. This sequence follows more closely the natural sequence of hormonal events during a normal cycle. Two additional variations have been introduced, primarily in

[14]*Manual of Family Planning*, p. 288.
[15]Celso-Ramon Garcia, "Clinical Aspects of Oral Hormonal Contraception," in *Manual of Family Planning*, pp. 302 and 318.
[16]*Manual of Family Planning*, p. 318.
[17]L. P. D. Tunnadine, *Contraception and Sexual Life: A Therapeutic Approach* (Philadelphia: J. B. Lippincott Company, 1970).

order to help the woman remember when she is to take her pill. Both techniques are based on a 21:7 sequence. In the first instance, the woman takes twenty-ones pills, stops for seven days, and then resumes her pills regardless of when her period began. In the second instance, she takes one pill every day but seven out of every twenty-eight in the sequence are placebos.

The advantages of the pill are obvious. It does not interfere with sexual intercourse, does not depend upon foreknowledge of when one is going to have intercourse, and, when taken properly, has the highest rate of effectiveness of any of the contraceptives yet made available. In principle, the effectiveness of the pill is 100 percent by the second month of usage. However, failure to take a pill reduces effectiveness. Missing one pill normally will not have serious consequences if two are taken the next day, but missing two or more days invites a fair risk of failure. The sequential pills are less effective than the combination pills: it is estimated that ovulation occurs in 2 to 8 percent of the cycles of sequential users. Whereas about 0.1 pregnancies per 100 women per year occur when "combination" oral contraceptives are used, this figure jumps to 0.5 pregnancies per 100 women per year with sequential types.[18]

Among the side effects of the pill, the most serious seems to be an increased risk of death from thromboembolic (clotting) disorders. About 3 out of every 100,000 women on the pill can be expected to die as a result of clotting caused by the pill. This is about three times the rate for non-pregnant women. On the other hand, women using other means of birth control have about 3.5 times greater likelihood than pill users of dying from complications caused by pregnancy, childbirth, and post partum problems, and women who use no contraceptive at all are 7.5 times more likely to die as a result of complications in maternity than pill users.

Many of the discomforts associated with use of the pill, such as dizziness, headaches, bleeding, weight gain, and the like, have not yet been reliably researched, largely because these symptoms also occur frequently in women not taking the pill. It is difficult to determine what percentages of instances are caused by the pill. Most of the symptoms pill users experience tend to diminish or disappear after a few months, but many women have become discouraged because of such discomforts.

Contraceptives Available without Prescription. *The Condom.* Perhaps the most widely used contraceptive in the United States is the condom. It is the only mechanical device used by males. It is cheap, easy to use, easy to obtain, easy to dispose of, and effective. The first condoms were made in England in the early eighteenth century from the intestines of

[18]Tietze, "Oral and Intrauterine Contraception," p. 378.

sheep. The Philadelphia World Fair of 1876 introduced the first vulcanized rubber condom.

The condom is a thin flexible sheath which fits over the erect penis. It measures about seven and a half inches in length. In common language condoms are known as "rubbers," "prophylactics," "french letters," and "skins." The rubber type is the most widely used; an estimated 750 million are sold annually in the United States. They come packaged, rolled and ready for use, sometimes with a small amount of lubricant. There are two major types of condom in use today—plain and reservoir tip. Choice between them is wholly a matter of personal preference as both are equally effective.

Unless a condom breaks during intercourse or slips off after ejaculation it offers almost 100 percent effectiveness. (Blowing into a condom or filling it with water before usage are effective means of assuring that there is no breakage.) What is more, the use of condoms in combination with spermicidal foam or cream increases their effectiveness. Even when used alone, however, the condom produces an effectiveness rate of 10 to 11 pregnancies per 100 women per year. The condom is also the best contraceptive method presently available for reducing the incidence of venereal disease.

Spermicidal Substances. Readily available in drugstores with a prescription, spermicidal substances are easy to use. They consist of various foams, jellies, creams, and suppositories that kill sperm. Plastic applicators enable women to inject the substance into the vagina before intercourse. This must be done at least ten to fifteen minutes before ejaculation and must be reapplied if intercourse is repeated. It has been noted that the foam type of spermicide (actually a cream packaged in an aerosol can) provides the best distribution within the vagina. Foam has a failure rate of about 3 to 10 pregnancies per 100 women per year when properly used—a somewhat better rate than that reported for creams and jellies.

Another chemical contraceptive is the vaginal suppository, a small solid cone that melts at 95 degrees Fahrenheit. These suppositories must be inserted at least fifteen minutes before ejaculation. Also available are vaginal tablets which are supposed to dissolve in the vagina. These tablets may present problems because they are very unstable in damp climates and may need more moisture than is present in the vagina in order to dissolve. Both tablets and suppositories are less effective than foam. They depend a great deal upon mixing with the natural lubricants and are difficult to disperse properly. The pregnancy rate with the suppositories is 5 to 27 pregnancies per 100 women per year; that of the tablets is 8 to 27.[19] Part of the reason for these high failure rates is

[19]*Human Sexuality*, p. 94; *Fundamentals of Human Sexuality*, p. 141.

the fact that if ejaculation occurs before the suppositories melt sufficiently to lubricate the vagina, mixing and dispersion of these agents does not occur to an adequate extent. Failure rates for foams, creams, and jellies are in the 20 percent range.

Douches. The term *douching* refers to washing out the vagina immediately after intercourse. It is one of the most ineffective methods of contraception in common use. Indeed, many physicians feel that douching is *less* effective than nothing inasmuch as the washing fluid, which is not a spermicide, may serve to increase the distribution of the sperm. About the best thing that can be said of the technique is that it is very simple. It requires only a douche bag and tap water, sometimes with the addition of some substance believed to make the douche more effective. Some of the common products used in this way include vinegar, lemon juice, soap, and salt. In actuality, these additions add little to the spermicidal qualities of tap water and may, in fact, irritate the vaginal tissues. Since it is possible for sperm to make their way into the cervical canal (beyond the reach of the douche) within one or two minutes after ejaculation, douching as a contraceptive method is quite limited. The failure rate is about 30 to 36 pregnancies per 100 women per year.[20]

Withdrawal. Probably the oldest known method of birth control is withdrawal, technically known as *coitus interruptus.*[21] This method, which is still common throughout the world, requires that the male withdraw his penis from the vagina before he ejaculates. Although many people find this practice satisfactory, others find it very frustrating because the man must withdraw at the crucial moment—or sooner—and must wait a considerable time before engaging in intercourse again. What is more, as was noted in Chapter 6, the secretion of the Cowper's gland, which is given off prior to ejaculation, may contain a few sperm which can impregnate the woman. The withdrawal method has a failure rate of from 8 to 40 pregnancies per 100 women per year.[22]

Rhythm. The rhythm method is the only contraceptive technique endorsed by the Roman Catholic Church. It requires that a couple engage in periodic abstinence from sexual intercourse during what is presumed to be the woman's fertile period. This method is unreliable, particularly in women whose menstrual cycles are irregular. Only about 30 percent of all women have sufficiently regular menstrual cycles to enable a rea-

[20]*Human Sexuality*, p. 94; *Fundamentals of Human Sexuality*, p. 142.
[21]Genesis 38:8–9 is thought by some to refer to this practice. See, however, the article by Blanchard cited in note 1.
[22]*Human Sexuality*, p. 95; *Fundamentals of Human Sexuality*, p. 143.

sonable pinpointing of the "safe" period. Add to this the fact that some women ovulate in response to sexual stimulation and the whole procedure becomes even more unreliable.

A more sophisticated variant of the rhythm method is based on the fact that a woman's temperature changes during her menstrual cycle. To use this method the woman must take her temperature every morning immediately before arising; she must do so before eating, drinking, or smoking. One of the major problems with this method is that many women have no marked or consistent temperature changes. What is more, colds or sore throats may throw off the temperature chart. Both rhythm and temperature methods have a medium pregnancy rate of 14 to 35 per 100 women per year.[23] As Herant Katchadourian observes, "The primary reason for using the rhythm method is that it is the only method approved for Roman Catholics."[24]

Choosing the Proper Contraceptive

Although the choice of a particular contraceptive technique should depend upon personal as well as technical considerations, one authority has suggested that if medical safety is the major desideratum, then the proper order of choice should be the diaphragm, the IUD, and then the pill. On the other hand, if clinical efficiency is the major desideratum, the ranking should be the IUD, the pill, and the diaphragm.[25] (Other professionals, it should be noted, rank the pill first for efficiency.) Of course, if prevention of venereal disease is a major factor to be considered, then the condom offers the greatest protection and the lowest risk short of abstention. These rankings admittedly reflect professional preferences as well as an evaluation of the data on the contraceptives themselves. Even the contraceptives that may be obtained without consultation offer considerable protection and certainly should be used rather than nothing at all if for some reason the more highly efficient techniques are unavailable.

Experimental Contraceptives Not Yet on the Market

There are a number of promising contraceptives still in the experimental stage.[26] The continuous progesterone pill (mini pill) may eliminate most

---

[23]*Human Sexuality*, p. 95; *Fundamentals of Human Sexuality*, p. 144.
[24]*Fundamentals of Human Sexuality*, p. 144.
[25]Hugh J. David, *Intrauterine Devices for Contraception: The IUD* (Baltimore: The William and Wilkins Company, 1971), p. 53.
[26]Much of the material used in this section is taken from Lawrence Crawley et al., *Reproduction, Sex and Preparation for Marriage*, 2nd ed. (Englewood Cliffs, N.J.: Prentice-all, Inc., 1973), pp. 209–13.

of the side effects commonly experienced with oral contraceptives, but it must be taken at the same time every day without fail or the woman incurs a risk of pregnancy. The "morning after pill," an oral contraceptive that has been around for twenty years or more, prevents the implantation of the fertilized egg. But the massive dose of estrogen (called Stilbestrol) interferes with the normal endocrine balance, producing endometrial changes which cause staining, bleeding, and disruption of the menstrual cycle. What is more, research findings indicate some dangers associated with it—particularly a higher rate of vaginal cancer in female offspring. In sum, it is erratic and unpredictable and leaves much to be desired at present. Continuous low dose progestin injections promise to be more effective than the mini pill, but at present the side effects seem much too costly. The implantation of a small capsule of progesterone under the skin will have lasting effects for a year, but it has the same costly side effects as the low dose progestin injections.

The vaginal ring is a chemical-mechanical device about the diameter of the diaphragm. It is filled with synthetic progesterone which suppresses ovulation. Menstrual cycles are achieved by removing the ring for seven days every twenty-eight days. Preliminary reports have thus far indicated low side effects. The insertion of very small amounts of progesterone—about the same dosage as in a typical pill—directly into the uterus in a time capsule device that releases the hormone over the course of a year promises to be a vast improvement over the pill. By using an extremely low dosage of progesterone that affects only the uterus, researchers hope to eliminate the side effects associated with oral contraceptives. However, there is such great variation from patient to patient in the effects produced by progesterone that it is very difficult to determine precisely the amount of the substance required to make the procedure effective at such low dosages. Copper devices inserted into the uterus prevent the implantation of the egg in the uterine wall. This variation on the IUD has been tested with over six thousand women, with encouraging results to date.

Male Contraceptive Research

In developing male contraceptives there are but three points of control: sperm production, sperm maturation, and sperm transportation. Under-the-skin capsules containing testosterone, a hormone which prevents sperm production, have been tested and evaluated, but determination of the effective dosage has thus far escaped researchers. Similar capsules are being tested with compounds that interfere with sperm maturation. A vasectomy—surgical cutting of the *vas deferens*—will stop sperm transportation simply and effectively, but it carries the disadvantage of irreversibility in most cases. Procedures that will enable vasectomies to be reversed are currently being evaluated. One of these involves the insertion into the vas of a plug that is anchored on the exterior surface of the vas and can be removed when contraception is no longer desired.

STERILIZATION

The sterilization of either the male or the female is a quite different kind of birth control from those we have been discussing because, for the most part, such operations are irreversible. Nevertheless, voluntary sterilization is becoming increasingly common in the United States: 750,000 vasectomies were performed in 1970 alone. Tubal ligation for the female is a more complex operation.

Vasectomy

Vasectomy is a simple procedure that can be done in a doctor's office. It consists of cutting and tying the vas deferens. A local anesthetic is injected into each side of the scrotum and an incision is then made on each side of the scrotum above the testicles. The vas is tied in two places. The segment between is then cut and usually removed.

The vasectomy does not affect a man's sexual response. Some men have difficulty with the idea of voluntary sterilization because they equate masculinity with fertility. Such men may have some emotional problems to overcome should they finally decide upon the operation. Occasionally the vasectomy may be reversed. As a surgical procedure, it is not 100 percent effective because some men have more than one vas deferens and one might be missed.[27]

Tubal Ligation

Tubal ligation, commonly called "tying the tubes," is the most common operation for sterilizing women. This operation is similar in principle to the vasectomy. The cutting of the Fallopian tubes prevents the egg from reaching the uterus. This surgical procedure is far more complicated than a vasectomy, requiring hospitalization for five days, followed by three to four weeks of post-operative recovery.

A recent variation for sterilizing women is called *laparoscopic sterilization* or *laparotomy*. Lawrence Crawley describes the procedure in the

[27] *Human Sexuality*, pp. 79–80.

following terms: "The laparoscope is a long instrument that is inserted into the lower abdomen via a small incision below the navel. The tubes are then blocked by cauterization and/or cutting."[28] The operation normally can be performed on an outpatient basis.

Three other procedures which result in sterility among women are the hysterectomy, the xoophorectomy, and the salpingectomy. They are, however, normally performed for the purpose of correcting various abnormal conditions rather than for birth control purposes.

Sterilization in either the male or the female can be either eugenic or therapeutic. A eugenic sterilization is undertaken to prevent the inheritance of genetic defects; a therapeutic sterilization is undertaken when the husband or wife have certain chronic diseases or disabilities. Some couples have themselves sterilized once they have had the number of children they desire. If the male stores some of his sperm in a sperm bank before he is sterilized, it then becomes possible for the couple to have children after his vasectomy in case they should change their minds about family size.

ABSTINENCE

The self-imposed denial of the sexual gratification of intercourse has long been the traditional means of controlling conception among the unmarried. That is to say, it has been the socially prescribed method of birth control, although the extent to which it has actually been used in practice varies considerably from culture to culture and from time to time. As Martin Goldstein and Erwin Haeberle have written, "One can safely assume that, on the whole, this moral demand cannot be, has never been, and is not now being met because sexuality is an integral part of human life which cannot permanently be suppressed by public opinion or individual effort."[29] Even within marriage there may be reasons for abstaining from sexual intercourse, such as during illness, late pregnancy, or early post partum. But abstinence as a regularly practiced means of birth control runs contrary to the normal sexual urges of most people. Unless it is to have troublesome side effects, the practice of abstention must be a mutual decision on the part of both partners. For one partner to make such a decision unilaterally is to disregard the needs of the other.

Although it is possible to abstain from sexual activity, it is not possible to turn off the biological sexual urges. Normal sexual urges gen-

[28]*Reproduction, Sex and Preparation for Marriage*, p. 20.
[29]Martin Goldstein and Erwin Haeberle, *The Sex Book* (New York: Herder and Herder, 1972), p. 13.

erally will find their outlets one way or another. Thus many persons who practice abstinence from intercourse experience nocturnal orgasms. For this reason, abstinence from one form of sexual behavior need not, and normally should not, mean abstinence from all sexual behavior. As we have observed before, even in those cases where abstinence is desirable, an imaginative couple still may enjoy sexual outlets such as mutual oral or manual stimulation.

ABORTION

Spontaneous abortion or miscarriage occurs in about one out of every ten pregnancies, usually within the first trimester.[30] Strictly speaking, this is not a form of birth control since it is not planned, although it may indeed have the effect of controlling population. Induced abortion is a term used to describe the intentional termination of pregnancy.

Historical Overview

Throughout history there have been a variety of attitudes toward abortion. A Chinese manuscript over four thousand years old is said to record the oldest method of abortion. Within the Judaic tradition there are no laws against abortion either in the Talmud or Judaic law, for Judaism, like Japanese Shintuism, believes that the fetus becomes human only when it is born. Aristotle reflected Greek thinking on this matter when he said that abortion was an acceptable means of birth control when other means failed. It is commonly believed that one Greek who dissented from the majority opinion was the physician Hippocrates, for the hippocratic oath, which was derived from his teachings, includes a clause prohibiting abortion. There is, however, reason to believe that this clause is based on a misunderstanding of Hippocrates, who formulated his oath primarily to prevent physicians from participating in political intrigues by administering potions to members of the ruling classes and who did not intend the oath to bind physicians to defend life under any circumstances. Be that as it may, the idea that abortion is a form of murder seems never to have occurred to the ancient Romans, who, like the ancient Greeks, viewed abortion as simply the removal of a portion of the body. Even when population control became a problem for the Romans as a result of the fact that the ruling classes practiced abortion so extensively that the ratio of citizens to slaves de-

[30]Much of the material in this section was taken from McCary, *Human Sexuality,* pp. 80–81.

clined alarmingly, attempts to outlaw abortion met with only partial success.

Today, the strongest and most vocal opponent to abortion is the Roman Catholic Church. It is not widely known that the Church's position on abortion has varied over the centuries. In the twelfth century, abortions were allowed if the fetus was not over forty days old if it were a male and eighty days old if female. (The Church did not say how in those days it was possible to make a determination of the sex of the fetus.) Four centuries later, in 1588, Pope Sixtus V pronounced all abortions a form of murder. Gregory XIV three years later reverted to the earlier law. Gregory's pronouncement remained canon law until 1869 when Pius XI condemned all abortion. The present attitude of the Church is thus only about one hundred years old.

Public opinion has gradually come to favor liberalized abortion legis-

lation. By 1972 eighteen states had greatly liberalized their abortion laws following the American Law Institute's model code, and four (Alaska, Hawaii, New York, and Washington) had made abortion a matter of a woman's choice in consultation with her physician, provided the abortion was performed early in the pregnancy.[31] A Gallup poll in 1972 showed that 64 percent of the American public, including a majority of Roman Catholics, favored the liberalization of abortion laws.[32] In 1973 the Supreme Court of the United States of America ruled invalid all existing state laws prohibiting abortion. This ruling permits abortion in the early months of pregnancy at the discretion of the doctor and the patient. It makes abortion a medical matter, not a legal one.

Hazards of Abortion without Proper Medical Supervision

Because of the legal restrictions on abortion, persons wanting abortions in the past have had to resort to illegal means. As a result, many abortions were performed under nonsterile conditions by unskilled persons. Understandably, the death rate under these conditions has been very high. With the legalization of abortions, allowing them to be performed in sterile conditions under proper medical supervision, there is reason to believe that the death rate will be much lower. Indeed, abortion under such conditions is less dangerous than childbirth. For example, in Czechoslovakia, where abortion is legal, there was not a single death in 140,000 abortions during 1963–1964.[33]

Four medical abortion procedures are available today: (1) dilation and curettage, (2) vacuum extraction, (3) the saline method, and (4) hysterotomy. The first two methods can be used up to the twelfth or thirteenth week of pregnancy. A fifth method, which makes use of chemicals called prostaglandins, is in the experimental stage.

Abortion is not something that a woman can bring about herself without running serious risks. Many women believe that they can readily terminate a pregnancy by taking a pill or by some mechanical means such as falling downstairs, pounding the abdomen, or inserting some foreign substance into the uterus. Although amateur attempts at abortion often succeed in terminating the pregnancy, they commonly do so with grisly results for the woman, causing permanent and serious injury in many cases and death in many others. There is no way short of sur-

[31]Ruth Roemer, "Legalization of Abortion in the United States," in Howard J. Osofsky and Joy D. Osofsky, eds., *The Abortion Experience: Psychological and Medical Impact* (New York: Harper & Row, 1973), pp. 284–86.
[32]As quoted in *Human Sexuality*, p. 82.
[33]Lawrence Lader, *Abortion* (Boston: Beacon Press, 1966).

gery that a pregnancy can be terminated without grave risks to the woman. The folk wisdom that says that pregnancy can be terminated by taking a "black pill" (ergot) neglects to mention that the dosage necessary to terminate the pregnancy may also terminate the mother's life. "Hot douches, strong purgatives, high diving, bouncing down stairs and parachute jumping are equally ineffective," Lawrence Crawley concludes.[34]

In addition to the purely medical problems associated with illegal abortions, there are psychological factors that must be taken into account. James L. McCary provides us with a succinct summary of this dimension:

Women who were denied therapeutic abortions have greater problems than those who were permitted abortions. . . . Better mental adjustment is reported in women who have sought and been granted therapeutic abortions than in women whose requests for therapeutic abortions were denied. Furthermore, the children born to those mothers who had requested and been denied therapeutic abortions have greater social and emotional handicaps than do their peers.

Most physicians, psychiatrists and psychologists agree that abortion in itself is a safe, simple procedure which does not result in emotional problems. The obstacles erected by laws against the procedure, however, caused it to become an emotionally traumatic experience. The Supreme Court's decision to remove early abortion from the jurisdiction of the law and make it a medical matter should help to end the needless suffering which women who were denied the right to legal abortion have endured.[35]

Of course, the liberalization of abortion laws should not be permitted to lead to a situation in which abortion becomes a major means of contraception. It should be a contraceptive technique reserved for use when all others have failed. The most rational, humane, and healthy social approach is to prevent conception in the first place when children are not desired.

**VENEREAL
DISEASE**

Venereal diseases get their name from the Roman goddess of love, Venus, because they are transmitted during lovemaking. At the present time syphilis and gonorrhea are, next to the common cold, the most common infectious diseases in the United States. The incidence of gonorrhea had remained relatively constant for decades until it began a rapid increase in the 1960s, reaching an estimated 1.5 million new cases

[34]*Reproduction, Sex and Preparation for Marriage*, p. 91.
[35]From *Human Sexuality: A Brief Edition*, pp. 85–86, by James McCary © 1973. Reprinted by permission of D. Van Nostrand Company.

during 1970. Syphilis also increased during 1970 to an estimated 300,000 new cases. As Lloyd Saxton notes, "Experts in communicable disease warn that gonorrhea has now passed epidemic proportions to become a national pandemic. If the present trend continues, by 1980 one in every two high school students will have contracted gonorrhea."[36]

Both syphilis and gonorrhea are treatable in most cases by the use of pencillin or other appropriate antibiotics.[37] With such relatively simple treatments available, it seems surprising that we are in the midst of a pandemic, but there are a number of reasons for this. Some persons who contract VD are unwilling to receive treatment because of feelings of shame or guilt. Those who do seek treatment often are unwilling to identify their sexual partners. Although physicians are required to report cases to the public health officials, they often fail to do this for their private patients. As a result, the person who infected the patient and those who were subsequently infected by the patient cannot be contacted and treated. Because there are so many unknowns it is difficult accurately to judge the number of cases. The true incidence of any disease is always greater than the reported incidence, and in the case of VD the discrepancy is likely to be very great indeed. "The American Health Association, in fact, estimates that the incidence is perhaps four times greater than is reported," McCary observes.[38]

Another factor complicating the reporting and treatment process is the nature of the diseases themselves. Both syphilis and gonorrhea often do not produce recognizable symptoms in the female. What is more, although syphilis has an incubation period of about three weeks, gonorrhea becomes contagious in three to eight days. Thus a person infected with gonorrhea may well pass the disease to another before any symptoms are recognized—if, indeed, they ever are recognized. Other factors which may be contributing to the increase in VD are the increased sexual permissiveness of our society and the popularization of birth control pills. Our increasing openness to sexuality results in a higher incidence of nonmarital copulation, and widespread use of the pill as a contraceptive has decreased the reliance on the condom—which offers reasonable

[36]Lloyd Saxton, *The Individual, Marriage and the Family* (Belmont, California: Wadsworth Publishing Co., Inc., 1972), p. 5.
[37]Some very popular books such as Alex Comfort's *The Joy of Sex* (New York: Delacorte Press, 1972), p. 252, suggests that one megaunit of pencillin can be taken as a preventative before sexual intercourse. However, more and more strains of the spirochetes responsible for the disease are developing immunity to penicillin. Furthermore, the amount of penicillin that it would be necessary to take to insure that one would not catch the disease is quite large. This is a highly doubtful prophylaxis at the present time and should not be relied upon.
[38]*Human Sexuality*, p. 174.

protection against gonorrhea, although not against syphilis. Venereal disease is a special problem of the fifteen to twenty-four year old group, which has four times the average incidence for all other age groups.[39] Because many of these persons are minors, the problem is compounded by the fact that various laws tend to make it difficult for them to obtain advice and treatment.

Clinical Symptoms

The clinical symptoms of gonorrhea (commonly referred to as "clap" or "strain") occur within three to ten days after contracting the disease. The site of the infection is the urethra. In the male, a yellowish pus is discharged from the penis. This discharge can disappear within twelve hours, but a thin flow may persist for a few days in a small percentage of patients. Urination is accompanied by a burning sensation and an itching within the urethra. This condition may subside within two or three weeks without treatment or it may continue. Other glands along the urogenital tract may become infected. Ninety percent of the cases clear up with proper treatment—usually penicillin.

In the female the symptoms may be mild or absent. There may be a yellowish discharge from the vagina, yet not all such discharges are indications of gonorrhea. The infection is usually in the cervix. In order to make a definite diagnosis the physician must make a microscopic examination of the bacteria present in the discharge. Penicillin is usually effective if the disease is recognized and treated promptly. Without treatment, the infection can spread to the uterus, Fallopian tubes, and other pelvic organs. During menstruation, the disease is apt to spread more easily.

The acute symptoms in the female are severe pelvic pain, distention and tenderness of the abdomen, vomiting, and fever. These symptoms may appear during or just after menstruation. If the disease is not treated it can result in infertility in the female.

The clinical symptoms of syphilis in the male are usually not recognizable for two to four weeks. The early stage is marked by skin lesions or chancres (shankers), which appear two to four weeks after contracting the disease. The chancre occurs at the site of contact—in the male this is frequently on the penis, the scrotum, or pubic area. In the female it most commonly appears on the external genitalia but it may appear on the cervix or in the vagina. The chancre, which is usually painless, consists of a large, round, raised open wound which may appear in other spots on the body besides the point of contact. It usually disap-

---

[39] *Reproduction, Sex and Preparation for Marriage*, p. 135.

pears with or without treatment in several weeks. This can lead the infected person to feel that he has gotten rid of the disease, or whatever he thought he had. The only sure test for syphilis in its early stages is a serologic (blood) test, but this will turn out negative, even if the disease has been contracted, if it is given less than four weeks after having contracted the disease. Most cases can be cured with penicillin during the time the chancre is present.

The chancre is only the first stage. If left untreated, syphilis moves into its second stage within weeks after the healing of the chancres. This stage is marked by a generalized skin rash that usually is not associated with the chancre. Some patients complain of vague symptoms such as headache, fever, indigestion, sore throat, and muscle pain.

All symptoms disappear at the end of the second stage, which is followed by a "latent" period. The latent period may last for years, during which time the syphilis producing organisms (spirochetes) invade the various tissues of the body, "particularly blood vessels, the central nervous system and bones."[40] The untreated disease is frequently fatal, but even in the third stage treatment with penicillin may be beneficial, depending upon the extent to which the internal organs have been damaged.

Prophylaxis

As noted already, penicillin, taken prior to or shortly after intercourse, could have some effect in preventing venereal disease. Overuse of the drug, however, entails serious dangers, not the least of which is the development of an allergic reaction to the drug. For this reason penicillin is rarely used for VD prevention, but is reserved for use in treatment. The prevention of venereal disease without the use of penicillin is a very complicated business. Crawley offers the following advice:

Before engaging in casual sexual relations, a man should obtain a condom and prophylactic kit from a drugstore. He should wash his genitals thoroughly with soap and water, avoid handling the genitals before the condom is in place on the erect penis, withdraw the penis immediately after ejaculation before the erection is lost, and make sure he grips the ring at the top of the condom on withdrawal to prevent its slipping off. Both partners should immediately urinate (to wash out any infectious germs from the urethra) and wash thoroughly the genitals and all exposed areas (chancres can be on areas not covered by the condom— e.g., testicles or inner thigh) with soap and water, as warm as is available and can be tolerated. These areas should be thoroughly dried. The male should then squeeze one half of the contents of the prophylactic tube into the urethra and smear the remaining half of the medication over the lining and skin of the organs

[40]*Fundamentals of Human Sexuality*, p. 301.

which touched during intercourse. About all the female can do is make sure the male follows these instructions. There is no prophylactic kit for her, and douching is not particularly helpful. The least she can do is urinate soon after intercourse, wash all exposed areas with soap, and dry thoroughly. These instructions may seem unrealistic and following them a nuisance, but there is nothing unrealistic about the disease.[41]

Venereal diseases are destructive and the probability of infecting others is very great. They often do not reveal themselves in clear clinical symptoms. If we are to be responsible about our sexual behavior, we must take the threat of VD seriously. A person should take every prophylactic measure possible. Some physicians are sufficiently alarmed by the problem to recommend taking a penicillin tablet before intercourse or within six hours after. Anyone who is not sexually monogamous should have a blood test every six months for syphilis and gonorrhea. A person who suspects that he has been exposed to the disease should seek diagnosis immediately.

[41]Crawley et al., *Reproduction, Sex and Preparation for Marriage*, 2nd ed., p. 142. © 1973. Reprinted by permission of Prentice-Hall, Inc., Englewood Cliffs, New Jersey.

SUMMARY

Contraception is not synonymous with birth control. This chapter has treated four major techniques to control birth: contraception, sterilization, abstinence, and abortion. Each one has its place as an effective and appropriate technique given the circumstances under which the decision to use a particular birth control method must be made. Obviously, it is better—if one is going to prevent birth—to do so before conception. Since the effects of contraceptives are generally reversible, contraceptives are likely to be preferred over sterilization in most cases. Abortion is more risky and raises many more ethical issues, but it too has its place as a means of birth control. For some individuals abstinence may be the preferable form.

The most reliable contraceptives require a doctor's prescription. Both the pill and the IUD are theoretically one hundred percent effective and nearly reach this theoretical efficiency in certain populations. However, not everyone can use them and so the diaphragm or cervical cap, both of which are slightly less effective in practice, may be the best option.

Of those contraceptives available without a prescription, the condom is the most effective and has an added benefit of providing some protection against venereal disease. Spermicidal substances vary greatly in their effectiveness and tend to interfere with the process of making love. Douches are virtually ineffective. Since only a third of all women have menstrual cycles regular enough to make the use of the rhythm method effective, about all that can be said for this technique as a contraceptive is that it is the only one officially endorsed by the Roman Catholic Church.

The rapid increase in venereal disease among the high school age population in particular is cause for genuine concern. While almost all cases can be effectively treated if caught soon enough, many people still are reluctant to undergo examination. A more helpful attitude is to view these diseases as we would view any other disease and seek quick and effective care. The symptoms described in this chapter should provide some clue, but among people who are sexually active in nonmonogamous relationships routine clinical checkups are advisable.

8

THE ART OF LOVEMAKING

Praise be given to God, who has placed man's greatest pleasure in the natural parts of woman, and has destined the natural parts of man to afford the greatest enjoyment to woman.

The Perfumed Garden

INTRODUCTION

Sex, to most of us, means sexual intercourse. Whether we talk about "doing it" or "making love," whether we use any of the crude but common terms or have invented our own tender euphemisms, the focal point of our meaning is the very specific act of genital intercourse. This focus is carried over into research on sexual behavior, which heavily concentrates on sexual intercourse or *coitus*, its more precise expression. But human sexual behavior is much more varied than that. As the noted anthropologist Bronislaw Malinowski has shown in his classic *Sexual Life of Savages*, sex is a social and cultural force pervading all of society.[1]

American lovemaking has been strongly influenced by our cultural heritage, which places a heavy emphasis on the reproductive function of human sexuality. Sex for the right purpose, with the right person, in the right way is a central element of our understanding of sexual intercourse that goes back at least as far as St. Thomas

[1]Bronislaw Malinowski, *The Sexual Life of Savages* (New York: Harcourt Brace Jovanovich, 1929).

Aquinas.[2] But sexual intercourse that is confined to the purpose of reproducing another human being is a very limited form of sexual behavior indeed. Such a heavy emphasis upon the reproductive aspect of human sexual behavior has greatly restricted the expressiveness of our sexuality, limited the scope of our lovemaking behavior, and made us overly concerned with the problems of sexual incompatibility, impotence, and frigidity.

Although sexual intercourse is an act that is pleasurable in and of itself, it seems to be most expressive when the partners are in love with one another. Persons in love are often more responsive to the touch of the beloved, and the meaning that their lovemaking conveys to each is deeper and richer because of their relationship. But to assert that sexual intercourse *must* always occur between persons in love for it to be either pleasurable or meaningful is simply to ignore a great portion of human lovemaking.[3] Such romantic and unrealistic attitudes make it difficult for many people to think of sexual intercourse as an activity that can be enjoyed simply for the pleasure it brings. Perhaps more importantly, such attitudes may tend to deprive those who hold them of the capacity to discover that sexual intercourse can indeed be a means by which a couple *make* love—that is, the act itself can initiate a loving relationship.

Many of us think of sexual intercourse as "doing what comes naturally." Perhaps in reaction to the numerous books about "how to do it" and the often misguided advice of marriage manuals that tell us that technique is the be-all and end-all of human lovemaking, many people jump to the opposite conclusion that everyone knows how to make love, or can soon discover how. In a limited sense, this is so. But if our lovemaking is to progress beyond the elemental act and become capable of expressing a wide range of meanings and nuances of pleasure, and if it is to provide us with a rich and rewarding way of expressing our love throughout our entire lives, then we must develop it as an art. This art is far more than technique. It involves the whole being of both partners and the total setting within which they make love.[4]

This chapter begins by discussing the context in which lovemaking occurs, including the setting and something of the expectations that we often bring to it. It then discusses stroking, the technique of verbally and physically comforting another, and the art of what Masters and Johnson have called "pleasuring." In pleasuring, couples discover how to arouse each other erotically and learn about the importance of being open in their lovemaking.

In the part of the chapter devoted to lovemaking itself, only a small portion of the many useful and pleasurable techniques will be discussed. Any one of a number of other excellent texts can provide more complete information about sexual techniques. The major portion of this section is to suggest the variety and to reassert the validity of sexual activity as a joyous, pleasurable means of making love.

[2]*See* Chapter 10 for further documentation of this idea.
[3]The "libertine" view of human sexual behavior is found in the works of Albert Ellis. See, for example, Albert Ellis, *The American Sexual Tragedy* (New York: Twayne Publishers, Inc., 1954).

[4]See especially Alex Comfort, *The Joy of Sex* (New York: Delacorte Press, 1972).

CONTEXT

The cultural context through which people in our society approach sexuality has been aptly described by James L. McCary as a "heritage of confusion."[5] This is not simply because sexuality means so many different things to different people—"different strokes for different folks"—

[5]James Leslie McCary, *Human Sexuality: A Brief Edition* (New York: Van Nostrand and Company, 1973), pp. 3–4.

but also because we understand ourselves so poorly as sexual beings. Human sexuality is not simply natural or instinctive. It is learned. Sexual intercourse is not simply the union of "two souls and the contact of two epidermises," it is a "secret coming together of two human bodies [in which] all society is the third presence." Our cultural heritage is the overarching context within which sexual intercourse occurs.

This heritage has been characterized by a woeful ignorance. In spite of all that is said about the subject, our scientific understanding of human sexual behavior is limited to about twenty-five significant studies.[6] Medical schools, seminaries, and universities have only recently begun to plan for course work and training in the area of sexual behavior, and among people who do not have access to such advanced resources, sex education is practically nonexistent. For years, doctors, clergy, and other professionals have been as a whole largely uninformed and prudish about human sexuality. Yet these were the people to whom individuals who were troubled about various aspects of their sexuality turned for advice. The extent of confusion in this area can be gauged by Alfred Kinsey's informed estimate that if the legal codes governing sexual behavior were ever enforced, something like 95 percent of American males would be condemned.[7] Furthermore, as McCary observes, "The mass communication media do not control our sexual behavior, they merely mirror our sexual anxieties. Confusion begets confusion, and there is a disturbing conflict in our social order. Our culture condemns illicit sexual relationships, but it also depicts them as desirable and exciting."[8]

It is within this cultural context that we Americans approach our lovemaking. There are signs, however, that the sexual renaissance may be changing many of our ideas, giving us a much more positive attitude toward our sexuality. More and more people are coming to recognize that human sexuality can communicate more than simple erotic attraction. It is becoming increasingly clear that any intimate partnership can be enhanced by an open and genuine sex life. We tend to think of communication, openness, and the giving of oneself as occurring primarily through words, but if the words are the only way a couple expresses who they are to each other, they have been cheated. The revelation and self-disclosure of two people in love and in bed together goes far beyond what can be put into words. This self-disclosure and joy in finding each other can continue throughout a relationship if a couple does not take their lovemaking for granted. Routine and monot-

---

[6]Winston Ehrman, "Marital and Non-Marital Sexual Behavior," in Harold T. Christensen, ed., *Handbook of Marriage and the Family* (Chicago: Rand McNally, 1964), p. 597.

[7]Alfred C. Kinsey et al., *Sexual Behavior in the Human Male* (New York: Pocket Book, 1948), p. 392.

[8]McCary, *Human Sexuality*, pp. 3–4.

ony in lovemaking can easily come to be the pattern in any long-term partnership, but this need not happen. Considering lovemaking as an art to be practiced leads one to anticipate and prepare for the pleasures it brings. Knowing how to make love skillfully enhances these pleasures. But discovering how truly to give each other pleasure in sexual relationships is not simply a matter of technique, however varied and elegant. It is a matter of openness, honesty, and communication as well. The longer and more deeply two partners have known each other and the more vital their love, the more they have to bring to their lovemaking.

Unrealistic Expectations

Although the changes in sexual mores generally described as the sexual revolution have helped many young Americans get over some of their hangups, these changes have produced some new problems. People today are coming to understand their sexuality as a rich and rewarding means of communication and a pleasure in its own right. They also are beginning to understand that women not only can find pleasure in sex but, indeed, as we saw in Chapter 6, have a much greater physiological potential to enjoy it than men. It is not common any more to think of sex in marriage as the man's pleasure and the woman's obligation, for the contemporary woman enjoys increased freedom to make her own demands. On the negative side, however, these generally beneficial changes have contributed to increased performance fears in many people. In the last thirty years various "experts"—many of whom are no more qualified than the average experienced adult—have offered numerous descriptions of what is expected of both partners in lovemaking. A rather humorous, but basically devastating, description of these changing expectations is found in Gina Allen and Clement Martin's book, *Intimacy:*

Once the goal was orgasm for him (essential for health). For her it was "satisfying him" (to keep him at home and preserve the marriage).

Then the goal was "satisfying her" for him (to prove he was a genuine sexual jock, not a run-of-the-mill athlete). Her goal was reaching orgasm (to prove her femininity). To prove she was also mature, it was necessary for her to reach "vaginal orgasm." That was a change in both rules and goals that unfortunately occurred just after the man had learned to find the clitoris. At first, reaching vaginal orgasm was thought to be her problem. But later, it became his problem, too, as he was expected to keep an erection and keep thrusting (and keep his mind off what he was doing) long enough to bring her to a mature, non-clitoral climax. Otherwise, he wouldn't earn his letter.

The stakes were later raised to a mutual climax, which if you were a real jock would shake the world. . . . Quantity rather than quality became the basis for scoring, with each player pitting himself against vague and varying national averages or healthful weekly requirements.

In the meantime, her performance was to be judged in a new way—as if competing for the Academy Award. She wasn't required to have an orgasm. (She got as much pleasure from pleasing her partner, the experts said.) But she was required to simulate an orgasm to make his performance look and feel better. To keep either partner from scoring too high, the experts gave him hints to tell if she was faking. Both lost points if her deception was detected.

And then came multiple orgasm (quantity still counts). Now he was able to give her at least three orgasms in the place of one. The first one of several could be clitoral, a pre-intercourse warmup. Then a mature vaginal climax or two after intromission. And finally—back to the mutual orgasm. A truly super performance by two superjocks!

The name of the game is Sexual Freedom, because it has freed sex from the bonds of reproduction, marriage, and love. The advertised prizes are health, happiness, and an end to anxiety.[9]

The demands made upon both partners by such unrealistic criteria for "excellent performance" may well have contributed to the increasing rates of impotence that are now being recorded. Masters and Johnson clearly point out that the "fear of inadequacy is the greatest known deterrent to effective sexual functioning" simply because it severely reduces an individual's ability to be receptive to the sexual stimuli that occur naturally in lovemaking.[10] No set of criteria can adequately measure the sexual performance of a couple save their own mutual pleasure. In lovemaking, as in all aspects of intimacy, being oneself rather than living up to the expectations of others is more likely to produce such pleasure. As Alex Comfort observes, "The whole joy of sex with love is that there are no rules so long as you enjoy, and the choice is practically unlimited."[11]

Setting

The immediate setting in which lovemaking takes place affects its quality, tone, and meaning.[12] To make love spontaneously under the pine trees in a secluded woods, on a sailboat in the privacy of a quiet lagoon, or hurriedly in the back seat of a car gives richness and variety to a relationship. Conversely, people who find it necessary—perhaps because both partners live with their parents—to confine their lovemak-

[9]Gina Allen and Clement Martin, *Intimacy: Sensitivity, Sex and the Art of Love* (Chicago: Corles Book Company, Inc., 1971), pp. 1–2. By permission.
[10]William H. Masters and Virginia Johnson, *Human Sexual Inadequacy* (Boston: Little Brown, 1970), p. 13.
[11]Comfort, *The Joy of Sex*, p. 17.
[12]Setting has always been an important factor in human lovemaking—in contrast to animal behavior, which is much less affected by this concern. See Malinowski, *The Sexual Life of Savages*, and Margaret Mead, *Sex and Temperament* (New York: Mentor Books, 1952).

ing to such unappealing places as motel rooms often find that the setting gives their sexual relationship a somewhat degrading quality.

Various physical features can be as important in their own way as the general ambience of the setting. A waterbed, for example, gives quite different rhythms to lovemaking than a feather bed or a standard mattress. Showering or swimming together during or after lovemaking may contribute to the comfort and pleasure to be found in making love. For some lovers the haste of a clandestine affair seems particularly appetizing, whereas others relish the intimate leisure of a long Sunday afternoon with the telephone off the hook and no visitors expected.

The couple who have an enduring partnership and the ability to select a permanent place in which to make love have the opportunity to see to it that certain amenities are present in their setting. A bed that is firm and large enough for adequate movement without undue noise seems ordinarily desirable, although lovemaking on the floor of the study or living room after the children have gone to sleep is sometimes a refreshing alternative for married couples. Pillows that are full and able to provide support, should they be called upon, are helpful additions. A chair that is sturdy enough to hold two people can add to the variety of positions to be enjoyed in intercourse. A great deal of effort can be put into making the bedroom of an ordinary apartment a much more comfortable and esthetically pleasing setting for lovemaking than it ordinarily is. This list of amenities that can enhance sexual relations could be extended indefinitely. The point is simply that where you make love does matter, so that efforts to improve the quality of the setting in which you make love generally will be amply rewarded.

DISCOVERING EACH OTHER

A great deal of the joy two people experience in coming together in sexual encounter is the discovery of each other's bodies. In the last analysis, we are our bodies. As George Downing observes, "Our emotions, our outer perceptions, our spiritual life, and even our conceptual understanding of the world around us all begin and end with this intimate shadowy mass which is our being."[13] A sense of touch is as important as a sense of sight in communicating pleasure. Indeed, our bodies are constantly communicating, whether we are aware of it or not. One of the gifts in lovemaking is to make use of the sense of touch in creating physical pleasure and excitement.

Exploration

Exploring each other's body heightens one's awareness not only of the other but also of one's own inner self. Touching can express tenderness,

[13]George Downing, *The Message Book* (New York: Random House, 1972), p. 134.

respect, understanding, trust, and of course, the sheer sense of mutual pleasure. When lovers caress, there is a fullness that can never be obtained by words. Touching and exploring each other can be an expression of deep self-giving, not simply a mechanical technique of arousal. But before this can become a reality, one must have developed some awareness of both oneself and one's partner.

Most of the time, our bodies are covered and held in reserve in the course of our daily interaction. Lovers, though, come to each other "without their clothing." If they take this condition of nakedness before each other as simply a convenient convention for facilitating access to their sexual organs, they will miss out on the opportunity their intimacy provides for exploring each other through an exploration of each other's body.

A person's feelings about his or her body are an important part of his or her self-image. Persons who are not comfortable with their bodies therefore find something threatening in the openness that is required for exploration and discovery. They tend to have a somewhat reserved attitude in their love-making, for their low self-estimates lead them to "hold back" from giving themselves freely. Conversely, people who are at ease with their bodies find it easier to be open and revealing with their partners. Often negative self-images are formed quite early in life, but a loving partner who convincingly conveys the sense of excitement he or she feels at discovering his or her partner's body can contribute greatly to repairing the damage done by low self-regard. A man or woman who fears that he or she is undesirable often can be convinced otherwise by sincere expressions of desire.

Pleasuring

Sex clinics such as Masters and Johnson's are constantly meeting persons who are uncomfortable with each other as lovers. They do not know how to give each other pleasure, are fearful of their inadequacies, and come to the clinic seeking help. An important part of the therapy that Masters and Johnson prescribe for many sexual dysfunctions is called "pleasuring." Basically, it is a simple means by which couples learn to become open to each other through touching. Initially, the couple is asked to engage in nongenital exploration. Commonly, the man rests against a pillowed headboard and the woman rests against him. If he is to give pleasure to her, she guides his exploring hands over her body and indicates by touch or sound what is pleasurable to her in his touching. Masters and Johnson describe the technique as follows:

The partner who is pleasuring is committed first to do just that; give pleasure. At a second level in the experience, the giver is to explore his or her own component of personal pleasure in doing the touching—to experience and appreciate the sensuous dimensions of hard and soft, smooth and rough, warm and cool, qualities of texture and, finally the somewhat indescribable aura of physical receptivity expressed by the partner being pleasured. After a reasonable length of time . . . the partners are to exchange roles of pleasuring (giving) and being pleasured (getting), and then repeat the procedure in similar detail.[14]

They thus come to experience the pleasure of giving as well as receiving by becoming more attuned to each other. This technique makes sure that couples learn to communicate with each other at a very basic level. It assumes something that most couples do not assume—that an individual becomes an expert lover by discovering his or her partner as a unique individual with specific sexual desires and a body that experiences sexual pleasure in a specific way. This process of discovery depends upon having a partner who is willing and able to respond to what is felt as pleasurable, who can say in effect, "I like that." This ability to respond openly to sexual stimuli is something that many people have never learned to express because of their cultural conditioning. Thus Masters and Johnson write:

The most unfortunate misconception our culture has assigned to sexual functioning is the assumption, by both men and women, that men by divine guidance and infallible instinct are able to discern exactly what a woman wants sexually and when she wants it. Probably this fallacy has interfered with natural sexual interaction as much as any other single factor. The second most frequently encountered sexual fallacy, and therefore a constant deterrent to effective sexual expression, is the assumption, again by both men and women, that sexual expertise is the man's responsibility. In truth, no woman can know what type of sexual approach she will respond to at any given opportunity until faced with the absence of a particularly desired stimulative factor. How can a woman possibly expect any man to anticipate her sensual pleasure, when she cannot accomplish this feat with consistency herself? How can any man presume himself an expert in female sexual response under these circumstances?[15]

Pleasuring seems to be a good general technique for discovering each other as lovers. It requires openness about oneself and one's body and willingness to provide the much-needed feedback that increases the pleasures of lovemaking. Many couples discover through pleasuring each other that their whole bodies can become "erogenous zones."

MAKING LOVE

Knowledge of one's own erogenous zones is essential if one is to move toward one's full capacity for sexual responsiveness. One learns sexual

[14]Masters and Johnson, *Human Sexual Inadequacy*, p. 73. © 1970 by Little, Brown and Company. Used with permission.
[15]Masters and Johnson, *Human Sexual Inadequacy*, p. 87. © 1970 by Little, Brown and Company. Used with permission.

responsiveness through experimentation and experience in a process which begins with acceptance and knowledge of one's own body. The full flavor of sexual responsiveness is discovered only by a person who has developed what Masters and Johnson describe as "a sensuous enjoyment and appreciation for the sight, smell, taste, feel and use of (one's) body in all its infinite capacities."[16]

Kissing

The erotic kiss, the most universal form of human lovemaking, has many variations. A kiss enables the lovers to taste as well as touch each other. In the intimacy of their embrace they can smell the fragrance of hair, perfume, and natural body odors. When the kiss becomes a deep kiss, the experience of penetrating and being penetrated becomes a part of their awareness of each other. Light stroking, tentative tongue caressing, gentle nibbling, and sucking all become part of mutual exploration and discovery. Sensitivity and timing with such a varied form of expressing become in themselves a show of responsiveness. Kissing can range over the entire body, greatly increasing the discovery and significantly stimulating both partners. The nape of the neck, the ears, the breasts, the palms of the hands, fingertips, thighs, feet, genitals— indeed any part of the body will respond to a lover's kisses. During this exploration, lovers come to discover the pleasantness of their own clean body odors.

Some lovers find the genital kiss especially stimulating. The genitals are particularly sensitive to erotic stimulation and so the genital kiss often proceeds to further exploration of the genital area. For some lovers such activities are psychologically very beneficial, for they encourage them to become intimate with parts of the body which the puritan strain in our tradition teaches us to regard as unclean and unacceptable. On the other hand, some people find oral-genital stimulation completely repulsive, despite that fact that, as Katchadourian points out, "If the genitals are clean, objections are difficult to support on hygienic grounds."[17]

Intercourse

Intercourse has many forms. Experimentation and discovery of new and satisfying positions enrich the lovemaking of a couple and reveal different aspects of the partners. Taking the initiative, being dominant or submissive, being aggressive or tender, imaginative or creative, can all

[16]*Human Sexual Inadequacy*, p. 76.
[17]Herant A. Katchadourian, *Fundamentals of Human Sexuality* (New York: Holt, Rinehart & Winston, Inc., 1972), p. 239.

be expressed in the various positions of lovemaking. "Marriage must continually vanquish the monster that devours everything, the monster of habit," the French writer Honoré de Balzac observed. Creative and imaginative couples who are free with each other can deal rather effectively with the monster of habit. The use of a variety of positions also provides a wide array of different sensations and can enable couples to continue their lovemaking in spite of pregnancy or various types of mild illnesses that might make intercourse in one particular position uncomfortable for one of the partners.

Four Basic Positions. Although there are many variations in the positions couples can assume while making love, there are four basic positions from which one can improvise by rolling, sitting, or standing. Artful lovers may assume several positions throughout an evening's lovemaking. There is no normal or natural position, although the so-called "matrimonial" or "missionary's" position enjoys wide acceptance in the United States.

Face-to-Face, Man Above. The face-to-face, man above position is the most commonly employed in the United States but its use is apt to be rare in many non-Western cultures. In this position—also known as the "matrimonial" or "missionary's" position—the woman lies on her back with her legs apart, sometimes with her knees bent. The man lying above her, supporting himself on his elbows and knees, can easily achieve intromission. Once his penis has been inserted, he is basically in control of the body movements because the weight of his body on her tends to restrict her movement to some extent. It is important for him to keep in contact with the clitoris. This may be accomplished by putting pressure on the pubic bone or by the woman's adjusting her position so that the clitoris is stimulated by the tensions in the clitoral hood. (Indeed, the clitoris is indirectly stimulated by the tensions in the clitoral hood in almost all positions of intercourse, including rear entry.)

FIGURE 8–1
Face-to-face,
man above.

Although, as noted above, the woman's body movements are somewhat restricted, she is relatively free to vary the position of her legs. During intercourse she may pull her legs up toward her shoulders, she may lock them around her partner's body, she may place her heels behind his knees to give her more control over her pelvic thrusting, or she may place her legs either inside or outside of his. By putting a pillow under her lower back and drawing her knees up toward her shoulders, she can receive the deepest penetration. Thus, by changing the position of her legs, she can alter the depth of penetration, relax, change the rhythm of the thrusting, and alter the amount of tension on the clitoral hood.

The advantages of this position are that it is one of the easiest to learn and one of the most adaptable. In addition, because the partners are facing each other they may express their feelings with their eyes and may continue their erotic kissing. This is also the position in which couples are most likely to conceive children because of the proper pooling of the ejaculate in the vagina. To increase the possibilities of conception, the woman should remain in this position after intercourse and the man should not withdraw hurriedly.

There are drawbacks to this position, however. The man's weight can be a burden for the woman, who is also hampered in her movements, particularly movements of her pelvis. What is more, because he must support himself, he is not free to caress, fondle, and stimulate his partner.

Face-to-Face, Woman Above. The woman above position provides a great deal more freedom for the woman. In this position she can control and vary the speed of the movement and the depth of penetration. Clitoral contact is frequently more intense in this position, which gives the woman primary control over this important source of stimulation. It is said that this position is less sexually stimulating to men, yet it does allow the man to be more relaxed. He also has easier access to his part-

FIGURE 8–2
Face-to-face,
woman above.

ner's body, and is able to see, touch, caress, and kiss many more areas of her body than in the man above position. Because she normally can rest her entire weight on him—whereas, in the man above position, his weight may be too much for her to support comfortably—she is equally free. By the same token, the man's body movements are not restricted as much by the woman's weight as the woman's are by the man's weight in the man above position. Thus the man frequently is able to delay ejaculation for a longer period of time in this position.

The woman may, if she wishes, lie full length against him with her legs inside or outside of his, attaining a fuller sense of body contact. Or she may more or less sit astride him. In this approach, the man also may vary his position. By resting on his elbows he may raise himself closer to her body. By raising his legs, he can provide his partner with a back rest.

An advantage of this position is that many women find it easier to experience an orgasm. On the other hand, there are certain disadvantages which appear to be caused by psychological factors. With the woman on top, some men feel threatened by appearing to be placed in a passive or subordinate position. There are certain indications, however, that this attitude is far less common than it used to be.

Face-to-Face, Side Position. The face-to-face, side position offers the opportunity for mutual control of body movements during intercourse. The couple lie on their sides facing each other. Often this position is arrived at by rolling from the man-above position. A thoughtful couple who plan ahead will have the freedom of their arms, legs, and hands after they have rolled over. With the arms, legs, and hands free, the couple has an infinite variety of opportunities for touching, caressing, and ex-

FIGURE 8–3
Face-to-face,
side position.

ploring. Because this is the most relaxing position for both partners, it is often possible to engage in intercourse for long periods of time in this fashion. After intercourse in this position a couple can lie together in the warmth of each other's body for a period of time and may even fall asleep without separating.

The variation of this position illustrated in Figure 8–3 is declared to be most satisfactory by Masters and Johnson, who encourage couples to try it because it permits the woman to vary the pelvic thrusting with more ease while at the same time allowing the man greater ejaculatory control.[18] Despite the fact that this position may be difficult to get into for inexperienced couples, it has the advantage of neither partner having to support the weight of the other. This position is especially advantageous if one partner is considerably taller than the other. Although penetration is normally shallower and the movements less active, the leisure and tenderness normally associated with this position make it desirable.

Rear Entry Position. Because animals typically copulate from a rear entry position, many people feel that this is an inappropriate position for human beings.[19] Nevertheless, this position can offer a great deal of

[18]Masters and Johnson, *Human Sexual Inadequacy*, pp. 310–11.
[19]In the Kinsey study, *Sexual Behavior in the Human Male*, only about 15 percent of the respondents reported having used this position.

FIGURE 8–4

Rear entry position.

pleasure to both partners. Many variations are possible: the woman sitting on a man's lap with her back to him; the woman lying on her stomach or kneeling; or both partners lying on their sides. The rear entry position offers the man greater freedom to caress the woman's breasts, clitoris, back, buttocks, legs, and almost all of her upper body. It also offers a wide variety of depth of penetration, depending upon the variation employed. As the couple moves from a distended position to a more seated position, the depth of penetration increases. Even in those variations that offer only slight penetration, some women find great pleasure in the stimulation of the introitus and either partner is able to compensate manually for any stimulation of the clitoris that may be felt to be lacking. The position is restful in most of its variants, and although there is lack of eye to eye contact, many of the other satisfactions can compensate for this. In this position the man can massage and caress his partner's back with much greater ease than in any other position.

These four basic positions in lovemaking can be almost infinitely varied to suit the couple's taste. The variations are very subtle. They cannot possibly be adequately described in terms of simple mechanics and techniques. They must be arrived at by exploration, discovery, and sensitive communication between loving couples.

Caring partners do not simply end their lovemaking perfunctorily after orgasm. Part of the great joy of lovemaking comes from bathing in the afterglow. Being together, recognizing what has happened to each other, caressing, lying in the warmth of each other's body are all part of the total experience of loving—a feeling well captured by the poet Dylan Thomas, who wrote, "Let me lie shipwrecked between thy thighs." More prosaically, Herant Katchadourian has observed, "The aftermath of coitus may signify the end of an episode of sexual activity or it may simply be an interlude between two acts of intercourse where afterplay imperceptibly merges into foreplay again."[20]

Thinking about lovemaking that has ended and anticipating lovemaking yet to come is a vital part of a partnership. One of the warm and endearing attributes that can be brought to a partnership is the experience of anticipating, planning, and preparing for lovemaking.

Lovemaking Roles

So much of our lovemaking in the past has been tied up with our understanding of masculine and feminine roles. Our culture traditionally has ascribed dominance to males and submissiveness to females, but today

[20]Katchadourian, *Fundamentals of Human Sexuality*, p. 254.

there is evidence suggesting that this sort of role stereotyping can be very crippling to the art of lovemaking.[21] A man and a woman in partnership should be free to define their own roles in terms of their own needs and the needs of their partners. Fortunately, there are some indications that this is becoming possible for an ever increasing number of people—thanks in no small part to the efforts of the women's liberation movement, which has succeeded in making large numbers of men and women sensitive to the problems created by restrictive definitions of sex roles. (This is an issue we will be discussing more fully in Chapter 9.)

**SPECIAL
CONCERNS**

When talking about lovemaking as an art, it is easy to drift into fanciful talk about some ideal mode of interaction wherein each partner is aware of and sensitive to the needs of the other and mutual satisfaction is readily obtained. In real life, however, this ideal and what is actually occurring may be quite different. Many couples have to work years before they are able to communicate at the deep level described in the portrait of an ideal relationship. Some never succeed. Most of us experience our lovemaking at times as completely fulfilling and at other times as inadequate or incomplete. Our sexual lives have their ups and downs as do our other ways of communicating with each other. The quality of the lovemaking of most couples thus varies a great deal. There are, however, a number of special concerns which commonly arise to inhibit or limit a couple's participation in lovemaking. In the next few pages we shall examine four of these.

Sexual Incompatability

Albert Ellis contends that for the most part the problem of sexual incompatibility is not related to differences in sex drives or hormonal imbalances between the partners; rather, it most commonly results from their inability to make the best use of their sexual responsiveness and expressiveness. In particular, he claims that most people are strongly influenced in their lovemaking by what he calls the "Great Coital Myth." The main premises of this myth are:

(1) That the only proper and manly form of sex relations is penile-vaginal copulation; (2) that whenever the husband is sexually desirous, it is his right to beg, cajole, or demand coital relations with his wife and that, to keep him happy, she must acquiesce just about as frequently as he desires; (3) that the wife must obtain her sex satisfaction, including orgasm, through the same type of vaginal-penile intercourse that satisfies her husband; (4) that if the wife wishes to have

[21]Masters and Johnson, *Human Sexual Inadequacy*, pp. 159, 160.

intercourse more than her husband that is just too bad for her; and (5) that, all told, the perfect union is one where husband and wife naturally and automatically desire intercourse exactly the same number of times per week or month, and where serious discrepancies exist in their desires, sexual incompatability is inevitable.[22]

The great coital myth is, of course, related to our traditional conception of appropriate sex roles. Although the influence of this myth may well be waning, the notion of sexual incompatibility nevertheless persists as a bothersome specter haunting many relationships.

Ellis suggests that a major step in dealing with sexual incompatibility in most partnerships is to change the attitude of the partners about what constitutes appropriate sexual behavior. Among the changes that often seem to be called for is a recognition that coitus is only *one* of many potentially satisfying human sexual experiences. For example, some women find it very difficult to achieve orgasm during coitus but easy to achieve it in noncoital lovemaking. The idea that both partners must be satisfied by one particular sexual technique places a great strain on many couples who in fact differ in their sexual desires.

Some readers may object at this point that such differences in desire, where they exist, constitute precisely what is meant by sexual incompatibility. Recognizing the existence of such differences, they may argue with some plausibility, is not a cure for incompatibility but simply an admission that the couple in question is indeed incompatible. This line of reasoning would be valid if it weren't for the fact that tastes and preferences are capable of considerable modification. Consider an elementary example involving some of the coital positions discussed earlier in this chapter. Assume that the woman finds she is unable to experience full sexual satisfaction from the man above position and that the man finds the woman above position objectionable. A simple case of incompatibility, it seems: either "The Great Coital Myth" predominates and the woman must resign herself to incomplete sexual satisfaction, or our recommendation that the couple expand their sexual vocabulary predominates and the man is obliged to engage in practices he finds repugnant. Neither solution seems satisfactory.

But a solution is possible if the partner who is trying to limit the couple's sexual repertoire—in this case the man—makes a sincere effort to open his mind to the possibility that the technique his mate favors is in fact an acceptable and legitimate option. We are not recommending that anyone engage in practices he or she finds repellent. But we do wish to point out that, objectively speaking, there is nothing inherently repugnant—that is to say, nothing either sinful or "unnatural"—about any of the practices we have been describing. If the reluctant partner

[22]Ellis, *The American Sexual Tragedy*, p. 187.

thus can bring himself to recognize that his reluctance is the product of a simple prejudice, he has taken the first step toward overcoming it. In the case in question, for example, the man may feel that it is unmanly for a male to engage in intercourse in woman above positions. Once he admits to himself that this feeling has no factual basis, he may feel bold enough to give it a try, and if his partner is patient, helpful, and tolerant there is every reason to expect that he may learn to enjoy this new option.

In short, what we are saying is that when incompatibility seems to consist of one partner's desire for a type of sexual experience the other partner does not want, there are two possible resolutions of the problem. One partner can learn to do without the desired type of activity or the other can learn to enjoy it. Either resolution would eliminate the incompatibility, but, given a choice between them, there seems to be no reason not to favor the resolution that offers greater richness and variety in the sexual lives of the couple.

Sexual Dysfunction

Sexual incompatibility sometimes may derive from sexual dysfunctions of one form or another. James L. McCary offers the following definition of sexual dysfunction:

A person is considered sexually dysfunctional if his or her efforts to gratify his or her sexual desires are continually frustrated in spite of an available and sexually functioning partner. The man who cannot achieve an erection and the woman who has never experienced an orgasm are examples of such individuals. [23]

Various researchers offer various definitions of sexual dysfunction and it is not possible to do justice to this complexity here. Therefore, only the most common dysfunctions will be mentioned and we will confine ourselves simply to setting forth the basic symptoms.

Impotence. There are two basic kinds of impotence. *Primary Impotence* is defined arbitrarily by Masters and Johnson as a condition in which "a male [is] never able to achieve and/or maintain an erection quality sufficient to accomplish successful coital connection. . . . No man is considered primarily impotent if he has been successful in any attempt at intromission in either heterosexual or homosexual opportunity."[24] All men have episodes of erective failure at one time or another in their lives as the result of fatigue, distraction, illness, or a poor relationship with their partner. When a pattern of erective failure persists, however,

[23] From *Human Sexuality: A Brief Edition*, p. 156, by James McCary © 1973. Reprinted by permission of D. Van Nostrand Company.
[24] Masters and Johnson, *Human Sexual Inadequacy*, p. 157.

clinical help may be called for. A man is arbitrarily defined as *secondarily impotent* if his "failure rate at successful coital connection approaches 25 percent of his opportunities."[25]

Female Orgasmic Dysfunction. *Primary orgasmic dysfunction* in the female is defined as *never* having experienced an orgasm through *any* form of sexual stimulation. *Situational orgasmic dysfunction* is defined negatively as orgasmic failure that is not primary. For example, a woman who reports inability to experience orgasm with her partner will be diagnosed as suffering from secondary orgasmic failure if she has ever experienced orgasm in the past—perhaps with a different partner, perhaps as result of masturbation. The definition of secondary orgasmic failure does not include any specific failure rate.

One of the frequent causes for orgasmic dysfunction is related to the woman's orientation to her partner and their relationship. The relevant questions here, according to Masters and Johnson, are as follows:

What value has the male partner in the woman's eyes? Does the male maintain his image of masculinity? Regardless of his acknowledged faults, does he meet the woman's requirements of character, intelligence, ego strength, drive, physical characteristics, etc.? Obviously, every woman's requirements for a partner vary with her age, personal experience, confidence and the requisites of her sexual value system.[26]

Premature Ejaculation. Premature ejaculation is common among men. It is defined as the inability of the man to delay ejaculation long enough to penetrate and satisfy his partner at least 50 percent of the time.[27] Premature ejaculation is commonly initiated by a few coital experiences early in life in which the male was expected to hurry up and get it over with as soon as possible. A few visits to a prostitute, a few exposures to the pressures to perform under the anxieties inherent in "doing it" in the back seat of an automobile often are sufficient to establish a lifelong pattern of premature ejaculation *in some males*.

Vaginismus. Vaginismus is defined as "a spastic contraction of the vaginal outlet, a completely involuntary reflex stimulated by imagined, anticipated, or real attempts at vaginal penetration.[28] It cannot be unreservedly diagnosed without a pelvic examination. Vaginismus is a classic example of a psychosomatic illness. Today a part of the cure consists of the clinical insertion of successively larger dilators, but early psycho-

---

[25]*Human Sexual Inadequacy*, p. 157.
[26]Masters and Johnson, *Human Sexual Inadequacy*, p. 241. © 1970 by Little, Brown and Company. Used with permission.
[27]*Human Sexual Inadequacy*, p. 92.
[28]*Human Sexual Inadequacy*, p. 250.

analysts did not attempt such a simple behavioral approach and therefore had relatively poor success in treating patients suffering from this disorder. Vaginismus is commonly caused by fright, guilt, or emotionally traumatic experiences associated with intercourse, rape, or homosexual contact.

As can be readily understood, sexual dysfunctions and the existence of any of the debilitating experiences associated with them can lead to devastating loneliness, frustration, and confusion in a partnership. Failure to communicate with each other concerning the feelings, longings, and understandings associated with what is taking place can have extremely destructive effects on a partnership. With the presence of increasing numbers of sex clinics, most—if not all—of these destructive influences can be eliminated or greatly reduced.

Age

As we saw in Chapter 6, the physiological processes associated with aging do not necessarily preclude the possibility of a vital, loving, sexual relationship, although advancing age generally does require that a couple make some adjustments in their expectations and behavior. Over the years, as a partnership develops and as each partner comes to appreciate a full range of sexual expression, they develop a history of significant sexual communication. With this as the base of their lovemaking, the warmth, tenderness, and caring that are so important in an individual's later years can find a variety of sexual expressions. The notion that people over sixty-five are no longer sexual beings with sexual desires and abilities is much more of a cultural conviction than a physiological fact.[29]

Homosexuality

Homosexuality is commonly viewed either as a criminal offense, a pathology, or a life style in its own right. The Kinsey scale suggests that people feel varying degrees of heterosexual/homosexual attraction. That is to say, the world is not neatly divided into "straight" and homosexual populations. In his sample, Kinsey found that 50 percent of the men and 38 percent of the women had responded erotically to a person of their own sex *at least once* in their lives.[30] Many more persons were erotically attracted to persons of their own sex but did not overtly respond. Erotic attraction to another person of the same sex thus seems to be experienced by a majority of people at least at some time during

[29]Isadore Rubin, *Sexual Life After Sixty* (New York: Basic Books, 1965).
[30]Alfred C. Kinsey, *Sexual Behavior in the Human Female* (New York: Pocket Books, 1967), pp. 472ff.

their lives. Just as most people have experienced some form of homosexual attraction, so most people have experienced some form of heterosexual attraction. The number of people who apparently have never experienced erotic attraction for persons of the opposite sex—Kinsey called such individuals "true inverts"—seems to be quite small.

The issue at hand, therefore, seems to be not who is or who isn't homosexual, but rather how the individual deals with whatever erotic attraction he or she may have for members of his or her own sex. This issue is far too complex to be dealt with fully here, but we should like to point out that one of the main dangers in this area is that an individual will torture himself or herself unnecessarily with fears of homosexuality. The 1960s and 1970s witnessed the emergence of the homosexual community of America as an outspoken minority group defending its right to its own choice of life style, and many people have come to agree with those homosexuals who insist that their sexual preferences are neither perverse nor pathological. From the point of view of this school of thought, fear of homosexuality is baseless for the simple reason that homosexuality is nothing to be feared; such people feel that a young person who is in doubt about his or her sexuality should examine his or her preferences as objectively as possible and then accept the verdict without guilt or recrimination.

It must be admitted that such a "liberated" view of homosexuality is far from predominant in American society at present. Yet even those who accept the idea that homosexuality is in some sense wrong—either immoral or pathological—must recognize in most cases anxiety is an inappropriate response to the discovery that one is capable of experiencing homosexual erotic attraction. While this book was in production, The American Psychiatric Association officially removed "homosexuality" from its list of pathologies. As Kinsey's data indicates, homoerotic attraction is an extremely common phenomenon and is by no means an indication that one "is" a homosexual—if, indeed, we can speak of people "being" either homosexual or heterosexual at all.

SUMMARY

We approach our lovemaking from a context of confusion. Conflicting advice fuses with often misguided folklore and mythology to make it difficult for us to come to an understanding of who we are as sexual beings. Yet our understanding of our sexual nature influences how we express this sexuality in making love. Sex, most observers will agree, is not something set apart; it occurs in a particular relationship with a particular partner in a particular setting which is in turn part of a particular culture.

Lovemaking takes on meaning and nuances of pleasure when it is developed as an art. The immediate setting establishes the general tone of the relationship, either providing greater opportunity for expressive behavior or restricting such expressiveness. Because lovemaking is a process of mutual discovery that can be either artful or clumsy, our discussion of the techniques of making love suggested how movement, touch, smell, and taste can be used as means of communication.

In dealing with various special concerns, we confined ourselves to an enumeration of the symptoms of some of the more common problems. Much has been done of late to make these problems more susceptible to treatment than they were just a few years ago. Age and homosexuality are "problems" only if they are made so in lovemaking. Aging in itself need not mean the end of lovemaking, though it may call for an alteration in style. Homosexuality becomes a problem when a person fears, or becomes anxious about, his or her attraction to members of the same sex.

In conclusion, we should like to point out that we have tried to be as unbiased as possible in our presentation of this material, some of which is of a hotly controversial nature. Some of our readers, we suspect, will not think we have succeeded in this aim. We should like to remind those who think they detect bias in our presentation that this is an era in which "fact" and "value" are tightly interrelated. This is because our understanding and expression of ourselves as sexual beings are matters that provoke passionate concern. Even the most sophisticated sex researchers bring deeply held values to bear on their work—and it seems unlikely that it can ever be otherwise. Nor would we want it to be.

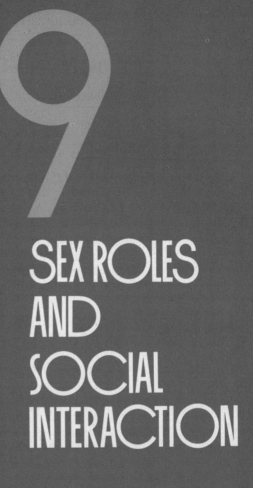

9

SEX ROLES AND SOCIAL INTERACTION

Sex, in its widest meaning . . . is rather a sociological and cultural force than a mere bodily relation of two individuals.

Bronislaw Malinowski

INTRODUCTION

When we discover each other as men and women, we bring to this experience an understanding of who we are that has been shaped by anatomical, psychological, and sociological influences. The complexity of these influences is perhaps something we do not understand, but it is something we have experienced, for these influences have shaped our understanding of what it means to be a man and what it means to be a woman. They have, in effect, determined our definition, our understanding, and our own personal comfort or discomfort with ourselves as men and women.

This chapter focuses primarily on the experiences and understandings about masculinity and femininity that are transmitted to us by the people around us. These can be called common stereotypes or sex roles. As we shall see, these stereotypes can serve as aids to social interaction; they also can be barriers to growing relationships. This is because it is impossible to develop deep relationships with other individuals if we relate to others on the basis of these stereotypes alone. Freedom and authen-

195

ticity are possible only if we relate to our partners in terms of their individual uniqueness and our own.

Conventional sex roles, in short, have a developmental task to play in our emergence as uniquely individual adult men and women. It is through them that we get our first clues as to what it means to be a man or a woman. But as we grow we must transcend the limits placed on us by these stereotypes. Toward this end, an awareness of the significance of these conventional roles is a first step toward transcending them.

Before our first breath is drawn, an essential part of our identity has already been established. A birth announcement that failed to say "It's a girl" or "It's a boy" would seem very incomplete to most people. Usually these are the first words that a doctor or nurse says to a new mother and a worried father. This sentence transforms an "it" into a social being with the beginnings of an identity. The ritual announcement of the sex of the infant initiates a whole set of culturally defined responses which will invariably further shape the emerging identity.

Men and women are different, although exactly why they are different remains something of a mystery. The Bible says, "God created them male and female," and for some people this pronouncement has closed the question for good: men and women are different because they are born that way and that's all there is to it.[1]

Our sense of the nature of these differences goes into the classification of characteristics we identify as masculine and feminine. Every word, every action, every nuance of behavior is affected by this elemental system of classification. When a mother says to her young son, "Little boys don't cry," she is telling him something very important about what it means to be a boy. When she says to him, "Little boys don't hit little girls," she is saying something to him about how men behave toward women. When a mother feels distressed about her daughter's desire to play baseball instead of playing with dolls, she communicates her sense of what constitutes the appropriate development of a woman. When a little girl is interrupted in a brawl with her brother and told, "Little girls shouldn't fight," she gets another clue as to how appropriate feminine behavior differs from appropriate masculine behavior. In all, it seems safe to say that no aspect of our bebehavior remains unaffected by these expectations of what is properly masculine and what is properly feminine.

As we grow up, these expectations become the "oughts" of our behavior. Generally speaking, we measure ourselves against these social standards, only rarely questioning their validity or appropriateness. Our feelings of self-worth and our comfort in relating to others depend in large part upon how we evaluate ourselves by these standards. And yet more and more people are coming to suspect that these standards are neither biologically determined nor socially necessary. In other places and at other times in history radically different understandings of mas-

[1]Genesis 1:27.

196

culinity and femininity have been in effect. The discovery that masculinity and femininity are not unalterable characteristics of human nature frees us to enter into the process of changing them to better meet our needs today.

Our Common Understandings

The process of changing our common understandings of appropriate sex role behavior is very complex. In contemporary American society much of the impetus for change comes from the women's liberation movement, which is at present leading the call for radical changes in how men and women are treated. This call is a plea for a redefinition of what it means to be a woman and a man. To better understand why such changes are felt to be necessary, let us look at our common expectations about masculine and feminine behavior.

It's a Boy! Both men and women in our society tend to have very strong expectations of what it means to be a man. Masculinity means aggressiveness, self-assertion, roughness of manner, fearlessness, adventurousness, rationality, and the ability to control one's emotions. In multimedia advertisements, men are shown in the great outdoors, engaging in dangerous sports, fighting against nature, enduring physically strenuous activities, and winning out. They are interested in tools and have highly developed mechanical skills. They are oriented toward rational pursuits such as the sciences, mathematics, and engineering. They are competitive beings—in sports, in business, and in every endeavor they engage

197

in. Finally, men are task-oriented and see their worth in the world in terms of what they can produce.

Men generally accept these expectations and try to fulfill them. They are encouraged to do so by the people around them, who tend to reward them for becoming more "masculine" and to punish them for failing to develop in this direction. Because men are supposed to be rational, achievement-oriented, and competitive, for example, they are urged to become professionals. As a result men dominate the professions, and their position of dominance gives them the power to encourage other males to follow this path and to discourage females who are foolhardy enough to try.[2] Thus men are seven and a half times more likely than women to hold doctorates and twice as likely to have masters' degrees.[3] In this way the common understanding of what masculinity means not only shapes the personal lives of individuals but also produces the conditions that secure the perpetuation of the stereotype.

The extent to which stereotypes permeate our culture is reflected in the responses men and women give in personality testing. Men score higher than women in such traits as dominance, suspiciousness, sophistication, experimentation, and self-sufficiency.[4] The fact that the majority of men develop in conformity with the stereotype—this is what gives the stereotype both its validity and its force—tends to make life difficult for those who do not match the standard picture. Thus the man who finds pleasure, excitement, and fulfillment in artistic endeavors may find it difficult to gain acceptance among a wide variety of persons who assume that he is not "masculine" enough. In his formative years he will have to deal with his parents and his peers, who are confused and troubled by his interest in the arts. He may even begin to wonder if there is something wrong with him, because all the cues that he receives say that he is not behaving in the prescribed manner. If he persists in following his own unique line of development, he is likely to run into problems with women, who also may assume that a man who prefers painting to football is not adequately "manly."

To be sure, the situation is not as simple as this picture may suggest. Numerous exceptions come to mind. Poets like Dylan Thomas succeed in being accepted as "masculine" in spite of their poetry because Irishmen are supposed to be somewhat romantic and, besides, he was a notoriously hard drinker and barroom brawler. Sports such as gymnastics place a high value on both strength and gracefully coordinated body movement. Male gymnasts thus gain recognition by mixing what are commonly thought to be masculine and feminine traits.

[2]U.S. Bureau of the Census, *Statistical Abstract: 1973* (Washington, D.C.: U.S. Government Printing Office, 1973), pp. 235–39.

[3]Richard J. Udry, *The Social Context of Marriage*, 2nd ed. (Philadelphia: J. B. Lippincott Co., 1971), p. 33.

[4]Udry, *The Social Context of Marriage*, p. 34.

These exceptions, though, only reinforce the general principle that for a man success in interpersonal relations—including both sexual relations and business relations—often depends on conformity to the sex role stereotype. What is more, a process of natural selection is at work here: successful men tend to conform to their society's expectations; because of their success, they serve as role models to encourage the next generation to conform; and so on. In short, stereotypes work as a sort of vicious circle: the more people conform to them, the more power they have to enforce conformity; and the more power they have, the more people conform.

Fortunately, the strength of a vicious circle is also its weakness, for once a stereotype starts to crumble, the process of collapse is self-accelerating. For example, if you are the only boy in your high school who likes reading Shakespeare, you are likely to keep quiet about it. If a few others join you, it becomes less necessary to hide this "unmanly" taste, and each successive defection from the conventional role makes it that much easier for the next boy to break rank. Indeed, precisely this process seems to be in operation in America today, largely under the urging of women's liberationists, who have been insisting on the absurdity of our sex role stereotypes. Whereas twenty years ago most men would have been afraid to be seen doing the family wash in the laundromat, today the number of men willing to undertake a fair share of the household chores is increasing, and as it becomes apparent to more and more men that doing a load of wash does not cost a man his virility, the stereotypical belief that such tasks are "women's work" will become harder to maintain.

It's a Girl! Unfortunately, our stereotypes of women are little more than the opposite of our stereotypes of men. This limitation to some degree reveals our lack of appreciation of maleness and femaleness, for, ideally, we should be able to describe what the two sexes are like without feeling compelled to hold the one over against the other.

Our common conception of femininity is that women are compassionate, sympathetic, tender, fastidious, aesthetic, emotionally sensitive, passive, and things of beauty. They are in touch with their emotions and are permitted, even urged, to express them. (Of course, they are then told that they are too "emotional" to hold most of the important jobs.) Their areas of skill reside in sociability, popularity, and attractiveness; they are most interested in domestic affairs. Paradoxically, unattractive women sometimes find it easier to enter the competitive "man's world" of business and professional life. Men can easily cope with the fact that a "plain" girl might want to enroll in MIT to become an engineer: they assume she is "compensating" for her inability to succeed as a woman. But when a pretty young woman makes this decision, men feel threatened by it and are at a loss to explain it: "Why should a lovely young thing like you want to be an engineer? You could have any man you wanted!"

Our common conception of women pictures them as homemakers, helpmates, mothers, and adornments to the household. If a woman does have an interest outside of the home, it is assumed that she will be engaged in the helping professions—caring for the young, the helpless, the aged, and the infirm. As far as sex is concerned, it is often assumed that women do not know much about it and are not particularly interested in it. They are expected to come to marriage as virgins and to participate in sex at the behest of the male.[5] In sex as in everything else, the woman's role is to be long-suffering, patient, and supportive of the goals established by her husband.

As we have seen in the case of the stereotypic understanding of masculinity, there is evidence to suggest that the same kind of self-fulfilling prophecy is at work in the case of femininity. Thus on personality factor tests women score higher than men in outgoingness, sensitivity, conscientiousness, eccentricity, and excitability.

Census data indicate that 42 percent of all married women who live with their husbands work.[6] On the surface this would seem to indicate that a major portion of women are career-oriented.[7] In fact, however, most of these women work in order to assist their husbands in providing for their families. Rather than breaking the stereotype, they are simply extending their maintenance function, normally exercised within the family, to outside the home. They work in service or clerical jobs rather than in the professions. Those who had appropriate training before marriage are likely to work in teaching, nursing, or social work—occupations that are simply extensions of the commonly prescribed female role.

There is no denying that women are, in effect, forced to spend the majority of their time taking care of their families. A thoughtless response would be to say they are doing this because they are naturally more dependent, compassionate, sensitive, and concerned about people. This simply is not true. Women tend to be weak on the "masculine" traits because any signs of competitiveness, rationality, and so forth are discouraged. A woman who is intelligent, competent, attractive, and achievement-oriented will find these qualities to be a liability rather than an asset. She will have to deal with the misgivings of her friends and acquaintances. If she chooses to exploit these qualities, she may have to do so with little help from personally known models. She can

---

[5]This component of the stereotype is rapidly changing, especially for college educated women. See Chapter 5 for further elaboration. Such a stereotype best fits working-class women today.

[6]*Statistical Abstract: 1973*, p. 223.

[7]Children's Bureau, *Youth in America* (Washington, D.C.: U.S. Government Printing Office, 1968).

Joel Gordon

emulate famous women, but will likely find very few personal friends who can share her interests and her understanding of what it means to be a woman. Breaking the stereotype and becoming a unique person can be costly when the people around you accept the stereotype without question. A woman who attempts to do so may have a particularly difficult problem finding a man who can accept her for the intelligent, competitive, achievement-oriented person she is.

Our Introduction to Sex Roles

We are introduced to sex roles from the moment we breathe our first breath. In most instances, the primary group in which this learning takes place is the family. The amount of time, the amount of energy, and the amount of interaction that takes place between a mother and child, or a father and child, constitutes the child's basic learning experience. From a very early age, a young girl has her mother as the model of femininity. Normally she will spend long periods of time with her mother in intimate situations. Eventually, the passive dependent role she is expected to play as a wife is not too different from her early childhood experiences, for it duplicates not only her mother's role as her father's wife but also her own role as a dependent member of the family.

Men become masculinized in quite a different way. Because fathers are apt to be absent from the family for considerable amounts of time, boys are often influenced by images of masculinity presented in the mass media or by peers.[8] What is more, whereas girls experience "femininity" (passive dependency) as something they have always had, boys have to achieve a masculine identity. A boy has to break away from his dependency upon his mother and live into such masculine characteristics as aggressiveness, independence, and self-assertiveness.

By the age of three, boys and girls in our society know the appropriate selection of toys for their sex.[9] They also can classify adult items as appropriate to one sex or the other. By the age of six to eight years, children can tell us about their concept of what is masculine or feminine. Boys are seen as stronger, larger, darker, dirtier, more angular, and more dangerous than girls. These early images are consistent with our adult images of masculinity and femininity. The fact that these stereotypes appear so early helps to convince us that they are natural. In fact, however, there is no biological inevitability that turns an infant with a penis into an aggressive, self-assertive, and independent adult while an infant with a vulva remains permanently in a state of relative passive dependency.

THE SOCIAL SHAPING OF APPROPRIATE SEXUAL BEHAVIOR

The awareness of sexual attraction arises in different contexts for men and women and is expressed in different ways. Among males there is an emphasis on doing things together, apart from females, and so men tend to learn about sex from their peers to a greater extent than do women. As boys get older, there is increasing interest in the techniques of sexual seduction and sex play.[10] Girls are interested in sex also, but

[8]Udry, *The Social Context of Marriage*, p. 67.
[9]Meyer Rabban, "Sex Role Identification in Young Children in Two Diverse Local Groups," *Genetic Psychology Monograph* 42 (1950), pp. 81–158.
[10]Winston Ehrman, "Premarital Dating Behavior," in Harold Christensen, ed., *The Marriage Handbook* (Chicago: Rand McNally, 1967), p. 339.

their conversation most frequently centers around the problems raised by the sexual advances of their boyfriends in dating situations, the threat of public exposure, expressed regret for sexual transgressions, or the justification of sexual activities as an expression of love, whereas the conversation among boys tends to be in terms of boastful accounts of sexual conquests.[11] The conversation among girls, therefore, tends to reinforce a romantic view of sex, while the boys encourage each other to see sex as a competitive game.

These basic differences in our approach to sexual response arise quite "naturally" out of the experiences that we have with other people. Men act out their sexuality in terms of personal gratification and conquest. Sex becomes, for them, a further means of proving their masculinity. Women discover their sexual responsiveness in the context of a romantic relationship. Because of the difference between these two approaches to sexual attraction, there is considerable likelihood of conflict and misunderstanding. As Richard Udry observes:

Sex emerges as something which boys "do to" girls, which girls "let them have" or which boys cheat girls out of. Accounts of boys' early coital experience with girls show the boys have been unconcerned with and largely unaware of the girls' own behavior. . . . It is sexual conquest.[12]

The Double Standard

The differing sexual attitudes just described serve to reinforce and fortify the traditional "double standard" code of sexual behavior. This "double standard"—in which men are expected to be sexually competent and experienced while women are not—governs a great deal of our understanding of appropriate sexual behavior today. Not only does it create problems between the sexes, but it also encourages self-deception. This was dramatically illustrated by a group of college students who were asked to respond to the question, "What do boys and girls talk about with their own sex under the traditional double standard?"

The girls said in effect, "In an all-girls group under the traditional double standard, no girl has ever had intercourse—each only knows of friends who have had. Or, if perchance some girl is known to have experienced intercourse, she needs to make it appear that it happened only once, she was practically forced into it,

[11]Ehrman, "Premarital Dating Behavior," p. 340. See also Donald L. Grummon and Andrew M. Barclay, eds., *Sexuality: A Search for Perspective* (New York: Van Nostrand, 1971), p. 76.

[12]Udry, *The Social Context of Marriage*, p. 78. The account discussed comes from Lester Kirkendall, *Premarital Intercourse in Interpersonal Relationships* (New York: An Angora Publication, 1971).

she didn't enjoy it and she would never do it again." The boys reported, amidst gales of laughter, "In an all-male group, under the traditional double standard, whether a boy has had intercourse or not, he needs to make it appear that he has had, that he enjoyed it tremendously, he is very proficient in his techniques, and all other boys should be seeking similar experiences."

As the groups stood up to leave, one of the girls put her finger squarely on the problem. In a reflective mood she turned to the group and asked, "Well, is it any wonder that we get into trouble with one another over sex? It appears that we can't even be honest with ourselves, to say nothing of being honest with one another."[13]

It is very difficult to establish meaningful relationships under this double standard, largely because the objectives for the male and female are different. What is more, the requirement that the man live up to certain norms of competence is likely to be a source of continual anxiety for him. Conversely, the woman's need to repress sexual feelings and repudiate any enjoyable sexual experience surely handicaps her in developing her own sexual response.

One of the most destructive aspects of the double standard is the fact that it puts both participants in an exploitative relationship with their mates. The code obviously contains an inherent contradiction in that it expects men to have intercourse with women and women not to have intercourse with men. This contradiction usually is resolved by the male's distinguishing between girls he will date and girls he will marry. A young man would not want to perpetuate a dating relationship with a woman with whom he did not have sexual relations, but on the other hand, when he feels he is ready to marry, he will look for a partner who has not disqualified herself by losing her virginity. One often hears boys say that they cannot respect a girl who does not "save herself" for marriage; on the other hand, they would not enjoy themselves with girls who do.

The double standard presents especially difficult problems for women. A girl is aware that boys will lose interest in her if she perpetually rejects sexual advances, yet she is also aware that by surrendering to her boyfriend's sexual advances she is creating a situation in which he will abandon the relationship when he is ready to look for a "suitable" marital partner. A girl thus seeks all the assurance she can get that the boy is "serious" about her, is "in love" with her, and considers their joint sexual activity as a down payment on a future marital relationship. And the boy lies to her eagerly, thankful for the opportunity to "take

[13]From Lester Kirkendall, "Sex and Human Wholeness," p. 283, in *Sexuality: A Search for Perspective* edited by D. Grummon and A. Barclay © 1971. Reprinted by permission of D. Van Nostrand Company.

what he can get," and all the while thinking that a girl who can be misled so easily is not anyone he would want to marry.

This may be a somewhat overdrawn picture of sexual relations under the double standard, but it is no exaggeration to say that the double standard, in its extreme forms, can be quite vicious. Even in its milder forms it is degrading to all concerned, encouraging dishonesty, hypocrisy, and a generally exploitative relationship between the sexes. Nevertheless, it is probably still the most common sexual code to be found in America today.

There are signs that this situation is changing, and it seems safe to say that the number of young people who can deal with their sexuality honestly is on the increase. Thus, to cite just one indication of this change, there is a dramatic increase in the number of coeds who are engaging in premarital sexual intercourse.[14] Presumably this indicates an increasing confidence that they will be able to find men who do not consider their sexual experience a disqualification for marriage. In some circles the double standard is being replaced by a "permissiveness with affection" sexual code, according to which it is acceptable for girls as well as boys to engage in sexual intercourse in the context of caring relationships.[15]

What About A Sex Drive?

Most people assume that there is such a thing as a sex drive, and most studies of sexual response have proceeded on this assumption. Recent research, however, calls this view into question. The sex drive, some researchers suggest, is "a theoretical invention." They contend that an individual's interest in sex, as well as his or her sexual behavior, comes from learning in the family and other social contexts. In contrast to a drive such as hunger, which can be traced to an internal bodily condition of lack of food, sexual interest seems to have little to do with any internal bodily conditions; rather, it is dependent upon external rewards and punishments.[16]

We all know that some physiological drives are more susceptible to

---

[14]See Chapter 5.

[15]Ira Reiss, *The Social Context of Premarital Sexual Permissiveness* (New York: Holt, Rinehart, & Winston, 1967). See also Lester Kirkendall, "The Key to the Sexual Rennaissance," *Journal of Marriage and the Family* (April 1966), p. 45; and Ira Reiss, "Premarital Sex Codes: The Old and the New," in Grummon and Barclay, *Sexuality*, p. 192.

[16]William Simon and John H. Gagnon, "On Psychosexual Development," in Grummon and Barclay, *Sexuality*, p. 74.

training than others. Some people get hungry and must eat every four or five hours while others train themselves to live on one or two nourishing meals a day and never get hungry between meals. The need for air, in contrast, is less modifiable; one can train oneself to do without it for no more than a minute or two. So the fact that the need for sex varies greatly between individuals does not in and of itself suggest that this is not a genuine physiological drive. But the extent of the variability does raise doubts about the status of sex as a natural drive. We cannot imagine a man dining regularly for a week and then going two months without eating anything at all; and we cannot imagine people living their entire lives without ever eating. Yet this is the range of variation we find in sexual behavior, and it is difficult to square such extreme variability with the notion of a sex drive.

Furthermore, if there is such a thing as a sex drive, we have not yet learned how to reinforce it. We have not yet discovered the aphrodisiac that will intensify the sexual drive, if there is one. As Katchadourian and Lunde note, "The search for substances that may increase the sexual drive or potency is as old and, so far, as unsuccessful as man's search for the fountain of youth."[17] Alcohol and marijuana, which some think of as aphrodisiacs, are truly not. They may affect sexual performance by releasing inhibitions, but they do not directly affect sexual desire. The most effective stimulant of sexual arousal for men seems to be a sexually aroused woman—and vice verse. But even this is not always effective.

Some Practical Implications

Contemporary sex research enables us to know more about ourselves as sexual beings than was ever before possible. It also provides forms of therapy that have only recently become available. A man and a woman who have questions about what really happens to them in their sexual encounters can come to better understand themselves as sexual beings in any one of a number of sex clinics. Couples who find that their degree of interest in sex differs greatly can get help in most instances. Many couples have a reasonable chance of becoming better matched sexually by freeing themselves from various of the myths that surround human sexual response.

The findings of the sex researchers have clear social implications for developing relationships. Young people learn about their own sexuality

[17]Herant A. Katchadourian and Donald T. Lunde, *Fundamentals of Human Sexuality* (New York: Holt, Rinehart & Winston, 1972), p. 97.

in heterosexual relationship before marriage. If Masters and Johnson's findings about women's sexual capacity and its repression under the double standard are correct, and if indeed we value sexuality and what it can bring to our relationships, then the destructive aspects of the double standard must be overcome. This means at the very least that women must have the same freedom to develop their sexuality as men. Indeed, all persons should have the freedom to adhere to the sexual code that seems to fit best their developing sexuality as they understand it.[18] Freedom such as this depends upon an informed awareness of the costs, the promises, and the risks of any choice that is made.

Some Class Variations in Sexual Behavior

A class is a large number of people who have roughly the same family income, who experience roughly similar economic and social opportunities, and who tend to share a similar style of life. Just as there are similarities in the way members of any one class dress or eat or spend their money, so also are there similarities in their sexual behavior. And by the same token there are differences between classes in sexual attitudes and tastes. Indeed, the most significant sexual variations in our society are to be found between social classes.

Researchers have indicated that the American middle class is decidedly limited in its ability to experience sexual satisfaction and enjoyment. Yet middle-class Americans seem to fare much better in this regard than do members of the lower class. This is in part because of a very different style of sexual behavior which is considered appropriate in the lower classes. Sherwin and Keller describe some of these differences as follows:

Upper level young people are much less sexually active but pet more. They tend to reserve sex for someone for whom they feel affection. Their sexual play usually has more prolonged foreplay, a greater readiness to use a variety of coital positions and a higher incidence of oral-genital contact. The males tend to treat women more as equals, and women tend to take a more active role, with the result that females at this level have a greater number of sexual postponements, masturbation is higher; college men masturbate about twice as often as those with only a grade school education. Persons at this upper level, though, have a low incidence of homosexuality. For the upper socioeducational group, sexual activity is less frequent but more variegated, more artful.

[18]There are a number of very thorough books about the ethics of sexual behavior. Among the best are Rustum and Della Roy, *Honest Sex* (New York: New America Library, 1968); Frederick C. Wood, *Sex and the New Morality* (New York: The Association Press, 1967); John Charles Wynn, ed., *Sexual Ethics and Christian Responsibility: Some Divergent Views* (New York: The Association Press, 1970).

Persons at the lower socioeducational levels have a radically different style. The frequency of male premarital sex is much higher; nearly one-half of the boys who do not go to college have intercourse by the age of fifteen. Many fewer females participate but those who do, do so with greater frequency. Persons at the lower level, especially the males, tend not to see sex as having a close relationship with affection or love. They are usually impatient with mere petting. Among this group, sexual play has greater simplicity and directness; there is less foreplay, less variety, greater speed. It tends to be male-oriented, and women at this level expect fewer orgasms and less emotional satisfaction. Masturbation is lower but homosexuality, especially among high school graduates without college educations, is higher. At the lower socioeducational level, sex is more frequent, more restricted in formal maneuver, and more slam-bang in approach.[19]

The working class still adheres more strongly to the double standard than does the middle or lower-lower class. The separation of the activities of the sexes is common in the working class and serves to support the double standard. Men typically do things with other men and a strong distinction is made between the woman's world and the man's. This distinction includes the separation of work patterns, leisure activities, decision-making roles, and friends. This kind of life style is technically described as "role segregation."[20] In societies where role segregation is pronounced, couples will tend not to develop close sexual relationships and women will not typically look upon sexual relations as gratifying. For the woman, sexual relations in this setting often become a symbol of stability in the relationship, but rarely a source of personal pleasure.[21] Sex is man's pleasure and woman's duty in such cultures. Thus men are allowed to have extramarital affairs but there are strong sanctions on women if they do.

Studies of the lower classes suggest that the interrelationship between enjoyment of sex and the public patterns of people's lives is significant. In looking at the lack of sexual gratification for women in highly segregated role relationships, we come to understand that the ability to participate in a gratifying sexual relationship depends to a considerable extent on the sharing of intimacies in other aspects of each other's lives.[22]

[19]Robert Veit Sherwin and George Keller, "Sex on the Campus," *Columbia College Today*, 15 (Fall 1967).

[20]Elizabeth Bott, *Family and Social Network: Role, Norm and External Relationships in Ordinary Urban Families* (London: Tavistock Publications, 1957).

[21]See a discussion of role segregation and attitudes toward marital sexual relations in Lee Rainwater, "Sex in the Culture of Poverty," in Carlfred Broderick and Jessie Bernard, eds., *The Individual, Sex, and Society* (Baltimore: The Johns Hopkins Press, 1969), pp. 130–40.

[22]See the discussion in Lee Rainwater, *Family Design* (Chicago: Aldine, 1965), pp. 71ff.

SUMMARY:
TOWARD
GREATER
FLEXIBILITY

Sex roles, we know from experience, describe much of what we know about masculinity and femininity. The concept of sex roles, however, is misused when it is taken to mean not merely a reasonable description of what is, but an assertion about what ought to be. In their quest to find general social laws, social scientists are apt to be quite conservative in their attitude toward change and quite insensitive to human needs. Others in the field are genuinely disturbed by the conservative use to which sex role theory is put; they object to the conversion of descriptive material into general laws of social behavior.

The man who knows that there is more to existence for him than aggressive competitiveness may very well suffer from the application of sex role stereotypes. The woman who knows that there is much to be lost in passive dependency is faced with an uphill struggle against those who would enforce conformity to the stereotypes. Such people know that sex roles need not be the standards by which they measure themselves. Why, for example, should male children be socialized for independence and self-assertion while females are left in a passive dependent state? Other cultures, such as the Tchambuli, reverse this process. Tchambuli men are passive, dependent, sensitive, and artistic whiile Tchambuli women are aggressive, self-assertive and independent. Such cross-cultural data indicate that there is no one "natural" way to define masculinity and femininity. [23]

Some social scientists approach the study of sex roles by looking at their function.[24] They see, for example, that a woman is called on to keep the family living peacefully together. This means that her major role is to be the "expressive leader" in the household. The man is identified as the provider and the person who is primarily concerned with the economic well-being of the family. He is therefore described as the "instrumental leader" of the family. But the notion of instrumental and expressive leadership comes out of the study of small groups. Researchers have found that small groups that are able to accomplish the tasks for which they are established seem to need these two types of leadership roles. Social scientists assume, therefore, that the family also needs these two types of leadership roles. But the family is anything but a task-oriented small group. Even if these two roles were needed, it is unreasonable to assume that the roles should be assigned on the basis of sex within the family when they are not so assigned in small groups. Indeed, in small groups the two roles are not even mutually exclusive; not only can men be the expressive leaders and women the task leaders, but the same individual

[23]Margaret Mead, *Sex and Temperament* (New York: Mentor Books, 1952); *Male and Female* (New York: Mentor Books, 1955).
[24]Talcott Parson, Robert Bales, and Morris Zeldich, *Family Socialization: An Interaction Process* (Glencoe, Ill.: The Free Press, 1955).

can serve in both capacities or change roles within the course of a group's life. We need this same kind of flexibility within the family.

What seems to be happening today is that men and women *are* seeking greater flexibility in their sex roles. Sometimes this flexibility arises out of the unique desire of an individual simply to be different. Sometimes it emerges out of necessity, as when it is imposed by divorce or death in the family. Sometimes it emerges out of a conscious desire for growth. There are often unanticipated benefits as well as costs from this greater flexibility, as the following account reveals:

In the steep, stony hills south of Los Angeles, Mike McFadden, a 34 year old free-lance writer, has been mothering his three young children for eighteen months. Not surprisingly, the vine-covered house of a morning is mayhem. Tiny, insistent storm-trooper feet stomp overhead before sunrise, heralding another dizzying day of bachelor fatherhood. Cats howl, noses need wiping, dresses need buttoning, tangled hair needs brushing. There are quarrels to mediate and hurt feelings to cuddle. But Mike McFadden minds neither the racket nor the incessant demands. "I get a lot more fun out of being with my kids than with most of the people I used to go out to business lunches with every day when I worked in an office," he insists.[25]

His wife also experienced some benefits from this "role reversal":

Although moving out to a nearby rented room in Laguna Beach was "amazingly simple" for Nancy, the self-accusations were harder to bear. She continued to see her children regularly, taking time off from her new ceramics business. "But I felt strange and bad. Then I realized I was seeing them out of guilt, just like I'd been living with them all those years out of guilt. It astounded me when I discovered I wasn't all that attached to them. At first they were angry and cut me off. That hurt. But when I became more positive, their attitudes changed. Now I'm kind of doing what men do. The children are no longer a major part of my life, in terms of the time I spend with them. But I feel the quality of my relationship with them is better."[26]

Mike and Nancy discovered their flexibility and adaptability after divorce. This need not and should not be the only way in which men and women discover such flexibility. The wish of psychologist Sidney Callahan seems to summarize the feelings of many people today:

Despite his biological limits, man being the free species should try to cultivate growing beyond polarity. Thus, I would wish for men to develop sensitivity, intuitiveness, personal concerns, cultural creativity, all of the things that have been

[25]*Newsweek*, March 12, 1973, p. 48. Copyright Newsweek, Inc. 1973, reprinted by permission.
[26]*Newsweek*, March 12, 1973, p. 48. Copyright Newsweek, Inc. 1973, reprinted by permission.

suspiciously labeled feminine. And I wish for women to develop more initiative, more aggression, more reponsibility for the wider world.[27]

This wish does not simply reflect a desire for changes in behavior; more importantly, it is a plea for wholeness. The fact of the matter is, men *are* capable of being sensitive, intuitive, creative, and women *can* assume more initiative, become more aggressive, assume more responsibility for the wider world. To have these capacities lie dormant in any individual is a waste. To the extent that the sex roles are the creator of this waste, they should be radically altered.

[27]From Sidney Callahan, "The Emancipation of Women and the Sexual Revolution," p. 214, in *Sexuality: A Search for Perspective* edited by D. Grummon and A. Barclay © 1971. Reprinted by permission of D. Van Nostrand Company.

PART THREE

THREE

MARRIAGE

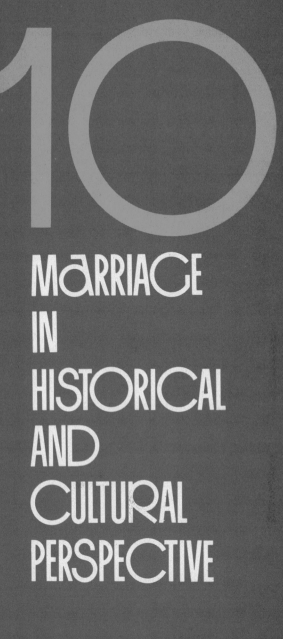

10

MARRIAGE IN HISTORICAL AND CULTURAL PERSPECTIVE

Romantic love as it occurs in our civilization, inextricably bound up with ideas of monogamy, exclusiveness, jealousy, and undeviating fidelity, . . . is a compound, the final result of many converging lines of development in Western Civilization, of the institution of monogamy, of the ideas of the age of chivalry, of the ethics of Christianity.

Margaret Mead

INTRODUCTION

Giovanni Arnolfini and His Wife by Jan van Eyck depicts an ideal marriage of early fifteenth-century Europe. The young couple is exchanging vows in their bridal chamber surrounded by symbols signifying the sacredness of marriage. The bridegroom has removed his shoes because he stands on holy ground. The little dog is a symbol of faithfulness; the single candle signifies Christ who is an all-seeing guest.

What strikes the modern eye first, however, is the bride's protruding abdomen suggesting pregnancy. The idea that a marriage is not truly consummated until the wife has conceived is more appropriate to the fifteenth century. Today sterility may be grounds for divorce in some states and married couples are expected to have children, but even so, we do not find it appropriate that a bride should come to her wedding so great with child.

In this chapter we will trace the evolution of the concept of love in our Western tradition from the time of the Greeks until the present.[1] The purpose of our investigation is to understand how we have come to think about love the way we do. The relationship between love and sexual desire has been interpreted differently at different times in our history, but generally people have put a much higher evaluation on love than on sex. Until quite recently, the institution of marriage was the only arena in which sexual relations were permitted. Nevertheless, as we shall see in our historical survey, love in its various forms always has transcended institutional limitations, so that even while Western culture has largely striven to contain sexual love within the institutional setting of marriage, attitudes toward other forms of love provide a rich heritage which can deepen our understanding of the ways in which people relate to one another, communicate with one another, and share their life experiences.

Although love has meant many different things in different times and places, what we commonly regard as its richest and most complete expression is to be found in sexual love. In the Western tradition, sexual love has meant mostly married love, and so a large part of our historical and cultural survey will be devoted to an examination of the institution of marriage. First we will look at marriage as a system of ideas, examining it in terms of the attitudes and ideals of marriage that are widely held in our culture and that shape the actual experiences of individual married men and women. Then we will turn to that experience itself, in an attempt to gain some understanding of the evolving reality of marriage in America today.

[1] In this investigation we are particularly indebted to Morton M. Hunt, *The Natural History of Love* (New York: Alfred A. Knopf, 1959), and Alan W. Watts, *Nature Man and Woman* (New York: Pantheon Books, Inc., 1958).

LOVE AND SEXUALITY IN WESTERN EXPERIENCE: THE HISTORICAL PERSPECTIVE

During the third century A.D., a lovely and talented lecturer in philosophy at the Alexandrian Museum, a virgin named Hypatia, expressed what was in her day a prevalent attitude toward sexuality. When one of her students professed his passionate love for her, she hoisted her dress above her waist and exclaimed contemptuously, "This, young man, is what you are in love with, and not anything beautiful."[2]

Her words and actions give evidence of the influence of Christian thinking, for by the third century the Christian conception of love had developed strong overtones of asceticism and antifeminism. Celibacy was being widely proclaimed as superior to marriage. Thus Ammon, a young man of Alexandria, was so strongly influenced by the teachings of Saint Paul that he decided to remain chaste in order to lead a more perfect life. When he was forced into marriage by his father, he promptly persuaded his bride that they should purify their marriage by jointly taking vows of celibacy. They lived a life of rigorous sexual denial without ever consummating their marriage. The fame of Ammon and his wife spread throughout the land and monks came to live near their separated huts in the desert in order to bask in the radiance of their purity.

During the same period many clergy chose to demonstrate their devotion to chastity and spiritual love by sleeping with naked virgins who, according to the record, in most cases remained virgins. It is difficult

[2] *The Natural History of Love*, p. 102.

today to understand what these priests were trying to demonstrate. In blatant contrast to the practice of earlier societies, where "vestal virgins" —that is, temple prostitutes—provided a means of worship through sexual intercourse, the virgins in this case, who were known as *Agapetae* —spiritual sisters or spiritual wives—provided a means of worship through sexual denial. They were dramatically portraying the tearing apart of sexuality from spirituality.

Of course, this antisexual bias is just one of the many images of love that have guided attitudes toward loving and lovemaking in the history of Western civilization. For contrast, consider the following quite different picture that appeared seventeen centuries later in a work of fiction by an American novelist:

And as they remembered, Angela and Adam, lost in each other's flesh, acted out the unceasing cosmic life drama. Slowly awakening to each other's touch, and responding to the amazing, panting wonder of being each other, they made love with a joyous laughing surrender that would dance in their heads for hours. And then lying in his arms, because their love had no before or afterwards but was continuous, Angela was partially aware that her charm for Adam was her own subconscious necessity to sway on the windseeds of his ideas, not losing her own roots as a person, but coming alive and blossoming for him and herself because neither of them alone could provide the cross-fertilization.[3]

Between these two extremes—on the one hand Ammon's view of sexual love as an evil from which one must purge oneself in order to enjoy spiritual love, and on the other hand the contemporary novelist's view of the intimate linking between spiritual and sexual expressions of love —lie all the various conceptions of love that have dominated the thinking of Western men and women.

The New Testament Tradition

We need not be surprised that Ammon and Hypatia regarded sexuality in the negative way just described. The Christian conception of love has been inordinately influenced by unmarried men. Jesus and Paul are prime examples. Although scholars have been able to uncover interesting information about the sexual adventures and misadventures of the church fathers and the celibate clergy and theologians who followed them, the historical record concerning the sexual behavior of these two men is completely blank. What is more, we know very little about their attitudes toward sexuality. To be sure, they did speak about love, but the love that they proclaimed as an ideal was the love that is generally described by the Greek term *agape*, meaning "God's love for man, or spontaneous altruistic love."[4] Christianity took this term from Plato, for

[3]Robert H. Rimmer, *Thursday My Love* (New York: Signet Books, 1972), p. 257.
[4]*Webster's New World Dictionary of the American Language, 2nd College Edition*

whom it meant the kind of love that is directed toward the eternal forms, or ideas, and centered it in the person of Jesus, the Christ, and in the life of the community that arose in response to him. Agapetic love is expressed as a kind of openness to all people, as a kind of joy or warmth. But it is decidedly not sexual. As experienced between men and men—or between women and women—it is the sort of love we associate with the concept of brotherhood or sisterhood. As experienced between men and women, it corresponds to what we commonly call "Platonic love."

There has been a tendency in Western religious thinking to look at the New Testament as a book about ethical teachings.[5] To a considerable extent this view does not correspond to the intention of its authors, who were more interested in proclaiming the "Good News" of Christ's coming and in inviting their hearers and readers to a new fullness of life, than they were in offering ethical instruction. Of course, the New Testament does contain numerous prescriptions or ethical teachings, particularly in the epistles of Saint Paul. These teachings, however, were colored by Paul's belief that the world was going to come to an end very soon—probably before he died. His basic advice, therefore, was to prepare for the end. This is the context of such Pauline statements as "To the unmarried and the widows I say that it is well for them to remain single as I do. But if they cannot exercise self-control, they should marry. For it is better to marry than to be aflame with passion."[6] The negative attitude toward heterosexual partnerships implicit in this statement may be traceable to the fact that Paul did not have a sense of time in this world in which to work things out. But the statement does not indicate that Paul would have looked with favor on Ammon and his

---

(New York: The World Publishing Company, 1970). The Greeks had another word for love in addition to *agape*. This was *eros*. We retain something like the Greek concept of *eros*, of course, in our notion of erotic love, except that for Greek men the most desirable object of erotic love was a young man. Plato's *Symposium* is thus a hymn to homosexual love.

[5]There are, of course, many understandings about what the Bible really is. As the authors see it, the Bible is a book written by many people over almost fourteen centuries of human history. It is a changing account of their encounter with their God and reflects numerous understandings about what that encounter meant. The New Testament, written over a period of about two hundred years, tells how this understanding was dramatically changed by the man Jesus of Nazareth, whom the Apostles called "The Christ." The Apostles and those who followed them saw that Jesus proclaimed the good news, "I have come that ye shall have life and have it more abundantly." Exciting interpretations of what this good news can mean to modern men are found in such books as: Paul Tillich, *The Shaking of the Foundation* (New York: Charles Scribner's Sons, 1948), and *The Courage To Be* (New Haven: Yale University Press, 1952); Joseph Fletcher, *Situation Ethics: The New Morality* (Philadelphia: The Westminster Press, 1966); and John Robinson, *Honest to God* (Philadelphia: The Westminster Press, 1963).

[6]I Corinthians 7:8–9.

wife, who married but chose to remain chaste, for their approach placed excessive and unnatural demands on the continence of even the devout. Indeed, a view like Ammon's could seem credible as a response to Paul's teachings only because Ammon lived three centuries after Paul and thus did not see his teachings about chastity in the context of his view of the imminent end of the world.[7] Thus a teaching that was intended to reflect the priorities relevant to a time when the end of the world was at hand was distorted into an absolute proclamation of the desirability of chastity for all people at all times.

If the New Testament is read as a proclamation of the "Good News" that Jesus is indeed the Christ and his presence in this world manifests the love of God for His creatures, its statements about spiritual love (*agape*) take on a completely different meaning. Christianity in its essence is an incarnational religion, for its central doctrine is that God chose to become incarnate in the world: God so loved the world that he took on our flesh and dwelt among us. Paradoxically, this religion based on a doctrine of incarnation produced a group of followers who saw it as their duty to struggle to escape bondage to the flesh. Indeed, it is this struggle to escape from the flesh that has characterized Christianity for most of its history.

The theologians who have left their mark on Western thinking about love have been intellectuals and scholars. On the whole, they were heavily influenced by Aristotle and Plato, so that the Platonic sense of *agape* as a love of ideas has never really left our tradition. Thus the Greek conception of *agape* fused with the Christian understanding of the agapetic and asexual love of God and one's fellow human beings to produce the dominant elements in Western thinking about love.

Augustine

Saint Augustine, a fifth-century Catholic bishop, had an enormous influence on Christian thinking about love, sex, and the sins of the flesh. After a lusty youth in which he sired numerous offspring and cavorted about with apparent abandon, he converted to Christianity at the age of twenty-seven, was ordained a priest four years later, and was consecrated as a bishop four years after that. In *The City of God*, his major work, he made a distinction which has had immense consequences for fifteen centuries. The sinfulness in human sexual intercourse, Augustine argued, was not to be found in the act of procreating offspring. It was, rather, in the passion which had to accompany the act. In it, a man and

[7]The notion that Paul was writing an "interim ethic" did not emerge until the nineteenth century. It arose out of the scholarly practice of seeing the Bible as the product of its own time—a stance fostered by the development in Germany of a school of critics who developed methods for interpreting the Bible in historical terms.

a woman lost control of themselves for the moment and were thus fair game for the constantly vigilant Satan. This passion Augustine labeled "concupiscence." By confining concupiscence within the context of the sacrament of marriage, however, this danger could be overcome because it was now divinely directed toward a good end—procreation. To Augustine, marriage is far more than a social contract between two parties; rather, it is a divine sacrament necessary for transforming the sinful passion of concupiscence into a divinely sanctioned procreative act.

For Augustine, then, it was not so much sex itself as erotic passion that stood condemned. This becomes clear in the following passage, in which he fantasizes about the passionless nature of intercourse in Eden before the Fall:

Those members [genitals], like the rest, would be moved by the command of his will, and the husband would be mingled with the loins of his wife without the seductive stimulus of passion, with calmness of mind and with no corruption of the innocence of the body. . . . Because the wild heat of passion would not activate those parts of the body but, as would be proper, a voluntary control would employ them. Thus it would then have been possible to inject the semen into the womb through the female genitalia as innocently as the menstrual flow is now ejected.[8]

In this fantasy Augustine made clear a distinction which has had profound consequences for Western sexual thought: procreation is exalted as a necessary and divinely ordained duty, but sexual passion is a "corruption of the innocence of the body."

Aquinas

By the Middle Ages the Church had pushed Augustine's notion of marriage as a divine sacrament even further. Saint Thomas Aquinas (1225–1274) asserted that the sacramental nature of the marriage bond meant that a couple, once joined, could never be separated except by death. Thus the sacrament of "holy matrimony" indelibly establishes a relationship between those who enter into it. Derrick Bailey sums up Aquinas's contribution to Christian thought about marriage and sexuality as follows:

[Aquinas] lays down a triple standard for the moral evaluation of sexual acts: They must be done for the right *purpose*, with the right *person*, and in the right *way*. Since the purpose of the genital organs is generation, any exclusion of the possibility of conception is sinful—and this can occur (in ascending order of gravity) in masturbation, coition in a manner unnatural or unbecoming in human beings, bestiality and homosexuality. Less serious is coition with the wrong person, as in seduction or rape (when the woman is under her father's authority),

[8]Saint Augustine, *The City of God*, Book 16, Chapt. 26.

adultery (when she is under that of her husband) and incest—and in the first two instances an important element in the offense is the infringement of another man's rights. Simple fornication, without any infringement of another's rights is a venial transgression, unless a child is conceived, when the offense becomes one of those against nature (since the child will lack a father's care and will suffer the stigma of illegitimacy) and is correspondingly grave. Kisses, touches and caresses are only sinful if inspired by a wrong motive such as enjoyment of forbidden pleasure.[9]

Much of our understanding of traditional marriage comes directly from Saint Thomas Aquinas. For example, the widely held sentiment that sex is a legitimate activity as long as it occurs for the right purpose, with the right person, in the right way is a direct reflection of Aquinas's teachings; similarly, the belief that marriage is the proper context for sexual intercourse for the purpose of procreation derives from the teachings of both Augustine and Aquinas. But in the Roman Catholic tradition chastity was still much preferred to marriage for the devout.

The Reformation

When Martin Luther broke from the Roman Catholic Church, he enthusiastically embraced the idea of the "married state." Marriage is "God's gift to man, a heavenly and spiritual state, a school of faith in love in which every menial task, every trouble and hardship, is a means of religious education."[10] Although he still saw sexual intercourse as a troubling and vexing problem, a source of temptation that could lead man to forget the spiritual side of his nature, his thinking on marriage represents some sort of advance on the Church's traditional position in that he emphasizes the companionship between the partners as an important element in marriage.

John Calvin was more original in his view of marriage. For Calvin, sexual intercourse was holy, not unclean. Marriage was a high calling, the primary purpose of which was to fulfill needs for belonging and acceptance. It was important to Calvin that each adult person belong to a family, for families were the elemental building blocks from which the religious community was built. In this system, woman was ordained to be man's companion throughout the gamut of his experience, and her specific calling was motherhood.

The preceding discussion obviously cannot do justice to the richness of the New Testament tradition. We have only touched upon some of the central elements of the teachings of only a few of the prominent thinkers who have contributed to this tradition. Nevertheless, we can

[9]Derrick Sherwin Bailey, "Sexual Ethics in Christian Tradition," in John Charles Wynn, ed., *Sexual Ethics and Christian Responsibility* (New York: Association Press, 1970), p. 148.
[10]Bailey, "Sexual Ethics . . .," pp. 150–51.

make the following broad generalizations about the impact of this tradition upon our understanding of love, sex, and marriage:

1. Spiritual love (*agape*) is held up as the highest form of love. It is divinely given and is held to be superior to the love that men and women experience when they "make love" (erotic love).

2. Erotic love (*eros*) is rooted in our humanness. It arises out of our capacity to feel, to sense, to be filled with passion. Whereas spiritual love can and should be extended to all of mankind, erotic love should be confined to marriage.[11] In spite of its usefulness in the act of procreation, erotic love is often portrayed as self-seeking, for in it each person is seen as expressing merely his or her own passion.

3. The only acceptable context for erotic love is one's relationship with one's spouse. Implicit in this view is the belief that the erotic satisfactions that derive from erotic love should always be subordinate to the necessity to procreate. Thus all forms of sexual behavior that do not offer the possibility of procreation are condemned.

No one brought up in the Western tradition can escape being influenced by these ideas. Whether we can identify their source or not, whether we agree with them or not, they are a part of our heritage. They affect how we feel, behave, and think in partnerships, even if only to the extent that we find ourselves in conscious rebellion against them.

Romanticism

The Christian tradition is not the only cultural force that has played a role in shaping our understanding of love, sex, and marriage and the expectations that we bring to them. Other currents within our tradition also have made important contributions. Among the most powerful of these is romanticism. It began as an ethic governing courtly love among the nobility of southern France in the eleventh century, was spread by troubadors and poets, and finally became the ideal of the European middle classes.[12]

The essence of romanticism is the distinction between "true love" and "false love." In a curious echo of the Christian distinction between agapetic love, which is nonsexual, and erotic love, which is confined to

[11]It is interesting to speculate upon the fact that erotic love seems so much more exclusive (in contrast to the inclusiveness of *agape*) as a result of our cultural conditioning as to what is beautiful, appealing, attractive, and erotic. When *eros* becomes inclusive we think it unnatural or perverted. To simply rejoice in the pleasure of sensuous love with anyone who will go to bed with you runs counter to all of our understanding of love—and yet caring can occur even here.

[12]Hunt, *The Natural History of Love*, p. 131.

marriage, romantic theory held that true love is experienced with a lover and not with one's wife. True lovers could kiss, touch, fondle, even lie naked together, but they could not consummate their love. Should a lady give herself in sexual intercourse to her lover, she was no longer an appropriate object of his adoration. Thus, although the object of true romantic love was a member of the opposite sex, their love was supposed to be as asexual as agapetic love in the Christian tradition. What is more, sexual love was confined to marriage, as it was in Christian thinking, and was held to be inferior to nonsexual love.

This strange ethic may have arisen, in part, in response to the fact that marriage in the Middle Ages had come to be more or less of a business proposition. It involved land, loyalties, and the production of heirs and future defenders.[13] As Morton Hunt has written, "The average Renaissance husband looked upon his wife with eyes which appraised rather than adored."[14] Romantic love thus offered an alternative to the mundane relationship of marriage. Lovers fought with their rivals, performed many acts of bravery and self-sacrifice, and yearned mightily and publicly for their beloved, and the fact that the union could never be consummated only added to its appeal. Thus the rewards of courtly love were basically to be found in the suffering, striving, and yearning of an unrequited love.

Although the courtly love convention may seem somewhat bizarre to us, it introduced for the first time into the emotional relationships between men and women in the West many elements that are familiar today. As Hunt observes:

. . . it brought into them tenderness and gentleness, exaggerated and sometimes absurd in form, but important nevertheless. It operated within a framework of adultery, yet it stressed as never before the importance of the fidelity of one man and one woman each to each.[15]

The "good" woman in both the romantic and the Christian tradition was never thought of as passionate. Maryolatry—the worship of the Virgin Mary—for example gives us an essentially romantic view of women. Strangely enough, one of the few contexts in Western experience where women were portrayed as sexually alive and passionate was as witches. An ancient symbol of the witch was lecherous Eve, who stood opposite the Virgin Mary and was hotly condemned in Christian thinking. The reaction of revulsion and fear to this aroused feminine sexuality is dramatically presented in the *Mallus Malefarum*:

A woman is beautiful to look upon, contaminating to the touch and deadly to

---

[13] *The Natural History of Love*, p. 137.
[14] *The Natural History of Love*, p. 190.
[15] *The Natural History of Love*, p. 192. Copyright © 1959 by Morton M. Hunt.

keep . . . a foe to friendship . . . a necessary evil, a natural temptation . . . a do-mestic danger . . an evil of nature, painted with fair colors . . . a liar by nature. . . . [She] seethes with anger and impatience in her soul. . . . There is not wrath above the wrath of a woman. . . . Since [women] are feebler both in mind and body, it is not surprising that they should come under the spell of witchcraft [more than men]. . . . A woman is more carnal than a man. . . . All witchcraft comes from carnal lust which is in women unsatiable. . . . These women satisfy their filthy lusts not only in themselves but even in the mighty ones of the age, of whatever sort and condition, causing by all sorts of witchcraft, the death of their souls through the excessive infatuation of carnal love.[16]

The status of women in the Middle Ages was thus mixed. Women were idolized in romantic poetry as virgin lovers, but they were subordinated in their status as wives and vilified as lustful witches. In short, they were stripped of their humanness by the assignment of various aspects of their humanity to different roles. As we saw in our discussion of the "double standard" in Chapter 9, this sort of splitting of women's roles is still very much with us, although in a sense the roles have been reversed with the lover now seen as a sexual object and the wife as a paragon of purity. Thus, both in our attitude toward erotic love and in our beliefs about the status of women, the romantic tradition is still alive today.

LOVE AND SEXUALITY: THE CROSS-CULTURAL PERSPECTIVE

When we compare the traditional Western understanding of love, sex, and marriage to the beliefs and practices found in other parts of the world, it becomes clear how truly unique our views are. The word "love" is rarely found in the indexes of anthropological studies of primitive peoples. It plays a far less significant role in the affairs of other men and women than it is proclaimed to play in our own tradition. In many cultures personal attraction or individual preferences often are not taken into consideration in the selection of a mate—as we saw in the statement of the Japanese girl quoted in Chapter 5. Anthropologists have a difficult time identifying anything similar to what we call "love." Sexual relationships are evident everywhere and marriage—even monogamous marriage—is a widespread phenomenon common to many cultures, but analogues to the Western understanding of love are quite rare. Indeed, in many primitive societies love relationships between husband and wife are suppressed on the grounds that they tend to estrange the couple from their kin. Because kinship relationships are often the basis of the social order in primitive societies, any exclusive tie of the married couple to each other would have serious disruptive consequences for the entire society.

[16]*The Natural History of Love*, p. 177. Copyright © 1959 by Morton M. Hunt.

Thus sociologist William F. Goode points out that many societies have evolved elaborate institutional patterns in order to control the potentially disruptive consequences of love.[17] He identifies five such institutional patterns in common use to control love:

1. Child marriage. Among the Tiwi of Australia, a man may promise to give his firstborn daughter in marriage even before she is born.[18]

2. Mate selection predetermined by the kinship structure. In societies using this system, kin of a given relationship automatically marry each other and the only decision the elders must make is to determine when the marriage is to occur. For example, a preferred choice of mate among many peoples of the world is a cross cousin—a mother's brother's child or father's sister's child. In societies such as the Murngin, cross cousins automatically marry each other simply because their position in the kinship structure decrees that they should.[19]

3. Institutional isolation of young women who are possible mate choices until the time of their marriage, as among the Manus.

4. Close supervision by duennas or close relatives, as among some Spanish-speaking peoples. Where such a tradition is in effect, young couples are constantly chaperoned because it is assumed that if they were not, there would be a natural tendency for them to engage in sexual intercourse.

5. A system in which love relationships are encouraged and in which the choice of mates is formally free, but which in fact contains informal constraints. Our own society is an example of this system, insofar as economic, ethnic, religious, and regional factors limit the choice of mate to a socially approved field of eligibles. For example, although we insist that love is the decisive criterion in selecting a mate, very few marriages are contracted between blacks and whites. The fact that we do not have formal rules determining who should marry whom does not diminish the effect of social expectations upon our choice of mate.

MARRIAGE IN AMERICA TODAY

Marriage, as social scientists look at it, is primarily a social institution. It can be defined as follows:

Marriage is the established institution for starting a family. . . . There is often an exchange of economic goods in a marriage, and involved is a legal, physical

[17] William F. Goode, "The Theoretical Importance of Love," *American Sociological Review* (1959), p. 40.
[18] C. W. M. Hart and Arnold R. Pilling, *The Tiwi of North Australia* (New York: Holt, Rinehart & Winston, 1960).
[19] Lloyd Warner, *A Black Civilization* (New York: Harper & Row, 1937).

and moral union between a man and a woman, continued through the raising of children. Marriage regulates relations between the sexes and helps establish the child's relation to the community. It is usually associated with a ceremony . . . which formalizes the group's approval. In marriage, the children produced by the woman are usually accepted as the legitimate offspring of the married couple.[20]

This definition, taken from a dictionary of anthropology, is intended to cover all known cases—including group marriage, polygamous marriage, and monogamous marriage. It does not define *how* the institution regulates relationships between the sexes; it does not specify the nature of the legal, physical, and moral union. Nor does it describe the characteristics of the ceremony which formalizes the group's approval. It merely describes the basic function of marriage in whatever form it occurs: a formally sanctioned economic institution which regulates procreation.

Attitudes and Ideals

The foregoing general definition can be compared with what most contemporary Americans would consider a minimal definition of marriage as it is found in our society. The majority of Americans would define marriage as a lifelong monogamous union between a man and a woman, involving exclusive sexual rights in the spouse, the acceptance of patriarchy, and the expectation of children. This conception fits the general definition well: it sees marriage as a union for the purpose of procreation, it establishes patriarchy as the specific form of economic relations within the family, and it establishes monogamy as the form which regulates relations between the partners.

Let us examine this definition of the contemporary American understanding of marriage in greater detail in order to learn what we can about the attitudes and ideals of our society with regard to this institution. In the first place, the definition tells us that marriage is a lifelong union. Of course, we all know perfectly well that, factually speaking, this is not the case. One hundred years ago or less, when divorce involved extremely expensive legal procedures, when it was granted only on a limited number of grounds, and when any divorced person—male as well as female—was an object of social scorn, it would have been reasonable to speak of marriage as a lifelong partnership in fact as well as in ideal. Today, as we shall see later in this chapter and again in Chapter 14, divorce is common enough to make it no longer factually accurate to speak of marriage as a lifelong relationship.

Nevertheless, the idea that marriage represents a permanent commitment to a partnership persists as an ideal which exerts considerable in-

[20]Charles Winick, *A Dictionary of Anthropology* (New York: New World Library, 1964).

fluence on people's attitudes. Thus, although divorce statistics tell us that Americans are quite willing to dissolve a marriage contract when they feel that their marriage no longer serves the purposes for which they entered the relationship, it is very rare indeed for any member of our society to enter into a marriage with the idea that it will be a temporary union. Although many young people today are realistic enough to recognize that they will be able to terminate their marriage if it doesn't "work out," they still regard permanence as the ideal toward which they are striving. Anything short of permanence is regarded as a failure.

The next stipulation—that marriage must be monogamous—is relatively straightforward. Monogamy is the only form of marriage that is legally valid in the United States. Occasionally, one hears of various forms of group marriage involving three or more partners, but such relationships have no legal standing at all. This sort of pseudo-polygamy is interesting from a sociological standpoint, but experiments in this direction have so far had little influence on the attitudes and ideals people bring to conventional two-party marriages and have had no influence whatsoever on the legal requirement that marriage can exist only between two people of the opposite sex. (In this later connection, it is interesting to note that various groups of homosexual activists have been fighting in courts and legislatures for legal recognition of their partnerships—so far without success.)

Next, we turn to the phrase in our definition which stipulates that marriage is a union "involving exclusive sexual rights in the spouse." Generally speaking, these rights exist both positively and negatively. That is to say, on the negative side, our conventional understanding of marriage holds that both partners are prohibited from giving themselves sexually to anyone but their spouses; on the positive side, it means that each party enjoys the right to receive sexual satisfaction from his or her partner. Although in most states both the positive and negative sides of these rights are legally enforceable—that is, both adultery and nonconsummation may be grounds for divorce or annulment—conventional understanding of what these rights imply varies considerably. For example, in some social circles these rights exist primarily for the benefit of the male. Thus, many people maintain that when a woman marries she incurs an obligation to satisfy the sexual demands of her husband, but the people who hold this belief rarely feel it important to add that the husband is obliged to satisfy his wife sexually. This difference results from the myth, discussed in Chapter 6, that women are sexually passive whereas men are sexually active. On the negative side, too, conventional understanding in some social circles favors the husband, whose infidelity is often tolerated as one of the facts of life a wife must learn to live with, whereas infidelity on her part would be regarded as a serious breach of the marriage contract.

Next, our definition describes marriage in America as a patriarchal institution. Patriarchy is a form of social arrangement in which the father serves as supreme authority in the family, and in which heredity is reckoned in the male line. In our society this is reflected in the widespread practice of having the woman adopt her husband's surname upon marriage; children, too, tend automatically to be given the husband's surname, so that the family as a whole is identified in terms of the male. It should be noted, however, that this naming convention is not legally obligatory in forty-nine of the fifty states. (Hawaii is the one exception.) In California, for example, the state attorney general recently found it necessary to answer a complaint by women who objected to the practice as a specimen of male chauvinism by pointing out that they were under no legal obligation to adopt their husbands' names. A married woman is perfectly free to keep her "maiden name"—that is, her father's surname —if she desires to do so. What is more, just as our patriarchal naming conventions are not legally binding, so in many states the laws governing the holding and transmission of property in a marriage partnership are not notably patriarchal. In this regard we have come a long way from the nineteenth-century British system—common also in many parts of the United States—in which all of a married woman's property belonged to the husband, including even property she held in her own name prior to marriage and income she earned in any way while married. Today, such blatantly patriarchal laws are practically nonexistent, and a number of states have community property statutes which make any property held by either member of a marriage partnership the joint property of both.

Nevertheless, American marriage still can be described as a patriarchal system in terms of the general social and psychological expectations we bring to it. Nonpatriarchal marriage is, of course, quite possible, but it is still the exception rather than the rule. Unless a couple explicitly agrees, either before marriage or in the course of their partnership, that they are to relate to each other as equals, male dominance tends to "go without saying." A situation commonly used to illustrate this point concerns decisions that may arise as to where a family is to live. Generally speaking, if both partners have careers, the practice is for the family to live where the husband can pursue his career to best advantage. If a husband gets an attractive job offer that requires the family to relocate, we consider it perfectly normal for the wife to give up her job, but only in abnormal situations do we consider it appropriate for the husband to give up his job if the shoe is on the other foot. This is a clear reflection of our patriarchal bias, which assumes, even when both partners are employed and earning equal salaries, that financial support of the family is the male's obligation and that the female's contributions in this area are optional and voluntary.

Finally, our definition stipulates that marriage is a partnership involving an expectation of children. Here, of course, the norm is not

Burk Uzzle, Magnum Photos

legally binding at all, but this is nevertheless one of the most important of all the conventional attitudes and ideals we bring to marriage. Advances in contraceptive technology have brought us a long way from the day when the birth of children was regarded as an uncontrollable accident, and except among the poor (especially the rural poor) and those whose religious beliefs preclude contraception, modern American society can be described as fairly sophisticated in its understanding of the possibility of controlling birth. For most people, however, the ability to practice birth control means that they can control when they will have children and how many they will have; rarely do they see it as offering them the choice of whether to have children or not.

Family and peer pressures in this area can be immense, and the couple who postpone the birth of their first child for a considerable amount of time are often told in no uncertain terms what is expected of them. Many married partners who are quite comfortable in their two-person partnership succumb to these pressures and decide to have a child without ever being able to articulate their doubts about whether raising a family is right for them. Thus, although couples are perfectly free to remain childless if they decide to do so, it is safe to say that when two people get married they generally expect to have children as a matter of course, without giving the question any conscious thought. What is more, even if they give it thought, their decision is likely to be heavily influenced by the expectations of interested onlookers—especially the couple's parents.

These, then, are some of the major attitudes and ideals that color and shape the expectations people bring to marriage in our society. Of course, no institution actually functions in precisely the way a generalized and abstract picture of it would lead one to expect. For example, on paper every corporation is a smooth-running machine with each part operating in a clear and unambiguous way to contribute to the total output, but in real life it is likely to be far more complex and confusing. Our attitudes and ideals tell us only what we expect the institution of marriage to be like, just as an organizational flow chart tells us only how a business institution is *supposed* to operate. The institution of marriage, like any corporate institution, must cope with a changing world, changing attitudes, and individual differences. In the remainder of this chapter, therefore, we will examine the evolving reality of marriage in America today. In some ways this reality will conform to our expectations, in many it will not. In any case, it would be unrealistic to expect anything as dynamic as an intimate relationship between two individuals to fit perfectly with any set of pre-existing norms.

The Evolving Reality

A fourteen-year-old acquaintance of the authors was able to identify at least five different life styles simply on the basis of her normal contacts in babysitting. These were as follows:

1. A traditional monogamous marriage with its characteristic balance of authority and permissiveness in child raising and a traditional involvement by the married couple in the "straight" social sense.

2. A divorcee with children whom our informant described as a "swinging single." She takes a tradtional approach to childrearing but makes no attempt to keep from anyone the fact that she spends weekends away from her children with any one of a number of boyfriends.

3. A divorcee who is living with a man without "benefit of clergy." In all outward aspects this partnership seems no different from any successful marriage in which the partners are bound to each other by the usual religious and/or legal forms.

4. A young upper-middle-class couple whose apartment consists mostly of makeshift furniture and has few of the mechanical comforts associated with modern living. This couple is deeply involved in mystical religious experiences; they seem to entertain a wide array of friends under a wide variety of circumstances, but our informant was not able to provide details.

5. A couple in which both partners have children by previous marriages, in addition to offspring from their own union. This family is structured along traditional lines with a normal middle-class style of social life, but there are occasions in which the tattered remnants of the previous marriages intrude upon the current relationship. All members of the family seem to be aware that the children can be divided into "his," "hers," and "theirs."

There is nothing representative about these styles and structures, but clearly they are all around us. The fact that they are not often distinguished in sociological studies of marriage does not mean that they do not represent significant departures from our common ideals, and that they do not demand different responses from the participants. They are a part of the rich variety of styles and structures that testify to the fact that the American institution of marriage is changing and evolving.

In the nineteenth century people were often amazed and appalled at the variations in marriage and family styles discovered by anthropologists, but it is now becoming increasingly clear that the greatest variation in marriage and family styles is to be found not in primitive cultures but in modern industrialized societies where affluence, leisure, and a critical stance toward one's culture both foster change and give increasing numbers of people the capacity and the motivation to try out new alternatives.

Some of the changes that are altering the structure of the institution of marriage in our culture are the result of conscious attempts to try out new styles of living together, new forms of marriage and family. The number of people involved in the intentional alteration of our marital style is probably quite small, however, although the public that sympathizes with such deliberate experimentation is undoubtedly considerably larger.

Why Is the Character of Marriage Changing?

The shortest answer to this question is to say, "Because our society is changing." To see how social change affects marriage, let us briefly examine six important dimensions of such change as they affect the character of the marriage partnership in America today. These are (1) the declining influence of religion; (2) the widespread use of products such as the birth control pill and the automobile; (3) the increasing antipersonalization of our society; (4) the creation of an enormous job market, including some 31.7 million jobs for women;[21] (5) the increasing demand for advanced training, which tends to increase the period of premarriage

[21]Bureau of the Census, *Statistical Abstract of the United States: 1973* (Washington, D.C.,: U.S. Government Printing Office, 1973), p. 219.

and encourages a critical stance toward our culture; and (6) the "population explosion," which has made us a very young country, with almost half of our population currently under twenty-five years of age.

The Declining Influence of Religion. When social scientists talk about the declining influence of religion, they are not so much concerned with church attendance as they are with the decline in importance of the sacred or holy in the daily lives of a people. Primitive peoples saw the entire world as essentially sacred, but with the advance of science and technology the sphere of the sacred has diminished drastically.

Since at least the time of Augustine, marriage has been regarded as a sacred contract, as indicated in the traditional wedding formula, "What God hath joined together let no man put asunder." By the Renaissance marriage had come to be less a sacred contract and more a social contract with important implications as a business transaction.[22] In the former view one was obliged to fulfill one's marriage contract much as one was obliged to obey any of the other precepts of one's faith; in the latter view breaking the marriage bond was as unthinkable as any violation of the norms of ethical business conduct. In the one case divorce was a sin against God, in the other it was a violation of the social order of the community. But today most people regard marriage as primarily a personal contract between two persons. Thus, neither the religious nor the secular community can have much influence on the couple that decides to terminate their marriage.

Some Pertinent Products. Modern technology has given us many products that affect both the style of our courtship and the character of our partnerships. Perhaps none have had more significant repercussions on the institution of marriage than the automobile and the birth control pill.

The automobile has affected our courtship and partnership patterns by increasing the autonomy of the young couple. Prior to the advent of the automobile, couples courted in the parlor; after it, they courted in the back seat. This greater freedom from parental supervision enabled couples to develop their own style of courtship, which generally included a much greater degree of sexual intimacy than was possible in the parlor. The automobile also increased the likelihood that a partner would be selected who lived at some distance—perhaps even across town or in the next town. As we saw in Chapter 4, in our discussion of differences in background and outlook, this change has created problems which did not exist when mate selection was limited, for all practical purposes, to the boy or girl "next door." Finally, the automobile has made it relatively easy for couples to establish their residence at some distance from

[22]Hunt, *The Natural History of Love*, p. 190.

both job and kin. The implications of this separation will be discussed below.

The birth control pill, along with other efficient contraceptives, has made it possible to effectively separate sexual pleasure from conception. The increased incidence of premarital sexual intercourse is directly related to the development of better and better contraceptives. Moreover, the ability effectively to separate sexual pleasure from conception has completely shaken our assumptions regarding the naturalness of the sequence of love-marriage-sex-reproduction, which is the basis of our traditional understanding of marriage.

An Antipersonal Society. To a considerable extent, the professional stance toward life militates against the growth of intimacy in one's private life. It is detached and impersonal. It is intended to be so. Although young professionals are supposed to be able to adjust, to move from the world of their profession into the world of their families with ease, most people do not do this well. The two worlds overlap in their concerns, and when this happens the world in which one earns one's living tends to dominate. This is particularly true in the middle class, where a large portion of the population is employed in a professional capacity, but it is also true, although to a lesser extent, in working-class families.

On the job people are rewarded for their success at aggressive competition in which they must manipulate people in order to further their personal objectives. The job places a high value on things and rewards behavior that is effective in producing those things.[23] At present, males are generally rewarded for their productivity more than females.

The personal world of most American men has two centers, the home and the place of employment. Normally, these are located in different places and generate quite distinct settings within which he acts out his daily routine. Women, on the other hand, typically have but one focus of their lives, their home. They may leave it for a number of reasons, but they do not ordinarily establish a separate setting within which they may try on new roles and fulfill different expectations. Thus, in spite of the advances made by the growing feminist movement, it remains true that in the typical case masculinity in America is defined primarily in terms of the expectations governing the job or career while femininity is defined primarily in terms of the expectations associated with childrearing and domesticity.

The net result is that men, because of the "cool" stance they are encouraged to adopt in their careers, and because their preoccupation with their careers and with the necessity of providing for their families, are

[23]See particularly Jules Henry, *Culture Against Man* (New York: Random House, 1963), pp. 11–12, and Erich Fromm, *The Art of Loving* (New York: Bantam Books, 1970).

less able to enter into intimate relationships than women. Equally as important is the related fact that marriage has a different valence for men than it does for women. For middle-class men, marriage is important for full social acceptability; it also provides the middle-class man with a means of demonstrating his professional competence indirectly through the standard of living he provides for his wife and children. For most women, on the other hand, marriage is a necessary step on the way to personal fulfillment. Because many women still see motherhood as essential for their personal fulfillment, they also see marriage as a necessity because it provides the only legitimate context in our society in which a woman can become a mother.

Working Women. About 42 percent of all married women who live with their husbands are employed outside the home.[24] The number has tripled since World War II. To the extent that women work outside the home and to the extent that such employment provides them with some degree of economic independence, to that extent marriage has less utilitarian value for them. A woman who is able to support herself does not have to remain in an unhappy marriage for economic reasons; her financial independence gives her an alternative.

It should be recognized, however, that the statistics on the number of employed women do not give an accurate picture of the extent to which women have achieved economic independence from their husbands. The average working woman's income is considerably below that of the average working man, so that in most cases if a working couple were to separate, each to live on his or her own income, she would be much less well off than he. Nevertheless, the fact remains that the more income a woman is able to command, the more she is free of the necessity to remain married for financial reasons. What is more, as more and more women are realizing the importance of pursuing careers rather than merely holding jobs, and as more and more worthwhile jobs are being made available to women, the force of the financial compulsion to marry will disintegrate. Sheer economic necessity was never a very good reason to remain in a partnership, but it was a real one. The progress of women toward economic equality with men makes it less so.

The Need To Be Trained. The amount of training required for many jobs and careers has been increasing steadily for decades and has had a considerable effect on the institution of marriage. This factor is particularly pertinent to the success-oriented upper middle class, but it applies also to the working class, although to a lesser degree. The decade of post-high school professional training involved in graduate education is an extreme case, but college education or technical training is becom-

[24]*Statistical Abstract: 1973*, p. 220.

ing an accepted part of our way of life for a huge portion of our population. In 1970, 48 percent of Americans between the ages of eighteen and twenty-one were in college; by 1980 it is estimated that this figure will reach 63.1 percent.[25]

Undoubtedly the most important reason why advanced education affects marriage has to do with the fact that it postpones the time when young people are economically independent. Because many men are reluctant to marry unless they can support a wife—and a family if that should prove necessary—increases in the number of years of schooling have the effect of postponing the age at which people marry. In turn this leads to a greater extent of premarital sex and an increasing number of nonmarital partnerships. What is more, college education often provides students with the intellectual equipment that makes possible a critical stance toward their culture and a greater degree of openness to alternative ways of doing things. This is reflected in the fact that college-educated people are considerably more likely than their non-college-educated peers to look favorably on freedom and experimentation in marital life styles.

A Nation of Young People. The so-called "population explosion," particularly the postwar "baby boom," has added an enormous number of new individuals to our society. Although the rate of growth for the nation as a whole is approaching zero, the size of our population will continue to increase as a result of the larger base of productive females. At present, America is a nation of young people, with almost half its population under the age of twenty-five.

Experimentation, innovation, and new departures always have been prerogatives of the young, but in the past, when the median age was considerably higher than it is now, young people could not help but feel that their ideas were more or less transitory. Young men and women were well aware of their minority status in a world populated mostly by older folk. Thus, although they might feel free to depart from the norms by "sowing their wild oats," they tended to be aware at the same time that this was simply a phase they were passing through on their way to taking their place in the adult world. Today, however, young people are not in the minority in America. Of great significance here is the fact that they are probably the largest and most influential group of consumers of cultural products such as music, literature, motion pictures, and television, so that to a considerable extent they are the trend setters in matters of taste.

Thus, instead of having a situation in which young people learn how to behave in the adult world, we have a situation in which the junior members of society establish the fashions and their elders struggle to

[25]*Statistical Abstract: 1973*, p. 129.

Carl Fischer

keep up. This was clear as long ago as the early 1960s, when middle-aged people started struggling doggedly but often vainly to master the Twist. Half a century ago, a typical twenty-year-old man probably would have been working somewhere where he was surrounded by fellow workers twice his age or older. A typical twenty-year-old male today is likely to be in college, surrounded by hundreds of fellow students his own age and taught by instructors half of whom may not be thirty years old themselves. In a nation of young people, in short, the unconventional behavior that characterizes the young in their approach to social institutions such as marriage can become itself a norm.

SUMMARY

Many Americans still think about sex, love, and marriage in essentially the same way that Saint Thomas Aquinas did: sex is only to be experienced in marriage with one's spouse, primarily for the purpose of procreation. Although most of us are persuaded that sex in marriage ought also to be enjoyable, we still tend to feel that any sexual behavior that cannot at least potentially lead to reproduction is perverted. That virtuous women should enjoy sex, even in marriage, is a very recent idea.

To a large extent, we have defined *agape*—spiritual love—as "good" and erotic love as "bad" because men lost themselves in passion in the process of lovemaking. The idea of the sin of concupiscence is traceable to Saint Augustine, who felt that the dire consequences of concupiscence (damnation) could be averted *if* the passion were redirected through the sacrament of marriage toward the goal of procreation.

From a cross-cultural perspective we have seen that many peoples feel that erotic love threatens to disrupt the social structure by isolating the lovers from their kin. Goode was able to describe five ways in which societies control the potentially disruptive aspects of this type of love: child marriage, arranged marriages by rules of endogamy, institutional isolation of young people until the time of marriage, close supervision of young couples (especially young women), and informal norms that define a field of eligible mates, as in our own society.

Today marriage is changing because our society is changing. The declining influence of conventional religion, the increasingly antipersonal nature of our society, the use of products such as the birth control pill and the automobile, the creation of an enormous job market, the increasing demand for advanced training, and the population explosion resulting in the predominance of young people in our population have all attributed to the changing norms and behaviors we witness. Consequently, even a fourteen-year-old girl engaging in the customary routine of babysitting is able to distinguish five differing life styles among her customers. The number of people who are intentionally experimenting with alternatives to traditional marriage probably is quite small, but one thing seems certain—the basically antisexual outlook of Aquinas no longer dominates our morality or our behavior in the way it did not too long ago.

11

HUSBANDS AND WIVES

In the view of the wise, Heaven is man and Earth woman: Earth fosters what Heaven lets fall.
When Earth lacks heat, Heaven sends it; when she has lost her freshness and moisture, Heaven restores it.
Heaven goes on his rounds, like a husband foraging for his wife's sake;
And Earth is busy with housewiferies: she attends to birth and suckling that which she bears.
Regard Earth and Heaven as endowed with intelligence, since they do the work of intelligent beings.
Unless these twain taste pleasure from one another, why are they creeping together like sweethearts.

Rumi

INTRODUCTION

This chapter begins with a continuation of the discussion of traditional expectations about marriage begun in Chapter 10. Traditional marriage, as we use the term, refers to what most of us mean by marriage. As we saw in Chapter 10, this involves the expectation of a lifelong monogamous union with exclusive sexual rights in the spouse. It involves the acceptance of patriarchy or a companionship type of relationship between husband and wife. It implies a common division of labor in which the husband provides for the family and the wife bears and raises children and takes care of the domestic chores. It involves an expectation that the husband and wife will share a great deal of their lives with each other. And fi-

Richard Frieman, Photo Researchers

nally, it involves an assumption that the small household unit formed by husband, wife, and children will be economically independent. Toward this end the husband and wife generally set up their own household from the beginning of their marriage and expect to maintain their independence from their families. Most people who intend to get married share this common understanding of the institution of marriage. In addition, they bring to this understanding all of their experience with married persons —primarily their parents.

All styles of partnership have their benefits and their costs, and this is no less true of traditional styles than of innovative ones. Persons entering any kind of partnership must decide what costs they are willing to pay to secure what benefits. The ideals and norms of traditional marriage are no more unrealistic or unrewarding than any other style. This is why large numbers of people find that they satisfactorily define the nature of marriage as it exists for them. Indeed, the traditional style has become traditional largely because for most people it is the preferred style of marriage, Thus, 45 to 50 percent of all married people in our society report that they are "happy" or "very happy" with their marriages.[1]

This chapter will explore some of the creative aspects of the institution of marriage as it is conventionally described. A successful traditional marriage, like any viable partnership, must be a dynamic process rather than a static condition. A man and a woman who are committed to their marriage will constantly grow and their relationship will grow. The expectations that they share after fifteen years of marriage will necessarily be different from those that they had when they began, for change is going on constantly both within the individuals and their partnership and within the society in which they live. Success in marriage requires that these changes be faced and dealt with.

The second half of this chapter will examine specifically some of the changes that

are observable in the way people relate to each other *within* the context of traditional marriage. We saw in Chapter 10 that various social factors have combined to bring about changes in the structure of marriage as a social institution. These changes include such things as higher divorce rates, higher incidence of premarital and extramarital sexual intercourse, and so forth—all of which have the effect of changing the context in which married people find themselves. Why this should be so becomes obvious if we compare a social context in which divorce rates are high with one in which divorce is a rare and unusual occurrence. In the latter case, neither party needs to be greatly concerned about dissolution of the partnership; if one partner, therefore, has a serious grievance against his or her mate, the pressure is on the aggrieved party to adjust to the situation because he or she lacks the power to use the ultimate threat of terminating the partnership if the mate does not alter the offensive situation. Where divorce is common, on the other hand, the relationship becomes more voluntary, and as a result both partners are aware that the partnership must be mutually satisfactory if it is to continue.

By the same token, the higher incidence of premarital intercourse has produced a situation in which more people enter marriage without the naive illusions about sex that were common in the past—and, indeed, are still common today. Among married partners who have no sexual experience other than with their mates, there was a natural tendency to assume that sex inevitably was whatever it was for the two of them; thus, it was especially common for women who led sexually unfulfilled lives with their husbands to assume simply that sex was an unfulfilling experience for a woman rather than that some adjustments could be made in the couple's lovemaking or that another partner might offer what the husband could not provide.

In short, changes in social conditions have produced changes in the expectations people bring to marriage, and these changes have affected the way people relate to each other within the institutional

[1]Lloyd Saxton, *The Individual, Marriage and the Family*, 2nd ed. (Belmont, California: Wadsworth Publishing Co., Inc., 1972), p. 267.

context of a traditional marriage. It is these latter changes we shall be examining in the section of this chapter entitled "Becoming More Flexible."

THE IMPLICIT MARRIAGE CONTRACT

Most wedding ceremonies include an exchange of vows between the partners. Commonly, the bride and groom promise "to love, honor, and cherish till death do us part." Such vows contain little in the way of specific content; they simply indicate the general nature of the relationship the two people intend to have with each other. Yet marriage is not usually entered into by people who do not have a clearer sense than the vows convey of what sort of relationship they expect. In a sense, then, behind the vague but explicit promises of the wedding vows lies an unspoken, implicit marriage contract which is shaped by the couple's expectations about marriage. In the next few pages we shall examine this "implicit marriage contract" in some detail.

Lifelong Monogamous Union

The central expectation of traditional marriage is that it is an indissoluble monogamous union. This understanding of marriage derives from the Christian tradition of marriage as a sacrament in which the ceremony makes the union indissoluble before God and man: "What God hath joined together, let no man put asunder." Even though marriage has been transformed, to a large extent, from a religious sacrament to a civil contract and then to a personal affirmation, it still remains as a symbol of the deep personal commitment of a man and a woman. For many people this symbol has validity and affirms their mutual commitment.

For example, we know of a couple who lived together for years without being married. After they got married, they reported that the marriage produced beneficial results for their partnership. "Sometimes we'd go through difficult periods," the husband explained, "and when we'd have a fight maybe it would end with one of us moving out for a few days. We always got back together again but it could get kind of scary. Whenever this happened there was a sense that maybe this time would be it. It tended to make both of us a little reluctant to bring up things that were bothering us; we were afraid to start a fight because of what it might lead to. But when we got married we more or less said to each other that we wanted to stay together for good. Instead of someone walking out when things get tough, we have to stay there and work the thing out. So it seems like we can be more open with each other now because by getting married we sort of said to each other, 'Look, if there are any problems, they're *our* problems. We've got a good—a beautiful —relationship and we're not going to let any temporary problems break it up.' "

Indissoluble monogamous marriage points toward a growing relationship where two persons look forward to time together in various stages of their lives. It offers them the exciting possibility of continued discov-

241

ery and interchange as they mature together. It sees the human personality as a richly changing resource upon which to build a relationship and assumes that there will always be mystery in the other partner that can constantly be discovered and can give new joy to the relationship. A part of the commitment to such a contract is the expectation that the partners will change and that they will share their changing selves with each other.

Exclusive Sexual Rights in the Spouse

As we saw in Chapter 10, traditional marriage involves an expectation of exclusive sexual rights in the spouse. This expectation reinforces the notion of monogamy as a lifelong commitment and emphasizes the uniqueness of the relationship. At one time not so long ago it was popularly believed that there was only one person in the world who was meant to be one's spouse.[2] Whether it derived from the religious or the romantic tradition, such a notion helped support the exclusiveness of the relationship.

As with lifelong monogamy, there is considerable variation in people's understanding of this expectation. In working-class families today, for example, the understanding is often that the husband has such rights over his wife but she does not necessarily have them over him. Sometimes a distinction is made in which casual sexual encounters, such as with a prostitute, are permissible but long-term affairs are not. In some upper-class social circles, extramarital sexual affairs are permitted for both husband and wife, with the couple understanding this clause in the implicit marriage contract as requiring only that they conduct themselves with propriety and not in a blatant manner. In many modern middle-class marriages the understanding is often that the wife's rights in this matter are the same as the husband's—that is, either both are free to engage in extramarital sexual activity or neither is.

Although it is often charged that the idea of exclusive sexual rights in the spouse necessarily implies a possessive relationship, this need not be so. On the contrary, it can simply be an indication of the dedication of the partners to each other, a symbol of the commitment of each to the other.

Common Residence and Economic Independence

The assumption of economic independence of the marital partnership from any outside support and the assumption of common residence give

---

[2]F. Ivan Nye and Felix Berardo, *The Family: Its Structure and Interaction* (New York: The Macmillan Company, 1973), argue that the sexual revolution has created a new obligation for the husband—to satisfy his wife sexually.

a distinctive economic identity to the married couple in modern American society. These assumptions, which probably derive from the characteristic American emphasis on rugged individualism, place an enormous responsibility upon the husband—and now increasingly upon the wife. Although many studies have shown that few American marriages are completely cut off from kin support, the extent to which we take it for granted that couples must "go it alone" is probably greater than in most societies of the world.[3] Although it is not uncommon for young people to marry while they are still in school and to depend upon parental support in the early years of their marriage, the general acceptance of the idea that marriage entails economic independence often leads such couples to feel that their marriage is not really complete—that they are merely "playing house" together—until they are on their own.

Division of Labor Patterns

Many changes are taking place in the traditional division of labor within marriage. It is possible to describe at least five patterns that women commonly follow in the assumption of their role obligations. Men have fewer alternatives at present. Although each pattern is a variation on how the work is to be divided up, all the patterns mentioned here tend to assume the other expectations of traditional marriage described above.[4]

Maternity-Homemaking Pattern. This pattern is the one that was almost universal in the earliest stages of the industrial revolution in this country. In this pattern, the husband accepts the entire responsibility for providing for the family while the wife assumes responsibility for housekeeping and child care. Under this arrangement, it is not possible for the wife to work outside of the home, but she makes a major economic contribution by processing food for the home and doing all the cleaning and domestic chores—with the help of her children when they reach an age at which it is possible for them to contribute. For this reason large families can be an advantage where this pattern is in effect. The pattern is still widely followed in rural America, but in urban and suburban settings it is less common and is less likely to be successful.

Companionship Pattern. In this pattern the maternal and economic roles of the wife are less important than they are in the maternity-homemaking pattern. Instead, the wife's attention and time are focused on her husband's interests and activities. In this pattern a wife might be expected

---

[3]See William N. Stephens, *The Family in Cross-Cultural Perspective* (New York: Holt, Rinehart & Winston, Inc., 1963), pp. 197ff.
[4]Fuller discussion of this role expectation can be found in Nye and Berardo, *The Family*.

to spend a great deal of time making herself attractive in order that she may respond in a sexual, recreational, and therapeutic manner to her husband, in whom she finds her fulfillment. Her social role as hostess to her husband's friends and business associates is also emphasized. This pattern, which is common in the upper middle class, has been a target of the women's liberation movement because it seems to center life around the male. This criticism has undeniable validity, but on the other hand, there is no denying that in such relationships women tend to have a great deal of power. Some men and women find intrinsic value in such a division of labor and do not feel that it makes the wife's role in any way inferior.[5]

Career Pattern. The career pattern is the other side of the coin from the maternity-homemaking pattern. Small families are favored and the birth of children probably will be planned so as not to interfere with careers. Outside persons are employed for child care and domestic chores. The woman assumes considerable responsibility for the support of the family and seeks part of her fulfillment in her career. In this pattern, as compared to any of the others, the husband is more likely to be assigned a share of household tasks. This style of partnership within traditional marriage is emerging as a dominant middle-class pattern. It is not to be confused with the working-class situation in which a wife works because she has to in order to maintain the family's standard of living or simply to pay the bills, for a job is not the same thing as a career. People take jobs primarily for money and other fringe benefits, whereas in a career they are likely to be looking primarily for personal fulfillment. One way to distinguish between these roughly similar situations is by asking whether the wife would continue working if the husband's income were such that it could satisfy the family's financial needs.

Family-Plus-Partial-Career Pattern. In this pattern, child care, childbearing, and household responsibilities are high priorities. Some or all of these tasks may be delegated to outside employees or agencies, but if these become unavailable or inadequate the wife is expected to relinquish her career. This simply means that the wife considers, or is expected to consider, the family interests first and the career second. A common variant of this pattern is for the wife to have a career until the birth of the first child, to suspend her career until the last child reaches a certain age, and then to resume her career as best she can. Naturally this variant is easiest to follow if the wife's career is one in which continuity of employment is not essential. In general, the family-plus-partial-

[5]See the response of 120,000 female readers of *Redbook* on this point. A significant *minority* favored the traditional roles. "How Do You Feel About Being a Women?" *Redbook* (January 1973), p. 1.

career pattern, like the full career pattern, is primarily a middle-class style of life.

Role Segregation Pattern. None of the patterns enumerated so far seems accurately to describe what Elizabeth Bott has called the "role segregation" pattern typical of the working class, although the closest approximation is the maternity-homemaking pattern.[6] The distinctive feature of the role segregation pattern is that the husband and wife really do not seem to see themselves as complementing each other's activities. Men typically engage in recreation with other men and women with other women. The sharp distinction between the "man's world" and the "woman's world" separates not only their major occupations—his job, her homemaking—but also their outside interests, hobbies, and social habits.

The Balance of Power

Much has been written about the balance of power within the traditional household.[7] This, too, is changing. Thus, although patriarchy was an almost universally accepted norm a few decades ago, its acceptance has declined markedly since World War II. To be sure, most middle-class husbands still make the major decisions about moving, buying a house or a car, deciding when to take a vacation, and so forth, but today it is considered far more acceptable for the wife to have an input in such decisions. Although the husband may still have the "last word" in many families, he generally can expect less support in case of an unpopular decision than, say, his father or grandfather would have expected in the same situation. The movement toward a companionship type of family has opened many of these decisions to debate within the family, even though, in the last analysis, it is still common for the father to make the final decision.

The Blessing of Children

As we saw in Chapter 10, the expectation of children is an important ingredient in the traditional understanding of marriage. Without children, it is often said, a marriage is not a family, and although a family has its good points and its bad points, it cannot be replaced with any other kind of relationship. Traditionally, large families of five or more children were thought of as highly desirable. Today, even though smaller

---

[6]Elizabeth Bott, *Family and Social Networks: Roles, Norms, and Extended Relationships in Working Class Families* (London: Tavistock Publications, 1957).
[7]See William Goode, Elizabeth Hopkins, and Helen M. McClure, *Social System and Family Patterns: A Propositional Inventory* (Indianapolis: The Bobbs-Merrill Company, 1971), pp. 558–61, for a list of references.

families have become more popular, it is still widely felt that the marriage without at least one or two children is incomplete. This topic will be discussed more fully in Chapter 12.

Togetherness

One of the more exciting experiences we can have as individuals is to share events, occasions, interests, and ideas with others. To laugh with someone who has come to know you intimately because she or he has shared so much of your life is to understand the private humor of personal involvement. Engaging in a common task, whether it be fixing up the house or going on a picnic with your spouse, is not only rewarding but also just plain fun. To have a spouse to whom you can turn in the midst of disappointment, frustration, and agony is one of the deepest and most significant rewards of intimate partnership. Cuber and Harroff capture a great deal of the positive value of the norm of togetherness in their example of a "total" relationship. In the following passage a consulting engineer describes his pleasure in being able to share a part of his job with his wife:

I invariably take her with me to conferences around the world. Her femininity, easy charm and wit are invaluable assets to me. I know it's conventional to say that a man's wife is responsible for his success, and I also know that it's often not true. But in my case I gladly acknowledge that it's not only true, but she's indispensable to me. But she'd go along with me even if there was nothing for her to do because we just enjoy each other's company—deeply. You know, the best part of a vacation is not what we do but that we do it together. We plan it and reminisce about it and weave it into our work and other play all the time.

His wife comments:

It seems to me that Bert exaggerates my help. It's not so much that I only want to help him; it's more that I want to do those things anyway. We do them together even though we may not be in each other's presence at the time. I don't really know what I do for him and what I do for me.[8]

In these statements the husband and wife have captured an aspect of togetherness that is often overlooked in superficial descriptions of doing things together. Often what is meant by togetherness is the sort of pseudomutuality we examined in Chapter 4. For Bert and his wife, however, their togetherness represents the fact that they enjoy a relationship in which communication has taken place at a deep level.

When we speak of togetherness, therefore, as one of the expectations implied in what we have been calling "the implicit marriage contract,"

[8]John F. Cuber and Peggy B. Harroff, *Sex and the Significant Americans* (New York: Appleton-Century-Crofts, 1965), p. 59.

we should distinguish between togetherness as a norm for conduct and togetherness as a product of a relationship. When people get married, they often regard togetherness as a norm; that is, they consider the kind of interested sharing described here as something they are entitled to from their mates and something they are obliged to give in return. They feel this is a part of the contract. As we saw in Chatper 4, however, such expectations can be damaging insofar as they deny the partners their unique, autonomous individuality. But this does not mean that togetherness is undesirable. On the contrary, when two people come to have genuinely mutual interests arising out of a pattern of intimate sharing, the results can be a deepening of their experiences compared to what they would have encountered if they followed their own interests alone.

**BECOMING MORE
FLEXIBLE**

In our presentation so far we have had repeated occasions to note that traditional marriage is undergoing some dramatic changes. The divorce rate is increasing, but the remarriage rate is increasing even faster. Counselors tell us that about half of the marriages in America are failures, as measured by the partner's own assessment of their relationship. It is safe to say that a large number of marriages could not be considered vital, growing relationships and are not considered such by the persons involved in them.

At the very time when an impersonal society is making increased demands upon marriage to fulfill the needs of its members for intimacy and a sense of belongingness, many people find the traditional institution incapable of satisfying their needs. Although this situation has led in some quarters to gloomy predictions about the future of marriage, many others feel that the problem is not with the institution itself, but that people often bring to marriage unrealistic and outdated expectations that are no longer relevant to the task of living together in today's world. There seems to be a need to make our expectations about marriage—and our marriages—more flexible, more in tune with our own unique needs and desires.

People who take this approach generally see their efforts as an affirmation of monogamous marriage, not a repudiation of it. They are operating on the assumption that the institution of marriage is worth saving. This affirmation comes at a time when others are contending that it has outlived its usefulness. What is more, it comes from people who are in touch with one another and care about each other rather than from partners who find themselves in a deteriorating relationship in which they have lost touch with one another. That is to say, the various attempts we see all around us to make marriage more flexible are not necessarily the desperate efforts of couples on the verge of divorce or of unhappy people looking for some alternative to their situation.

On the contrary, those who want to improve marriage, to make it more responsive to their own needs and desires, tend to be couples who already have a reasonably good human relationship and want to make it better.

Such people are attempting to build a vital relationship in which the growth of the partners is an important consideration. Good communication between the partners is essential if this end is to be achieved. So is a creative effort to transcend the conventional roles of married life where these roles are felt to inhibit personal growth and the growth of the partnership. Role transcendence is aimed toward the ideal of nondependent living—that is, a way of living together in which the relationship between the two individuals does not force either one to give up so much of herself or himself that she or he becomes dependent on the other. People striving for more flexible marriages also hold as a high priority the personal growth of each partner and recognize that individual freedom is a necessary ingredient of such growth. Each individual, they feel, must have the freedom to decide for himself or herself what the most creative activity or use of his or her time might be. And finally, most immediately related to role transcendence, is the ability to be flexible in the definition of the roles of husband and wife.

Nondependent Living

According to popular lore and popular songs, the aim of marriage is for two people to live together "as one." But according to the ideal of nondependent living, each partner in a marriage should strive to become more of a person in his or her own right and should try to avoid surrendering his or her own personhood to the partner. As each partner becomes more of a person through developing his or her own talents and interests, the two of them save themselves from becoming dependent upon one another. Each one brings to the relationship a growing, manyfaceted personality that could, if the occasion called for it, stand alone and adequately manage the problems of everyday life.

In describing his own marriage, the noted psychologist Carl Rogers presents a picture of a partnership in which nondependent living is evident as one of the major qualities of the relationship:

We complemented each other. . . . I tend to be a shy loner; Helen is more naturally and comfortably social. I tend to persevere at what I'm doing; she is the one to say, "Why don't we do this or that?" "Why don't we take a trip?" I grudgingly agree, but once under way I'm the more adventurous and childish and she is more steady. I've been a therapist, with an interest in research; she has been an artist and a lifelong worker in the planned parenthood movement. Each of us has had the opportunity to learn much from the other's field of interest. We have also been able to deal constructively with most of our conflicts and differences.[9]

[9]Carl Rogers, *Becoming Partners* (New York: Delacorte Press, 1972), pp. 27–29.

In contrast to this picture, Rogers cites the case of a woman who lost her independent status upon marriage:

Jennifer, before her marriage, had been an extremely independent, creative, innovative person, always starting things and carrying out projects which others were not bold enough to do. Yet in her marriage, she adopted the role of being her husband's support, of doing what he wanted done in the way he wished it done. She felt this was the way a wife should behave.[10]

Such a loss of self in a relationship follows naturally from trying to live up to the ideal of two people "becoming one." In order to succeed in this aim, either both partners must surrender a part of themselves or one of them—in our society this is generally the woman—must surrender entirely. Because such relationships generally meet with social approval, especially when it is the woman who is called upon to renounce her own development, the loss of autonomy frequently goes unnoticed. As the nineteenth-century Danish philosopher Soren Kierkegaard observed: "The greatest danger, that of losing one's own self, may pass off quietly as if it were nothing; every other loss, that of an arm, a leg, five dollars, etc., is sure to be noticed."[11]

Because the loss of self in dependency can readily go unnoticed, it is very important that partners be alert to the importance of retaining their distinctiveness and personhood. They should look out for such signs as habitually deferring to the other person's wishes or trying to assess what the partner thinks about something before venturing to express one's own views. As the poet Kahlil Gibran wrote in *The Prophet*, "Let there be spaces in your togetherness!"[12] Without a significant degree of personal autonomy, it makes no sense to talk about freedom or personal growth. In order for two people to "come together" there first have to be *two people*.

Personal Growth

Personal growth is the movement away from simple conformity to social expectations and toward a discovery that each of us has an internal center of evaluation that can provide us with adequate guidance. Personal growth involves coming into contact with the vast array of feelings, emotions, ideas, and attitudes that are within us and responding to the world in terms of this complexity. It is a discovery of how we feel personally about the world and the cultivation of the courage to act on these feelings. It means that as we become more of who we are, we have a richer variety of alternative responses to any situation.

[10]*Becoming Partners*, p. 15.
[11]Soren Kierkegaard, as quoted in *Becoming Partners*.
[12]Kahlil Gibran, *The Prophet* (New York: Alfred A. Knopf, 1952), p. 16.

To illustrate what we mean by personal growth, consider the fact that most people have the capacity to engage in simple athletic skills such as swimming, baseball, tennis, and skating. Although a lot of books, a lot of words, and a lot of instructions have been lavished on young children who are trying to master one of these skills, in fact no child is ever going to learn any of these skills until he or she tries it. Then the child's own body, sensations, and perceptions are what will enable him or her to perform successfully. Indeed, a few afternoons at a baseball park will convincingly demonstrate that few of the really good hitters have batting stances that look like the stances illustrated in the "how-to" books. Over the course of time they have developed styles of their own that suit their own specific talents best.

In much the same way, personal growth in partnerships requires a developing reliance on how one feels in the partnership rather than a concern about how one ought to feel. In one of Carl Rogers' case studies, Roy and Sylvia convey how they feel about their growing partnership:

We want our relationship to be such that each is given the freedom and encouragement to develop his [her] full potential. We want our marriage to be an exciting exploration of new avenues. We want to share so deeply that even the forbidden, the shameful, the jealous, the angry feelings that we have are as fully expressed and as much accepted as the tender and loving feelings. . . . We want to be the complexity of our feelings, which are by no means always simple and clear.[13]

It is important to note at this point that although personal growth often entails a willingness to disregard or defy convention, it is not a matter of simple rebellion. Personal growth is the process of becoming one's real self, and this means following conventions where one is comfortable with them as well as rejecting them where one is not. Rebellion for the sake of rebellion is not personal growth, it is simply living into your own neuroses. Personal growth involves an awareness and affirmation of the meaning of one's behavior. In partnerships when personal growth is taking place, Rogers observes, ". . . a worthy partner [is] not a slave or slaveowner, not a shadow or an echo, not always a leader nor always a follower, not a person to be taken for granted, and certainly not a boring person."[14]

Individual Freedom

The ideal of nondependent living and the ideal of personal growth both imply that the partners in a marriage have a considerable degree of

[13]Rogers, *Becoming Partners*, p. 69.
[14]*Becoming Partners*, p. 208.

individual freedom. At the simplest level, this freedom means that willingness to dissolve what Nena and George O'Neill call the "couple-front"—a term the O'Neills coined to describe acceptance of the norm that married partners should always outwardly manifest solidarity.[15] Acceptance of the couple-front as a norm means that the couple should always go places together, do the same things, and not allow any other person to have intimate access to either partner. Inevitably, this demand legislates against individual freedom.

True individual freedom does not mean merely the freedom of time and resources to do things separately. Equally important is an awareness that the partners are free to make contacts, cultivate friendships, and develop separate interests and activities. One of the O'Neills' respondents remarks:

Both of us have shared interests along with different individual interests. So how can we live our whole lives attached to one another? Her to me, me to her? Is she going to get all her humor from me, all her sympathy, all her intellectual interests from me? Christ, I can't fill that role. I'm smart, but let's face it, I'm not God. So when you get down to it, what does it mean, that I can't be everything to her? It means she has to live with other people too. So if she meets another person, another man, say, who is a musician, it's all right for her to go to dinner with him. Is it all right for her to go to a ballet or a concert with him? Sure. Sometimes we go to the ballet together, too. But I can't possibly supply the same type of stimulus and companionship at a ballet or concert that she can get with a musician.[16]

For many readers, we are well aware, this husband's statement conjures up the specter of sexual infidelity. Indeed, the O'Neills' book *Open Marriage*, from which this statement is taken, is widely assumed—by people who have not read it—to be a defense of a new style of marriage in which the partners are free to engage in sexual activities with people other than their mates. To a large extent, this mistaken interpretation of the O'Neills' views about individual freedom in the context of marriage is the result of sensationalist journalism, which has singled out the potentially most lurid implications of their argument. But to an equally large extent this misinterpretation of the idea of freedom in marriage derives from the suspicion, widely held in our society, that close personal friendships of a nonsexual nature are not possible between men and women. Americans in general tend to be quite cynical on this issue,

[15]George and Nena O'Neill, *Open Marriage* (New York: M. Evans & Company, Inc., 1972), p. 166.
[16]From *Open Marriage: A New Life Style for Couples*, p. 167, by Nena O'Neill and George O'Neill. Copyright © 1972 by Nena O'Neill and George O'Neill. Reprinted by permission of the publisher, M. Evans and Company, Inc., New York, New York 10017.

imagining that the husband just quoted is being hopelessly naive: if he thinks his wife can go to concerts, ballets, and dinners with another man, he is, such people would say, asking for trouble.

In a sense, these skeptics are not completely wrong, for their dire predictions can tend to be a self-fulfilling prophecy. That is, in a society where married men and women are not trusted to socialize with members of the opposite sex freely, even totally "innocent" contacts are likely to be looked at suspiciously, and so the two people involved may feel it necessary to be somewhat furtive about their relationship. What is more, this sort of furtive secrecy, which is natural in illicit sexual relationships, makes it all the easier for the relationship to turn into a sexual one—even though that was contrary to the original intentions of the man and the woman.

Consider, for example, the case of a male college teacher who finds that a certain female faculty member is the colleague with whom he can enjoy the most stimulating conversations about his academic specialty. They find themselves spending five or six hours a week together engaged in "shop talk" after classes. If his conversational companion were another male, he probably wouldn't give this a moment's thought, and neither would his wife. But socializing with a woman is another matter. Perhaps his wife shows signs of jealousy, or perhaps he imagines them; in either case, he reasons—quite rightly—that he has done nothing wrong and that there is no reason to terminate his friendship. But he doesn't want to upset his wife, and he especially doesn't want "people to start talking," so he and his female colleague stop meeting in public places on campus and he begins to lie to his wife about where he spends his afternoons. He justifies the lying by telling himself that the truth in this case would only upset his wife needlessly. But the point is that he is no longer honest in his relationship with his wife and has transformed a perfectly innocent friendship into something he feels guilty about. Psychologists tell us that people frequently engage in behavior they know to be wrong in order to "justify" feelings of guilt they already have; the child who misbehaves because he feels he deserves punishment is a common example of this phenomenon. In the case at hand, this mechanism may well work to drive the teacher and his colleague into an affair neither of them really wants.

On the other hand, if the man in this case had felt perfectly free to form whatever close friendships he felt his development as a person and as a professional required, his association with his female colleague would not have been surrounded with an aura of guilt, and insofar as it was guilt feelings that led him to escalate a friendship into an affair, this outcome would have been that much less likely. This is not to say that sexual infidelity will not occur in a marriage governed by the principle of individual freedom. But when we recognize that in American society today the norms are generally against a married person's freedom to form friendships with members of the opposite sex, and nevertheless about 50 percent of married people report that they have engaged in extramarital sexual activities at one time or another, the conclusion is inescapable that limiting freedom is not an effective way to secure marital fidelity. What is more, from an ethical point of view it seems clear that sexual exclusivity practiced in a context of freedom is far more valuable and meaningful to the couple involved than the same exclusivity when it is the result of enforced seclusion from members of the opposite sex. The man or woman who secures his or her partner's sexual fidelity by assuring that the mate is never alone with a member of the opposite sex may get the desired result, but such fidelity does not serve as an expression of the value the partner puts upon the relationship. Indeed, any act in an intimate partnership that is not the result of free choice is inevitably meaningless as a communication of how the partners feel about each other.

Role Flexibility

It is impossible for any individual to be completely free of the influence of social expectations about appropriate behavior or roles. Roles provide the framework within which social interaction can take place even

Hanna Schreiber, Rapho Guillumette

among strangers in the same culture. They are accretions of a people's past experience that lend stability and order to social living. Despite their obvious values, however, simple acceptance of preestablished social roles leads to domination by them. On the other hand, awareness of the roles an individual is called upon to fulfill and reflection on them in terms of the individual's own unique situation enables people to make their roles more flexible and more suited to their own peculiar needs.

At the simplest level, the level of daily living, role flexibility means a willingness to share and exchange chores. Role flexibility in an intimate partnership means that the man becomes more involved in the raising of children, in cooking, and in other domestic tasks while the woman takes on decision-making responsibilities that are reserved for the male in the traditional role system. Some couples are deliberately experimenting with role reversal over an extended period of time. One such couple devoted an entire year to reversal: the wife went to work and paid the bills while the husband stayed home and took care of their two children. They reported that the process resulted in an increased understanding of each other and considered it a creative contribution to their marriage. The O'Neills observe, "Any task normally undertaken by one mate can be exchanged with the other. None is likely to be glamorous, but all are necessary, and by shifting these chores back and forth, marital partners can relieve boredom, learn something new, become more versatile, and gain additional respect for the other's efforts."[17] Scandinavian countries such as Sweden have given experiments in role reversal extensive testing. Predictably, both partners usually take several weeks or months to become adjusted to the new routine, but the results are generally gratifying. The wives seem to be better able to adjust to the job than the husband to the home and domesticity.[18]

MUTUAL TRUST AND EXPANSION THROUGH OPENNESS

Couples striving for greater flexibility generally replace the norm of togetherness with an emphasis on mutual trust and expansion through openness. One of the couples in the O'Neills' study defines trust as follows:

[17] From *Open Marriage: A New Life Style for Couples*, p. 158, by Nena O'Neill and George O'Neill. Copyright © 1972 by Nena O'Neill and George O'Neill. Reprinted by permission of the publisher, M. Evans and Company, Inc., New York, New York 10017.

[18] Olof Palme, "The Lesson from Sweden: The Emancipation of Man," in Louise Kapp Howe, ed., *The Future of the Family* (New York: Simon & Schuster, 1972), pp. 247–58.

Glenda: Trust is a confidence you have in the other person, a belief in him. I believe in Robert, he believes in me. Sure, it takes time, but we love each other enough to be honest with one another. If we weren't honest with each other, it wouldn't be possible.

Robert: You know, trust is freedom—a lack of fear. When you get down to it, trust is really faith. We have a faith in the fact that what we have together is much more than any temporary relationship could ever be. So we aren't afraid of one another's relationships with other people.[19]

The fact that Glenda and Robert's relationship is open and honest and based on mutual trust gives it a kind of vitality that is rarely possible in partnerships that are limited by conventional role assignments. They share an exciting experience of the sort that builds confidence in one's partner and in oneself. In such a partnership, the partners know that the relationship has durability, and the inner security they derive from this knowledge gives them the freedom to expand and grow in an open and trusting way. That is to say, in an intimate partnership trust has a spiraling effect: the more it is given and reciprocated, the more secure the partners become in the essential soundness of their relationship, and hence the more trusting they can be.

Openness involves the capacity to hear, understand, and realize who another person is. It means assuming responsibility for yourself first and then sharing that self to whatever degree seems appropriate. Every couple must define these limits for themselves, for openness means not only communicating freely with one's partner but also respecting the partner's need for privacy, the partner's need to have an independent, autonomous life, parts of which he or she may not wish to share. The couple who pride themselves on the fact that they "have no secrets from each other" may not have as much openness in their partnership as they imagine. What is missing in this case is the freedom to have private lives.

We can realize how important this is by considering the case of a wife who has a friend who would like to confide some personal secret to her but does not want the husband to know. If the friend is aware that the husband and wife "have no secrets," she will be reluctant to talk confidentially, knowing that anything she tells her friend will pass directly to her friend's husband. She finds it impossible, therefore, to treat her friend as an autonomous individual; instead, she has to regard her as

[19]From Open Marriage: A New Life Style for Couples, p. 226, by Nena O'Neill and George O'Neill. Copyright © 1972 by Nena O'Neill and George O'Neill. Reprinted by permission of the publisher, M. Evans and Company, Inc., New York, New York 10017.

merely one half of the husband-wife duo and can share with her only those thoughts she would be willing to share with him. This simple but rather common case involving an outsider indicates how easily the ideal of openness and sharing can be misunderstood and pushed too far. Openness should never become a pretext for invading the individual privacy of the partners. Properly understood, the ideal of openness means not only the freedom to communicate fully with one's partner but also the freedom not to communicate when one does not want to.

Another important ramification of the concept of openness involves the controversial subject of whether or not opening up marriage to outside sexual contacts is a beneficial thing. We will return to this subject shortly, in our discussion of the role of jealousy in intimate partnerships, but for the time being we should like to observe that there is some evidence to suggest that in some cases expanded sexual relations can indeed bring new life to individuals and to their partnership. Raymond Lawrence, a therapist, provides an example in his case study of Susan, a patient of his in her mid-twenties who had been married for over six years when she came to him for therapy. "She was thinking of having an affair with a young pediatrician and she felt she needed to talk to someone about it," Lawrence explains.[20]

Over a series of sessions, various areas of Susan's marriage were explored. It was revealed that Susan's husband was deeply immersed in his work and was able to spend little time with her. Throughout this experience, Susan felt herself deteriorating and her feelings about herself becoming less and less positive. Although her meetings with the pediatrician were accidental at first, she found they had the effect of making her feel more and more stimulated and excited about life.

During the sessions with Mr. Lawrence, the therapist sought to examine with Susan whether she was possibly acting out a desire to communicate something to her husband, to even the score with him for her sense of dullness, to get revenge on her husband for something that he might have done, or simply to get his attention. None of these typical motivations seemed to be present behind Susan's desire to have an affair with the pediatrician. Susan revealed a commitment to her marriage even with its limitations. "Susan is like innumerable married persons who have come to me for counseling," Mr. Laurence observes. "They are persons stifled and burdened by the total and exclusive dimension of the marriage contract."[21]

After having secured reasonable assurance that there were no ulterior

[20]Raymond Lawrence, "The Affair as a Redemptive Experience," in Robert Rimmer, ed., *Adventures in Loving* (New York: Signet Books, 1973), p. 65.
[21]"The Affair as a Redemptive Experience," p. 66.

motives and that the projected affair was not an assault on her husband, the therapist explored the whole area of guilt with Susan. He tried to help her understand the serious moral questions involved in her interest. He asked Susan to consider if she was capable of bearing the guilt feelings such an affair was likely to entail.

At the end of this careful process of guided self-examination, Susan decided to have her affair. It lasted six months. During that time marked changes in her appearance, her manner, and her functioning within her family became apparent. These changes in Susan evoked increasing interest and response from her husband. He exhibited some anxiety and at the same time began to focus more and more of his attention on her and their marriage. Both Susan and her husband were pleased with the new vitality they found in their marriage.

From this case history, we can understand something of the contribution outside relationships may bring to a partnership under certain conditions. It must be noted, however, that in this case the therapist explored many possible ulterior motives, unconscious drives, and other psychological mechanisms that could have been used to turn this affair into a very destructive liaison for all involved. The same sort of caution should always be employed whenever the question of engaging in sexual intercourse outside of marriage is approached because this is likely to be an area in which hidden psychological motivations may be at work. It may not always be necessary to seek professional guidance, but a careful examination of one's own feelings is advisable if one is to feel confident that the end result will be an opening up of the relationship to greater freedom rather than a plunge into a tangled situation involving self-deception and feelings of guilt.

Coping with Jealousy

Jealousy is an integral component of our understanding of love. The extent to which we feel jealous is often taken as a measure of our love. If the husband or lover does not experience jealousy when the beloved bestows her time and attention on another, then he must not love his partner very much. What is more, anthropologists tell us that jealousy seems to be a fairly widespread phenomenon in human experience; it occurs even in polygamous households among co-wives.[22] Nevertheless, there is little evidence to support the assumption that jealousy is a necessary ingredient of deep and loving relationships. Jealousy is a learned

[22]George Peter Murdock, *Social Structure* (New York: Free Press, 1965), p. 294. William N. Stephens, *Comparative Perspectives on Marriage and the Family* (New York: Holt, Rinehart & Winston, 1963), p. 59.

response. Far from being a natural way of indicating the depth of one's love, it is a technique we learn for expressing the insecurities that arise in possessive relationships. As the O'Neills observe:

The idea of sexually exclusive monogamy and possession of another breeds deep-rooted dependencies, infantile and childish emotions and insecurities. The more insecure you are, the more you will be jealous. Jealousy, says Abraham Maslow, "practically always breeds further rejection and deeper insecurity." And jealousy, like a destructive cancer, breeds more jealousy. It is never, then, a function of love, but of our insecurities and dependencies. It is the fear of a loss of love and it destroys that very love. It is detrimental to and a denial of a loved one's personal identity.[23]

The fact that jealousy is a deep-rooted tradition in our culture and that, in personal terms, it may express deep unconscious feelings, does not mean that it is natural, inevitable, or something to be encouraged. Many people, in their efforts to achieve trusting and open partnerships, have been able to overcome it. Such people often report that their struggle with jealousy has been successful to the extent that it does not prevent them from developing meaningful and loving relationships outside the primary partnership of their marriage. They have come to view outside relationships as a natural right to be enjoyed by themselves and their spouses.

When two partners in an intimate relationship are secure in their own self-identity and are capable of trusting each other, each is free to know, enjoy, and share relationships outside of the marriage that can actually serve to augment the primary partnership and make it more creative. Occasionally, the partners may even agree that their outside relationships may include sexual intercourse. At present, this extreme form of openness is relatively rare, and the situation is difficult to discuss objectively because of the deep feelings many people have on the subject. Although discussions in the popular press of the O'Neills' book *Open Marriage* might lead one to suppose that the concept of openness necessarily refers to extramarital sexual relations, in fact this is only one special case of openness which does not figure centrally in the O'Neills' thinking.

The important point to be borne in mind is that openness means a relationship based on mutual trust and equality; in an open relationship there is no room for jealousy because the feelings of insecurity and possessiveness out of which jealousy grows are absent from the relationship. Thus it may well be that some couples in an open relationship can enjoy outside sexual contacts that enable them to bring back to their primary relationship the love and pleasure experienced outside without jealousy disrupting their partnership.

On the other hand, recognizing that openness can be of immense value in creating a dynamic and growing partnership should not blind us to the fact that there are many good reasons why a couple may choose to limit their sexual activities to each other. Many people find that their sexual pleasure and their ability to communicate through sex are heightened by the fact that this communication is something inviolately private between just the two of them. For such people sexual exclusivity would not be inconsistent with an open relationship. But when exclusivity is based on proprietary feelings about one's partner, openness is indeed impossible. In short, the couple who want an open and trusting relationship should strive to eliminate feelings of possessiveness and jealousy from their interactions, but this does not mean that they have to or even should open up their sexual relationship to outside contacts. On the contrary, sexual exclusivity can be an important and meaningful part of an open and creative partnership so long as it is not based on jealousy and possessiveness.

A NEW MARRIAGE CONTRACT: A SAMPLE

Some couples today are beginning their marriages—or redefining already established marriages—by writing out their own formal marriage contracts.[24] Such documents may not have legal standing because they are inconsistent with various state laws governing marital relationships, but efforts to establish legally valid precedents in this area are gaining momentum. In the future it may become possible to be increasingly creative in the drawing up of a marriage contract that will accurately reflect a given couple's understanding of their relationship.

The contract reprinted below was drafted by Harriett Cody and Harvey Sadis with the aid of a lawyer. The couple intended it to be the guideline for their marriage.[25] They were legally married in the State of Washington by signing a marriage license on the same day as they signed this contract. It is not at all clear whether the State of Washington would uphold such a contract, but Harriett and Harvey, who have

[24]Another contrast is to be found in Rimmer, *Adventures in Loving*, pp. 133–35.
[25]"Marriage Contract of Harriett Mary Cody and Harvey Joseph Sadis," *Ms.* (June 1973), pp. 63ff. Reprinted by permission of Ms. Cody and Mr. Sadis.

MARRIAGE CONTRACT

OF

HARRIETT MARY CODY and HARVEY JOSEPH SADIS

THIS CONTRACT is entered into this 24th day of November, 1972, by and between HARRIETT MARY CODY and HARVEY JOSEPH SADIS, as the parties enter into a marriage relationship authorized by a Marriage License and by an Official of the State of Washington, County of King.

RECITALS OF FACT

1. HARRIETT MARY CODY is a woman 27 years of age, born on August 23, 1945, in Norfolk, Virginia, and the child of Hiram S. Cody Jr. and Mary V. Cody.

2. HARVEY JOSEPH SADIS is a man 26 years of age, born on April 12, 1946, in Seattle, Washington, and the child of Jean Sadis and Joseph Sadis.

3. HARRIETT and HARVEY are presently residing together in Seattle, Washington.

HARRIETT and HARVEY desire to enter into a marriage relationship, duly solemnized under the laws of the State of Washington, the rights and obligations of which relationship differ from the traditional rights and obligations of married persons in the State of Washington which would prevail in the absence of this CONTRACT. The parties have together drafted this MARRIAGE CONTRACT in order to define a marriage relationship sought by the parties which preserves and promotes their individual identities as a man and a woman contracting to live together for mutual benefit and growth.

HARRIETT and HARVEY are of sound mind and body, have a clear understanding of the terms of this CONTRACT and of the binding nature of the agreements contained herein; they freely and in good faith choose to enter into this MARRIAGE CONTRACT and fully intend it to be legally binding upon themselves.

NOW, THEREFORE, in consideration of their affection and esteem for each other, and in consideration of the mutual promises herein expressed, the sufficiency of which is hereby acknowledged, HARRIETT and HARVEY agree as follows:

Article I. Names

HARRIETT and HARVEY affirm their individuality and equality in this relationship. The parties reject the concept of ownership implied in the adoption by the woman of the man's name; and they refuse to define themselves as husband and wife because of the possessory nature of these titles.

THEREFORE, THE PARTIES AGREE TO retain and use the given family names of each party: HARRIETT MARY CODY and HARVEY JOSEPH SADIS. The parties will employ the titles of address, MS. CODY and MR. SADIS, and will henceforth be known as PARTNERS in this relationship.

Article II. Relationships With Others

HARRIETT and HARVEY believe that their partnership will be enriched by the extent to which their respective needs can be met by relationships with others, rather than by a total dependence on each other to fulfill their needs. The parties have strong individual identities, with their own families, friends, careers, histories, and interests, and do not view themselves as an inseparable couple who do not exist apart from each other.

THEREFORE, THE PARTIES AGREE to allow each other as much time with other friends individually as they spend with each other. The parties also agree that invitations extended to one of them will not be assumed to have automatically been extended to the other.

The parties freely acknowledge their insecurities about sexual relationships beyond the partnership.

THEREFORE, THE PARTIES AGREE to maintain sexual fidelity to each other.

Article III. Religion

HARVEY freely admits the break with Jewish tradition represented by this CONTRACT with HARRIETT. But he fully intends to maintain the cultural and religious traditions of his Sephardic community insofar as possible. HARRIETT chooses not to embrace the Jewish religion.

THEREFORE, THE PARTIES AGREE to respect their individual preferences with respect to religion and to make no demands on each other to change such preferences.

THE PARTIES AGREE to continue the traditions associated with their respective religious holidays (Christmas, Hanukkah, Passover, Easter, Rosh Hashanah, Yom Kippur, Thanksgiving) and to include each other in the celebrations thereof.

Article IV. Children

The joy and the commitment of the parties' relationship are not dependent on raising a family. HARRIETT and HARVEY will not be unfulfilled as individuals or as partners if they choose not to have children. At this time, the parties do not share a commitment to have children.

THE PARTIES AGREE that any children will be the result of choice, not chance, and THERE-FORE the decision to have children will be mutual and deliberate. FURTHER, THE PARTIES AGREE that the responsibility for birth control will be shared. In the event of a pregnancy unwanted by either party, THE PARTIES AGREE to obtain an abortion of such pregnancy. A decision by one party to be sterilized will be supported emotionally and financially by the other.

Article V. Careers; Domicile

HARRIET and HARVEY value the importance and integrity of their respective careers and acknowledge the demands that their jobs place on them as individuals and on their partnership. Commitment to their careers will sometimes place stress on the relationship. It has been the experience of the parties that insofar as their careers contribute to individual self-fulfillment, the careers strengthen the partnership.

THE PARTIES AGREE that, should a career opportunity arise for one of the parties in another city at any future time, the decision to move shall be mutual and based upon the following factors:

(a) The overall advantage gained by one of the parties in pursuing the new career opportunity shall be weighed against the disadvantages, economic and otherwise, incurred by the other;

(b) The amount of income from the new job shall not be controlling;

(c) Short-term separations as a result of such moves may be necessary.

HARVEY HEREBY WAIVES whatever right he may have to solely determine the legal domicile of the parties.

Article VI. Care and Use of Living Space

HARRIETT and HARVEY recognize the need for autonomy and equality within the home in terms of the use of available space and allocation of household tasks. The parties reject the concept that the responsibility for housework rests with the woman in a marriage relationship while the duties of home maintenance and repair rest with the man.

THEREFORE, THE PARTIES AGREE to share equally in the performance of all household tasks, taking into consideration individual schedules and preferences. Periodic allocations of household tasks will be made, in which the time involved in the performance of each party's tasks is equal.

THE PARTIES AGREE that decisions about the use of living space in the home shall be mutually made, regardless of the parties' relative financial interests in the ownership or rental of the home. Each party shall have an individual area within the home in an equal amount, insofar as space is available.

Article VII. Property; Debts; Living Expenses

HARRIETT and HARVEY intend that the individual autonomy sought in the partnership shall be reflected in the ownership of existing and future-acquired property, in the characterization and control of income, and in the responsibility for living expenses.

THEREFORE, THE PARTIES AGREE that this Article of their MARRIAGE CONTRACT, in lieu of the community property laws of the State of Washington, shall govern their interests and obligations in all property acquired during their marriage, as follows:

A. Property

THE PARTIES HAVE MADE full disclosure to each other of all properties and assets presently owned by each of them, and of the income derived therefrom and from all other sources, and AGREE that each party shall have sole management, control, and disposition of the property which each would have owned as a single person, all as specifically described in EXHIBIT A, which is incorporated by reference and made a part of this CONTRACT.

THE PARTIES AGREE that the wages, salary, and other income (including loans) derived by one of the parties will be the separate property of such party and subject to the independent control and/or obligation of such party. In order to avoid the commingling of the separate assets, THE PARTIES AGREE to maintain separate bank accounts. At the present time, HARVEY's income consists of his salary as a full-time teacher with Seattle Public Schools; and HARRIETT's income is derived from her savings and government loans,

while she is a full-time student at the University of Puget Sound School of Law in Tacoma.

Ownership of all future-acquired property, tangible and intangible, will be determined in accordance with the respective contributions of each party, even in the case of property which is jointly used. Annually or sooner if required, THE PARTIES AGREE to amend EXHIBIT A of this CONTRACT to include future-acquired property and any changes in the ownership of property presently described in EXHIBIT A. The parties may, by mutual agreement, determine their respective interests in an item of property on a basis other than financial contribution, but such agreement shall not be effective until reduced to writing in EXHIBIT A to this CONTRACT. Gifts, bequests, or devises made to one of the parties will become the separate property of that party, while gifts made to both of the parties will be considered to be jointly owned.

THE PARTIES AGREE to name each other as full beneficaries of any life insurance policies which they now own or may acquire in the future.

B. Debts

THE PARTIES AGREE that they shall not be obligated to the present or future-incurred debts of the other, including tuition and other educational expenses.

C. Living Expenses

THE PARTIES AGREE to share responsibility for the following expenses, which shall be called LIVING EXPENSES, in proportion to their respective incomes: (1) Mortgage payment or rent,

(2) Utilities, (3) Home maintenance, (4) Food, (5) Shared entertainment, (6) Medical expenses. Other expenses shall be called PERSONAL EXPENSES and will be borne individually by the parties.

THE PARTIES RECOGNIZE that in the absence of income by one of the parties, resulting from unemployment or extended illness, LIVING EXPENSES may become the sole responsibility of the employed party; and in such a situation, the employed party will assume responsibility for the PERSONAL EXPENSES of the other, including, but not limited to the following: (1) Insurance, (2) Transportation, (3) Clothing, (4) Miscellaneous personal items.

THE PARTIES AGREE that extended periods of time in which one or both of the parties will be totally without income will be mutually negotiated.

HARRIETT HEREBY WAIVES whatever right she may have to rely on HARVEY to provide the sole economic support for the family unit.

Article VIII. Evaluation of the Partnership

HARRIETT and HARVEY recognize the importance of change in their relationship and intend that this CONTRACT shall be a living document and a focus for periodic evaluations of the partnership.

THE PARTIES AGREE that either party can initiate a review of any article of the CONTRACT at any time for amendment to reflect changes in the relationship. THE PARTIES AGREE to honor such requests for review with negotiations and discussions at a mutually convenient time.

THE PARTIES AGREE that, in any event, there shall be an annual review of the provisions of the CONTRACT, including EXHIBIT A, on or about the anniversary date of the execution of the CONTRACT.

THE PARTIES AGREE that, in the case of unresolved conflicts between them over any provisions of the CONTRACT, they will seek mediation, professional or otherwise, by a third party.

Article IX. Termination of the Contract

HARRIETT and HARVEY may by mutual consent terminate this CONTRACT and end the marriage relationship at any time.

FURTHERMORE, THE PARTIES AGREE that the breach of a material provision of this CONTRACT for a sustained period of time shall constitute "cruel treatment or personal indignities rendering life burdensome" and shall serve as a ground for termination of this CONTRACT, according to the divorce laws of the State of Washington, under RCW 26.08.020.

THE PARTIES AGREE that in the event of mutual consent to terminate this CONTRACT or breach thereof, neither party shall contest the application by the other party for a divorce decree or the entry of such decree in the county in which the parties are both residing at the time of such application.

In the event of termination of the CONTRACT and divorce of the parties, the provisions of this Article and Article VII of this CONTRACT, as amended, shall serve as the FINAL PROPERTY SETTLEMENT AGREEMENT between the parties. In such event, this CONTRACT is intended to effect a complete settlement of any and all claims that either party may have against the other, and a complete settlement of their respective rights as to alimony, property rights, homestead rights, inheritance rights, and all other rights of property otherwise arising out of their partnership.

At such time as there may be a child born of this partnership or adopted by the parties, THE PARTIES AGREE to amend this CONTRACT to make provisions for their respective rights and obligations in regard to the child in the event of termination of the CONTRACT (including provisions for support and education of the child).

Article X. Decision-Making

HARRIETT and HARVEY share a commitment to a process of negotiations and compromise which will strengthen their equality in the partnership. Decisions will be made with respect for individual needs. THE PARTIES HOPE to maintain such mutual decision-making so that the daily decisions affecting their lives will not become a struggle between the parties for power, authority, and dominance. THE PARTIES AGREE that such a process, while sometimes time-consuming and fatiguing, is a good investment in the future of their relationship and their continued esteem for each other.

NOW, THEREFORE, HARRIETT and HARVEY make the following declarations:

1. They are responsible adults.
2. They freely adopt the spirit and the material of this MARRIAGE CONTRACT.
3. The MARRIAGE CONTRACT entered into in conjunction with a Marriage License of the State of Washington, County of King, on this 24th day of November, 1972, hereby manifests their intent to define the rights and obligations of their marriage relationship as distinct from those rights and obligations defined by the laws of the State of Washington, and affirms their right to do so.
4. They intend to be legally bound by this MARRIAGE CONTRACT and to uphold its articles before any Court of Law in the Land.

THEREFORE COMES NOW, HARRIETT MARY CODY who applauds her development which allows her to enter into this partnership of trust, and SHE AGREES to go forward with this partnership in the spirit of the foregoing MARRIAGE CONTRACT.

HARRIETT MARY CODY

THEREFORE, COMES NOW, HARVEY JOSEPH SADIS who celebrates his growth and independence with the signing of this CONTRACT, and HE AGREES to accept the responsibilities of this partnership as set forth in the foregoing MARRIAGE CONTRACT.

HARVEY JOSEPH SADIS

FINALLY, COMES JANICE NIEMI who CERTIFIES that HARRIETT and HARVEY did freely read and sign this MARRIAGE CONTRACT in her presence, on the occasion of their entry into a marriage relationship by the signing of a Marriage License of the State of Washington, County of King, at which she presided as an Official Witness and as an Official Authorized to Solemnize Marriage in this state. FURTHER, SHE DECLARES that the Marriage License of the parties bears the date of the signing of this MARRIAGE CONTRACT.

JANICE NIEMI

agreed to abide by it, have gone a long way toward specifying their own understanding of their relationship.

Basically oriented toward an egalitarian relationship, the contract covers many areas that really need exploration and discovery. It arose out of the desire on the part of two individuals for a partnership based on a system of rights and obligations that do not seem to be available in the traditional style of marriage. Although many of the specific points made in this contract may reflect the desires of a great number of people today, it is important to remember that this document represents the specific desires of two specific individuals. As they say in Article VIII, they intend this contract to be "a living document and a focus for periodic evaluations of the partnership." We offer it here simply as a sample of the type of approach which some couples feel can provide a framework within which they can grow.

Whether or not we agree with the details of this contract, we can acknowledge that it is a sincere effort to reach an understanding of many important facets of the marriage partnership. It attempts to specify the ground rules for handling some of the problems that Harriett and Harvey know will confront them in their marriage. Some people do this informally and often quite effectively, but most never raise the issues at all. What is important here is the effort to deal openly with many of the unconscious assumptions we make as a result of our conventional expectations about marriage. Such an effort reflects a willingness to engage in a partnership which encourages nondependent living, personal growth, individual freedom, flexible roles, mutual trust, and expansion through openness.

SUMMARY

This chapter began with an examination of the implicit marriage contract, which is the set of expectations that determines the roles, rights, and obligations married partners generally expect to see fulfilled in their relationship. A partnership that follows the norms described in the implicit contract will be characterized by (1) lifelong monogamy; (2) sexual exclusivity; (3) economic independence of the partners from outside support; (4) a division of labor pattern that will vary from case to case but generally will fall within certain broad patterns; (5) a pattern of dominance in which the male generally holds the balance of power; (6) an expectation of children; and (7) an acceptance of the ideal of togetherness.

Although there is nothing wrong with any of these conventional expectations, it seems to be generally true that a couple can increase their chances of building a dynamic and growing relationship by adapting the conventional expectations to their own unique situation. By becoming more flexible, a couple can achieve a relationship characterized by nondependent living, personal growth, individual freedom, role flexibility, mutual trust and expansion through openness, and freedom from jealousy.

Although this sort of flexibility can be built into a marriage on an informal basis, the formal contract drawn up by Harriett Cody and Harvey Sadis was used to provide a sample of the way one articulate contemporary couple approached the problem of building a framework within which a dynamic partnership could flourish. Their intent was to establish a free and egalitarian relationship in which the partners can find mutual growth and enjoyment.

12
PARENTS AND CHILDREN

In the revised edition of *Decent and Indecent* . . . I now start . . . with the needs of infants and young children for a sensitive, enthusiastic kind of care if they are to develop into warm-hearted, creative people. They can receive this from loving fathers, mothers, grandparents. But each year it is harder to hire a full-time substitute caretaker whose personality and attitude approach those of good parents. . . . If neither parent is willing to take part time off from a job for a few years, they might do better without children.

Benjamin M. Spock

INTRODUCTION

By common understanding, children make a family. A young couple very often hesitate to call themselves a family until children are born; indeed, some young couples do not really feel themselves to be married until they have children. In some areas of the world today, such as rural Sweden and among the Swazi of Africa, a marriage is not considered consummated until the wife has borne a child.

Parenthood has been even more romanticized than love in American Society.[1] Thus most young people look forward to growing up, getting married, and having children as the normal and natural sequence of events. In this context, the idea of someone's not wanting to have children seems

[1] E. E. LeMasters, *Parenthood in America*, 2nd ed. (Homewood, Ill.: The Dorsey Press, 1974), pp. 8–32.

Joel Gordon

269

as unnatural and perverse as not wanting to grow up. For this reason some misguided marriage counselors occasionally have advised people who were having trouble in their marriage to have a child, apparently on the assumption that this would "bring them back to normal."

The notion that a marriage relation or a partnership can be improved because the partners participate in the procreation of new life is clearly not founded in fact. Thus, for example, studies have shown that marital satisfaction commonly decreases over the childbearing years and begins to recover after the children leave the home.[2] Any realistic assessment would have to conclude that children are an additional responsibility and burden—as well as a joy—that should be assumed only by mature partners who consciously decide that they are willing to become parents.

This chapter deals with a question every couple must face at some time in their partnership—the question of whether or not to have children. This choice is complicated by the fact that a great number of factors must be considered in arriving at an answer. The first of these concerns the health and the biological capacities of the partners and their prospects for a normal birth. Second, in light of the increasing concern for population control, the choice to have or not to have a child cannot be made re-sponsibly today without some awareness of the issues involved in controlling the world's population. Third, the changing life style of women, particularly those who want to develop careers, adds new dimensions to the choice, inasmuch as having children normally places some constraints upon the mother's career development. Fourth, the teaching of various religious denominations may come into play if one belongs to a faith that limits one's options as far as birth control and abortion are concerned.

Finally, the decision to have children involves a long-term commitment of resources. It is difficult to specify how the conditions of life will change during the period of the child's growing up, but once a child is born the decision is irrevocable. On the other hand, under most circumstances the decision not to have children can be reevaluated at any time, although, of course, increasing age diminishes the effectiveness such reevaluation can have. After forty, most couples would probably find it very difficult to decide to have children.

The choice *not* to have children is an exceedingly difficult one for a couple to make in our society simply because it is so widely assumed that they should have them. The discussion that follows is offered with the intention of making it possible for couples to deal with this vitally important question in an honest and open way. By doing so, they can avoid being led into parenthood when they don't really want it and also can feel confident, when and if they decide to have children, that the decision actually reflects their own desires.

[2]See the summary in Boyd Collins and Harold Feldman, "Marital Satisfaction Over the Family Life Cycle" *Journal of Marriage and the Family* (February 1970), pp. 20–28.

DO WE REALLY WANT CHILDREN?

Most couples can have children. The question is, Do they really want them? To raise the question in this way is perhaps misleading, for it implies that a couple can somehow know enough to answer it rationally. In fact, however, the consequences of whatever decision is made are hard to predetermine. Couples in the second year of their marriage have different resources and liabilities than couples in their fifth or fifteenth. Their personalities change, their life changes and life styles change, and the world in which they live changes. Then how is it possible to answer such a question with any assurance that the answer will still seem right a number of years in the future?

Although it is difficult to reach any answer with certainty, an important step is taken as soon as the question is raised. In the past, the factors that seem to have had the most influence upon whether or not couples have babies were economic. During the Depression, for example, the birth rate fell drastically, presumably because people were immediately aware of the economic hardships of raising children in such hard times. Today the birth rate is rapidly declining, but economics do not fully explain this phenomenon. Young couples may well see children as economic liabilities in an urban world, but other factors also seem to be involved. Not only have young couples become aware of the problems associated with overpopulation, but they also no longer unquestionably assume that the woman's destiny is motherhood. But what specific factors actually influence these decisions in specific cases? And on what basis can a couple have reasonable assurance that they have made the right decision?

One of the interesting things about asking the question, "Do we really want children?" is that very few people have bothered to offer arguments in favor of having children. It is simply assumed that nine out of ten couples will want children and that is that. As a result, there is little research on the issue, for until quite recently neither researchers nor the general public have seen the issue as critical. As the arguments against having children have become more and more pronounced, however, the counter-arguments in favor of children have had to be consciously developed. Thus we have a paradoxical situation in which having children is still assumed to be the natural choice for married couples but the arguments in favor of this decision may tend to seem idealistic and a bit unconvincing. Conversely, it is easy to argue convincingly that the public interest is best served by controlling the number of children, but the decision not to have children is a difficult one to make.

Most people who decide to have children today do not really sit down and weigh the alternatives before reaching a decision. The costs of having children, or more children than one can afford, may lead to a consciously made and rational decision *not to have* children, but in most cases the decision to *have* children is not made on the basis of such explicitly developed reasons. This is why we think it important that the arguments both for and against children be sketched out, so that either decision can be reached on a rational basis that will satisfy any particular couple's sense of needs, values, and desires.

In Favor of Children

Among the factors that affect the decision to have children, probably the most significant is the fact that society normally expects this of two people who get married. Childless marriages are commonly subject to criticism, and there tends to be a general suspicion that there must be something wrong, either physically or psychologically, with a couple who do not have children after a reasonable period of married life. Because of these expectations, many women feel that fulfillment as a woman depends upon giving birth to a child and experiencing motherhood. Thus women frequently decide to have children because they feel it necessary to do so in order to fully realize their own identity. What is more, for both men and women accepting the responsibility of parenthood is ordinarily regarded as clear evidence that one has reached maturity.

In addition to these social factors, there are many personal rewards that derive from living into the roles and expectations of parenthood. In a very real sense, the decision to have a child is really a decision to begin developing a new and different kind of an environment in which to grow. Being one member of a couple certainly can provide a feeling of group identity and belongingness, but being a member of a "family," even a small one, multiplies the possibilities for intimate interaction. Self-actualization, self-respect, and self-esteem can develop within families to a richer and fuller extent than in dyadic (that is, two-party) relationships simply because the web of intimate connections is fuller and more complex. For this to happen, however, the children must be regarded as participants in the companionship system of the family, not simply as dependents. Where children enjoy participant status, their contribution to the growth and development of their parents can take place at several levels. Simply by interacting with their parents they may bring about a deeper understanding of what it means to be a person. Children often feel freer than their parents to express such basic human emotions as affection, love, and respect. Contact with them thus often serves to help adults get back in touch with their feelings. What is more, children's awe and wonder at the commonplace, and their curiosity about all things, often provide their parents with refreshing opportunities to see the mundane world in a different and more exciting way. In this sense, children can create a richer environment within which growth can take place, so that it seems fair to conclude that the family is a socializing agency for the parents as well as the children.

A final reason for having children is the elementary fact that the propagation of the human species appears to be an intrinsically worthwhile goal. Implicit in the commandment, "Be fruitful and multiply," is the assumption that procreation is beneficial both for the species and for the couple. Indeed, some people see this as the overarching reason for having children. In this context even the contemporary recognition of the necessity of controlling the size of our population does not appear as an injunction against having children. On the contrary, it is a recognition of the fact that it is necessary for some people to limit the size of their families or to have no children at all if we are to provide the best possible environment for the species as a whole. But of course this does not mean that *no one* should choose to become parents. The fact that many people are making the choice to have no children or few means that those who want children are freer to have them without feeling that their decision is socially irresponsible.

Against Children

The arguments against having children seem to be gathering some strength today because of concern about the population explosion. People concerned with the population problem generally argue that young couples should learn to *want* fewer children, not that they should have fewer than they want. Insofar as this general argument serves to take some of the pressure to have children off those couples who are really hesitant about having them for a variety of reasons, it tends to increase the number of couples who do not in fact have children. But it is clearly not an argument against having children per se.

By far the most powerful arguments against having children are linked to attempts to overthrow the myth that motherhood is instinctive and that women cannot fulfill themselves unless they have children. The simple truth of the matter is that some women, perhaps a large number of them, should not have children because they are not suited, either socially, psychologically, or biologically, to the role of mother or because having children and raising them can effectively destroy or at least hamper careers they value more than they value motherhood. At the present time, day-care facilities are not adequate to permit many mothers to find suitable substitutes for maternal care at a price they can afford. Given this state of affairs, the choice to have children and the choice to pursue a career may be mutually exclusive.

Because of the belief that the maternal role is in some sense natural or instinctive, the decision to say "no" to motherhood is regarded as a nonconforming choice and earns the woman who chooses this option few social supports and rewards. Although this situation is slowly changing, making it easier for some middle-class women to decline motherhood, this is still by no means an easy choice for a couple to make. The choice not to have children places both the man and the woman in relatively unexplored territory as they experiment with the rather new style of voluntarily childless families. The guidelines are not as clear, the expectations are not as precise, and the social benefits— ranging from tax advantages to social approval—are not as great as are the benefits deriving from parenthood.

Children place numerous constraints upon their parents. Parents are not as free as nonparents to move, change jobs, travel, change life styles, or engage in various recreational activities. Children demand time and resources, and any significant change in living conditions must be considered in terms of how it is likely to affect them. Thus people who do not want to accept these constraints are provided with a powerful argument against having children. Unfortunately, couples who decide to remain childless for this reason are often denounced as selfiish and self-indulgent. They should recognize that this criticism—which can be quite disturbing, especially when it comes from the couple's parents—has absolutely no validity. Seeking to find personal satisfaction through a childless life style is no more self-indulgent than seeking personal fulfillment through parenthood.

In light of our society's interest in training and education, it is surprising that Americans spend so little time and effort in training people to be parents. At a time when more is expected of parents than at any other time in our history, parents have few resources to fall back on and often find themselves feeling inadequate in the role. In the past, when extended families were common and young couples tended to live with or near their own parents, new mothers could count on readily

Burt Glinn, Magnum Photos

available guidance from their mothers or mothers-in-law. Today this is less likely to be the case, and the trend for young couples to establish residence in suburban communities consisting largely of their age-group peers means that in all likelihood the inexperienced new mother will be surrounded by friends no more experienced than she.

It is easy enough to tell the young couple who doubt their competency in this role that "everybody feels this way" and "you'll get over it," but it is not necessarily clear that it is wise to do so. Obviously, anyone beginning a new experience is likely to feel somewhat apprehensive about it; in some cases these apprehensions may be no more than a natural nervousness about a new role. But in other cases feelings of inadequacy may be quite justifiable. When one considers how many disturbed and unhappy children there are in our country, one cannot help wishing people had not always been so eager to convince couples who doubted their ability to be good parents that their doubts were unfounded. Parenthood is undeniably a more difficult and demanding role in our fluid and changing society than it was in the relatively more stable social situation of a few generations back, yet the psychological rewards it offers have remained unchanged. The fact that there has been an increase in the costs and no compensatory increase in the rewards tends to make it a less attractive role than it used to be. There is no reason why couples who do not find the role appealing should be encouraged to become parents.

Economic considerations often provide an important reason not to have children. As a rough guide to cost we can estimate that it takes three times the annual family income to raise each child to the age at which he or she achieves economic independence. Thus a family earning about $15,000 will spend about $45,000 on each child, including education. This is a heavy expenditure that will increase as inflation, rising expectations, average years of schooling, and cost of education rise. What is more, the money lost from the wife's income when she must stop working or reduce her work schedule to care for the baby must be taken into account. Campbell estimates that for families living at poverty levels this cost is about $2,000 annually; for middle-income people it would, of course, be much higher.[3]

As we saw in Chapter 7, many contraceptive techniques are available to couples who choose not to have children. Some of these means (such as sterilization) make the choice essentially nonreversible, but many of them merely make it a choice that can be changed readily at a later stage in a marriage. As never before, intentionally childless marriage

---

[3]See the discussion in F. Ivan Nye and Felix Berardo, *The Family: Its Structure and Interaction* (New York: The Macmillan Company, 1973), pp. 349–53.

has become an available and viable life style option for increasing numbers of people, either for part of their marriage or as a lifelong arrangement. The choice to remain childless should not be seen in negative terms. The decision not to have children requires thinking and examination of alternatives, but giving this matter thoughtful consideration also means that the decision to have children—if and when it is made—becomes more of a conscious choice.

PREPARING FOR PARENTHOOD

We have just examined some of the arguments for and against having children. As time passes, young couples in our society are more and more likely to make the matter of having or not having children a conscious decision rather than assuming that it is simply natural to have children. As matters stand at present, however, about nine out of every ten married couples will have one or more children. And in most cases where couples do not have children it will be because they cannot have them. Yet very little is being done to prepare young couples for parenthood either before or after marriage.

Despite common assumptions to the contrary, learning how to be a parent does not come naturally. Bringing children into the world and raising them can be exciting and interesting, but it can also be a very difficult and arduous task. In our society these difficulties are often glossed over, for parenthood is even more romanticized in America than marriage. This romanticism can intensify the problems new parents face, inasmuch as it leads them to approach parenthood with a great many naive and misguided notions. Thus many young mothers are terrified and frightened when they first experience intense negative or even hostile feelings toward their screaming infants. They have been taught that "good mothers always love their babies" and they are ill-prepared for temporary lapses from this norm. Young mothers and fathers often find it difficult to cope with the complex feelings that arise in response to this new person who is making demands on their lives.

In one sense, there is not much a young couple can do to prepare themselves psychologically for the arrival of their first child. Caring for an infant of one's own is so unlike any other experience that in most important respects it will be something entirely new for the couple. Even people who grew up with younger brothers and sisters and who may have assumed a fairly heavy share of responsibility in caring for them do not have the experience that is really analogous to having one's own child. For example, we have already mentioned the fact that new parents

"We parlayed a twenty-seven-year trial marriage into six years of wedded bliss."

Drawing by Geo. Price; © 1974 The New Yorker Magazine, Inc.

often go through periods during which they resent intensely the demands placed upon them by the infant. But the fact that they may have had similar feelings toward a younger brother or sister does not really provide them with guidelines for responding to their own baby, for our social values tell us that it is quite acceptable to resent a demanding younger sibling but quite unacceptable to resent the demands of one's own child. Thus familiarity with the feelings does little or nothing to assuage the sense of guilt they are likely to generate.

In this regard, perhaps the most important thing young couples can do to help themselves in preparing for or adjusting to parenthood is to get as unromantic and realistic a picture as possible of what is involved. Something like consciousness-raising sessions for new parents can be quite helpful, as can serious conversations with candid and honest people who have experience with children. The candidness is the key ingredient here, for many people are reluctant to admit the existence of certain problems; such people, far from providing helpful information, can deepen the new parents' sense of confusion, disorientation, and guilt by reinforcing unrealistically rosy and romantic expectations about what parenthood is like.

Another appealing idea, which seems far less radical today than it did a mere decade ago, concerns something called "trial marriage" or "marriage in two stages."[4] The idea of trial marriage is to break the link that connects childbearing and marriage as though one were the inevitable consequence of the other. In trial marriages couples agree to marry simply for the sake of becoming partners and discovering each other. Children are specifically *not* part of the contracted expectations at this stage. (Divorce from such a marriage should be relatively easy to obtain because no children are involved.)

Only after satisfying themselves that the "trial" was successful would a couple approach the decision as to whether or not parenthood was a desirable next step for them. If it was, then the couple would remarry, this time on the basis of a marriage contract that included an expectation of children. Divorce from the second stage of this marriage should be more difficult to obtain, but because of the great amount of thought that went into making a specific contract for parenthood, it is reasonable to assume that divorce would be less likely to occur than in conventional one-stage marriages. Of course, if the couple should decide to remain childless, after living in such a trial marriage for a number of years, then there is no reason why they should not be free to perpetuate the partnership on its original basis.

It is not unlikely that something like trial marriage will become a legal reality in the not too distant future. It makes good sense from a number of points of view. The contract recorded in Chapter 11 attempts to bring such a trial marriage into effect, for it specifically states that Harriett and Harvey do not wish to have children at the time of their entering marriage. They also state that they intend their marriage contract to stipulate the terms of the divorce in the event they ever decide to separate. If this document is considered a legally binding contract in the state of Washington, where it was entered into, then trial marriage, for all intents and purposes, has become a legal option. The precise legal status of this document, however, has not been determined.

LIVING WITH CHILDREN

With the advent of their first child, a young couple is faced with a totally new situation. Many adjustments will be necessary. Simply because there are now three people instead of two, there is a more com-

[4]The notion of a trial marriage has a number of well-known advocates. See especially Judge Ben V. Lindsey, *Companionate Marriage* (New York: Boni & Liveright, 1927); Lord Bertrand Russell, *Marriage and Morals* (New York: Bantam Books, 1968).

plicated interaction pattern in the family and a more complex network of relationships. What is more, a growing child needs to be treated differently at different stages in her or his development. Thus the parents must continually learn new response patterns. And as the child's world expands through school, friends, and other outside contacts, her or his parents will be drawn into more active participation in the society outside their family.

When a family contains three people instead of two, it becomes possible for coalitions to be formed, and this possibility by itself is enough to bring about changes in the family power structure. The mother and her child can easily drift into an alliance that effectively excludes the father; or a father and child may form a coalition that leaves the mother out of the action; or the husband and wife can join forces against their child, producing what may well become a psychopathological condition called "scapegoating."[5] If another child is added to the family, the potential for paired relationships increases from three to six and it becomes

[5]Ezra Vogel and Norman W. Bell, "The Emotionally Disturbed Child as the Family Scapegoat," in Bell and Vogel, eds., *A Modern Introduction to the Family* (New York: The Free Press, 1960).

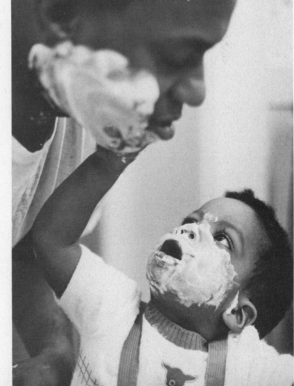

Burk Uzzle, Magnum Photos

possible for three-party coalitions to emerge. The larger the family, the greater the increase in the complexity of this family interaction network. Coalitions can emerge simply as a function of the increasing size of the family and they can have little or nothing to do with the particular personality characteristics of the family members. They can come about simply because it is now possible for them to occur.

Lest the reader become alarmed about what sounds like a frighteningly tangled situation, we should point out that in most cases coalitions between family members are not stable, long-term alliances. Most coalitions arise on an issue-by-issue basis. There is nothing wrong with coalitions of this sort; in fact, they are quite unavoidable. If a family is undecided about even such an elementary matter as whether to eat at home or go out for a pizza, the simple mathematics of the situation tell us that two members will favor one option and one will favor the other; after all, if all three agreed there would be no decisions to make. This means that a coalition forms between the two who are in agreement. Such a coalition, however, probably will not last beyond dinner time; by then a different coalition may have been formed about what television show to watch or some other matter.

Coalitions become a problem only when consistent patterns begin to emerge. For example, imagine a marriage in which one of the partners generally prefers an active social life while the other tends to favor spending most evenings at home alone. When such a couple is childless, they probably will work out some compromise in which sometimes the more active partner goes out alone and at other times they take turns going along with each other's desires. With the arrival of a child the situation changes, however. Many small children do not like their parents to go out and leave them with babysitters. Thus, it becomes very easy for the more socially passive partner to form an alliance with the child, who quickly learns that it is possible to keep Mommy and Daddy home by strategic intervention at the appropriate moment in the parents' discussions about whether to go out or not.

Such a situation is dangerous because it can easily escalate into a permanent arrangement. At first it may be limited to one recurring issue, such as going out or staying home, but as one parent—say the mother—grows to resent the persistence with which her child and husband "gang up" against her, she may deepen the alienation, thus generating further coalitions. When children get a sense that one parent is more sympathetic to their desires than the other, it is easy for them to form a coalition with the parent they see as the "good guy" and against the one they see as the villain. This situation commonly arises over the issue of discipline, when husbands who are away from the children all day are reluctant to play a role in disciplining them when they get home. The father thus becomes the child's natural ally while the mother is cast as the enemy. The situation then worsens when the father, unconsciously recognizing what is going on, becomes even more reluctant to discipline the child because he does not want to jeopardize his favorable position in the child's eye. Even small children can be remarkably adept at exploiting such situations for their benefit, thus intensifying the alliances and deepening the divisions they cause in the family structure. For this reason couples are well advised to watch for the emergence of any such patterns. Husbands and wives should listen attentively whenever their partners complain that they are being victimized by this sort of "ganging up." Coalition patterns arise so naturally and easily, and often without any conscious intent, that the aggrieved party is very likely to be right on this score. Fortunately, most coalition patterns can be easily broken if they are caught before they harden into destructive antagonisms.

The birth of a child not only changes power relationships within a family by making coalitions possible, but also necessitates the reorganization of many other aspects of the family's life style. Many studies indicate that the birth of the first child is a crisis for a couple regardless of whether the child was planned or not.[6] This crisis involves reorganizing the spending and often the earning of the family income. It involves new demands for space, time, and attention. What is more, the partners must reestablish patterns of intimacy and renegotiate the responsibilities and privileges, the patterns of power and authority that may have been disrupted by the period of pregnancy and post partum abstinence. The young husband may become increasingly aware that the demands upon him to earn a living may be in conflict with the demands that he be present as a family member as much as possible. The young wife becomes increasingly aware that child care can become a full-time occupation and she may resent the unexpected extent to which her other interests have to be pushed into the background.[7]

The birth of a child makes it necessary for the couple to reestablish a satisfactory sexual relationship under different circumstances. Because of increased demands on their time and energy, both partners are more likely to be tired when they come to their lovemaking. The infant's cries and the toddler's demands may interrupt sexual activity. The preservation of husband-wife intimacy thus becomes more difficult. Conversation between partners tends to get more disciplined; some research has indi-

[6]E. E. LeMasters, "Parenthood as Crises," *Marriage and Family Living* 19 (1957): 325–55.
[7]Helen Z. Lopata, *Occupation Housewife* (New York: Oxford University Press, 1971). See also the response to *Redbook*'s questionnaire, "How Do You Feel About Being A Woman?" *Redbook* (January 1973), p. 1.

cated that young parents talk to each other only one half as much as newly married couples, and when they do talk, they tend to talk about the children rather than themselves or their relationship.[8] In sum, the frequency of intercourse declines, as does the amount of shared leisure. Under these circumstances, any difficulties the couple already may have had in their sexual relationship may become magnified. If adequately handled, however, none of these problems need result in family crisis or marital dissatisfaction. In this regard, perhaps the best defense is knowing what to expect. The couple who imagine that having a baby will simply mean turning the study into a nursery but will not otherwise affect their life style is in for some shocking surprises which they may not be prepared to deal with creatively.

[8]William F. Kenkel, *The Family in Perspective* (New York: Appleton-Century-Crofts, 1966), p. 455.

SUMMARY

Most Americans are less prepared for parenthood than they are for marriage. Our folklore has done us a great disservice for overromanticizing parenthood as an unqualified happy experience and one that is capable of bringing a couple together if their marriage is in difficulty. Like marriage, parenthood is commonly taken for granted as natural. As a result, most couples tend to have children as a matter of expectation whether they are qualified for parenthood or not. The proposal to make marriage a two-stage contract is one way of dealing with this situation. In the first stage the two partners marry each other but children are definitely *not* a part of the contract. After they have tried out marriage, they may then make a second contract to become parents if they so desire. Because no children are involved in the first stage, it should be possible to obtain a divorce without much trouble, whereas obtaining a divorce in the second stage would be much more difficult.

Coping with the problems of children is a difficult task. Studies demonstrate that the first child presents many problems of adjustment for the young parents, whether the child is planned for or not. The possibility of forming two-party coalitions against the third member of the household becomes a reality. What is more, time and resources must be rearranged to meet the demands of the new member of the household. The intimacy that may have been developing between the parents must be developed further under the trying circumstances of reduced emotional capacity to cope with frustrations, and interruptions in the private time that the couple had become accustomed to before there were any children.

Because we tend to take it for granted that couples should have children, the arguments that might be advanced in favor of them seem trite or unpersuasive to increasing numbers of persons who view the population explosion and the drain on resources as cogent social reasons for not having children. The decision to not have children in a marriage is becoming more and more of a personal decision as the once overpowering expectation that married people should have children is now losing some of its force.

13

THE DEVELOPING FAMILY

Every society consists of [people] in the process of developing from children into parents. To assure continuity of tradition, society must early prepare for parenthood in its children; and it must take care of the unavoidable remnants of infantility in its adults.

Erik Erikson

INTRODUCTION

When a meaningful partnership such as marriage is entered into, the lives of many people are changed. Parents become in-laws and some old friends either lose their place of importance in the life of one of the partners or take on new importance to both. Relatives approach the couple in a new way. All these changes are bound to affect how the partners relate to one another.

Because marriage is a socially approved partnership with a long tradition behind it, it provides both the young couple and those who come in contact with them with a set of guidelines that help to shape appropriate behavior, thus easing the couple's transition into a new set of relationships. Couples without such guidelines must improvise with care if they are going to retain valued external relationships and still develop their partnership. For example, when a daughter invites her parents to meet the young man with whom she has been living for a number of months, how should the parents behave? How should the young man respond?

What can the daughter reasonably expect of any of them in this situation? As yet there are no clearly defined norms governing such situations, which as a result tend to be fraught with anxiety and confusion.

Like any enduring partnership, marriage changes over the course of time. Some of these changes result from the ongoing process of mutual discovery as the partners get to know each other more intimately and the relationship grows in maturity and depth. The birth of a child, or the addition of another member to the partnership, also sets up a whole new set of demands and interactions that change the nature of the relationship, and as the child grows and develops the parents must change their mode of relating to the child and to each other. An expanding family with several children of differing ages is quite a different kind of environment than a family with only one child or no children. What is more, as the partners themselves grow older, their needs and expectations with regard to one another and their partnership change.

Finally, when the children have all left home, their parents enter what is commonly called the "empty nest" period. In this period both partners, but particularly the mother, must make some dramatic readjustments in their style of life. Just as the transition to the empty nest phase is particularly difficult for the woman, so preretirement and retirement generally tend to be difficult times for the American man. His job or career has been the center of his life—just as the children may have been the center of his wife's—for such a long time that it is difficult for him to adjust to not being needed on the job. A great deal of patience and understanding is demanded of both partners at this stage of their relationship.

This chapter will examine the developmental course through which most partnerships pass.[1] Although the focus is clearly on marriage, in fact any form of partnership that lasts for a significant period of time will face many of the same problems described here. Three basic developmental stages will be covered: (1) Beginning families, up to and including the first years after the arrival of children; (2) families in the middle years, as the children grow to maturity; and (3) aging families in the empty nest and retirement phases.[2]

[1]The approach taken to marriage in this chapter is called the "developmental approach." This way of looking at partnerships such as marriage sees that they pass through stages of development. There can be as many as ten or as few as four stages, depending upon who is doing the research. At each stage there are certain tasks that must be accomplished in order for the relationship to develop smoothly.
[2]This is a condensation of the eight stages proposed by Evelyn Duvall, *Family Development*, 4th ed. (Philadelphia: J. B. Lippincott, 1972), p. 151. A much more sophisticated treatment of this approach is found in Roy Rogers, *Family Interaction and Transaction: The Developmental Approach* (Englewood Cliffs, N.J.: Prentice-Hall, Inc., 1973).

BEGINNING FAMILIES

Usually, American couples have about two years at the beginning of their marriage before they have children.[3] During this time they can focus on the problems of beginning a lifelong partnership. Among the tasks appropriate to beginning families, the following six seem especially important and will be considered in some detail: (1) developing competency in decision making; (2) working out mutually satisfying realistic systems for getting and spending the family income; (3) adjusting to the status of being "married"; (4) developing ways of expressing and accommodating differences creatively; (5) developing satisfactory relationships with relatives, particularly the husband's and wife's parents; and (6) working out satisfactory household routines and schedules

[3]Duvall, *Family Development*, p. 121.

that facilitate smooth functioning in the world of work and pleasure.[4]

These are common tasks which all couples must face in one way or another. How they deal with them depends upon their personalities, the constraints placed upon them by their social situation, their self-understanding, and the kind of life style they wish to develop.

Decision Making and Planning

All couples must work out some satisfactory way of making those decisions that they must make together. Decision making is not simply a

[4]William F. Kenkel, *The Family in Perspective* (New York: Appleton-Century-Crofts, 1966), p. 409.

matter of getting the job done or the problem solved, for the whole style of a couple's life together is affected by the way in which they make their decisions. The style of the decision making process and the style of the partnership are closely related. Couples must decide what areas they want to make subject to collective decision making. Will they each have areas of interest or activity in which only their own decisions will count? For example, will he have anything to say about how the household budget is spent or will she have anything to say about the kind of car they will own? Will they have joint or separate bank accounts? These considerations involve more than just a discussion of skills or areas of privacy. They are tied closely to the couple's notion of an appropriate division of labor in the home.

Using decision making as a planning process is important to some couples and not to others. Some people are quite organized about the way in which they handle their lives while others favor a more spontaneous, ad-lib approach. If two partners are at opposite ends of this spectrum they will have to come to grips with the difference in their style of decision making. The young man who calls his wife from the office Friday afternoon and says, "Honey, let's see if we can get someone to take care of the kids and we'll go away somewhere for the weekend," may not meet with an enthusiastic response if his partner is someone who feels that a weekend trip should be a carefully planned event.

Shared Decision Making. In the early years of a marriage, shared decision making very often comes quite naturally. This initial period is often characterized by a sense of excitement and mutuality. Yet the use of shared decision making at this stage does not always foretell the future. Shared decision making requires time, energy, and a spirit of accommodation; all things considered, it is a "costly" way of reaching decisions. In the early years of a marriage a couple might derive a great deal of pleasure and excitement from deciding on a piece of furniture for their living room, but after a number of years this approach may come to seem too time consuming and inefficient. If shared decision making is not a conscious mode of behavior to which the couple is committed, it tends to slip into a process of unilateral decision making as the partnership matures.

The fact that equality between the members of an intimate partnership is an important value often leads people to assume that shared decision making is always to be preferred over unilateral decision making. This is not necessarily the case. In general, shared decision making seems to be preferable under two conditions: (1) when both partners want to have a say in the decision; and (2) when both partners have an equal or nearly equal interest in the outcome of the decision. The first condition is simply another way of saying that it is not necessary for partners to feel obliged to take part in all decisions simply for the sake of keeping decision making on a shared basis. In our furniture buying case, for example, the husband may have learned from experience that he tends to favor furniture that looks good in the showroom but doesn't wear well at home. He has learned to trust his wife's judgment in this area and to be suspicious of his own. In such a situation, his choice to refrain from participating in the decision making process certainly seems reasonable.

The second condition concerns the question of what "right" each partner has to involve himself or herself in a particular decision. The simplest case occurs when one partner is not in the least concerned with the outcome; here, obviously, the partner who is concerned should be free to decide unilaterally. But most situations are not that simple. What if a wife wants to enroll in a late afternoon class at the local university? In itself, the decision as to whether or not to take a course involves her alone, but if she decides to take it she will be unable to prepare dinner on the three days a week when the class meets. This means that the husband, too, is concerned. But is his interest in the outcome of the decision the same as hers? It doesn't seem, on the face of it, that the inconvenience entailed in eating frozen dinners a few nights a week is as important as the opportunity to engage in a fulfilling educational experience; he, therefore, has less right to shape the final decision than she does. This is not to say that the couple should not discuss the situation, but it is to say that in many situations it is more appropriate for one party to have the "last word" than for the decision to be mutual.

Decision Making as Process. Decision making is a process, not simply a choice at a particular point in time. Every decision involves the past history of the person or couple, their wishes at the moment, their perceptions, and their feelings. Decision making in most families is thus not the cool, rational process it is often thought to be.[5] It involves feelings about ourselves and who we are, feelings about our partner and who he or she is, and feelings, either distorted or realistic, about the limits placed upon us in the particular situation, including an assessment of the costs and benefits of each of the available alternatives. An adequate decision must take all of these dimensions into account.[6] The following

[5] It is clear that the decision making process outlined here assumes that the partners choose to make the process of decision making a means by which their partnership can grow. If they decided that, for them, the most efficient decision making process should be utilized, a somewhat different approach would be taken. Unilateral decision making seems more efficient but can also be disruptive of relationships.
[6] Again this process is concerned with adequacy more than efficiency or verification of data. Most decisions of consequence in our lives, it would seem, are made with inadequate information. We must nevertheless invest a great deal of ourselves in the decision and assume the responsibility for the consequences. This is risky. Em-

account of a young couple in a small midwestern town faced with a decision about moving and changing jobs illustrates the complexity of the decision making process:

The new job is a junior executive position with an advertising company in a large West Coast city. Jim and Shirley have lived in their home town all their lives, except for a period away from home attending the state university. Their four parents and numerous other relatives are an important part of their lives. They are prominent people in their home town. Their social circle tends to be closed and comfortable.

Jim and Shirley have to explore numerous areas, including some self-examination, if they are to make an adequate decision. An adequate decision in this case would be reflected in their ability to move to the large West Coast city, knowing that they personally could survive, that their relationship could stand it, and that their new life and their work would contribute to their growth. Or it could be a decision to stay and achieve some of the same goals in their home town; this decision would be based on a recognition that they value the life style they have achieved more highly than they value the sort of career advancement that is at stake.

In the process of reaching a decision, Jim will have to come to some understanding of himself, some perception as to whether he is the kind of person who could make a contribution in the demanding field of advertising in this much larger cosmopolitan community. Does he have the stamina, drive, and creativity required? Does he see himself in this role, or does he find the small-scale, low-pressure life that he lives more in keeping with who he is? Shirley, too, has many questions to answer. Does she have the strength to leave the comfortable social circle she already knows? Is she the kind of person who is comfortable developing new friendships and discovering new modes of entering into relationships? How will she take the new experience? Is the source of her strength her close friendships and relations with her relatives? How will she fare without this support?

Moving to this new community will require them to sell their modest home and live in an urban apartment. The new job will require them to live in the city, which means that the pleasure that they enjoy in small-town life will be taken away from them. In making a decision, therefore, they must assess the constraints and limits that the new job will place upon them.

In their new home Jim and Shirley will have to cope with the fact that at first they will not know many people and will not have a familiar social scene in which to move. They will have to learn how to live in an urban situation, which demands a different style of life from what they are used to in a small town where they knew everybody and had a clear sense of their status. The promise is, however, that this may be a starting point from which Jim can develop many of his potentials that he felt were not being adequately used in his home town. The job holds the possibility of advancement and greater economic rewards.

---

phasis on the adequacy of the decision making process helps us cope with the risks. The kind of decision making described here is more appropriate for "commitment-type" choices involving long-term consequences than it would be for simple market choice situations such as what cereal to buy.

As Jim and Shirley face this decision, they will have to weigh the costs on the one hand against the promises. Does Jim's career have higher priority than the life style they had established in their home town? Can they make an adequate adjustment to the new life style? Will he really develop his potential?

Because this is a decision that deeply affects both partners, it seems appropriate that it be made jointly rather than unilaterally. In making the decision, therefore, each should contribute not only his or her knowledge and feelings about the objective situation but also his or her feelings about both of them. Jim must have some sense of how Shirley will react to the new situation just as Shirley probably has some assessment of how well Jim will adjust to the new job. They both face many unknowns, but each can help the other understand the situation as fully as possible.

It is impossible to know everything about a given situation, so there is always an element of risk in any decision. But if a couple has developed a method of decision making that is a creative process for both of them, they stand a good chance of making adequate decisions and are in a good position for coping with the situation in case their decision turns out to have been an inappropriate one. It is simply easier to live with a troublesome situation if one can feel confident that the decision that brought it about was the best that could have been made under the circumstances. For this reason, building a decision making process in which one can have confidence is an important task for all couples, regardless of the particular decisions they will have to face.

Some Common Patterns. Although it is important that a young couple starting out develop a style of decision making that suits their own unique partnership, a great many studies on decision making in marriage have uncovered the following patterns and trends:

1. The personality of the partners "can be seen to play a significant part in decision making, but only as it is mediated by the strong cultural influence of sex roles."

2. For the vast majority of couples, age has no effect on the relative power of the partners with regard to decision making; husbands who are at least ten years older than their wives, however, tend to have more influence in the decision making process.

3. Ordinarily, the mate with more education is more influential in the decision making process.

4. A wife who is employed outside the home normally has more influence in family decision making than a wife who does not have outside employment.

5. The husband dominates the decision making process more in high status families than in low status families.

6. Several studies have shown that marriages in which the entire decision making process is left in the hands of the wife tend to be unhappy. Researchers interpreting this finding generally assume that the wife's dominance is a result of the unhappiness and not its cause.

7. There is a discernible trend among young couples toward the development of separate fields of authority.

8. Very little is known about the influence of children on the family decision making process, but clearly they have considerable impact. Presumably the older the child, the greater the influence.

9. Finally, couples in the early stage of their marriage tend to be "syncratic" in their decision making—that is, they decide by mutual discussion and resolution. As the family expands by the addition of children, however, the wife's influence declines, although it is partially restored as the children leave and the parents approach middle age. Middle-aged married life is almost as egalitarian as the preparental stage.[7]

These patterns are closely related to the traditional understanding of sex roles and the traditional nuclear family structure. In partnerships that differ significantly from these norms, the patterns just described may not be in evidence.

Income Management

One of the most important tasks facing the beginning partnership concerns income management. Mutual decisions must be made about the patterns of acquiring income and spending it. These decisions must be sufficiently in tune with reality to allow the couple to survive financially. Except for this constraint, the partners are free to decide who should earn the money and how it should be spent in a number of different ways. What is important, however, is that they both freely consent to whatever division of labor they decide upon.

Getting the Income. At the beginning of marriages in which the husband is the sole producer of the income it is very often the case that the wife must accept a lower standard of living than she is used to. If both partners are working, however, this is not apt to be the case; indeed, young couples starting out with both working often enjoy more disposable income than at any other time in their relationship. The arrival of chil-

---

[7]For a more detailed discussion of these findings, see Richard Udry, *The Social Context of Marriage*, 2nd ed. (Philadelphia: J. B. Lippincott, 1973), pp. 315–18.

dren, often accompanied by home mortgage costs and other indebtednesses along with loss of the wife's income, often puts a severe strain on family resources. At the other end of the developmental spectrum, although disposable income may be higher than ever after the children have left the family, the need to plan for retirement and to provide for the uncertainties of old age often leaves older couples without much financial flexibility. Thus, ironically, the young couple starting out is often in one of the most favorable economic positions of their married life, although frequently they fail to appreciate this fact and do not adequately plan ahead for the increasing demands soon to be made upon their income.

Women are increasingly contributing to the family income. In 1900, about 5.6 percent of married women worked outside the home; by 1972, about 42 percent were working.[8] Clearly, this change has important implications for role assignments with regard to housework and child care. Indeed, many factors may enter into the decision as to who will engage in income-producing work, and often income itself will not be the most important of them. In cases where financial necessity dictates that the wife must work, the only decisions to be made will concern compensatory arrangements so that she is not saddled with the double workload of housekeeping responsibility and employment while her husband is responsible only for his job. But in cases where financial needs do not make it necessary for the wife to work, factors such as the personal satisfaction that may derive from a career, a suitable distribution of the domestic workload, and the benefits of added income all must be weighed against each other.

In a truly egalitarian partnership, it may be felt that the decision as to whether the woman works should primarily rest with her. After all, there is no inherent reason why the husband should be given first crack at the choice between making an income and doing the housework. Yet this is in effect what most commonly happens. That is to say, the partners recognize that they are faced with the twofold task of supporting and running a household; the husband automatically undertakes the support function and the wife is then free to join him in working only if the couple can reach a mutually satisfactory agreement about how the household is to be run. We would consider it almost unthinkable, when two gainfully employed people marry, for the wife to tell the husband, "I'm keeping my job; let's figure out if we can afford a housekeeper so that you can keep yours too." The fact that this statement sounds obviously unfair should be an indication that it is just as unfair when the husband says it to the wife.

[8]Bureau of the Census, *Statistical Abstract of the United States. 1973* (Washington, D.C.: U.S. Government Printing Office, 1973), p. 223.

Once we look at the issue in this light, we can see that the just solution is for each partner to decide, on the basis of his or her preferences, whether or not to work. If one decides to work and the other elects not to work, the division of labor between running the household and supporting it is automatically settled. (It is conceivable, on this basis, that the wife might decide to work and the husband to stay home. Why not?) If both decide to work, then they must divide up the housekeeping responsibility by some system of negotiation. This should not be regarded as a matter of his choosing what areas of housework he will undertake to "help her out"; if both partners are working, the housekeeping responsibility belongs to both of them and he is no more "helping her out" when he does the dishes than she is "helping him out" when she does the laundry. Finally, if both decide not to work, they must start over and go through the deciding process again, for unless they are financially independent this simply is not an option that is available to them.

The issue of earning money—and spending it, a subject to which we shall turn in a moment—is often the question around which the autonomy of the partners comes into focus. Many cultural factors shape the expectations that help or hinder a young couple in deciding on a division of labor that is appropriate for them. Parents, friends, and professionals are often all too ready to give advice, both asked for and unasked for, on this score. In this context, a creative step forward for a young couple is to establish their own priorities and follow them.

Spending the Income. In the beginning of a partnership, one of the things the partners quickly learn is the spending habits of their mates. Spending habits vary by personality but also by class, region, and ethnicity. Despite the fact that money problems of one sort or another are almost inevitable, and despite the fact that money may well be the most common source of conflict within marriage, a recent study on engaged couples indicates that they were "almost completely unaware of potential differences over the use of money."[9]

The problems young couples in our society face as they learn to manage their money are exacerbated by the cultural conditioning to spend. Even economic experts have been known to advise young couples to overcome their prejudice about going into debt. Banks and credit card companies advertise services that make it no longer necessary for people who want some expensive product to take into consideration whether they can afford it or not. Very often one partner will be caught up in

[9]Judson T. Landis and Mary G. Landis, *Building a Successful Marriage*, 6th ed. (Englewood Cliffs, N.J.: Prentice-Hall, Inc., 1973), p. 358.

this consumption orientation and the other will not. Such differences can lead to very heated showdowns unless the couple takes the trouble to work out mutually satisfactory ground rules for spending the family income.

There are many ways in which couples can divide up the task of spending the income. Duvall and Hill have described five common types of spending patterns:

1. *The Dole System.* In this system, one of the partners hands out small amounts of money at a time to the other partner and to other family members.

2. *The Family Treasurer System.* In this system, each member is allowed a certain amount of money to spend as he or she sees fit; one member dispenses these allowances and keeps the rest of the family's income for paying bills and for making the majority of the family's purchases.

3. *The Division of Expenses System.* In this system, the various spending tasks are assigned to either one partner or the other, with an appropriate amount of money allotted to each. For example, the husband may be responsible for the mortgage, the insurance, and the automobile while the wife is responsible for the food, clothing, and recreation. Any other spending is undertaken after a joint decision.

4. *The Joint Account System.* Earnings are placed in a joint account from which either partner can withdraw funds to meet his or her needs.

5. *The Budget System.* The couple plan together in advance what their expenses will be and establish this as the basis of their spending.[10]

Each of these systems has its advantages and disadvantages. For example, both the dole system and the family treasurer system have the advantage of simplicity and clear accountability in that there can be no doubt about who is responsible for maintaining the family on a stable economic basis. They have the disadvantage of giving one partner more power than the other over disposing of the income. If the wife is the treasurer, for example, and her husband wants to buy a new suit, he must ask her for the money, whereas she does not have to ask anyone's permission to buy a new dress. The joint account system has the advantage of providing a greater equality in the power to spend but the disadvantage of unclear lines of responsibility. The various advantages and disadvantages must be weighed against each other and each couple should work out their own system that best preserves their individual

[10]As described in Richard H. Klemer, *Marriage and Family Relationships* (New York: Harper & Row, Publishers, 1970), p. 271.

needs for autonomy and best meets their day-to-day need for control over their spending habits. Because it is not unlikely that the two partners may have come from homes in which different systems were employed, deciding upon an appropriate system may prove difficult. Nevertheless, it is important that this difficulty be faced, for as Richard H. Klemer has observed:

> . . . the most important knowledge that a marriage partner can have is his [or her] awareness of his [or her] mate's personal spending idiosyncracies. Given such an understanding plus a great deal of motivation, a lot of planning and some intelligent use of readily available information, young marrieds can make up spending-knowledge deficiencies as they go along.[11]

Being Married Is Different

Marriage is a social as well as a personal event. For couples who go through the normal stages from courtship through engagement to marriage, a good part of the engagement period ordinarily is devoted to working out the wedding arrangements and making plans for the new home. A certain amount of mutual exploration and adjustment is possible during this period, but being engaged is not the same as being married. Unmarried cohabitation is probably the closest approximation to marriage available, but even here there are some subtle but nonetheless real differences. The fact that many unmarried couples who are living together decide to get married is clear proof that, at least in their eyes, marriage is different.

From one perspective, the marriage ceremony itself is a superb labeling process. It impresses upon the "just married" and their friends, neighbors, and relatives that a contract has been negotiated that involves public as well as personal expectations. Even though Americans are not generally a people who put much emphasis on ritual, weddings are social occasions that make definite impressions upon most who attend them. What is more, even though we are not a particularly religious nation, three-fourths of all couples who marry prefer a church wedding.[12] Curiously, there is a weak but significant correlation between "success" in marriage and having been married in a religious ceremony, although it is not clear why this is so.[13] It is probable that this correlation reflects

[11]*Marriage and Family Relationships*, p. 275.
[12]Leonard Benson, *The Family Bond: Marriage, Love and Sex in America* (New York: Random House, 1971), p. 173.
[13]For an excellent survey of the factors commonly thought by social scientists to be important predictors of marital success see William F. Stephens, ed., *Reflections on Marriage* (New York: Thomas Y. Cromwell Company, 1968).

the conforming or conservative character of those who prefer church weddings more than it reflects any sort of independent commitment to marriage.

Weddings dramatize the commitment of the couple to each other and to their social and familial responsibilities. One theory holds that the heavier the responsibilities the couple is expected to assume, the more elaborate the ritual of the wedding and its associated events. It is clear, of course, that weddings also provide an occasion to display publicly the wealth of the families that are being related by this event—particularly the status of the bride's family, which is expected to pay for most of the wedding.[14]

To a young woman, the label "Mrs." and the adoption of her husband's surname provide a shorthand way of referring to a whole set of expectations regarding what is now demanded of her as appropriate role behavior. The man, of course, does not undergo any such dramatic transformation of identity—a fact which has led feminists to denounce the naming customs as symbols of the possessive nature of the marriage relationship. The woman, these critics point out, becomes immediately identifiable upon marriage as the man's wife, but nothing in the way the man identifies himself indicates that he is her husband. For this reason it is becoming increasingly common for young women to retain their "maiden" names after marriage and to use the label "Ms.," which avoids identification in terms of marital status.

Even without the name change, however, marriage often entails more of a dramatic change for the woman than for her husband. This change is especially marked when the woman retires from her career or job upon marriage and becomes a full-time housewife. The couple, therefore, should not be surprised if the woman experiences somewhat greater difficulty than her husband in adjusting to the new situation.

The ancient tradition of a honeymoon trip was probably designed primarily for the purpose of easing the transition into the new roles both partners are expected to assume when they marry. During the honeymoon the couple can begin to adjust to each other as husband and wife in a setting where they will not be bothered by the more pressing problems of everyday life. The honeymoon is one of the few socially sanctioned occasions for a "dyadic withdrawal." Philip Slater interprets the pranks usually attached to the event as signs of society's anxiety that the couple will "drop out" more permanently and forget their social obligations.[15]

[14]Benson, *The Family Bond*, p. 174.
[15]Philip Slater, "Social Limitations on Libidinal Withdrawal," *American Psychological Review*, 25 (June 1963), 339–64.

Dealing with Differences

Although the mate selection process tends to favor couples who are similar in such areas as religion, socioeconomic class, ethnicity, age, and community background, thus producing a situation in which the partners coming to a marriage tend to be alike in a great many ways, nevertheless the individual personalities of the partners inevitably will differ in significant and critical ways. The problem of learning to cope with differences in spending patterns was suggested above. The issue of dealing more creatively with differences was discussed at length in the sections on "Differences in Background and Outlook" and "Mate Selection" in Chapters 4 and 5, respectively.

Relating to Relatives

Beginning a marriage means establishing some kind of relationship with in-laws and redefining relationships with other relatives. Kinship ties normally are maintained most closely through the mother-daughter relationship, a fact which is reflected in the folk saying, "A son's a son till he takes a wife, a daughter's a daughter for all of her life."[16] Probably as a result of this situation, the wife is more likely than the husband to feel that in-laws are a problem.[17] Indeed, the classic situation of conflict in the American kinship system is the relationship between mother-in-law and daughter-in-law.[18]

The importance of kinship ties varies with socioeconomic class in a curvilinear fashion.[19] Kin are most important in the lower and upper classes and less important in the middle class, where friendships often play a role in the couple's life analogous to the role played by kin in other socioeconomic classes.[20] Several studies suggest that there is a positive relationship between marital happiness and establishing good relationship with in-laws.[21] Thus couples who make a reasonably good adjustment in other areas of their partnership and who develop a sense of working together as partners tend to have less problems with their in-laws than do couples who are less well adjusted to each other. On the other hand, disagreements on how to relate to in-laws are frequently cited as a source of marital unhappiness.

Kin are the persons to whom marital partners are most likely to turn

---

[16]Udry, *The Social Context of Marriage*, p. 337.
[17]*The Social Context of Marriage*, p. 337.
[18]*The Social Context of Marriage*, p. 337.
[19]See the discussion of the American kinship system in relation to the conjugal family in David A. Schulz, *The Changing Family: Its Function and Future* (Englewood Cliffs, N.J.: Prentice-Hall, Inc., 1972), pp. 113–38.
[20]Udry, *The Social Context of Marriage*, p. 337.
[21]Landis and Landis, *Building a Successful Marriage*, p. 296.

when they need help or support that they cannot get from their mates. This is true even in middle-class marriages where kinship may otherwise be relatively unimportant. Bott's classic study of working-class England showed that couples who did not share very much with each other commonly shared a great deal with their kin.[22] This seems to be the case also with lower- and working-class Americans, although to a lesser degree than Bott found her English population. Thus the kinship network is related to the nuclear family unit in a complex way and has subtle effects upon the pattern of marital interaction.

When couples are asked to identify the source of in-law problems, both partners tend to name the mother-in-law most often. The reason for this is quite obvious. The mother in our society is the parent specifically oriented to caring for the children, and it is not easy for her to relinquish this role when they marry. Very often this tendency is exacerbated when one of the partners has not fully separated himself or herself from the mother-son or mother-daughter role. The husband who wants his wife to cook like his mother did is inviting his mother's interference in her daughter-in-law's kitchen; the wife who turns to her mother rather than her husband for advice in establishing her new home is likely to make her husband resent his mother-in-law, whose presence, he may be justified in feeling, is an intrusion in the couple's privacy which is all the more irksome because his wife actually seems to welcome it.

For all these reasons, and many others, three-generational households are very difficult to maintain satisfactorily in our society. They are typically resorted to when there is no other economic alternative to having the parents move in with their children; less frequently, the children "come home" to live with the parents. Part of the problem comes from the fact that our society has no specified way of dealing with the allocation of authority in such a household. Is the daughter to retain her authority over the household and its chores, or does she relinquish these responsibilities to her mother when she moves in? And what if it is her husband's mother rather than her own mother with whom she must live? Each couple must work out their own arrangements for coping with such situations, and we must frankly confess that none seems to work very well in our society.[23]

Working Out the Routine

In the early years of their partnership young couples are seldom aware of how many hours of just plain routine will go into their relationship.

[22]Elizabeth Bott, *Family and Social Networks: Roles, Norms and Extended Relation in Orderly Families* (London: Tavistock Publications, 1957).
[23]Klemer, *Marriage and Family Relationships*, pp. 277ff.

Caring for bodily needs, cleaning the house, buying the food and preparing it, picking up after each other—these and many other mundane matters consume a great deal of time. Because these aspects of living involve deeply ingrained habits that are often taken for granted, couples can find themselves struggling through a great deal of conflict without really knowing why they are getting angry at one another. Yet a great deal of marital conflict arises out of the apparently inconsequential things that may seem too unimportant to matter.[24]

The problem of dealing with these questions of detail and routine is half solved as soon as it is realized that they are not unimportant. If persistent feelings continue to point up a disturbing pattern, this should be brought out into the open and discussed in such a way as not to offend the other. Often these "little things" (such as leaving underwear hanging in the bathroom to dry or never filling up the car until the tank is practically empty) are laughed at before marriage; thus the offending partner may feel that the other has understood his or her idiosyncracy and can live with it. But after marriage the humor often rapidly fades and the matter becomes an irritant.

The developmental tasks described in the preceding sections may or may not be adequately met in the beginning stage of a partnership. If they are adequately met, the assumption is that the partnership will develop smoothly and the partners will be relatively free to deal with new tasks that confront them as their relationship matures. If they are not adequately met, however, the partners are likely to experience increasing tensions that may disrupt their partnership or slow its development. In either case, however, if the partnership endures it is quite likely that the issues discussed in the first stage will tend to fade from prominence as new ones arise and require the couple's attention. The later stages in the developmental sequence will be discussed briefly in the remaining pages of this chapter.

FAMILIES IN THE MIDDLE YEARS

The time after the children have left their parents' home and become independent has been called the "empty nest" stage in the developmental sequence through which the parents are passing. This stage covers the time from the departure of the last child to retirement—an average of about fifteen years. If the trend toward earlier retirement continues—as now seems quite likely—then this stage will become shorter.

[24]Peggy Marcus, "In-law Relationships in Couples Married Two or Eleven Years," *Journal of Home Economics* (January 1951), pp. 35–37.

Couples in these middle years have an opportunity to experience a new sense of independence, to rediscover each other, and to regain greater intimacy. Middle-aged persons are generally healthier and more vigorous today than they were at the turn of the century. What is more, their income is apt to be near its maximum. On the other hand, the couple may find that their relationship has changed during the period of child rearing and they have grown apart. The wife may find, when she tries to return to her career, that it is impossible for her to compete with younger people and those her own age who did not have to drop out in order to raise children. What is more, the couple may discover that they lost the ability to spend leisure time creatively. Thus time may weigh heavily upon couples in their middle years. This is a problem which is likely to affect women more than men. The wife who can no longer find her fulfillment in bringing up her children, who finds no particular pleasure in housework, and who cannot return to a job or career is faced with a major problem of adjustment.

Most couples enter the middle stage of their marriage at around the age of forty-five or fifty. Before the turn of the century it was not common for couples to have many middle years together after the children left, for the average life expectancy simply was too short. As a result, we do not have well defined, traditional expectations about what such couples should do. They must face the fact that children can no longer be the center of their lives and that they have reached the stage in their lives when their economic status has pretty much been established. Either they have "made it" or they have not. A man must accept the fact that he is no longer a promising young executive on the way up; at forty-five, either he has "peaked out" or, in most professions, he should be able to make a reasonably good estimate of how much farther up the ladder of success he is likely to climb. If he has realized his personal objectives, he can take satisfaction in his accomplishments; if he has not, then he should adjust himself to the fact that it is not likely that he will have another chance. The self-awareness required for such adjustment often comes as quite a jolt to working-class men who, at forty-five, may find themselves earning less than their sons who went on to college—in fact, less than their sons who went to work right after high school but who are more valuable to employers than the "old man" because of their youth, greater agility, and greater strength. In the lower levels of the working class, men often are laid off or "retired" early so that companies can avoid paying maximum pensions—if there is a pension program—and can keep the payroll down by minimizing the number of higher salaried, more experienced workers.

For women, menopause marks the transition in life as dramatically as retirement does for men—perhaps more so. With menopause, women end their childbearing period and must cope with the effects of aging that become apparent as a result of changes in hormone balance. For many women, the end of their menses symbolizes the end of their youth. Often this is a traumatic time in a woman's life when she may come to doubt her own womanliness. These doubts may be aggravated by suspicions that her husband is losing interest in her. Ultimately, most women adjust to this new stage in their lives, but this does not mean that the psychological pain often associated with menopause should be taken lightly. A husband is no more entitled to assume that "it's just something she'll get over" than a wife is entitled to disregard the husband's gloomy feelings of uselessness and obsolescence as he faces retirement. In both cases, an understanding partner is an invaluable aid in getting through what sometimes tends to be a rather tough transition.

The physical process of aging, of course, changes the character of both men and women. Bodies lose their tone, their shape, and begin to wrinkle. Physical stamina declines. Men and women either accept these changes as inevitable and take reasonable steps to minimize the rate of aging by means such as exercise, diet, cosmetics, and dress. Or they can strive to "maintain their youth" by not admitting what is happening to them. In either case, the physical process of aging will continue, so that the former strategy is clearly preferable in that it enables the person to cope with a situation that must be coped with at this time.

During the middle years the need to plan for retirement becomes evident. Awareness of this is often quite limited in earlier years, as is evidenced by the fact that the majority of couples in America do not adequately prepare for retirement.[25] Couples with limited resources often find it simply impossible to prepare for this stage of life. Thus a large majority of couples have made no provision for retirement income. Social Security is a very inadequate source of retirement income, yet it remains the major resource upon which most retired couples must depend.

Planning for retirement income is but one aspect of the problem of planning for retirement. Retirement for most men means coming to grips with the fact that they are no longer of use to society. To avoid this feeling of uselessness, it is better to retire *to* something than retire *from* something; if possible, therefore, hobbies, community activities, and avocations should be cultivated during the middle years. Unfortunately, even in our "affluent society" many American families can afford neither the outside activities that can lend a sense of purpose to the retirement years nor the luxury of being able to put aside savings for the time when employment income disappears. For countless such families

[25]Harold Shepard, "The Poverty of Aging," in Ben B. Seligman, ed., *Poverty as a Public Issue* (New York: Free Press, 1967), pp. 86–87.

retirement means poverty, and that in itself is a lonely and frightening specter.

AGING FAMILIES

A couple fortunate enough to have adequate income in the post-retirement years generally can look forward to good health and an extended period of post-retirement life together. Because of the longer life expectancy of women, the wife can expect to be the survivor and can anticipate a widowhood of eleven years on the average. The problems of aging families are closely tied to the problems of our economy, which tends to produce workers who accumulate like the waste products of our industry, to be disposed of or discarded when the industrial system is through with them. Severe economic constraints are placed upon the elderly, either as a result of their own lack of planning or as a result of society's inability to provide adequate income through earnings, social insurance, or outright grants.[26] Descriptions of this phase in a couple's life often seem to gloss over the hardships and emphasize the autonomy of the aging couple.

With all this information, it is not difficult to see that one of the primary tasks facing an aging couple is to recognize that they can be useful persons and to find a way to express this. Often, however, the husband simply retires into the home when he loses the one thing that gave his life meaning—his job. Having no other outlets through which to express himself, he may slouch around the house meddling in his wife's established routine, which did not undergo such radical changes upon his retirement. Very often he loses his sense of purpose, direction, and meaning in life. Statistics show that many die within five years after retirement.

With the increased time a husband and wife have together after his retirement, many conflicts which formerly had been suppressed or ignored now become very important. What is more, the once independent breadwinner loses status and the once dependent wife gains in status and power, producing role changes to which the elderly couple may have difficulty adjusting. Another common pattern is for the aging couple to become increasingly dependent upon their children. All these hazards must be dealt with if the aging couple is to stand any chance at all of enjoying the retirement period.

A happier scenario is recorded in the case of those husbands who are able to find a sense of usefulness and purposefulness in their post-retirement years by participating more actively and helpfully in the

[26]F. Ivan Nye and Felix Berardo, *The Family: Its Structure and Interaction* (New York: The Macmillan Company, 1973), p. 578.

Thomas Hopker, Woodfin Camp

household chores and emphasizing their value as loving, affectionate companions to their wives and children. Middle-class men generally are able to make this role change more readily and more effectively than lower-class men. Because the upper middle-class man is likely to have experienced some degree of role flexibility prior to his marriage, he is often able to change roles with a fair degree of self-confidence while basking in the afterglow of the accomplishments of his successful career. If his success and self-esteem are secured, he can look forward to this kind of role change as an opportunity to participate in an expressive life style and to explore feelings that he may have overlooked on his climb to success. If the relationship is one of caring and understanding, both husband and wife can evoke from each other a new sense of purposefulness at this late time in their marriage.

SUMMARY

Looked at from the developmental point of view, partnerships such as marriage face certain critical tasks at various stages in their development. Beginning families must develop decision making patterns and adjust in other ways to the uniqueness of the married state. Families with children face the task of incorporating new members and dealing responsibly with these new persons. During the "empty nest" period the partners need to rediscover each other and prepare for the retirement period.

In this chapter we have touched on all these stages briefly but have devoted most of our attention to the stage of beginning families. In particular, we have explored six tasks that are of major importance at this stage: (1) developing competency in decision making; (2) working out mutually satisfying and realistic systems for getting and spending the family income; (3) adjusting to the status of being "married"; (4) developing ways of expressing and accommodating differences creatively; (5) developing satisfactory relationships with relatives, particularly the couple's parents; and (6) working out satisfactory household routines and schedules.

DISORGAN-IZATION AND DIVORCE

For an unknown, but indubitably large number of people, marriage isn't a comfort, a source of companionship or a means of sexual satisfaction. . . . Making divorce more obtainable is a relief for people caught in the agony of a hateful marriage, but legal farewells are difficult, unpleasant and sometimes traumatic. A better solution would be to change the institution of marriage to fit the needs and desires of husbands and wives.

Nicholas von Hoffman

INTRODUCTION

All partnerships must come to an end. In a book about self-actualizing partnerships it is important to note that most marriages do not end voluntarily. In spite of all that we hear about the rising divorce rate, death ends more marriages than any other factor. Most couples, it seems, are committed to the ideal of a lifelong marital contract, but this should not obscure the fact that many of these lifelong commitments seem quite empty to the people involved in them.

In characterizing intimate nonmarital partnerships, it is commonly assumed that, in contrast to marital relationships, they represent a high degree of voluntary commitment. Why else would two people who weren't married to each other live together if they didn't want to? There is really not much information about this kind of issue at the present time. It should be obvious, however, that this view of the voluntary character of nonmarital partnerships is probably an oversimplification. Great dependency needs may bring couples together and keep them together whether they are married or not. The extent to which such relationships are entered into, maintained, and terminated with conscious awareness and voluntary intent, therefore, is probably overstated.

Because we know so little about this matter at present, it is more useful to look at marital relationships if we want to understand the processes involved in the disruption and termination of partnerships. This chapter will do so first by discussing some of the factors that create stress in a marital partnership. These forces tend to disorganize partnerships and frequently end them. Thus we can talk about partnerships in terms of the kinds of disorganization that tend to predominate in any given partnership.

In the bulk of this chapter, however, we will look at divorce. Who are getting divorces, at what rates, and why? Assuming that the possibility of divorce is necessary if marital partnerships are to be truly voluntary, what can be done to minimize the destructive effects of divorce upon the partners and their children? It is a sad thing when any partnership breaks up, and particularly sad when the partnership is a marriage of long duration. But it is to be hoped that the decision to terminate a marriage (or any other partnership) will be as voluntary as the decision to enter it and made with at least as much consideration of what is at stake.

Most of those persons who divorce will remarry within a few years, but some will never do so. For them a "single" style of life may become more fulfilling. In Chapter 15 we briefly consider some of the consequences that the way in which a partnership terminates creates for this single life style.

FAMILY DISORGANIZATION

Sociologist William Goode helps us understand divorce by placing it in the larger context of family disorganization. As Goode sees it, there are at least five major types of disorganized families: the uncompleted family; the empty shell family; the family disorganized by external catastrophe such as bankruptcy, scandal, or imprisonment; the family disorganized by internal catastrophes such as illness or death; and the family disorganized by willed departures such as divorce.[1]

The Uncompleted Family

Families that have never been formed in the first place are a part of Goode's classification. These result when a child is born outside of wedlock and the couple fails to assume the socially expected role obligations of parenthood. The child born of such a union creates a fundamental problem for society as it is now structured because it has no acknowledged place. This is symbolized by the fact that it cannot reasonably take the name of its biological father. Very often such a child takes the name of its mother unless it is adopted. In this case the adoptive parents bestow their name upon it and fix its place in the social structure. This has the practical consequence that now the child can inherit from its adoptive parents and can legally expect all of the support we assume a non-adopted child has by virtue of its birth.

[1] William J. Goode, "Family Disorganization," in Robert K. Merton and Robert A. Nisbet, eds., *Contemporary Social Problems*, 2nd ed. (New York: Harcourt Brace & World, Inc., 1966), pp. 479–552.

While it is true that a few women openly prefer to be mothers without getting married, most who do so with some degree of success are in the upper class and have sufficient economic power and resources to overcome many of the social handicaps of not having a socially recognized husband and father for the child. A child born outside of marriage in the lower class does not ordinarily suffer as much from the stigma of illegitimacy as he or she would in the working or upper classes, but economic hardships are to be expected.

Sociologist Kingsley Davis points out that it is possible to eliminate illegitimacy in one of two ways: either a society can institutionalize marriage to such an extent that no one can conceive outside of it, or it can establish marriage so weakly that few, if any, persons marry.[2] In either case illegitimacy would be no problem. One society, the Tiwi of Australia, has made it impossible for a woman to be unmarried. A female is often bestowed in marriage before she is born (and certainly before she reaches puberty) and if her husband dies before she does she is remarried at the graveside of her deceased husband. At no time in her reproductive life is she unmarried. Any child born to her is considered to be her husband's regardless of its biological origins. Thus, there can be no such thing as an illegitimate child among the Tiwi.[3]

We do not know of any society that has taken the other option of disestablishing marriage to the same extent that the Tiwi have established it. In some of the Caribbean islands, illegitimacy rates of around 70 percent of the live births are not uncommon. These rates are so high because, in addition to the normal number of unwanted or accidental pregnancies that eventuate in live births, the islanders have accepted a visiting relationship in which a man and woman live together for extended periods of time and care for each other without getting married. To some extent these illegitimacy rates are artificially high because of the fact that the government considers only Roman Catholic marriages valid and thus children born to other marriages are considered illegitimate. Nevertheless, the islanders clearly seem to prefer marriage despite the fact that they are quite willing to accept a nonmarital alternative.

The Empty Shell

By calling attention to the empty shell type of disorganization, Goode recognizes that partnerships may be terminated for all intents and purposes although the partners remain living together. Many of the couples described by Cuber and Harroff in *The Significant Americans* as having

[2] Kingsley Davis, "Illegitimacy and the Social Structure," *American Journal of Sociology* (1939), pp. 215–33.
[3] C. W. Hart and Arnold R. Pilling, *The Tiwi of North Australia* (New York: Holt, Rinehart & Winston, 1962).

Hella Hammid, Rapho Guillumette

a "utilitarian" kind of partnership may fit into this category.[4] The utilitarian reasons for staying together—because the pattern of everyday life is reasonably comfortable, the expenses of living together are less than if the partners lived apart, and so forth—do not really compensate the couple who live in empty shell partnerships. They remain together because they can perceive of no other alternative. A heavy sense of despair may hang over their hopeless situation, or they may simply be seen as not having much going for them. By describing this type of partnership as an "empty shell," Goode notes that, in either case, there does not seem to be anything to it.

External Catastrophes

Wars, depressions, floods, imprisonment, bankruptcy, or scandal may cause a partnership's termination. The stress these events generate simply may be too much for the partners to cope with. Sociologist Reuben Hill has pointed out that different partnerships handle the same events in quite different ways. In the 1930s, after all, the Depression did not

---

[4]John F. Cuber and Peggy B. Harroff, *Sex and the Significant Americans* (Baltimore: Penguin Books, Inc., 1968).

cause all marriages to break up but it did disrupt quite a few. On the other hand, it seems to have strengthened some couples as they rose to the occasion and saw it through. In Hill's view a family's inability to handle a stress-inducing event is a function of six interrelated variables: degree of role conflict, adequacy of interpersonal relationships, extent of cultural diversity, extent of unrealized aspirations, class memberships, and economic resources. Partnerships which have reasonably compatible role patterns, adequate communication channels, similar frames of reference, an adequate history of realized aspirations, and adequate economic and sociopolitical resources are much less likely to become disorganized by stress-inducing events.

Internal Catastrophes

Events that occur within the family—such as the illness, disability, or death of one of the members—also can be causes of family disorganization. The family's capacity to cope with these events follows much the same pattern as its ability to cope with external catastrophe. In the case of a partnership in which there are no children, however, the disabled partner may not be able to fully participate in the crisis definition or its resolution, so that the dynamics of coping with these types of crises are probably much different. Some of the aspects of coping with bereavement are treated in Chapter 15.

Willed Departures

Finally, partnerships such as marriage may be disorganized by the willed departure of one of the partners, as occurs in desertion, separation, annulment, or divorce. At the outset it must be pointed out that the extent to which any given separation or divorce can be said to be willed or intentional varies. This is a point that will be developed in the remaining portion of this chapter. At this point it is sufficient to note that the disorganization of lower-class partnerships is characterized to a greater extent by such "willed departures" than is the disorganization of upper-class partnerships. Taking divorce statistics alone, however, the upper classes rank higher. This is largely a matter of their being able to afford the amenities of a divorce. It has rightly been stated that desertion is a poor man's divorce. Thus it seems reasonable to argue that the lack of income is as likely to account for the "instability" of low-income marriages as is any lack of intentional commitment.

A further advantage of viewing partnerships in terms of these kinds of disorganizing factors is that it becomes apparent that society has more of an interest in one kind of disorganization than in another. We are rightly concerned about rising divorce rates and approve of increased resources to cope with them through family enrichment programs and marital counseling. We have even begun to expect corporations to become conscious of the effect of their demands upon the home. Thus partners can receive a considerable amount of help in coping with problems likely to lead to divorce. At the same time the increasing rate of divorce means that more and more divorced people find themselves with others in a similar state and can feel freer to talk about their problems. But on the other hand, very little is being done about the empty shell type of family. In part this is because partners involved in empty shell relationships are able to conceal this fact from others by being slightly withdrawn from normal social activities. In part, too, it derives from our general unwillingness to probe into the private lives of others. This means that persons in empty shell partnerships must cope with their problems largely on their own.

DIVORCE

Divorce Rates

At present there is one divorce or annulment for every three marriages that take place each year. In 1972, for example, 2,269,000 couples got married and about 839,000 terminated their marriages.[5] Figure 14–1 shows that since 1961 the rate of divorce has been increasing more rapidly than the marriage rate. The rate at which couples remarry, however, is rising even more rapidly. About 20 percent of all remarriages end in divorce. Alvin Toffler observes, "As conventional marriage proves itself less and less capable of delivering on its promise of lifelong love . . . we can anticipate public acceptance of temporary marriages."[6]

In general marriages last longer and the rate of remarriage is lower as the income and education of the partners increases. For example, in those marriages where both husband and wife are college graduates, 90 percent have been married only once. Eighty-three percent have been married only once in those marriages where both partners are high school graduates, and 75 percent of the partners have been married only once in the case where neither husband nor wife have graduated from high school.[7] If the percentage of marriages in which the partners have been married only once is used as an index of marital stability, the majority of marriages are stable; on the whole in 1971 about 33 million— or 81 percent of all married persons—had been married only once. On the other hand, there is a small but increasing number of couples in

[5]U.S. Bureau of the Census, *Statistical Abstract of the United States: 1973* (Washington, D.C.: U.S. Government Printing Office, 1973), p. 65.
[6]Alvin Toffler, *Future Shock* (New York: Bantam Books, 1972), p. 251. Copyright © 1970 by Random House, Inc.
[7]*U.S. News and World Report* (October 30, 1972), p. 39.

FIGURE 14–1

Marriages have been increasing steadily, but divorces are rising even more sharply. For every three new marriages today, one old marriage ends in divorce or annulment. A decade ago, the rate was one divorce or annulment for every four marriages.

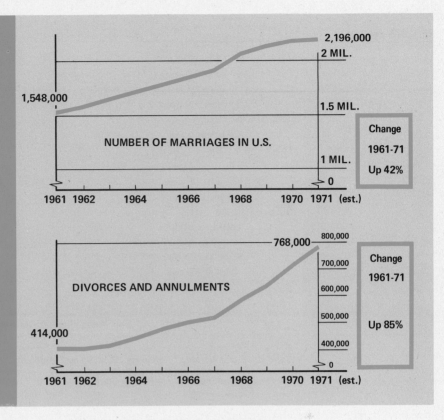

Source: *U.S. Department of Health, Education and Welfare.*

which each partner has been married three or more times. In 1971 there were about 200,000 such instances.[8]

A Closer Look

Divorce is becoming a part of the experience of more and more people. Thus, while only 2.8 percent of the men and 4.3 percent of the women were divorced in 1973, a recent study by census experts Paul Glick and Arthur Norton indicates that about 15 percent of all men and 17 percent of all women who were seventy years old or older and who had ever been married had experienced divorce.[9] Persons who marry at a younger than normal age are more likely to become divorced. For example, white men who married between the ages of fourteen and twenty-one and

[8]*U.S. News and World Report* (October 30, 1972), p. 39.
[9]Paul Glick and Arthur Norton, "Frequency, Duration and Probability of Marriage and Divorce," *Journal of Marriage and the Family*, 33 (May 1971), 310.

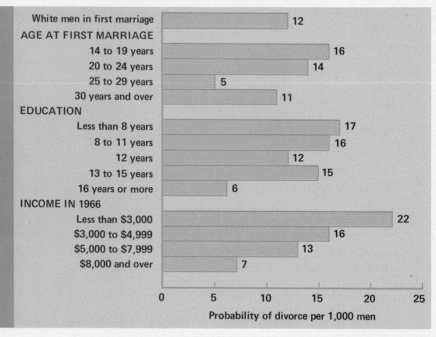

FIGURE 14–2

Average annual probability of divorce per 1,000 white men in their first marriage less than 5 years by selected characterstics, 1960–1966.

Source: *Glick and Norton, "Frequency, Duration and Probability of Marriage and Divorce,* Journal of Marriage and the Family *33 (May 1971), 314. Copyright 1971 by National Council on Family Relations. Reprinted by permission.*

white women who married between the ages of fourteen and nineteen are more divorce prone than those who first married at older ages. When these persons were examined twenty years after their first marriage, 25.4 percent of the men and 24.8 percent of the women had obtained at least one divorce.

The figures for black men and women are notably higher across the board. Forty-six percent of all black men who first married between the ages of fourteen and twenty-one had obtained at least one divorce twenty years later, as had 47 percent of all black women who had married between the ages of fourteen and nineteen. Glick and Norton conclude, "Barring marked change in current trends, it seems plausible to expect that during the lifetime of those who are now entering marriage at correspondingly young ages, close to one third of the whites and one half of the Negroes will eventually end their marriages in divorce."[10]

Persons who marry at a later age can expect divorce rates about one-half to two-thirds as high as these. Figure 14–2 illustrates how the probability of divorce varies for white men according to the selected variables: age at first marriage, education, and income in 1966.

[10]Glick and Norton, "Frequency, Duration and Probability of Marriage and Divorce," 310.

When looking at divorce statistics, it is important to realize that marriage is still a quite durable partnership for most Americans. For example, sociologist P. Krishman calculates that a married female aged twenty has a chance of 29 in 100 of becoming divorced during her lifetime, she can expect divorce during childrearing at a lower probability of 25 in 100, and thereafter can look forward with confidence to twenty-five years of uninterrupted married life during her reproductive years.[11] For those who do divorce, however, the typical first marriage is much shorter. Figure 14–3, taken from the Glick and Norton study, illustrates how the duration of marriage varies for white males by selected characteristics. On the average the first marriage lasts 7.6 years. Lowest expectancies are found in the cases of men who married between the ages of twenty and twenty-four, or who had some high school education but did not graduate, or who earned between $3,000 and $4,999 in 1966. Glick and Norton observe, "Income is more significant than education in determining which men obtain divorce, particularly during the first 10 years of marriage."[12]

[11]P. Krishnan, "Divorce Table for Females in the United States," *Journal of Marriage and the Family*, 33 (May 1971), 318.
[12]Glick and Norton, "Frequency, Duration and Probability of Marriage and Divorce," p. 316.

FIGURE 14–3

Median duration of first marriage for divorced white men by selected characterstics, 1960–1966.

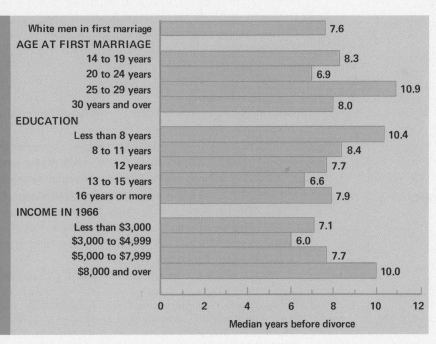

White men in first marriage	7.6
AGE AT FIRST MARRIAGE	
14 to 19 years	8.3
20 to 24 years	6.9
25 to 29 years	10.9
30 years and over	8.0
EDUCATION	
Less than 8 years	10.4
8 to 11 years	8.4
12 years	7.7
13 to 15 years	6.6
16 years or more	7.9
INCOME IN 1966	
Less than $3,000	7.1
$3,000 to $4,999	6.0
$5,000 to $7,999	7.7
$8,000 and over	10.0

Median years before divorce

Source: *Glick and Norton, "Frequency, Duration and Probability of Marriage and Divorce,"* Journal of Marriage and the Family 33 (May 1971), 311. Copyright 1971 by National Council on Family Relations. Reprinted by permission.

William Goode summarizes the characteristics which seem to be associated with divorce proneness:[13]

Greater Proneness	Lesser Proneness
Urban residence	Rural residence
Married young (15–19)	Average age at first marriage (male 23, female 20)
Married after short acquaintanceship	Knew each other at least two years
Short engagement or none	Engaged at least six months
Parents unhappily married	Parents happily married
Non-attenders at church or from mixed marriages	Regular attenders at church, same faith
Kin and friends disapproved of marriage	Kin and friends approved of marriage
Dissimilarity of background	Similarity of background
Different conceptions of husband and wife roles	Similar conceptions of husband and wife roles

All of these indicators of divorce proneness can be seen as obstacles which a couple must overcome if they seek to preserve their marriage—or any other durable partnership. Most manage to preserve their marriages in spite of some of these obstacles. Nevertheless, if a couple marries young and has inadequate income and dissimilar background, it is statistically quite likely that a divorce will occur.

Divorce Laws

The cause of divorce is normally quite different from the legal grounds for divorce. Unfortunately, the law plays only a limited role in controlling divorce. Sociologist Eugene Litwak argues that this is so because marital breakup is a complex matter such that a more adequate matching of a particular type of law with a particular type of breakup is required. The law, for example, can be primarily punitive, as in cases where costs of divorce are high and grounds are few; it can be therapeutic, as in those instances in which it requires counseling; or it can be primarily educative, as when it requires certain tests before marriage. It is least effective when it is purely punitive.[14]

One consequence of the predominantly punitive orientation of tradi-

[13]From "Family Disorganization," p. 517, by William J. Goode in *Contemporary Social Problems*, 2nd Edition, edited by Robert K. Merton and Robert A. Nisbet, copyright © 1961, 1966, by Harcourt Brace Jovanovich, Inc., and reproduced with their permission.

[14]Eugene Litwak, "Divorce Law as Social Control," *Social Forces*, 24 (March 1956), 217–23.

tional divorce laws is that the legal grounds for divorce are often faked or trumped up. Thus, before New York passed its "no fault" divorce law, the only ground for divorce was adultery. Standard procedures in such a case were either to obtain a divorce in Nevada or to provide evidence—often deliberately staged—of adultery in New York.

Goode's classic study, *After Divorce*, found that couples gave the following as the main causes for their divorces regardless of what they claimed as grounds:[15]

Desertion	33%
Husband dominant	32
Non-support	31
Drunkenness	30
Personality factors	29
Unsatisfactory home life	25
Differing values	21
Other lovers	16
Relatives	8

The percentages total over 100 percent because the respondents were allowed to pick more than one cause. Adultery does not rank high in this listing. In contrast, the grounds for divorce seem to reflect solely the preferences of state law, as illustrated in Table 14–1.

The Uniform Marriage and Divorce Act is not law at present anywhere, but it is intended as a model to guide state legislation. It does not require a couple to produce grounds for a divorce. Rather, it permits them to seek legal redress of grievances when they perceive that their relationship has reached an "irretrievable breakdown." It recognizes that it is more than likely that the couple, not one particular partner, is "at fault." Marriage counselor Marie Kargman observes,

If unhappily married people could have access to the courts for the dissolution of their marriage before marital infidelity seems the only way out, before desertion seems the only way out, before the hostilities have seriously wounded either one or both partners, before either one or both parties are driven in desperation to dope, to drink, or to mental illness; then the parties could be encouraged to make responsible agreements for their marital obligations, especially where there are children, and the family could be "recycled" with diminished damage to all concerned.[16]

Divorce Counseling

Those who are concerned with marriage counseling are beginning to take a new look at their role in regard to divorce. At least one counselor

[15]William J. Goode, *After Divorce* (New York: Free Press, 1955), p. 123. Copyright © 1955 The Free Press.
[16]Marie Kargman, "The Revolution in Divorce Law," *The Family Coordinator*, 22 (April 1973), 245.

TABLE 14-1   GROUNDS FOR DIVORCE BY STATE

State	Cruelty	Desertion	Non-support	Alcohol	Felony	Impotency	Pregnancy at Marriage	Drug Addiction	Fraudulent Contract	Other Causes	Residence Time	Time between Interlocut'y and Final Decrees
Alabama	x	x	x	x	x	x	x	x	–	Q-K-W-F-MM	1 year*	None-R
Alaska	x	x	x	x	x	x	–	x	–	F-K-B	1 year	None
Arizona	x	x	x	x	x	x	x	–	–	X	1 year	None
Arkansas	x	x	x	x	x	–	–	–	–	B-Y-K-DD	3 months*	None
California	–	–	–	–	–	–	–	–	–	K-KK	6 months	6 month
Colorado	–	–	–	–	–	–	–	–	–	MM	90 days	None
Connecticut	x	x	–	x	x	–	–	–	x	K-F	3 years*	None
Delaware	x	x	x	x	x	–	–	–	–	F-K-Y-DD-FF	2 years	3 months
D.C.	–	x	–	–	x	–	–	–	–	Y-Z	1 year	None
Florida	x	x	–	x	–	x	–	x	–	A-M-BB-DD-K-X	6 months	None
Georgia	x	x	–	x	x	x	x	x	x	K-M-AA	6 months	1
Hawaii	x	x	x	x	x	–	–	x	–	K-Z-B-X	1 year	1
Idaho	x	x	x	x	x	–	–	–	–	X-K	6 weeks	None
Illinois	x	x	–	x	x	x	–	x	–		1 year*	None
Indiana	x	x	x	x	x	x	–	–	–	K	1 year*	None
Iowa	–	–	–	–	–	–	–	–	–	MM	1 year*	None-S
Kansas	x	x	–	x	x	x	x	–	x	K-F-CC	6 months	None-T
Kentucky	–	–	–	–	–	–	–	–	x	AA-PP	1 year	None
Louisiana	–	–	–	x	–	–	–	–	–	X-Z	1 year*	None
Maine	x	x	x	x	–	x	–	x	–	X	3 months	None
Maryland	x	x	–	–	x	x	–	–	–	Y-K-W	1 year	None
Massachusetts	x	x	x	x	x	x	–	x	–	LL	2 years*	6 months
Michigan	–	–	–	–	–	–	–	–	–	No Fault-MM	1 year*	None
Minnesota	–	x	–	x	x	x	–	–	–	K-W-OO	1 year*	None-T
Mississippi	x	x	–	x	x	x	x	x	–	K-M-DD	1 year*	None-U
Missouri	x	x	–	x	x	x	x	–	–	B-J-DD	1 year	None

Source: Compiled by William E. Mariano, Council on Marriage Relations. Inc., 110 East 42nd Street, New York, N.Y., 10017. Published in *The World Almanac and Book of Facts*. New York: Newspaper Enterprise Association, Inc., 1974, p. 1026.

(1) Determined by court order. (2) No minimum residence required in adultery cases. (3) Or 5 days after action is set for trial, whichever is sooner (4) Except one year when defendant is a non-resident, or personal service of a summons is impossible. (A) Violence. (B) Indignities. (C) Loathsome disease. (D) Joining religious order disbelieving in marriage. (E) Unchaste behavior after marriage. (F) Incompatability. (H) Any gross misbehavior or wickedness. (I) Wife being a prostitute. (J) Husband being a vagrant. (K) 5-yrs. insanity; permanent insanity in Utah; incurable insanity in Calif. Exceptions 18 mos. Alaska; 2 yrs. Ga., Nev., Ore., Wash., and Wyo.; 3 yrs. Ark., Fla., Tex., Minn., Colo., Kan., Hawaii, Md., Miss., W. Va.; 6 yrs. Idaho. (M) Consanguinity. (N) In cruelty cases, one yr. to remarry. (O) Plaintiff, 6 mos.; defendant 2 yrs. to remarry. (P) If guilty spouse is sentenced to infamous punishment. (Q) Crime against nature. (R) Sixty days to remarry. (S) One year to remarry; Hawaii one year with minor child. Except Iowa, 90 days (T) Six months to remarry; in Kan. 60 days. (U) Adultery cases, remarriage in discretion of court. (W) Separation for 2 yrs. after decree for same in Ala. and Minn.: 4 yrs. in N.J.; 18 mos. in N.H.; 5 yrs. in Wis. and Md. (X) Separation, no cohabitation—5 yrs. Exceptions La., Va., Wyo., and (under agreement), W. Va. 2 yrs.; Tex. and Maine 3 yrs.; N.C. 1 yr. and R.I. 10 yrs. (Y) Separation, no cohabitation—3 years. Exceptions: Vt., Wash., 2 yrs.; Del., Md., 18 mos.; D.C. and Wis., 1. (Z) Separation for 2 yrs. after decree for Dist.

State	Cruelty	Desertion	Non-support	Alcohol	Felony	Impotency	Pregnancy at Marriage	Drug Addiction	Fraudulent Contract	Other Causes	Residence Time	Time between Interlocut'y and Final Decrees
Montana	x	x	x	x	x	–	–	–	–	K	1 year	None*
Nebraska	x	x	x	x	x	x	–	–	–	K-LL	2 years*	6 months
Nevada	x	x	x	x	x	x	–	–	–	K-Y	6 weeks	None
New Hampshire	x	x	x	x	x	x	–	–	–	D-GG-HH-II-KK	1 year*	None
New Jersey	x	x	–	–	x	–	–	x	–	NN-K	1 year*	None
New Mexico	x	x	–	–	–	–	–	–	–	F	6 months	None
New York	x	x	–	–	x	–	–	–	–	X-Z*	1 year	3 months*
North Carolina	–	–	–	–	–	x	x	–	–	Q-K-X	1 year	None
North Dakota	x	x	x	x	x	–	–	–	–	K	1 year	None-U
Ohio	x	x	–	x	x	x	–	–	x	BB-CC-DD	6 months	None
Oklahoma	x	x	–	x	x	x	x	–	x	F-K-BB-CC	1 year	90 days
Oregon	–	–	–	–	–	x	–	–	–	KK	1 year*	None
Pennsylvania	x	x	–	–	x	–	–	–	–	B-M-DD-K-Y	1 year*	None
Rhode Island	x	x	x	x	x	x	–	–	x	H-X	2 years*	6 months
South Carolina	x	x	–	x	–	–	–	–	x	Y	1 year	None
South Dakota	x	x	x	x	x	–	–	–	–	K	1 year*	None
Tennessee	x	x	x	x	x	x	x	–	–	A-B-DD-EE	1 year	None
Texas	x	x	–	–	x	–	–	–	x	K-X-F-PP	1 year	60 days
Utah	x	x	x	x	x	x	–	–	–	W-K	3 months	3 months*
Vermont	x	x	x	–	x	–	–	–	–	Y-K	6 months	3 months-O*
Virginia	–	x	–	–	x	x	x	–	–	I-B	1 year	None-U*
Washington	–	–	–	–	–	–	–	–	x	B-K-Y-KK	6 months	None
West Virginia	x	x	–	x	x	–	–	–	x	X-K	2 years*²	None
Wisconsin	x	x	x	x	x	–	–	–	–	X-W	6 months	120 days⁴
Wyoming	x	x	x	x	x	x	x	–	–	B-J-K	60 days	None

of Col.; 1 yr for La. (AA) Mental incapacity at time of marriage. (BB) Procurement of out-of-state divorce. (CC) Gross neglect of duty. (DD) Bigamy. (EE) Attempted homicide. (FF) Plaintiff under age at time of marriage. (GG) Treatment which injures health or endangers reason. (HH) Wife without state for 10 yrs. (II) Wife in state 2 yrs.; husband never in state and has intent to become citizen of foreign country. (JJ) Seven years absence. (KK) Irreconcilable differences. (LL) Life sentence dissolves marriage. (MM) Breakdown of marriage with no reasonable likelihood of preservation. (NN) Deviate sexual conduct. (OO) Course of conduct detrimental to the marriage relationship of party seeking divorce. (PP) Incompatability without regard to fault.

Adultery is either grounds for divorce or evidence of irreconcilable differences and a breakdown of the marriage in all states.

The plaintiff can invariably remarry in the same State where he or she procured a decree of divorce or annulment. Not so the defendant, who is barred in certain States for some offenses. After a period of time has elapsed even the offender can apply for special permission.

The U.S. Supreme Court in 5 to 4 opinion, ruled April 18, 1949, that one sided quick divorces could be challenged as illegal if notice of the action was not served on the divorced partner within the divorcing States, excepting where the partner was represented at the proceedings.

Enoch Arden Laws. Disappearance and unknown to be alive—Conn. 7 years absence; N.H., 2 years; N.Y., 5 years (called dissolution); Vt., 7 years.

contends that in reality the term "marriage counselor" is misleading. A better way of labeling the profession would be "marriage and divorce counselor."[17] Adding the "divorce" suggests the new stance. Esther Fisher contends that the role of counselor is not limited to improving the character and quality of the partnership's dissolution, for the counselor's role must shift as the stages in the process change. In pre-divorce the issue is whether or not a divorce should be sought. During the process of divorce itself, support must be provided to one or both partners so that they will not abuse each other before the law and will not make hostages of their children. After legal divorce has been granted the role of the counselor is to help the client achieve the transition from ex-spouse to single person. Fisher points out that divorce can be seen as a three-stage process itself. Emotional divorce occurs when the couple realize that their relationship is ended. Physical divorce follows upon separation from bed and board. Legal divorce is really an anticlimax; it simply records for posterity what has already been accomplished and permits the divorced couple to legally remarry.

Divorce as a Process

Paul Bohannan describes divorce as a process involving at least six stages.[18] It is a complex social phenomenon and can be a traumatic personal experience. Because people often mistrust the emotions associated with the dissolution of a partnership, they tend to withdraw from the situation and allow the crisis to come to their awareness slowly so that they can more readily manage the unpleasant experience. Socially, this tendency to hide from the situation is reflected in inadequate legislation, support, and role guidelines for divorcing persons. Bohannan lists the following six stages of the divorce process:

(1) The emotional divorce which centers around the problem of the deteriorating marriage; (2) the legal divorce based on grounds; (3) the economic divorce which deals with money and property; (4) the co-parental divorce which deals with custody, single parent homes and visitations; (5) the community divorce surrounding the changes of friends and community that every divorcee experiences; and (6) the psychic divorce, with the problem of regaining individual autonomy.[19]

These six stages are not related sequentially to one another, as any of them may occur simultaneously. Each stage involves distinctively different tasks.

[17]Esther Fisher, "A Guide to Divorce and Counselling," *The Family Coordinator*, 22 (January 1973), 55.
[18]Paul Bohannan, *Divorce and After* (Garden City, N.Y.: Doubleday & Company, Inc., 1970).
[19]As quoted in Marcia E. Lasswell and Thomas E. Laswell, *Love, Marriage, Family: A Developmental Approach* (Glenview, Illinois: Scott, Foresman & Company, 1973), p. 475.

Emotional Divorce. The first stage is obviously the most significant in that marital breakdown is taking place. This is what provides the initial impetus for considering the possibility of divorce. Conflict already has taken its destructive toll and the partners, in one way or another, have withdrawn from the giving of themselves to each other. Although they may appear to function adequately in the social dimensions, they have ceased to aid each other's growth and are involved in increasing amounts of divergent feedback. In a healthy growing partnership, two people naturally grow apart to some extent as they mature, but they also continue to build up their interdependence at the same time as they increase their autonomy. In emotional divorce, however, two people grate upon each other simply because they interpret whatever interdependence remains between them as hated evidence of dependency.[20] Sadly, two people can remain emotionally divorced from each other for a lifetime without ever obtaining a legal divorce.

Legal Divorce. An emotionally divorced couple may seek a legal divorce. The courts in each state specify the "grounds" for divorce; that is to say, they have determined what will be acceptable reasons *before the law* for obtaining a divorce. The legal grounds for obtaining a divorce, of course, may be different from the "real" reasons a couple have for wanting a divorce. This is why, in large measure, divorce proceedings are so often a travesty of justice and an additional pain to the couple seeking a divorce. They often have to lie or trump up charges against each other in order to obtain a legal divorce.

Proving the case in court—that is, demonstrating that one does indeed have legally valid grounds for divorce—is quite a different process from discovering the reasons why a couple want a divorce. This is clearly reflected in the statistics:

Some divorces are granted on bizarre grounds and are picked up by reporters as "human interest" stories. But, according to the statistics gathered by the Department of Health, Education and Welfare, about three-fourths of all divorces are granted on three legal grounds: desertion (or abandonment), nonsupport (or neglect), and cruelty (physical or mental). In some states, 90 percent or more of decrees granted are on one particular ground. Cruelty is the ground for more than 90 percent of the divorces granted in Idaho, Iowa, Michigan, Nebraska, Oregon, Utah and Wisconsin; desertion is the ground for 90 percent or more of the divorces granted in Virginia; incompatability is the ground usually given in Alaska, and "indignities" in Wyoming.[21]

Although several states are moving to modify their divorce laws and

---

[20]Lasswell and Lasswell, *Love, Marriage, Family*, p. 476.
[21]Gail Fullerton, *Survival in Marriage* (New York: Holt, Rinehart & Winston, 1972), p. 407. Taken from U.S. Department of Health, Education and Welfare, *Divorce Statistics Analysis, U.S.: 1963* (Washington, D.C.: U.S. Government Printing Office, 1967).

speak of the "dissolution of marriage" in a proceeding which essentially asks the court to determine if there is, in fact, evidence that the marriage cannot be continued, forty-six states have not changed their laws in decades. They still operate on the old "adversary" notion that one partner must be found "at fault" in order for the divorce to be obtained. New York, California, and Florida have adopted "no fault" divorce laws in which a couple can obtain a divorce for a nominal fee without the need of a lawyer. In California the divorce rate is one divorce for every two marriages contracted at the present time.

The actual divorce proceedings take but a few minutes; few go longer than fifteen. Many divorcees are disappointed, having expected that their grievances would be heard when they had their "day in court":[22]

I thought there would be more to it than that. My attorney just asked a few questions and the judge asked something without even looking up from the papers in front of him, and my attorney indicated that I should step down. It couldn't have taken five minutes and my marriage had lasted five years. I still feel married.[23]

With all of the problems and the hypocrisy involved in divorce proceedings as they are commonly conducted at present, legal divorce does accomplish one thing that cannot be obtained otherwise:

Divorce can be varyingly defined as the pronouncement of a court, the paper on which pronouncement is recorded, or the legal situation which arises from this pronouncement. In this situation the parties, or occasionally only one of them, are free to do something which they could not do before; they are now free to enter upon new relationships capable of being recognized as legally valid marriages.[24]

Economic Divorce. Because couples in the United States are recognized as an economic unit not unlike a corporation in many ways, divorce must involve a property settlement. The assets of the couple must be divided in two. This division is complicated by tax laws, so the divorce lawyer must have a great deal of knowledge of the details of tax law or must make use of an assistant who has such specialized knowledge. Varying kinds of emotional and sometimes irrational decisions are made at the time of the property settlement. Anger and frustration often impede a just settlement. Although most things are clear in terms of separating the household goods, various items of value to which one or the other partner may have an emotional attachment can become critical conflict-provoking issues.

Involved in the economic settlement is, of course, the matter of ali-

[22]Lasswell and Lasswell, *Love, Marriage, Family*, p. 482.
[23]Fullerton, *Survival in Marriage*, p. 406.
[24]Max Reinstein, *Marriage, Stability, Divorce and the Law* (Chicago: The University of Chicago Press, 1972), p. 266.

mony. In most cases, the husband is required to pay alimony, the amount of which is established by the court. Some recent decisions, however, maintain that in given economic situations the wife may be quite capable of maintaining herself. Alimony is usually based on the wife's needs and the husband's ability to pay. Other factors which are often considered are the wife's educational background and ability to be a breadwinner, her state of health, his state of health, the income tax question, children, and the general life styles of both.

Child support is figured separately from alimony on a similar basis of determining need and ability. Because both alimony and child support are established by the court, failure to pay represents an act of contempt of court. This is the only legal sanction that can be invoked to ensure that these payments are made, but it is not really adequate in dealing with husbands who refuse to pay. Many post-divorce conflicts arise out of failure adequately to deal with the economic aspects of divorce.

Co-parental Divorce. Co-parental divorce is necessary if there are children. Perhaps one of the most painful and agonizing aspects of divorce is determining who will live with whom after the household breaks up. Custody of the children is decided by the court on the basis of what will be in the best interest of the children. The custodian may be either of the parents or even a third party if the court feels that such an arrangement is necessary. Traditionally, under English common law, the father had absolute property rights in the children, but the tendency to give the mother custody is more common today. Some women refuse child support on the mistaken assumption that they can thus deny the father the right to see his children. In fact, however, his visiting rights are not contingent upon his continual support, but derive from his parental role. Nevertheless, some fathers accept this tradeoff, although it is not likely that it would stand up in court should they contest such a decision. In Chapter 15 some of the problems of single-parent families will be discussed.

Community Divorce. The change in status of the divorced sometimes means isolation from the community of friends and neighbors that is difficult to cope with or overcome. Personal inadequacies are now seen in a different context and loneliness can become all-pervasive. With the increasing options available to single people in our society, however, the surface of this loneliness can be broken much more easily today than in the past. This aspect of divorce also will be treated briefly in Chapter 15.

Psychic Divorce. The most difficult stage in recovery from divorce, yet probably the area in which one is most free to be creative, involves the regaining of individual autonomy. In one sense, a partnership such as a marriage never ends, particularly if there are children. It may be legally broken, but the ties inevitably go on for a while, sometimes for a lifetime.

The problem of regaining autonomy is related to the extent to which autonomy was given up in the partnership. Men and women who continued to retain a great deal of individual autonomy in their partnership will have less difficulty upon divorce. (It is also less likely that they will divorce in the first place, however.) Regaining autonomy means

. . . learning to live without somebody to lean on—but also without someone to support. There is nobody on whom to blame one's difficulties (except oneself), nobody to short-stop one's growth and nobody to grow with.

Each must regain—if he [or she] ever had it—the dependence on self and faith in one's own capacity to cope with the environment, with people, with thoughts and emotions.[25]

There is evidence that "divorce breeds divorce" in the sense that restrictions on obtaining divorces influence the rate of divorce, although the data on this issue is far from clear. Nevertheless, the trend toward increased divorce rates need not be a cause for alarm. Qualitatively, there is reason to believe that divorce, whatever its frequency, is preferable to conflicted, destructive partnerships. As Max Reinstein observes:

If we regard family stability as a social good, a situation of high incidence of marriage breakdown constitutes a social evil. Its reduction deserves to be an aim of social policy. But what about divorce? It does not occur by itself but only as a sequel to marriage breakdown. Insofar as divorce opens the door to legitimate remarriage and thus to the creation of new homes free of any taint of illegitimacy, it is a social good rather than an evil. But if the easy availability of divorce is conducive toward a high incidence of marriage breakdown, good social policy requires that the incidence of divorce ought also to be reduced.[26]

[25]Lasswell and Lasswell, *Love, Marriage, Family*, p. 488.
[26]Reinstein, *Marriage, Stability, Divorce and the Law*.

SUMMARY

Because we know so little about how nonmarital partnerships terminate, in this chapter we have chosen to focus exclusively on how marriages end. Following Goode, we can describe five types of family disorganization: the uncompleted family, the empty shell, the family disorganized by external catastrophes, the family disorganized by internal catastrophes, and those terminated by willed departures such as divorce.

Although death terminates more marriages than any other cause, divorce receives the most publicity. Currently, one divorce takes place each year for every three marriages that are contracted in that year. While 81 percent of all married persons have been married only once, about 15 percent of all men and 17 percent of all women who are seventy or over have been divorced at least once.

Divorce laws are rapidly being modified to better fit the realities of modern marriage and permit couples to have access to legal redress of grievances without having to prove "fault." This change amounts to another factor that is making marriage more voluntary and thus contributing to the increased divorce rate. Divorce counselors are beginning to take a more active role in reducing the damage that can be inflicted by divorce.

Paul Bohannan describes divorce as a six-stage process, each stage of which has its own problems that divorcing couples must face: emotional divorce, legal divorce, economic divorce, co-parental divorce, community divorce, and psychic divorce.

PART
FOUR

ALTERNATIVES

15

DEVELOPING STYLES FOR SINGLES

Just what life will offer single individuals is up to them. They can follow any or all roads today and any or all life-styles. From the quiet, dull rural life one can enter the hustle-bustle of the big city. Living alone or in a singles building, joining a singles club or finding your own dates are simple choices in this day and age. There is now, away from the small communes, something for everyone.

Rosalyn Moran

INTRODUCTION

The category of persons frequently lumped together under the title "singles" is much more heterogeneous than most groupings we make. If we mean by "single" anyone who does not happen at a particular time to have a legal mate—is not married—then we must include in this group those who have never married, those who are divorced or separated, and those who are widowed. The only factor all these people have in common is that at the time in question they are not married.

Because of the tremendous pressure to marry in our society, few researchers seriously consider the single life style as a viable alternative in its own right. Indeed, until recently, few Americans seriously considered remaining single as a viable lifelong life style; for most people, being single was the result of failure to marry, failure at marriage, or the accidents of fate that determine widowhood. Because marriage is often considered the only life style any reasonably well-adjusted person would willingly choose, those who elect to remain single or find themselves single must forge their own life style as best they can.

Recently, however, more and more industries have begun to cater to the tastes, interests, and problems of single persons. It is becoming possible to consider seriously a single style of life as a positively valued alternative to traditional marriage. Thus, in this chapter it is particularly important that we think in terms of man-woman relationships and partnerships rather than in terms of marital or nonmarital relationships. With this focus, the designation of a person as a divorcee, widower, single parent, or what have you becomes a shorthand way of referring to certain experiences that these persons have had in their past that have an effect upon the way in which they live out their single life style. But such designations do not presume that the marital state is inherently more desirable than the single state. In keeping with the intent of this book, the focus is upon the quality of whatever kind of partnership emerges rather than upon the formal structure of that partnership.

WHO THEY ARE

We do not know much statistically about how the average American goes about establishing partnerships other than marriage. It is, therefore, not possible to provide any estimate of the amount of time people spend without any kind of partnership at all. It has been estimated, however, that the divorced who remarry live in partial families—that is, families consisting of one parent plus dependent children—for an average of 5.9 years. Three of these years are spent in a state of either legal or de facto separation prior to divorce; the other 2.9 years follow the legal divorce. The widowed live in partial families for an average of 3.5 years.[1] Some in each category, of course, never remarry.

The overall figure of about 22 million persons over the age of eighteen who were not married in 1971 includes within it a sizable number of persons who are going to get married as soon as they can.[2] Many of them already had their marriage partner picked out and some undoubtedly were engaged. It also includes all of the divorced and widowed persons without children and a number of persons who will never marry, either because of circumstances beyond their control or because they really never intended to marry. One study estimates that there are at least 8 million involuntarily single females over the age of eighteen in our society. Not included in the 22 million are people living in single-parent families. This category includes the never married who have had children, as well as the divorced, separated, and widowed who have children. There were about 7.5 million single-parent families in 1972.

Thus, although the fraction of the population in any given year who are without marital partners is around 27 percent of the total number of persons over eighteen, the total number of persons who have lived a significant part of their adult lives without a marital partner is much

[1] Ivan F. Nye and Felix Berardo, *The Family: Its Structures and Interaction* (New York: The Macmillan Company, 1973), p. 529.
[2] U.S. Bureau of the Census, *Statistical Abstract of the United States: 1973* (Washington, D.C.: U.S. Government Printing Office, 1973), p. 40.

larger. With the pressure to marry diminishing as our society comes to give increasing recognition to the value of nonmarital partnerships, the number of persons who will choose not to marry—or not to marry again —will continue to increase.

THE DIVORCED

The single person who has been married one or more times brings to the single style of life he or she is developing a distinctive heritage, for good or for ill, arising out of the fact of having been married. In developing relationships, determining the marital status of one's partner is one of the first pieces of information one collects about the partner, and "divorced" has certain implications in the common understanding. "Whenever a guy hears that I am a divorcee, he thinks that I am ready to go to bed with him at the drop of a hat," a divorced woman reports. "When I go out with a woman and tell her I'm divorced," a man testifies, "I can see the wheels start turning immediately. Before she's willing to let herself get interested in me she wants to find out what my problem is. She's afraid maybe I'm impotent or have a violent temper or something like that."

Divorce frequently carries with it an aura of failure that affects both the divorced people themselves and those around them. Thus a certain insecurity is frequently a part of the heritage of divorce. "After being married to George for thirty years, I really don't know how to respond fully to other men," one woman laments. "God, I don't even know how much soap to put into the washing machine," a divorced man says, expressing what he obviously sees as a symbol of his general incompetence. On the other hand, divorce offers some people a new lease on life: "I never really knew I was such a sexual person until I started dating other men"; "I didn't realize how much I lost track of the meaning of relationships during those twelve years." Divorce has different significances for the persons involved depending on whether it occurs when they are relatively young or when they are in middle or old age, on whether they were married for many years or only a few months. It makes a difference if children are involved, particularly if the family is poor. In the 1960s well over three-fifths of all divorcing couples had minor children.[3] Only those divorced persons without children will be considered in this section.

How Do We Live?

Because of the strong expectations that adults be independent from their parents, divorced people who do not have children rarely return to live in the parental home. "I couldn't possibly go back and live with my par-

[3]Nye and Berardo, *The Family*, p. 475.

ents," a divorced woman explained. "Of course I was very lonely but it was better to be lonely than to burden my parents with my sadness. After all, it wasn't their fault that John and I couldn't get along. I simply would have made them hate John, and that's not fair."

If the couple followed a traditional division of labor during their married years, the requirement that they now live on their own will mean that each has to develop the skills formerly contributed by the spouse or pay for such services. The man who moves into an apartment usually buys as many of the domestic services as he can afford. He eats out, sends his clothes to the laundry, and hires a housekeeper. If he is paying alimony, this means that in effect he is paying to run two households. The woman's predicament in this regard is usually more serious than the man's if she limited her work during marriage to performing the housekeeping duties. While it is possible for him to continue in his specialty—earning the income—and hire someone to provide her services, it is not possible for her to hire someone to support her while she remains a homemaker. If there is no alimony or if the amount is inadequate for her needs—or if it is not paid regularly, as often happens—she must seek employment even though her inexperience as a worker puts her at a disadvantage in the job market. The woman who worked during marriage, on the other hand, is in a position not unlike the position of the divorced husband.

What Do We Do About Friends?

Divorce not only means the loss of a partner, but over a period of time it usually means the loss of some of the friends the partners knew as a couple. Divorce can create an awkward situation for the friends of a formerly married couple. The problem from the friends' point of view is, "Which one do we invite?" Often in friendships between couples the relationship is primarily a friendship between the wives and another friendship between the husbands. When one of the couples gets divorced, therefore, it is likely that the husband in the still married couple will favor maintaining relations with the ex-husband while the wife wants to keep the friendship of the ex-wife. Settling this difference may produce a strain that is most easily resolved for the still married couple by simply cutting off relations with both divorced partners. "I'd like to have you to dinner more often, Helen," the friend of a divorced woman might explain, "but my husband thinks it wouldn't be fair to Bob."

To a large extent, divorced people are unable to control such developments. Thus, over the course of about a year, they will find that their friendship patterns have been radically changed. "After eight months I began to realize that I was getting fewer and fewer invitations to go out. I still had occasions for luncheon with my old girlfriends, but I was

spending more and more time alone at night," a divorced woman explained. At this point the divorced person usually recognizes the need
to discover new friends. Although this is no easy task even today, it is
getting easier all the time. Compared to single women aged twenty-five,
divorcees are more likely to marry; their chances are 99 out of 100,
compared to the single woman's 88 out of 100.[4] What is more, divorcees
with children are more likely to remarry than those without, and statistics show that they are able to do so in about the same amount of time.
In fact, children seem to be an incentive to marry. The problems they
create for divorced people—especially divorced women—will be discussed in a following section.

But what if the divorced person really doesn't want to remarry? Two-
fifths of them do not remarry. What kind of a life can they expect to
realize as single persons? Again, times are changing. Any one of a number of organizations can provide social and recreational opportunities
that were once lacking for single persons in our society. This is truer,
perhaps, for divorced people under thirty-five than for older people. It is
also truer for people who are temperamentally more gregarious. The life
style of the young unmarried single, to which the young divorced could
return, is discussed in a later section of this chapter.

A less frantic sort of life style can be sustained by making use of
activities provided by churches such as the First Singles Church and
various civic organizations.[5] Many places of entertainment are now open
to single men and women, where once they catered largely or even exclusively to couples. The problem of getting to know people is not so
much a matter of where to go as it is a matter of money and incentive.
If the divorced person is young and has at least a middle-class income,
there are numerous opportunities for social contact of many sorts. Without money, the problems are quite different. Because most low-income
persons who become divorced have children, their style of adjustment
will be discussed in the section dealing with single-parent families.

What About Sex?

While at one time it was popular to suppose that divorced persons
should abstain from sexual intercourse just as they were supposed to
have done before marriage, it is now becoming widely recognized that
this is nonsense. The sexual needs of divorced persons are likely to be
greater than those of single people their own age.[6] Discovery of this
fact, of course, is nothing new; for a long time it was intuitively sensed

[4]Richard Udry, *The Social Context of Marriage*, 2nd ed. (Philadelphia: J. B. Lippincott, 1973), p. 460.
[5]"First Singles Church, U.S.A.," *Newsweek* (June 12, 1972).
[6]Nye and Berardo, *The Family*, p. 519.

by the men who created the stereotype of the divorced woman as an easy target for sexual advances. Today, however, as attitudes toward sex are changing, it is becoming increasingly easy for divorced people to openly acknowledge their sexuality.[7] The fact that divorced men and women are not expected to be sexually "innocent," in the way never-married single people are, may be one of the real advantages they enjoy over the never married as they attempt to adjust to a single life style.

Living with a Label

In spite of the opportunities now beginning to appear for divorced persons to make a better reentry into single life (and to achieve a better remarriage if they want one), there are still many problems associated with the role. The label "divorced" still means failure both to the society at large and to the divorced person. Although this can be beneficial, in the sense that expectations of lasting partnerships like marriage may be more realistic the "next time around," it can also mean that the divorced person feels less sure of himself or herself in social and intimate interactions.

It is unfortunately true that not many divorced people are permitted to emerge from the experience with their sense of themselves as solidly intact as the woman who gave us the following testimony: "Look, getting divorced is a lot like getting married in some ways: both are voluntary decisions to change your living arrangements. Sure, in a lot of cases people get divorced unwillingly—I mean, their husbands or wives divorce them against their will or their marriage is so bad they feel they have no choice. In those cases, I suppose, people should sympathize with them. But my husband and I both *decided* to get divorced. It wasn't anything that happened to us, it was something we decided. I don't want people's sympathy and I don't think Andy does either. When we got married people had the courtesy to assume we knew what we were doing. They didn't say, 'Oh, I'm sorry things didn't work out for you when you were single'; they said, 'Congratulations.' Well, this is a decision to change the way we're living, too, and I wish people would take it that way. When someone I haven't talked to in a while calls and I tell them I'm divorced, they always say, 'I'm sorry to hear that,' or 'Oh, that's too bad.' Well, it's not too bad; I think it's the best thing for both of us."

In the same vein, many divorced people do not feel that they should be stigmatized as individuals who failed in marriage, which is how they are most commonly regarded and the way they are encouraged to regard

[7]Udry, *Social Context of Marriage*, p. 460.

themselves. "I don't think my marriage with Diane was a failure just because it didn't last forever," one man reported. "We had a lot of good years together; we helped each other a lot and we grew a lot with each other. That's not what I call a failure. We just reached a point when we stopped growing and we both felt we could do more with ourselves if we each went our own way. I look at it this way: a person learns a lot in college, but it reaches a point when college doesn't have all that much more to offer him. He graduates. Does that mean that he was a failure at college because he couldn't go on learning there forever? I know the analogy doesn't really fit, because when you enroll in college you only intend to go four years but when you get married it's supposed to be for the rest of your life. But that only means we were wrong about that part. It doesn't mean our relationship was a failure."

Both of these statements indicate that the stereotype that labels divorced people as individuals who "couldn't make a go of it" in marriage is, like all stereotypes, often inaccurate and contributes to the problems divorced people face in our culture by encouraging them to see themselves as misfits. This is not to deny that in a great many cases divorce does represent a traumatic failure of one sort or another. Thus, for example, divorced persons have higher death rates and suicide rates than the married.[8] They frequently report great personal stress and strain after divorce. Researcher William Goode found this to be especially true of divorced women with children. They reported increased difficulties in the following areas: difficulty in sleeping, 62 percent; poorer health, 67 percent; loneliness, 67 percent; low work efficiency, 43 percent; memory problems, 32 percent; increased smoking, 30 percent; increased drinking, 16 percent.[9] Clearly, divorce can have a significant negative impact on an individual's performance and health. On the other hand, for many people divorce is a positive step toward reestablishing themselves as autonomous, growing individuals. The decision to get divorced, because it is viewed so critically by many people, sometimes requires an act of great courage and may be more difficult than the decision to remain in an unsatisfactory or unfulfilling relationship. Summoning up the courage to make this decision, therefore, may be a significant triumph in an individual's development, and in this sense we do the divorced an injustice when we think of them as failures.

The divorced person without children can cope with the stress and disorientation often involved in divorce by traveling, by "losing" herself or himself in a job, by moving to a new location, by dating new people, or by becoming a hermit and simply suffering for a time. The divorced

[8]Nye and Berardo, *The Family*, p. 520.
[9]William Goode, *After Divorce* (Glencoe, Ill.: Free Press, 1956), p. 186.

person with children obviously does not have as many options, for he or she must consider the impact of all of these decisions on the children. Because the children most often live with their mother, it is usually the divorced woman who must cope with this problem.

THE WIDOWED

Death dissolves more marriages than any other cause of marital dissolution. Although death can come at any age, the widowed population is, as one might expect, on the average considerably older than the divorced. For every five divorcees among persons in their late twenties, for example, there is one widow. Because of the difference in life expectancy of men and women, being widowed is more commonly experienced by women than by men. Forty-three percent of all women between the ages of sixty-five and seventy-four are widowed.[10] In 1972 there were 11,435,000 widowed persons over the age of eighteen in the United States, over 9.5 million of whom were women.[11]

In the past, men survived their wives with greater regularity than they do now. The tombstones of New England bear witness to the death of many women in childbirth and note with awe the man who survived several wives. Today, a man's life expectancy is about seven years less than his wife's and the average woman who becomes widowed outlives her husband by eleven years. But the fact that women are widowed more often than men is really beside the point. What is not beside the point is the fact that, except in those relatively rare and generally accidental cases where two partners die simultaneously, all couples can expect that one or the other of them will have to go through a period of widowhood.

Grief Work

When a spouse dies, the widow or widower must cope with a myriad of experiences for which she or he is not prepared. Our society in general deals with the question of death in a most inadequate way, for we do not have the heritage, as other cultures do, of a rich and complex ritual response to death. Not only does the widow or widower not know what her or his role in mourning should be, but on top of this, she or he must handle the lack of knowledge of how to respond to this event in the majority of people who have known the deceased partner. Because of the lack of guidelines and the anxieties provoked by the crisis of death,

[10]Gail Fullerton, *Survival in Marriage* (New York: Holt, Rinehart & Winston, 1972), p. 421.
[11]*Statistical Abstract: 1973*, p. 38.

the majority of people want to *do* something, but the fact of the matter is that there isn't that much to do. Thus the widowed person is forced to become in some respects the "project director" for condoling friends and relatives.

In grief work there is an initial period of unreality when the bereaved feels not quite sure what has happened. A kind of automatic response to the situation helps the bereaved make the decisions that need to be made, but she or he may very well not remember having made them. A decided memory lapse is not uncommon among the newly widowed, who also often feel a need to place blame for the partner's death somewhere; this fluctuates from guiltily blaming oneself to lashing out and blaming others. Much has been written about grief work, and in general psychologists are agreed that it is important for the psychic health of the bereaved that grief be expressed; if it is not, it will frequently result in neurosis.[12]

Once the widowed person has performed the appropriate grief work, she or he in some sense joins the ranks of the singles. Although widowed people are generally older than the average divorced person (better than 70 percent of the wives widowed in 1964 were over fifty-five; over 30 percent were older than sixty-five), the widowed and the divorced face many of the same problems of reentry into the singles life style.[13] Both widows and widowers have lower probabilities for remarriage than divorced persons at all age levels.[14] Those that do remarry, however, do so in a shorter period of time than the typical divorced person (if the period of separation from the spouse is included in our computation of remarriage time for divorced people).

What About Friends?

Old friendships tend to dwindle for the widowed, in part as a result of the death of friends and in part as a result of a pattern similar to the one experienced by divorced persons. The upper-class woman who has been involved in a great many activities outside of her marriage will have a less difficult time maintaining friendships than the lower-class person or the person for whom marriage has been the center of her being. The widowed form a large portion of the impoverished population of our society, and thus the widowed person with inadequate income often faces old age and death in a terrifyingly lonely environment.

[12]Stanley G. Stergis, "Understanding Grief," *Mennenger Perspective* (April-May 1970).
[13]Nye and Berardo, *The Family*, p. 602.
[14]*The Family*, p. 606.

Sylvia Johnson, Woodfin Camp

Coping with Inadequate Income

The problems of most widowed people are compounded by inadequate income—a result of the fact that most couples in America are financially ill prepared for old age.[15] They come to retirement with little more than Social Security as a dependable source of income, and this is rarely sufficient for their needs. For some time it was widely believed that older persons really needed less than younger persons because they already had bought most of the things they need in life; besides, they were less active than younger people and therefore their expenses were necessarily less. Yet it is clear that, given adequate income, older persons can put it to good use. They can travel, buy condominium apartments, move to warmer climates, and generally maintain a level of social interaction not too different from that which they experienced in middle age. This is especially important for widowed older people, for whom the resources that make an active social life possible provide an opportunity to rebuild a life that was probably seriously disrupted by the death of the spouse. Indeed, the needs of the widowed elderly may well be greater than those of the elderly in general if for no other reason than the fact that the pleasures of companionship, which cost nothing, may be missing from their lives. It is thus often necessary for them to get out of the house if they do not want to be alone, and most outside activities cost money.

SINGLE-PARENT FAMILIES

The problems of all solo parents seem similar, even though some of them may be single because they have never married, some because they have

---

[15]For an excellent description of the economic plight of the elderly, see Harold Sheppard, "The Poverty of Aging," in Ben B. Seligman, ed., *Poverty as a Public Issue* (New York: Free Press, 1965), pp. 98–99.

been divorced, and some because they are widowed. Whatever the cause, the solo parent must cope with the task of trying to raise one or more children without a spouse. This requires a considerable commitment of the parent's time, even while she or he is also striving to provide an adequate income. (Divorced women may have it a bit easier on this score because child support is commonly available to them whereas, obviously, it is not available to the never-married and the widowed.) Single people with children are not nearly as free to make choices about partners, residence, and how they will spend their own time as single persons without children.

By far the larger number of single-parent families are headed by women.[16] The way of coping with solo parenthood varies by class. Lower-class men rarely assume the responsibility for heading a family without a spouse because they have very few resources either for housekeeping or earning a living; besides, most of our welfare legislation favors families headed by women. Upper-class professional men may head a partial family, in which case they usually compensate for their spouse's absence by buying the services of a maid, housekeeper, or "nanny."

"Broken Families"

Single-parent families are often thought of as "broken," "partial," or "disorganized" nuclear families. It has been commonly argued that both parents are necessary in order properly to socialize the child. In particular, "fatherless families" have been correlated with increased rates of schizophrenia in children, juvenile delinquency, inability to delay gratification, and a host of other disorders.[17] In recent years, however, it has become increasingly clear that many of these studies are based on faulty and inappropriate comparisons. As Nye points out, the assumption that "any father is better than no father at all" is commonly held by psychologists but often denied by sociologists.[18] The family in which there is conflict and continuing tension between the spouses is clearly not to be preferred to a single-parent family in which there is warmth and acceptance. Frequently, studies of fatherless families overlook the extent to which there is, in fact, a viable male role model in the house. This is particularly true of the lower-class black families in which a boyfriend assumes the role of a quasi-father.[19]

[16]*Statistical Abstract: 1973*, p. 40.
[17]Thomas F. Pettigrew, *Profile of the Negro American* (Princeton, N.J.: D. Van Nostrand Co., Inc., 1964), p. 1.
[18]Nye and Berardo, *The Family*.
[19]For a more detailed discussion of the role of the boyfriend see David A. Schulz, *Coming Up Black: Patterns of Ghetto Socialization* (Englewood Cliffs, N.J.: Prentice-Hall, Inc., 1968).

In sum, a good case can be made for abandoning pejorative labels such as "broken" when describing single-parent families. Many single-parent families provide their members with as complete and unbroken a family environment as many two-parent families. The term "broken" implies a value judgment which simply does not do justice to the successful efforts of numerous single parents who are adequately fulfilling the demanding task of raising their children in a society in which two-parent families are decidedly the norm.

Boyfriends

Recent sociological studies of lower-class black families reveal that boyfriends are frequently much more supportive of a woman and her children than had previously been imagined. The boyfriend may not "live in" with the family, but in his care and concern for all the members of the family he clearly demonstrates that his relationship to the family is not simply limited to his tie to the mother as a sexual partner. "He believes in survival for me and my children," one mother said in describing the concern of her boyfriend. This care may take the form of purchasing a significant part of the week's groceries, buying furniture, taking the family to the movies or the park, and helping the mother with her young children when she is sick. Such boyfriends often discipline the younger children and are generally respected in the household. Given their concern, it seems reasonable to assume that more would marry if they had an adequate and dependable source of income and if welfare laws in various localities did not make it disadvantageous for them to do so.

Having a boyfriend allows the low-income woman to make a better assessment of the man's ability to care for her and her family in a context in which this is not easily determined in any other way. Women who have been disappointed in one marriage do not find it easy to commit themselves to another when there are fewer social constraints to keep the marriage together and many factors that tend to pull it apart. Therefore, they say frequently of their boyfriends, "If he wants to love me he has to love my kids first."

Aid to Families with Dependent Children

The problems of providing aid to families with dependent children have been with us since the 1930s. It seems clear that many of the greatest difficulties of single-parent families are directly related to the fact that they often lack adequate income. Nye observes:

Our society seems to be saying: "We will support life in these families and nothing more."

Sociologically, the question may be stated: Do the roles of child care. socialization and housekeeping constitute an adequate occupation for a woman who has no husband for whom she may render these and other services?

Currently, it seems American society has not accepted the maternal role as a sufficient contribution to society and, in effect, by providing a submarginal level of subsistence for partial families, it tries to motivate them to become self-supporting. However, it has not yet provided the institutions that are necessary for the solo parent to function efficiently and to share in the rewards of the society.[20]

Undoubtedly the most significant of the institutions which society could provide to benefit solo parents at all income levels is an adequate day care program. Without some such program, solo parents with dependent children are placed under severe stress, both economic and psychological. Working would be almost counterproductive for a single parent who could expect only a low-income job and would have to pay a large portion of that income for day care for the children. What is more, time away from the children is important to all parents, but particularly to solo parents who, in the absence of a spouse, cannot find companionship with other adults in the family setting. Lack of adequate day care facilities ties the single parent to his or her children, making both work and a healthy social life nearly impossible.

The Influence of the Absent Spouse

The question of how to handle the absent spouse can be a vexing problem for divorced persons. If the children are young—say under the age of six—when the divorce occurs, and if the parents have been able to be relatively open about their conflicts and disagreements, they may not be very close to their biological father or their mother and can, therefore, accept a stepparent more readily. Presumably, they also might not have a great deal of difficulty accepting any other kind of partnership the mother or father might wish to establish. Older children are more likely to find it difficult to accept another intimate partner for their solo parent.

It has been argued that divorce laws should be modified in such a way as to minimize the damage to the children's relationship to their parents. When the conjugal bond is broken in divorce, it is not in fact necessary to sever the parental bond. Indeed, in most instances it seems highly desirable for all concerned to cultivate these parental relationships even after divorce. If a divorce is to be minimally harmful to the children involved, the following guidelines should be followed:

1. The responsibility for the decision to divorce must belong to the adults and not the children. Some couples on the verge of divorce con-

[20]Nye and Berardo, *The Family*, p. 5.

sult the children in order to solicit their feelings on the subject. Unless this is done very carefully, it can have the effect of making them feel responsible for the decision when it is made—a tactic which is hardly fair to a child.

2. The divorcing couple should agree on realistic reasons for the divorce.

3. They should share this information with their children in an understandable fashion.

4. The divorcing couple should work out their settlement with as wide an understanding of their personal needs as possible; flexibility and responsiveness to the children's needs should be the primary consideration in establishing visiting patterns.

5. The departing parent will help his or her child if he or she continues to show interest in the child; some visible symbol of their continuing relationship is often helpful in this regard.

6. The separated couple should continue to plan together for the children's future. Important decisions about the children—such as decisions about schooling—should not be left exclusively to the parent with whom the child is living.

7. The parents should be willing to discuss the divorce with the children even after the divorce; both of the former partners should be honest about the facts of the divorce at all times. In this regard, honesty about human frailties can help the children cope with the fact of divorce without blaming either one parent or the other.[21]

THE NEVER MARRIED

In our society about 8 to 10 percent of the population chooses never to marry. Since the 1960s the needs, wants, and tastes of single people have been given increasing attention. Singles housing, bars, clubs, and dating systems, along with a deemphasis upon the "couples only" requirement in restaurants, excursion cruises, and other public recreational facilities have brought about many new opportunities for singles to get together in groups or as individuals.[22] This public recognition that there is an alternative single style of life has also encouraged a kind of "singles" consciousness that enables single people to think positively about their alternative rather than to view it as a liability. The greatest amount of singles activities is concentrated in New York and California, the two states with the largest number of adult single persons. Many of these

[21]Jack Westman and David W. Kline, "Divorce Is a Family Affair," *Family Law Quarterly*, No. 5 (March 1971).
[22]Computer dating, a popular fad in the sixties, has declined in popularity, largely as a result of the many abuses associated with it. See Rosalyn Moran, "The Singles' Life Styles," p. 338.

persons are immigrants from small towns or rural areas; a large percentage of them are office workers and professional people.[23]

Housing for Singles

The 1960s and 1970s have seen a rapid increase in the availability of housing for singles only. Closed communities of singles in rather posh settings cater to the housing and recreational needs of upper middle-class singles. These housing units, often located in suburban communities, offer "a millionaire-like atmosphere with pool, saunas, jacuzzis, air conditioning, outdoor barbecues, recreation rooms and billiards, plus a wild and exciting decor!"[24] Many of these places also provide a hostess or program director who organizes and manages dances and group games and generally oversees the social life. It should be noted that many young people tend to criticize this particular kind of single life style as little more than an extension of the college dormitory, sorority, or fraternity. Nevertheless, the fact that large sums of money have been invested to develop these complexes indicates that there is a considerable market for them.

A Quieter Style

In large urban areas, bar hopping has provided a more or less traditional way for single people to meet people of the opposite sex. Many urban areas have what are called "body shops," bars that are well known as places where it is possible to find a sexual partner. Criticism of this side of our emerging new singles society has been widespread. It is often charged that, in effect, such establishments cater to men and degrade women. Men in the various bars, complexes, clubs, and other social settings for singles often behave like "buyers at a slave market," as Roslyn Moran points out.[25] Indeed, there is no denying that men in these settings typically do not stop long enough to develop a conversation, much less a relationship, in their quest for "progress" among the prospective females available.

Fortunately, the evolution of the singles style of life has reduced the necessity for single people to meet under these circumstances. Many single women and men are pleased with the emergence of a new style of singles club where they can engage in social encounters in a context that is not specifically sexual. What is more, many of our large cities offer a fairly wide variety of apartments of all sizes and prices, making it in-

[23]Moran, "The Singles in the Seventies," p. 338.
[24]Moran, "The Singles in the Seventies," p. 341.
[25]Moran, "The Singles in the Seventies," p. 339.

creasingly easy for single people to find suitable living accommodations. Thus it is possible for some single people to work out a rich and varied life style that has little in common with the hassle of the "swinging" singles scene so widely publicized in magazines and films.

Ann is one such person. Forty-two years old and a graduate of a university not far from her current residence, she has never been married. She has a wide circle of friends of both sexes. Some of her friendships date back to her days in the university, some were formed at work, and others resulted from her membership in numerous organizations. She dates often and establishes varying degrees of intimacy in her relationships with the men she dates. Ann travels a lot, particularly for skiing in Europe, which she is able to afford on the salary she earns as a professional. She manages her money well, feels excited about what she is doing, seems to enjoy a considerable amount of freedom in her relationships, and in general seems happy and adjusted in her singles style.

Ann has developed a life style which she finds rewarding, despite the fact that her experience runs counter to the prevailing myth that true fulfillment—especially for women—is not to be found outside of marriage. There are various factors, of course, which have made it relatively easy for her to do this. Living in a community where the university from which she graduated provides a network of social interaction is

Ray Ellis, Rapho Guillumette

important. She is fortunate, too, in that she benefits from a financial position that gives her much more flexibility than less well-off people are likely to enjoy. And finally, the fact that she is apparently at ease with her own sexuality has enabled her to be much freer in her relationships with others than is commonly the case. Her general approach to life enables her to expend her energy on things that help her to grow as a person.

Many people like Ann have developed very adequate life styles as single persons, but even today many of them are unnecessarily burdened by the fact that their society tends to see them as in some sense inadequate because they are single—that is, because they have "failed" to marry.

Changes in sexual mores over the last decade or so may be decreasing the burden placed upon single people, but there is no denying that they still face some serious problems. As Rustum and Della Roy point out:

Traditional monogamy does not deal humanly with its have nots—the adult singles and the widowed and divorced. Statistically speaking, we in America have more involuntarily single persons above the age of 25 or 30 than those who have had no choice about a socially and economically disadvantageous color for their skin. The latter have had to bear enormous legal and social affronts and suffered the subtler and possibly more debilitating psychological climate of being unacceptable in much of their natural surroundings. But this disability they share with voiceless single persons in a marriage-oriented society. Our society proclaims monogamy's virtue at every point of law and custom and practice, as much as it says white is right. Biases, from income tax to adoption requirements and Emily Post etiquette all point to the traditional monogamists as the acceptable form of society.[26]

[26]Rustum and Della Roy, "Is Monogamy Outdated?" *The Humanist* (March/April 1970). Reprinted by permission.

SUMMARY

If for no other reason than the simple fact that the number of males is not equal to the number of females in our society, marriage cannot be a reality for all people. Nor should it be. Yet we live in a society which either covertly or overtly measures people by whether or not they are married—despite the fact that a large portion of our population is unmarried either by choice, by accident, or by fate.

This chapter has tried to describe persons who are unmarried for a variety of reasons. It has attempted to sketch some of the variety of ways in which single people form partnerships distinct from marriage. In analyzing the various life styles of the different classes of single people, we have used the labels "divorced," "widowed," "single parent," and "never married" to define some of the unique problems single people face as well as some of the opportunities open to them in terms that are relevant to the particular ways of being single in our society.

A divorced person may bring to new relationships deeper insights into who he or she is along with a deeper longing for a partnership. This wisdom and knowledge may not always be pleasant, but the experience of marriage and divorce certainly offers an opportunity for reflection and growth. The widow or widower, if she or he successfully grows through the period of grief work, has on the one hand a tougher time than the divorced person in adjusting to a single life style because she or he generally comes to be single at a later age. On the other hand, the widowed person often brings to her or his single style of life memories of a meaningful partnership. Solo parents have some very practical limitations placed upon them regardless of their economic background, but obviously the difficulties are greater for low-income persons than for the more well-to-do. Children are both a hindrance and an aid in forming new partnerships, depending upon many factors in the parent-child relationship.

Today the never-married are experiencing their single life style at a time when it is becoming possible to think positively about that style of life for the first time in our history. Although the seemingly hectic life style of the singles complex may not appeal to all young single people, in fact modern urban settings offer the single person a rich variety of resources to help him or her establish a life style of practically any sort.

It is important that our society learn to develop more adequate ways of responding to all of these types of "singles" life styles. Being single can no longer be taken to mean being a second-class citizen in a society that prides itself on recognizing individual differences and affirms the right of all men and women to develop freely in a style of life best suited to their own unique personhood.

16

COMMUNES AND MULTIPLE MARRIAGES

The better life! Possibly, it would hardly look so, now; it is enough if it looked so then. The greatest obstacle to being heroic is the doubt whether one may not be going to prove one's self a fool; the truest heroism is, to resist the doubt; the profoundest wisdom, to know when it ought to be resisted, and when to be obeyed.
    . . . Whatever else I may repent of, therefore, let it be reckoned neither among my sins nor follies that I once had faith and force enough to form generous hopes of the world's destiny— yes!—and to do what in me lay for their accomplishment; even to the extent of quitting a warm fireside, flinging away a freshly-lighted cigar, and travelling far beyond the strike of city clocks, through a drifting snow-storm.

Nathaniel Hawthorne

INTRODUCTION

Throughout the whole of human history there have been people for whom the conventional is much too confining and for whom the forging of a new way of life becomes a compelling necessity. Whether driven by their dislike of the establishment, or lured by their vision of a new way to live, they set themselves apart from the majority and try, with varying degrees of success, to make their dream a reality. This chapter discusses two basically different approaches: the commune, which seeks to redefine a whole life style, and multiple marriage, which seeks to redefine marriage.

The word "commune" has been linked by the mass media to a particularly unsta-

Bonnie Freer, Rapho Guillumette

ble form of hip community in which the main social institution is the drug abusers' crash pad. To the average reader this scene is more likely to suggest a kind of modern-day "skid row" than a vision of a bright new world. Not often recognized is the fact that the function and orientation of most communes are quite different from those of a crash pad. The communes to be discussed in this chapter tend to be relatively stable social arrangements characterized by a common commitment to a way of life that involves a degree of sharing. A commune is a community with a purpose and a philosophy. Among the perhaps 250,000 persons who have lived in the approximately three thousand communes in the United States, there is great variation in purposes and philosophy.[1] About the only thing they all have in common is that they can be described by the adjectives "intentional" and "experimental," which are commonly attached to the word commune to emphasize the *conscious intent* to create a new life style. Most persons who choose to live in a commune today do so because they desire to live in a much more person-centered kind of community than they can find in our modern impersonal society.

[1]Benjamin Zablocki, *The Joyful Community* (Baltimore: Penguin Books, Inc., 1971).

COMMUNES: A BRIEF HISTORICAL SKETCH

The Essenes, a monastic community of men that flourished in Palestine from about the second century B.C. to the second century A.D., formed possibly the earliest communal society.[2] Some Biblical scholars contend that John the Baptist was an Essene. Members of this commune lived an austere life on the shores of the Dead Sea. They held all property in common but allowed each member to pursue his own occupation. The New Testament refers to Christian communities living in Jerusalem during the first century A.D. who "own all things in common." Indeed, because of the persecution of Christians during the first three centuries after Christ, many Christians were forced to support one another in closed secretive communities that undoubtedly had many characteristics commonly associated with communes.

Richard Fairfield, in his study of communes, points out that Christianity throughout its entire history has spawned communities that established separate distinctive life styles and sought the restoration of true personhood through various kinds of sharing. Monastic communities and sects such as the Lollards, Cathars, Waldenses, and Anabaptists all espoused a communal way of life. As Fairfield explains:

The anabaptists were the most radical and the most democratic of the sects that separated themselves from traditional society. They uncompromisingly opposed government restrictions on the individual. They refused to fight in wars or pay taxes or submit to any outside religious authority. They believed in direct inspiration from God as their guide to behavior, Biblical interpretation and religious practices. They were, as a result, the most persecuted of sects. Even Martin Luther cried out for the church authorities to "stab, crush and strangle" these deviant utopians.[3]

[2]Richard Fairfield, *Communes, U.S.A.: A Personal Tour* (Baltimore: Penguin Books, Inc., 1971), p. 11.
[3]Fairfield, *Communes, U.S.A.*, pp. 12–13.

Communal living in the New World was inspired by secular as well as sacred ideologies. Socialist communities such as New Harmony, Brook Farm, Red Bank, and the Icarians, and religious communities such as Amana and Oneida are among the more famous of the nineteenth-century experiments in communal living.

Oneida (1848–1880)

Oneida is perhaps the most famous of the American communal experiments. It was founded on the banks of the Oneida Creek in midstate New York by a perfectionist theologian named John Humphrey Noyes. Perfectionism was a heterodox version of Christianity that preached against the notion of original sin and proclaimed that men could become perfect "even as your father in heaven is perfect." Although many thousands of persons were caught up in reading perfectionist tracts and attending the lectures of its leading advocates, Oneida at its peak housed only 288 persons, the majority of whom lived in the settlement in New York. It took ten years of struggle and some forty thousand dollars in capital investment to make Oneida a solvent economic venture at a time when there were some sixty-odd communes in America, all of which failed sooner or later.[4] Oneida itself survived thirty-two years as a community. In 1880 the community disbanded, with its members giving up the practice of "complex marriage," the community's distinctive style of marriage, and opting instead for conventional monogamous unions. Although Oneida no longer exists as a commune, it persists as an economic venture to the present day, in Oneida Ltd., a company known for its fine silverware. When it disbanded its community its assets totaled over $600,000.

Mutual Criticism. One of the significant features of life in the Oneida community was the practice of mutual criticism, a technique for dealing with interpersonal problems as they arose. If a member deviated from the norms of the community, or if personality or character deficiencies were troublesome, the offender would be asked to meet with a committee of peers to undergo criticism. If an offense against the basic understandings of the community was involved, the community would act as a committee of the whole. As the community developed, the practice of mutual criticism came to be seen more as a means of self-improvement than as a means of correcting deviant behavior.[5] It also became a test for determining who among the new postulants could stand up to the rigorous demands of Oneidan life. In effect, mutual criticism provided members

[4]William Kephart, "The Oneida Experiment," in Arlene S. Skolnick and Jerome H. Skolnick, eds., *Family in Transition* (Boston: Little, Brown and Company, 1971).
[5]Kephart, "The Oneida Experiment," pp. 485–86.

of the community with feedback that helped them socialize themselves to the norms of the community as a whole.

Complex Marriage. Noyes' perfectionist theology contended that monogamous marriage was a violation of the first and second commandments. As Maren Lockwood writes in setting forth the Oneida position:

Monogamy makes a man or woman unfit to practice the two central principles of Christianity, loving God and loving one's neighbor. "Exclusive attachment" to a spouse turns the attention from God and one's fellow man. It is preferable for a man to love everyone equally and to give the greatest love to God. If there are sexual relations in the kingdom of heaven, then the ideal state is one in which all men are viewed as married to all women. If the kingdom is to be established on earth, it must include such a system of "complex marriage."[6]

From the very beginning of Oneida, Noyes made it clear that romantic love and monogamous marriage were to have no place in the community's life. To him, these two ideas were simply expressions of selfishness, exclusiveness, and possessiveness.[7]

Instead of romantic love, with its ideal of a passionate attachment to one lover, Oneida cultivated a generalized affection for all members. Passion, even in lovemaking, was considered inappropriate to the perfectionist way of life. Thus the Oneidans were able to practice a form of contraception called "male continence." Oneidan men—particularly the older, more experienced members of the community—trained themselves to be able to engage in sexual intercourse for as long as an hour without ejaculating or feeling the need for ejaculation. The woman, of course, was free to experience orgasm.[8] Although this form of contraception was not perfect, it did enable the community to establish a eugenics program with about 80 percent effectiveness.

We do not know for certain what factors caused the Oneida community to disband. Before it dissolved in 1880, its records were burned, making it impossible to reconstruct a detailed history of the internal affairs of the community. Nevertheless, Lockwood speculates that the problem lay in the fact that the Oneidans could not effectively socialize their second generation. What is more, after Noyes' death his sons were unable to perpetuate his charismatic leadership. Jealousies developed between factions within the community, thus helping to end its life. Complex marriage, however, seems to have been valued by the Oneidans as long as they lasted as a community.[9]

[6]Maren Carden Lockwood, *Oneida: From Community to Corporation* (Baltimore: The Johns Hopkins Press, 1971), p. 16.
[7]Kephart, "The Oneida Experiment," p. 486.
[8]Havelock Ellis, *Studies in the Psychology of Sex*, Vol. 6: *Sex in Relation to Society* (Philadelphia: F. A. Davis, 1961), p. 533.
[9]Lockwood, *Oneida*. It should be pointed out that Kephart, in "The Oneida Experi-

**MODERN
COMMUNES**

The most successful modern experiment in communal living is not an American venture. The Kibbutzim, socialist-zionist communities in rural Israel, number some 255 settlements and currently contain approximately 93,000 people.[10] The movement is in its third generation and has become famous for its distinctive method of collective child rearing.[11]

These communities began with a single settlement, Degania, in 1910, and have spread throughout the state of Israel. They have opened up the Negev and other arid regions of Israel to farming. During the Protectorate period they provided a major part of the resistance movement against Britain and today they defend a goodly portion of Israel's border and staff a significant portion of her air force. Thus they represent a considerable political force in contemporary Israel even though they face many problems, not the least of which is the increasing pressure to industrialize, accompanied by a rising standard of living, a reemerging interest in private property and the nuclear family, and a growing awareness of inequality. Nevertheless, the Kibbutzim have drastically changed the traditional family system of the European Jewry from which most members came, and have achieved perhaps a greater degree of equality over a longer period of time than any other socialist venture.[12]

In America, the most successful modern commune—at least in terms of persistence—is much less well known. Like the Kibbutzim, the Bruderhof is also in its third generation.[13] It arose out of many of the same elements that generated the Kibbutzim. Although the Bruderhof is a Protestant sect, with Anabaptist-Hutterite origins, whereas the Kibbutzim are clearly Jewish, both owe a great deal to the German Youth Movement and the socialism of early twentieth-century Europe. Strong feminist elements also are present in both, though to a lesser extent in the Bruderhof. At present, the Bruderhof numbers about 750 members residing in three settlements. The community was first established in Germany in the 1920s, adding settlements in England, Paraguay, Uruguay, and, finally, the United States in 1957.

Although the focus of loyalty in the Bruderhof is clearly the community itself, the nuclear family structure persists and is supported by community members. Each family has its own quarters, but they all send

ment," disagrees with Lockwood's conclusions about the causes of the collapse of the community.

[10] Dan Leon, *The Kibbutz: A New Way of Life* (New York: Pergamon Press, 1970).

[11] See Bruno Bettelheim, *Children of the Dream* (New York: The Macmillan Company, 1969).

[12] Several good books have been written about the Kibbutz in addition to those already cited. See especially Melford Spiro, *The Children of the Kibbutz* (Cambridge: Harvard University Press, 1958), and Yonina Talmon, *Kibbutz and Community* (Cambridge: Harvard University Press, 1972).

[13] An excellent analysis of the Bruderhof is found in Zablocki, *The Joyful Community*.

their children to the community school where a distinctive kind of collective child rearing takes place. The major source of income for the Bruderhof comes from the manufacturing of Community Playthings, a strong classic line of wooden toys manufactured primarily for schools.

In the Bruderhof, children are deliberately kept ignorant of their sexual natures until they are ready for marriage. As might be expected, this presents problems when the children must leave the community school to attend public high schools. Nevertheless, supported by religious ideology, ritual, and a strong sense of community—which visitors to the community characteristically describe as a source of great joy to the members—marriages among the members seem to be quite stable and durable. This may be explained by the fact that in such a community many of the tensions and troubles that beset married couples in society at large are borne by the whole community, so that the strong sense of community identification provides a type of support unavailable to most marriages outside.

A Typology of Communes

Richard Fairfield, in his book *Communes, U.S.A.: A Personal Tour*, defines a commune as "three or more persons among whom the primary bond is some form of sharing, rather than blood or legal ties."[14] He divides modern communes into six basic types:

1. *Religious communes* (Bruderhof, The Oregon Family, The Lama Foundation, Hutterites), which today commonly profess some mixture of Christianity and various Eastern faiths.

2. *Ideological communes,* which adhere either to socialist doctrine or to doctrines arising out of behavioral psychology (Cold Mountain Farm, Twin Oaks).

3. *Hip communes,* which tend to be based on some sort of drug culture and generally have a more or less mystical quality about them (Drop City, Morning Star Ranch).

4. *Group marriage communes,* which set themselves the task of developing new family styles (Harrad West, The Family).

5. *Service communities,* which are created to provide a total work-recreational environment for disadvantaged persons (Camphill, Synanon).

6. *Youth communes,* which usually are composed of college graduates or dropouts who simply wish to share the advantages of group living.[15]

[14]Fairfield, *Communes, U.S.A.,* p. 1.
[15]*Communes, U.S.A.,* pp. 2–3.

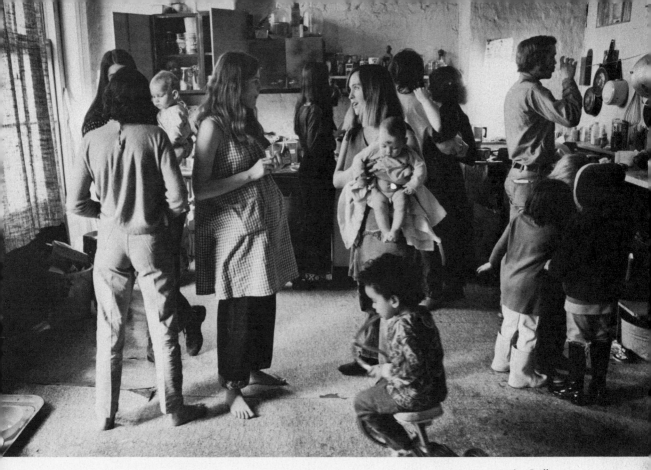

Bonnie Freer, Rapho Guillumette

The discussion that follows will be limited to a brief examination of one major specimen of the ideological type of commune, Twin Oaks, and one example of a hip commune, Morning Star Ranch.

Twin Oaks: A Behavioristic Commune

Twin Oaks arose out of the convergence of several persons who had been strongly impressed by psychologist B. F. Skinner's modern utopian novel *Walden Two*.[16] Walden House was founded in Washington, D.C., in 1965.[17] In the summer of the following year, several members of Walden House met with other enthusiasts at the first annual Walden Two Convention in Michigan. A group of participants at this conference determined to put the ideas of *Walden Two* to the test by buying a farm and adhering to an experimental way of life based as much as possible on the principles of behavioral psychology.

[16] B. F. Skinner, *Walden Two* (New York: The Macmillan Company, 1948).
[17] The history of Twin Oaks is found in Kathleen Kinkade, *A Walden Two Experiment: The First Five Years of Twin Oaks Community* (New York: William Morrow & Co., 1972).

On June 16, 1967, Twin Oaks was founded on a farm near Louisa, Virginia. In six years it has gone from a few members to about forty and has a waiting list of persons eager to join the community as soon as there is room. Thus, although it has not been in existence very long, it seems to have come to grips with the basic issues of supporting and regulating a growing population. Insofar as this is true, it seems to offer a viable alternative style of living to its members. As one participant explains, "The biggest single misconception in the public mind about communes is that they are an escape from reality. . . . We answer patiently that far from running away from life or our social responsibilities, we are trying to make a new and better society . . . and that this world is as real as they come."[18]

The Labor-Credit System. Twin Oaks works as well as it does because it has found a way in which to make work acceptable to all of its members. Ever since the first weeks of its existence, the labor-credit system has been the means for regulating and accomplishing the tasks necessary for the community's survival. In its early form the system worked as follows: The labor-credit manager devised a list of jobs that needed to be done. Each person then signed up for the job he or she most desired. The sign-up sheet became the basis for determining which were the most desirable and the most undesirable jobs in the community's collective opinion. A job for which many people signed up was rated highly desirable and a job for which no one signed up was ranked as highly undesirable. Credit was then assigned to the jobs on the principle that the more desirable jobs were given less credit—after the fashion outlined in Skinner's *Walden Two*. All members were expected to contribute the same number of labor credits to the community per week. Thus one could choose between working at a very undesirable job for a few hours or working at more desirable jobs for a longer period of time.

This system worked well for about three years. There was, however, a lack of quality in some of the work under this system. Indifference and carelessness occasionally defeated the projects of the labor-credit manager. Moreover, the frequent changes of shifts resulted in a lack of continuity on a job, which often manifested itself in sloppy performance. To correct these problems the system was revised in the tradition of an experimental community. The work was assigned in blocks of longer periods of time, such as from fourteen to twenty-one hours, but because the longer blocks of time did not lend themselves well to the sign-up system a new plan had to be devised for assigning the work. Kathleen Kinkade, one of the founders of Twin Oaks and its current historian, writes:

[18]Fairfield, *Communes, U.S.A.*, p. 201.

Our current system asks each member to take a list of all the available jobs and place them in the order of his [or her] personal preferences. After that, he [or she] doesn't have to sign up at all. The labor clerical people take over and work for two days filling out everyone's schedule as close to their personal preferences as possible. These days, one gets high credit for doing work which one finds personally disagreeable. Two people might be shoveling manure side by side, and the person who enjoys the work is getting less credit for it than the person who doesn't.[19]

Planners and Managers. Twin Oaks works also because the community has been able to satisfactorily settle the problem of management through the manager system under a board of planners. This structure may sound vaguely bureaucratic and authoritarian, but in practice it is much more personal and humane than the establishment titles suggest.

A great deal of thought goes into the selection of the people who govern the community. The three-member board of planners is self-generating on an eighteen-month term basis. Although the board of planners is expected to appoint its own successors, the community meeting as a committee of the whole can overrule the planners' selection by a simple majority vote. "In other words, we don't vote *for* our planners, but we vote against them," one member explains.[20] Planners are expected to appoint the various managers who oversee the work routines of the community, decide ideological issues, and settle conflicts between managers. They do a great deal of thinking about where the community is going and why. Most of the real authority and decision making of the community, however, is vested in the managers, who are selected on the basis of interest and work ability. Generally, the men and women who become planners at Twin Oaks are people who are in tune with the community's policies and have an ability to think through problems in a logical way. Basically this involves an ability to separate their opinions from their feelings—a task which requires a high degree of self-awareness.

Expertise is highly valued in the Twin Oaks community, but it does not automatically provide a person with status and power. The expert must earn his or her place within the community by discovering how this expertise can contribute to the total life of the community. Early on, the members recognized that the contribution of an expert, if it does not fit the needs of the total life of the community, poses a threat to the community as a whole. For example, a Twin Oaks venture into cattle raising ran into problem after problem, until finally the member who was the community's cattle expert left. The community lost some $1500 invested in feed and other expenses because with the cattleman's de-

[19]Kinkade, *A Walden Two Experiment*, p. 164.
[20]Fairfield, *Communes, U.S.A.*, p. 88.

parture they could not bring enough of their calves to market. Ever since, the members of Twin Oaks have been more careful to stay out of ventures that do not reflect the interests of a significant portion of the community. Thus they avoid the problems that can arise when the community as a whole relies too heavily on the expertise of a single member. Putting it in more positive terms, in Twin Oaks a person is valued for his or her expertise only insofar as that expertise meshes with the desires of the commune as a whole.

The problem of finding a way to incorporate expertise and make use of the unique contributions of each individual without either setting up a class system or subjecting the community to the excessively narrow guidance that comes from overspecialization is one which contemporary American society has not solved. All communes must face this problem, whether they are aware of it or not. A community that is trying to build a better society must take into consideration as far as it is able the total context of its world. Expert information gathered through specialized training has a place in such a world *if* it is compatible—economically, ideologically, and in terms of social psychology—with this total context. It seems that Twin Oaks has made advances toward solving this dilemma that could well prove instructive for American society as a whole.

Marriage. Unlike the fictional Walden Two, Twin Oaks opted for sexual freedom. This includes the option of choosing a monogamous style of partnership for couples who so desire. Thus the community leaves its members free to select from a wide variety of types of love-sex relationships. From the beginning the community made no effort to regulate love-sex relationships, but actual sexual freedom did not become a reality until Twin Oaks was two years old. This came about as a result of the influx of a large number of young single persons. When asked about how married couples generally fare in the commune, Kathleen Kinkade points to the fact that because the commune removes the external supports of a marriage, married couples must work especially hard to maintain their relationship:

It's very simple. Marriage is a very weak institution. It's supported on the outside by all sorts of pressures which are removed as soon as you get into the community. We remove the pressures and make alternatives available and people do what comes naturally. They will choose to stay married only if that's reinforcing. If it isn't reinforcing, what for?[21]

"The only reason for a couple to stay married in a community is that they like each other," Kinkade writes.[22] Of the nine married couples

[21]Quoted in Fairfield, *Communes, U.S.A.*, p. 85.
[22]Kinkade, *A Walden Two Experiment*, p. 165.

who were at one time or another members of Twin Oaks, six stayed married after they met each other in the community.[23]

Jealousy over love-sex relationships does not present much of a problem in a close community such as Twin Oaks. As Kinkade explains:

The biggest bulwark against jealousy is our heavy communal disapproval.

Twin Oaks has taken a firm stand in favor of sexual freedom and nonpossessiveness, and that brings its problems with it. But problems notwithstanding, we did not have any real choice about taking this stand. Any group that settles on monogamy as a norm has to figure out how to defend it. Without a heavy puritan religious bias that is very difficult. Philosophy isn't the only problem with monogamy, either. Sexual rules are hard to enforce in any society, and more so among free-thinking communitarians. The closer people live together, the higher will be the incidence of opportunity for attraction. A commune has to take the choice between dealing with jealousy in an open way or dealing with complicated questions of sin, dalliance, adultery. I conjecture a group norm of free choice in sexual matters is not only philosophically consistent but literally easier to manage than any compromises would be.[24]

Self-Criticism at Twin Oaks.

Twin Oaks consciously borrowed the idea of self-criticism from the Oneida community. The practice, however, does not seem to be as productive for them as it was for the Oneidans. Members of Twin Oaks seem to experience some fear about being too honest, so that the criticism often does not raise the issues of interpersonal relationships that should be raised. Many members of the community feel that self-criticism is an inappropriate technique for Twin Oaks and, because it is a voluntary commune, they do not attend the self-criticism sessions. By 1971, the number of people not attending had become quite large and the sessions were discontinued.[25]

Prior to the introduction of self-criticism, Twin Oaks tried out the idea of an institutionalized "Generalized Bastard" whose task it was to reprimand persons for their social shortcomings. Since this role was understood as the bearer of grievances, the person fulfilling it met with more toleration than might have been the case if the grievance was brought by the personally affronted person. However, this practice also fell into disuse.

Morning Star Ranch: A "Hip" Open-Land Commune

One of the better known hip communes is Morning Star Ranch, located on thirty-two acres of virtually unfarmable land in the hill country of Sonoma County, California.[26] Lou Gottlieb, a member of the pop-folk

---

[23]*A Walden Two Experiment*, pp. 165–66.
[24]*A Walden Two Experiment*, pp. 168–69.
[25]*A Walden Two Experiment*, p. 158.
[26]The history of Morning Star Ranch is recorded in Fairfield, *Communes, U.S.A.*

singing group The Limelighters, is currently battling to keep it an open-land commune in the face of state laws to the effect that no one but himself and his family can stay on the land. Sonoma County brought an injunction against Gottlieb prohibiting him from using the land as he had intended because of problems created by overuse and poor relations with the neighbors. Gottlieb responded by deeding the land to "God." As of this writing he is fighting in the courts to make this a legal deed which, he believes, would have the effect of providing a sanctuary on which individuals could live as they pleased without fear of the law.

An open-land commune operates on the principle that anyone who wants to can build on the commune's land. But it has a much deeper meaning for Lou Gottlieb. "Morning Star," he says, "is a training replacement center, or rest and recuperation area, for the army of occupation in the war against exclusive ownership of land."[27] With free access to the land and no rules governing anyone, the founders of Morning Star felt that people could become reborn by living in harmony with the earth.

The reality of Morning Star seems to be quite a different thing. Started in 1966, when the loosely structured "hippie" community in the Haight-Ashbury section of San Francisco was beginning to turn sour, Morning Star attracted thousands of visitors and "hangers-on" who, by the ground rules of the community, had as much right as anyone to be there. Although some of the original members claimed private space that was respected by the mob, the hundreds of people who would sometimes crowd the food lines on weekends soon tore the place apart. The buildings were wrecked, the land was deprived of its topsoil, trees were indiscriminately cut down, and the rains gullied the land. There were only two toilets for the whole community, and often they did not work; when the hoards of people who flocked to Morning Star used the surrounding woodland without making latrines, they created a health hazard. It was at this point that the county closed the commune as a health hazard and brought the injunction against Gottlieb prohibiting him from opening up his land to anyone. Ironically, the structure that began to evolve out of the meetings called for the purpose of dealing with the visitor problem could have developed procedures for handling the sanitation problem if it had been created sooner. Although Gottlieb contends that the land now holds no more people than it can properly accommodate, the cost of achieving this meager balance has thus far been enormous and it is far from clear whether the land or the people can recuperate.

However, another open-land commune spawned by Morning Star—Wheeler's Ranch—seems to be doing much better.[28] It has its rituals

[27]Quoted in *Communes, U.S.A.*, p. 252.
[28]Interview with Bill Wheeler in *Communes, U.S.A.*

and common life and its "center" in the young man, Bill Wheeler, who bought the land with part of an inheritance. Wheeler deeded his ranch to the Ahimsa Church, a tax-exempt, nonprofit organization that he founded on the ranch. Although in principle Wheeler's Ranch is an open-land commune, in practice a very poor road prevents many people from taking advantage of the land offer. Despite constant court battles, Wheeler's Ranch was still in existence in 1972 and persons who passed through reported "good vibrations."

MULTIPLE MARRIAGE

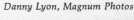

Multiple marriage is to be distinguished from communes in that the people who practice it are interested primarily in redefining the institution of marriage but not necessarily in producing an entirely new way of life. Communes may practice group or multiple marriage as a part of their life style, but multiple marriages often exist in the midst of suburbia, where only their distinctive style of marriage differentiates the practitioners of multiple marriage from their neighbors. In some cases the partners in a multiple marriage do not even share a common residence. Because such marriages are illegal, and in some states a felony, persons who practice them are understandably cautious about discussing their living arrangements.

Danny Lyon, Magnum Photos

The idea of multiple marriage, or polygamy, has been a common feature of American thought though never a dominant one. The Mormons were the last group to practice polygamy openly, but their marriages were forceably broken up in the early 1960s.[29] The Mormon version of polygamy was polygyny, a marriage arrangement wherein one husband has several wives. Although this works fairly well in some cultures, the Mormon style of polygyny seemed to create many unnecessary difficulties. In the first place, a man was not required to treat his wives as equals in his affection, and as a result his playing of favorites often created considerable tension within the household. What is more, there was no effective means of organizing the household under a senior wife, as is commonly done in Africa, and so the problem of status and authority was being negotiated continually. Nevertheless, Mormon polygamy survived for many decades and helped establish the state of Utah.

Recently, the idea of multiple marriage has been given much publicity in the fiction of Robert Rimmer and Robert Heinlein.[30] Rimmer, the nation's leading advocate of multiple marriage, describes a wide variety of styles in his novels, which generally are based on the theme that it is not only possible but highly desirable to love erotically more than one person at a time. Since the publication of *The Harrad Experiment* in 1966, many people have experimented with multiple marriages. Harrad West, which is described below, was a group marriage experiment that owed much of its original inspiration to Rimmer's novels. All of the other examples given in this section come from a compilation of case studies assembled by Rimmer entitled *Adventures in Loving*.[31]

Larry Constantine prefers to call the group marriages he has studied "multilateral marriages." He distinguishes multilateral marriage from historically and comparatively similar styles of marriage as follows:

The contemporary multilateral marriage has intrinsic elements which contrast it with its precedents. It is based not on male (or female) dominance or on implied property or possession as in polygynous and polyandrous marriages, but on essentially equal and mutual bonds among all partners (hence "multilateral"). Nor is it necessarily communal, in the sense of focusing on extended community, unlike many prior and current utopian attempts.[32]

[29] Alvin Toffler, *Future Shock* (New York: Bantam Books, Inc., 1972), p. 48, reports that Mormon polygamy has "gone underground" and that perhaps thirty thousand people still live in polygamous households in Utah alone.
[30] Robert Heinlein, *Stranger in a Strange Land* (New York: Berkeley Publishing Co., 1971), and *The Moon Is a Harsh Mistress* (New York: Berkeley Publishing Co., 1968); Robert Rimmer, *The Harrad Experiment* (New York: Bantam Books, 1968), *Proposition 31* (New York: New American Library, 1969), and *Thursday My Love* (New York: New American Library, 1972).
[31] Robert Rimmer, *Adventures in Loving* (New York: New American Library, 1973).
[32] Larry Constantine and Joan Constantine, "Where Is Marriage Going," *The Futurist* (April 1970), p. 44. Published by the World Future Society, PO. Box 30369 (Bethesda), Washington, D.C. 20014.

Harrad West and the other examples described below all seem to fit Constantine's definition of multilateral marriage.

Harrad West

Harrad West was founded in Berkeley, California. Richard Fairfield, publisher of *The Modern Utopian*, had rented a twelve-room house in Berkeley with the intention of establishing a commune. A year earlier he had organized a group of people who were interested in setting up intentional communities. In this group was a couple, Don and Barbara, who had been married for fourteen years. They had been involved in "swinging" types of relationships for some time but because they were now interested in relationships of more depth they decided to try group marriage. This couple set the tone for Harrad West. Fairfield moved out and Don and Barbara (and their three children, aged twelve, ten, and eight) were joined over a period of time by Bill and Karen and Jack and Molly. Thus the group marriage consisted of six adults and three children.

The Harrad West group published their credo in *The Modern Utopian* in 1970. It said:

We feel that a larger number of concerned persons learning and growing together often can deal with stresses that would overwhelm two individuals. In addition, children in a group marriage can be more certain of the continued existence of their families and have more than two adults to rely on.

All adult members of Harrad West are considered married to all other adult members of the opposite sex. "Pair bond" relationships do exist since most of the members entered the community as couples, one with three children. These couples and those who have entered as singles do not demand exclusive rights with each other. Relationships are on all levels. . . .

We believe that sex is vital in a successful marriage. We find our more ample number of loving relationships helps us to become more affectionate persons. We feel our friendships deepened, our capacity for warmth and understanding increased, and our lives enriched as a result of this community. The development of this rational and agreeable means of helping fulfill our social and sexual nature has enabled us to become more honest with ourselves and others.[33]

On balance, however, the experience of Harrad West does not appear to have been nearly as creative as its founders expected. The first couple to be accepted after the credo was issued moved out within a month. They cited as reasons for their departure hostilities, complaints, and tensions existing within the community which were not resolved even with the help of a professional therapist. One member was hospitalized for what appeared to be a mental breakdown. There seemed to be a lack of understanding about the issues involved in group marriage, as evidenced

[33]As recorded in Fairfield, *Communes, U.S.A.*, p. 297.

in the credo's suggestion that those who wanted to find out about group marriage should try "swinging" first. Fairfield observes:

In my opinion, the advice about swinging was very unsound, for it seemed to me that the Harrad West members' ability to relate had not been improved through mate swapping. As I understand the notion about the swinger route to group marriage fulfillment, group marriage is an intimate personal *relationship* among people; while swinging is essentially sex among people. Now, if you don't know the difference, you're a swinger, and if you do then *maybe* you're ready to go from swinging with others to living with them.[34]

It would appear that Harrad West simply could not live up to the reality of its own dreams. The honesty that it professed in its credo was not able to blossom in its life. The reality fell far short of the ideals and the members were apparently ill equipped to deal with the discrepancy. Indeed, they did not even seem capable of recognizing it.

A New England Experiment

A quite different experience in multilateral marriage is described in the case study "First Annual Report," included in Robert Rimmer's *Adventures in Loving*.[35] It is not possible to do justice here to this detailed account of personal growth of an open foursome who look forward to another contracted year together, but because this experiment seems to have been successful for at least its first year it is worth sketching here, even if incompletely.

Involved in the first year's venture were John and Kit Brinton, a couple in their early forties, and Michael and Rene Stuart, a couple in their early thirties. All four are professional persons with advanced degrees. John is a physicist with a local corporation, Kit is a professor in the English department of the state university, Michael is an assistant professor of anthropology at the state university, and Rene is a psychologist at a nearby college.

John and Kit lived in an unconventional open marriage for twenty years before meeting Michael and Rene. They have three children, two boys aged seventeen and eighteen and a twelve-year-old girl. The Brintons, "one of the few university families in town, have attitudes toward politics, civil rights, the war in southeast Asia, drugs, adolescent sexuality, lifestyle, always just a little more radical than those of their neighbors."[36] Kit had had several long-term lovers and John one brief unsatisfying affair before they launched their foursome.

Michael and Rene had moved to New England from California. They

[34]*Communes, U.S.A.*, p. 298.
[35]Michael Stuart and Kit Brinton, "First Annual Report," in Rimmer, *Adventures in Loving*, pp. 98–120.
[36]"First Annual Report," p. 100.

"had been each other's first lovers, but after several years of marriage they began to talk about the possibility of opening their marriage so it might include depth relationships with others, even sexual relationships. So, long before either entered into such a relationship, they had integrated the possibility into their understanding of marriage."[37] During Michael's years in graduate school, they found themselves involved in a number of sexual relationships. Their move from California to New England was traumatic for them, not only because of the change in culture but also because of the need to leave the lovers behind.

The Process of Commitment. It took a year for this foursome to work out the nature of their commitment to one another. Kit and Michael originally met when they worked together on an interdisciplinary course at the university where both taught. After three months of close professional cooperation, it became clear to them that they could express their feelings and emotions for one another in a sexual relationship. Even John and Rene saw this as a natural and almost inevitable development. Thus Kit and Michael came to provide each other with intellectual, emotional, and sexual excitement in a deepening relationship. By the end of the semester, John and Rene had developed a parallel relationship.

Given the set of interlocking relationships that had spontaneously developed, it seemed natural to all four that they should spend the midwinter break together. During this holiday, they found the time for discussions, mutual discovery, and long leisurely hours of lovemaking. It was during this time that they first talked about living together. "We acknowledged even then that some of our interest arose out of our somewhat objective professional fascination with experiments in alternate lifestyles and out of our rather general commitment to self-conscious responsible deviance of many kinds. But clearly, our interest was more than abstract; each of us felt genuinely pulled toward wanting to try it sometime."[38]

As they saw it, there were three major advantages of a foursome living together: (1) economic advantages of group living; (2) child rearing advantages resulting from the fact that the Brinton children would be able to grow up with more than one set of role models; and (3) the advantage of a dynamic setting which would keep the participants growing.[39] The third of these reasons seems to be most dominant in their concerns and the account of their growth during their year's experience together clearly indicates that this was taken most seriously.

Having broached the subject of living together during the midwinter break, they then took the next several months to think about it. They

[37]"First Annual Report," p. 103.
[38]"First Annual Report," p. 105.
[39]"First Annual Report," p. 106.

discussed the idea with the Brinton children, who seemed generally to favor it. Kit talked it over with Peter, a man with whom she had been intimate and with whose family she and John had hoped to live at some future time. The children could see their mother's involvement in such an arrangement much more easily than they could see their father's: "They were not wholly confident that he could give this its space and also fulfill his responsibilities as husband and father the way they were used to."[40]

After the discussions with the appropriate others and the period of waiting had passed, the foursome began to plan in earnest. They talked about the ground rules, the structure their four-adult household would take, and their expectations. Michael and Rene were more accustomed to planning ahead than were John and Kit, and the foursome opted for the more structured approach favored by the Stuarts. They made arrangements for the house to be remodeled to provide ample space for the two couples and also an appropriate amount of "private spaces" for all four.

Moving into the Brinton's house as a family, the two couples formalized their commitments. They committed themselves to a psychological adventure in depth, rather than to a long-term relationship. They vowed to maintain the privacy of their respective marriages and explicitly stated that they did not intend to place them in jeopardy by this experiment. All agreed, however, that the foursome would not be a closed system, but would be open to other relationships as well. They agreed that they would regard the year-long experiment as a success if at the end of it they remained "open, trusting and caring" for one another, even if they did not wish to live together for another year.

The First Annual Report. Insights into what happened after the Brintons and Stuarts had lived together for one year are found in their first annual report. The major focus of this report is on the inner growth of the four adults involved. Each adult is described as having developed a more wholistic view of himself or herself and his or her world as a result of their intimate interaction. Unfortunately, very little is revealed about the practical dilemmas that they must have faced. Perhaps it can be taken as a positive sign of the success of the experiment that they did not think of these problems as especially significant. As of this writing it seems reasonable to conclude that this group has been able—with a considerable degree of effort—to achieve their objectives. They reoport that their first year was a very successful venture for all four participants:

We are happy with how this year has been for us, and believe its importance may at least somewhat transcend what it has meant personally to us. We

[40]"First Annual Report," p. 106.

are convinced of the social significance of experiments like ours. We know that there are others wanting to read about such attempts written up in as honest and human a way as the participants can manage. It seems important to share the complexities, the problematics, the sense of movement and to show how similar they are to the dynamics that accompany any two-person marriage, especially in its first years.[41]

The Complexities of Group Marriage

There are serious difficulties that must be faced by anyone who wants to live in a group or multilateral marriage. First of all, it is very difficult to find four adults who can comfortably live together for any length of time. Any newly married couple has difficulty adjusting to differences in states, interests, schedules, and the patterns the partners have evolved in their personal styles of living. Four persons coming together must face a potentially greater problem because not only do they have to deal with their own personal differences, but also they must make some allowances for the mutual styles they have developed as couples. What is more, interactions are inevitably more complex among four people than between two simply because of the complex system of temporary alliances that naturally develops. As Albert Ellis has noted, another factor that makes group marriage difficult is that "The usual kind of utopian-minded individual who seeks out such group marriages today is very frequently a highly peculiar, often emotionally disturbed and exceptionally freedom-loving individual."[42] Finally, getting four people together who find each other sexually attractive is no easy task. In casual sexual relations this does not present too many difficulties, but when the four people expect to live together in the same household with the intent of establishing a deep relationship, much greater demands are placed upon the sexual relationships. All kinds of problems involving sex, love, and jealousy can easily arise in such ventures and must be handled in varying ways.

These problems and others clearly were responsible for the early demise of Harrad West and many other group marriages that are now being reported in the literature. The New England experiment cited above seems to have fared much better in meeting these difficulties, although we are not given all the details we need to understand how they accomplished their task. The four people involved in this experiment were clearly unique individuals who possessed unusual talents and skills that helped them cope with such issues.

Larry and Joan Constantine have been conducting extensive research on group or multilateral marriages for some time. They conclude, tenta-

[41]"First Annual Report," p. 120.
[42]Albert Ellis, "Is Group Marriage an Alternative?" in Herbert Otto, ed., *The Family in Search of a Future* (New York: Appleton-Century-Crofts, 1970), p. 92.

FIGURE 16–1

Stable and unstable structures of group marriage.

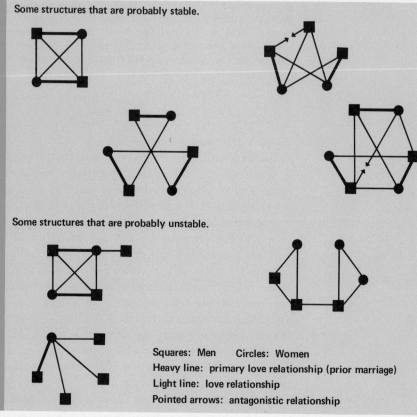

Some structures that are probably stable.

Some structures that are probably unstable.

Squares: Men   Circles: Women
Heavy line: primary love relationship (prior marriage)
Light line: love relationship
Pointed arrows: antagonistic relationship

Source: *Constantine and Constantine, "Where Is Marriage Going? The Futurist (April 1970), 45. Published by the World Future Society, PO Box 30369 (Bethesda), Washington D.C. 20014.*

tively, that some structures are more stable than others. Although ideally all persons in a group marriage should love each other equally, this is not always possible and may not even be necessary. Figure 16–1 indicates some structures that are probably stable and some that are not.

The Constantines predict that in the future group marriage will be an option available to a "significant minority"; it will be "socially, if not legally, condoned." Albert Ellis is in essential agreement when he writes:

It seems very doubtful, however, that a great many people will rush into group marriages in the near future; it seems even more unlikely that this form of mating and family life will replace monogamy or polygamy on a world-wide or even a national scale. . . . Group marriage, then, is a logical alternative to monogamic and to other forms of marriage for a select few.[43]

[43]Ellis, "Is Group Marriage an Alternative?" pp. 96–97, in Herbert A. Otto, *The Family in Search of a Future: Alternative Models for Moderns* © 1970. Reprinted by permission of Prentice-Hall, Inc., Englewood Cliffs, N.J.

SUMMARY

For most Americans, communes and multiple marriage are radical alternatives to conventional life styles. Indeed, many aspects of these alternatives—particularly their styles of marriage—are illegal in most American states. Communes have, nevertheless, existed in Western experience since at least the second century B.C. One of the most famous experiments in American history, the nineteenth-century Oneida community, introduced the notions of complex marriage and mutual criticism to many individuals in the modern commune movement through the numerous books that have been published about this perfectionist community.

In the twentieth century, the Kibbutz in Israel and the Bruderhof in America have proven to be the longest lived communes, with each now in its third generation. The Kibbutzim presently count some 93,000 members, the Bruderhof about 750. Richard Fairfield distinguishes six types of communes: (1) the religious commune such as the Bruderhof and the Lama Foundation; (2) the ideological commune such as Cold Mountain Farm and Twin Oaks; (3) the hip commune such as Morning Star Ranch and Wheeler's Ranch; (4) the group marriage commune such as Harrad West and The Family; (5) the service communities such as Synanon and Camphill; and (6) the youth commune. All but the last two types were discussed in this chapter.

Multiple marriages differ from communes in that persons who live in group or multilateral marriages are primarily interested in redefining marriage but not necessarily in establishing a whole new style of life. Practitioners of multilateral marriage characteristically live in the midst of suburbia, retain their professional jobs, and remain in close contact with the society surrounding them.

Although perhaps as many as 250,000 persons have lived in communes in the United States in this century, the number of persons experimenting in multilateral marriage is unknown. Because of the many hazards of such a relationship, it is not likely that it will ever become a popular style of marriage. For some, however, it seems to offer a rich and highly rewarding opportunity for growth.

PART

FIVE

THE
FUTURE
OF
MARRIAGE

17

FANTASIES, FORECASTS, AND TRENDS

. . . in principle [man] has the possibility of recreating himself at every moment of his waking life. It is difficult but possible to reinvent one's identity, because man is human, the embodiment of freedom; his body and his situation are raw material out of which a way to be can be created, just as a sculptor creates forms out of clay or steel. . . . It is possible to play games with a relationship, to experiment with new forms, until a viable way is evolved. What seems to thwart this kind of interpersonal creativity is failure in imagination on the part of either partner, dread of external criticism and sanctions, and dread of change in oneself.

Sidney M. Jourard

INTRODUCTION

Looking into the future is not something that the social scientist does with any degree of accuracy. Unlike the astronomer who studies stars and planets whose macroproperties, at least, are readily predictable, or the experimental scientist, who can predict because he can control the environment that influences his experimental subjects, the social scientist has little control over the environment in which he finds himself. Demographers, who have some of the most reliable data in the social sciences, hesitate to predict with assurance beyond five years. The variables that influence social institutions such as marriage and the family are numerous, complexly interrelated, and poorly understood.

This chapter, therefore, will be broken

into three major sections. In the first section there will be a brief discussion of some of the techniques that can be used to predict change. Some of the trends commonly thought to effect change in the family will be discussed. The second section will contain some evaluation of the experimentation now taking place in partnerships. The first part of this discussion assumes that the traditional structure will be preserved so that the focus is upon changing roles within the traditional structure. The future of group marriage and the commune movement also will be discussed. The final section of this chapter will consider some of the more radical proposals about what is happening to marriage and the family. It may be that future marriage forms are not at all predictable from either present trends or present experimentation. If such is the case, then the world of the future is only vaguely foreseeable and the capacity of men and women to adapt to a constantly changing environment will be taxed to the utmost.

LOOKING INTO THE FUTURE

Many ingredients go into the assumptions a social scientist makes about how things are changing. Some of the major issues with which he or she must deal are presented below. Simply extrapolating from present trends usually does not produce accurate projections. As we shall see, Hill's three-generational technique seems to make some important improvements over the statistical approach, but only for the next generation.[1]

In making any projection, value judgments must be made about what is desirable as well as what is probable. These value judgments are particularly critical because human beings are free to choose between alternatives. Thus new developments do not follow automatically from what has gone before in some mechanical way. From a technical point of view, the family is usually treated as the dependent variable—that is to say, it is ordinarily assumed that the family will adapt to its environment. As the environment changes under the influence of such forces as a developing technology, population growth, and changing attitudes toward human rights, the family responds. But it is also true that the family exerts an independent effect. This book has assumed throughout that partners can control the kind of partnership they desire to a considerable degree. To the extent that this is so, the interdependence of the partnership and its environment is a critical factor that must be taken into account in assessing the future.

Students of marriage and the family sometimes wish that they could tell us more about what is going to happen to these institutions simply by projecting present trends into the future. In many areas of science this is an acceptable and reliable procedure, but even in the area of demography, where the aggregate data seem to form reliable and consistent patterns, simple extrapolation is not a reliable tool for predicting the future.

[1]Reuben Hill, "The American Family of the Future," *Journal of Marriage and the Family*, 26 (1964), 20–28.

For example, consider the problem of projecting the future population of the United States. The Bureau of Census generally makes three different projections under three different sets of assumptions. It then revises its projections as more reliable data is gathered. For the first time in recent years, the Bureau of the Census has revised one of its projections to take into account the effectiveness of efforts by young couples to control family size voluntarily. As a result, one projection now assumes zero population growth over the next decade. This is a dramatic shift in assumptions when we realize that it was not more than five years ago that we were caught up in the rhetoric of a population explosion.[2]

If we were to take census type data on marriage and project it into the future, one of the important trends we would want to describe is the changing age at which people in our society first marry. The average age at first marriage declined steadily from 1890 to about 1960.[3] After 1968 it began to increase. Which is more reliable, the long-run trend or the short-run tendency that appeared recently? On logical grounds it would seem reasonable to place greater trust in the long-run trend, but most social scientists feel that the short-run trend is going to continue. Many factors are involved in determining the age at which persons typically enter marriage for the first time. One factor is the size of the field of eligibles at a given time. This, in turn, is dependent upon a host of other factors, such as the sex ratio, the fertility rate, war, the state of the economy, and probably many unknown variables as well. It is not accurate, then, to take any one of the statistics on marriage and simply plot it on a curve based on the extrapolation of the present trend. How one answers questions such as, "Will more and more women continue to compete voluntarily with men for jobs and careers?" and "Will graduate education become more and more of a requirement for men and women in the future?" and many others will affect how the projection is made. Thus, although the projections made by social scientists are certainly better than no projections at all, it is very important to realize their inherent limitations.

Three-Generational Studies

Reuben Hill's three-generational approach offers a significant improvement in projective techniques.[4] Hill's technique utilizes the changes that have taken place over a period of three generations within the same extended family. In noting how the life styles of married children differ from the life styles of their parents' and grandparents' families, Hill

[2]U.S. Bureau of the Census, *Statistical Abstract of the United States: 1973* (Washington, D.C.: U.S. Government Printing Office, 1973), p. 4.
[3]*Statistical Abstract: 1973*, p. 65.
[4]Hill, "The American Family of the Future," p. 23.

holds constant many factors that would be peculiar to the socialization of a particular family line. Thus he can observe intergenerational changes that presumably are responses to a changing environment. His work is based on a study of three hundred families: one hundred married child families (ages twenty to thirty), one hundred parental families (ages forty to sixty), and one hundred grandparental families (ages sixty to eighty). All these families lived in the Minneapolis–St. Paul area.

Hill's study revealed a number of intergenerational changes: (1) the educational level of the husbands increased to near equality with that of their wives; (2) the age of first marriage and the difference in the ages of the spouses at marriage decreased over the three generations; (3) the youngest generation had a larger family than their parents, much closer to the size of their grandparents, but their child rearing period ended earlier than that of their grandparents; (4) there was a pattern of accelerated advancement on the job; (5) the youngest generation was more optimistic, less fatalistic, and more future-oriented than the older generations; (6) although role integration was deteriorating, there was a trend toward developmental child rearing, egalitarian idvision of labor, improvement in family value-consensus, and increased planning in economic matters.[5]

Hill concludes from his study that

. . . a picture emerges of increasing effectiveness, professional competence and economic well being, of greater courage in risk taking accompanied by greater planning, of greater flexibility in family organization with greater communication and greater conflict between spouses.[6]

Although Hill reaches the conclusion that the family as we know it does have a future, like so many others who make projections, he does not specify the period of time over which his projection is supposed to hold. All indications lead us to expect that the family of the near future will be very similar to the family as we now know it. But what about several generations into the future? When the children of Hill's married children marry, in all probability they will depart only slightly from the marriage and family styles of their parents—unless some unforeseen catastrophy makes the world in which they live a quite different place indeed.

Factors Likely To Influence Changes in the Family

We already have pointed out that the assumptions made about the social factors one considers likely to influence the trend one is attempting to project have a critical effect on the final projection one makes. Although

---

[5]"The American Family of the Future," pp. 23–25.
[6]"The American Family of the Future," p. 26.

Hill's three-generational technique reduces some of the uncertainty involved in making these assumptions, it is still necessary for us to be clear in our own minds about the social factors which we assume are likely to affect family change in the future. In the next few pages we will examine this issue in some detail.

One factor that undoubtedly will continue to have a considerable effect upon the family is our changing technology. Some observers have noted that the cybernetic revolution amounts to a sort of second industrial revolution with far-reaching implications for our life style. If we can make machines do the work so that men and women can get on with the thinking, a major transformation will have taken place. As Bernard Faber analyzes it, the following results of the cybernetic revolution will have profound effects on the family: (1) fewer workers employed in agriculture; (2) expanded automation; (3) more workers employed in service occupations; (4) increased social density as a result of continuing migration to the cities; (5) increased mobility; (6) increasingly effective communication and transportation networks; (7) increasing bureaucratization with fewer entrepreneurs relative to the number of workers involved; and (8) continuing control of disease through improved medical techniques and, concomitantly, increasing longevity.[7]

Harold Christensen places the emphasis on somewhat different aspects of this revolution. He identifies four social trends which will continue to influence the family: (1) increasingly higher standards of living as a result of technological innovations; (2) continued population growth and a continued search for ways to control it; (3) increasing individualism and a reduction in familism; and (4) continuing decline in religious values and the sense of the sacred and increasing confidence in the ability of science to solve the problems of a secular world.[8] F. Ivan Nye adds to these factors a conviction that the human rights revolution will continue to improve the status of women and of racial and ethnic minority groups before the law and in social interaction.[9]

Most social scientists who study the family see it as a highly adaptable institution that is capable of responding to the changes likely to be brought about by these social forces.[10] They therefore assume that the nuclear family structure and monogamous marriage will undergo dramatic changes in role and style, but will persist as the dominant forms of intimate partnership. Some, however, feel that the structure will change dramatically because it cannot meet the increasing needs for

[7]Bernard Faber, *Family: Organization and Interaction* (San Francisco: Chandler Publishing Company, 1964), pp. 232–81.

[8]Harold T. Christensen, "Changing Roles of Family Members," paper presented in 1965 at a workshop at Michigan State University, pp. 1–25.

[9]F. Ivan Nye and Felix M. Berardo, *The Family: Its Structure and Interaction* (New York: The Macmillan Company, 1973), p. 632.

[10]Faber, *Family*; Christensen, "Changing Roles of Family Members"; Nye and Berardo, *The Family*; Hill, "The American Family of the Future."

nurturance in an increasingly impersonal world.[11] Many more hope that a greater variety of styles will be acceptable in the future.

The dominant tendency in family analysis is to assume that *if* these societal trends continue as projected, *then* the family and marriage will change in certain predictable ways. F. Ivan Nye, for example, epitomizes the sociological perspective when he predicts, on the basis of the social factors listed above, that the family will change in the following ways:

1. Family life will become increasingly affluent and women will continue to make an increasing contribution to this affluence on an increasingly voluntary basis.

2. An increasing percentage of married women will work.

3. It will be necessary, therefore, to provide increasingly adequate child care facilities; the government will have an increasing hand in this.

4. The life styles of American families will continue to converge as their consumer habits become increasingly similar; young people, however, will continue to experiment with divergent alternatives.

5. There will be more families, both because an increasing percentage of Americans will decide to marry and because of increasing life expectancy and the concomitant reduction in widowhood.

6. Both the divorce rate and the remarriage rate will continue to increase.

7. The age at which young people marry will continue to increase.

8. Power within the family will become more equally distributed as two types of marriage continue to increase: the companionate marriage and the colleague marriage in which the two partners are equal in terms of professional skills and status within the family.

9. Women will approach nearer and nearer to equality with men in terms of the regulation of their sexual behavior; increasing numbers of both men and women will experience nonmarital intercourse.

10. Effective contraceptives will become increasingly available to more and more people at a price they can afford, and they will be used with increasing effectiveness.

11. The average work week will continue to shrink so that family members find they will have increasing amounts of leisure time.

12. Family roles will continue to change, but not dramatically. Men will still be expected to be the providers. Women will increasingly participate in this role on a voluntary basis. The housekeeping role increasingly

[11]See especially Warren Bennis and Philip Slater, *The Temporary Society* (New York: Harper & Row, Publishers, 1969); Sidney Jourard, "Reinventing Marriage"; and David Cooper, *The Death of the Family* (New York: Vintage Books, 1971).

will be carried on by outsiders and the family will eat out more often. Child care during the day will more and more become the responsibility of schools and other public agencies. Parents will have more time to give to their children and will increasingly share the responsibilities of child care. A more continuous pattern of socialization will emerge as children spend more time with peer groups under professional supervision. Thus when they reach the age at which they are expected to go to work with age peers, they will experience less radical disjunction in their expectations and behavior than is presently the case.[12]

These sociological predictions do not seem particularly startling. Few of us would be surprised by them. They suggest a family life style not too different from what we now experience, except that it will be increasingly adapted to the needs of its members as the changes listed above occur. This is essentially an "optimistic" view of family life.

ASSESSING CURRENT EXPERIMENTA-TION

The changes in marriage outlined in the preceding discussion were predicted on the assumption that marriage will evolve in response to changes in the sociological environment. Yet as we have seen repeatedly throughout this book, people can and do exercise considerable choice about the type of partnership they will have. Thus, while some changes in the structure of the institution of marriage will occur automatically in response to environmental changes, others will be brought about intentionally. In this regard it is important to consider what role today's intentional experimentation will play in shaping the marriages of tomorrow.

Transforming the Traditional Structure

The character of monogamous marriage and the nuclear family is changing as we observe these institutions today. The most widely publicized transformation is the increasing equality in sex role definition and in job opportunities for women.

Role Redefinition. A recent poll by *Redbook* magazine indicated that women generally did not yet feel that they had achieved equal status with men.[13] The respondents to this poll, generally young women in their thirties of middle-class background, felt that women who do the same work as men generally receive less money, that most men do not

[12]Nye and Berardo, *The Family*, pp. 633–644.
[13]Carol Tavis and Toby Jayaratne, "What 120,000 Young Women Can Tell You about Sex, Motherhood, Menstruation, Housework—and Men," *Redbook* (January 1973), pp. 11–14.

take women seriously, and that the communications media degrade women by portraying them as sex objects. Forty-nine percent of the sample felt that women were exploited in this country as much as minority groups were. In regard to the home, the majority felt that although raising children provides many rewards, the role of mother does not satisfy most women as a full-time job. They also felt that the housewife-mother role does not really provide women with enough opportunity for self-fulfillment. Although their responses cannot be considered as typical of the responses of American women as a whole, they do suggest that an educated and articulate segment of the female population desires equality of opportunity and a redefinition of sex roles and is dissatisfied with the progress that has been made to date.

Not surprisingly, evidence indicates that the chances of marital happiness for both husband and wife are increased in families in which the wife chooses to work outside the household.[14] At least five studies confirm that the husbands tend to assume a greater share of the household responsibilities in situations in which the wife works.[15] The difference in the amount of housework undertaken by the husbands was not great (15 percent where the wife did not work, 25 percent where she did), but it was a real increase. As more and more women become trained for rewarding occupations within the labor market, and as the shift to service occupations opens up more desirable types of work for women, it is likely that more married women will work outside the home. This will have a considerable impact on the structure of marriage because there is a pronounced tendency for working women to have greater authority within their households than women who are not gainfully employed. In this connection the prediction of Orden and Bradburn is especially significant:

In the public sector, if society moves toward its national goal of better educational opportunities for all its members, there should be an increase in the proportion of women who choose to enter the labor force in prestigious occupations to which they have a real sense of commitment. We predict that this phenomenon will not be detrimental to the institution of marriage. On the contrary, there is evidence to support the contention that there might well be a strengthening of the marriage relationship both for the husband and for the wife.[16]

There is no evidence to indicate that children suffer any harm as a result of their mothers' working so long as they are properly cared for. Indeed, Bruno Bettelheim, the noted child psychologist, contends that

[14]Susan R. Orden and Norma Bradburn, "Working Wives and Marriage Happiness," in Joann S. Delora and Jack R. Delora, eds., *Intimate Life Styles: Marriage and Its Alternatives* (Pacific Palisades, Calif.: Goodyear Publishing Co., Inc., 1972), p. 250.
[15]See Robert O. Blood, "The Effect of the Wife's Employment on the Husband-Wife Relationship," in Jerold Heiss, ed., *Family Roles and Interaction* (Chicago: Rand McNally, 1968), pp. 255–69.
[16]Orden and Bradburn, "Working Wives . . .," p. 250.

children of working mothers are often happier than children whose mothers are not employed outside the home. "It benefits neither the child nor the mother if all the 'do's' and 'don'ts' come from her, the most important person in the child's world," Bettelheim writes.[17] It is his contention that the most important transformation that can occur in our society as far as working mothers are concerned is for us to get over the idea that they are somehow not good mothers.

Just as the mother's role within the family is changing as more and more women work outside the home, so the father's role is changing also. A few decades ago it was not uncommon for fathers to play little active role in family affairs outside of providing economic support. This pattern was especially common in suburban settings. Today, as women take upon themselves an increasing share of the responsibility for providing income, many men are finding themselves more deeply involved in family affairs. As Leonard Benson points out, there is a tendency for the family to become more important to father as the father's importance as the family's sole means of support decreases.[18] Within the family, however, he is called upon more and more to meet the emotional needs of family members—a role once exclusively the mother's

Some couples have been deliberately experimenting with role reversal in which the wife is expected to earn the family's income and the husband to take care of the home and the children. One such couple is Marge and Steve Everett. The following conclusion resulted from their year-long experiment in role reversal:

Marge is convinced that her year of role reversal saved her from a second rate existence. She is no longer living entirely through Steve and the children. She and Steve still argue about some of the same things, but the bouts are fewer and faster, thanks to greater mutual understanding and clearer communication. "Fights that would have gone on for eight or nine hours before are now over in a half an hour."

Although it might seem that a year of being housebound would prompt Steve to get out and stay away as much as possible, he comes home earlier, spends more time with the family than ever before. "I have more of a feeling now that I belong."[19]

Such deliberate experiments merely highlight the experience of countless couples who have changed traditional role definitions without any conscious intention to engage in experimentation with alternative styles of partnership. Role reversals as dramatic as the Everetts' may never be very common, but role transformations of a more limited extent are very likely to be a significant feature of the marriage of the future.

[17]Bruno Bettelheim, "Why Working Mothers Have Happier Children,"
[18]Leonard Benson, *Fatherhood: A Sociological Perspective* (New York: Random House, 1970), p. 324.
[19]*Newsweek* (March 1973).

Open Marriage. There has been little evaluation to date of the modification of traditional marriage described in Chapter 11. Becoming more flexible, eliminating the emphasis on the norm of togetherness, and incorporating outsiders into intimate relationships are not unlikely developments for tomorrow's marriages. There is little reason to doubt that marriage in the future will be increasingly open as far as role flexibility and individual autonomy are concerned. Whether this openness will include an increase in permitted extramarital sexual intimacy remains in doubt, however. At present it is not known under what conditions it is desirable to cultivate such relationships. It seems clear that not everybody can cope with jealousy or manage the increasing tensions that inevitably emerge along with the pleasure to be found in such outside activities. In the following dialogue Denise and Eric, a couple interviewed by Carl Rogers, express their feelings about trying to incorporate others into their sex lives:

Denise: I still think it could be done and I think it is an enlarging of one's life experience or thoroughness of living life, but I think we play with it too much. You have to have a good, strong bond in the marriage going—nothing can be wrong there, very seriously wrong, because that's the one thing we found out. When we worked this thing with the other couple, that one link was a little weak and the whole thing went down the drain—the other man was not really ready to do this.

Eric: But damn it, I am not willing for Denise to have lovers. I mean, I don't want to think about her making love to another man. I've always felt that way, I mean the jealousy of thinking about you and Gus or you and Ed together just tore my guts out. And we got into this a little while back, you know, and finally we got into a sort of funny kind of bind where we said, in terms of all our values, everything we believe, all our rational kind of approach to the thing, we say my having a lover or Denise having a lover if she wants one, may add to the marriage, it may enhance our growth, there is no reason it needs to be destructive, yet—I mean we're not free, you know, we're not free independently choosing organisms.[20]

In spite of all the swinging marriages, group marriages, and open marriages now being attempted, it is not yet clear who can and who cannot satisfactorily partake in such relationships. There is no evidence so far as to what effects such activities may have upon long-term partnerships. Perhaps in a decade or so we will know more about the possibilities and the consequences.

[20]Carl Rogers, *Becoming Partners: Marriage and Its Alternatives* (New York: Delacorte Press, 1972), pp. 181, 183.

The Cluster Family. The cluster family is essentially an attempt to get upper middle-class people to work together cooperatively to a far greater extent than is ordinarily found in most neighborhoods today. In a sense, cluster families aim at recreating, in an urban or suburban environment, the intimate network of families characteristic of Southern cooperatives, the amiable smalltown neighborhoods of rural America, or religious communities such as the Amish and the Quakers. All these types of family networks share some of the characteristics called for by such advocates of cluster families as Frederick H. Stoller:

Briefly defined, an intimate network of families could be described as a circle of three or four families who meet together regularly and frequently, share in reciprocal fashion any of their intimate secrets, offer one another a variety of services and do not hesitate to influence one another in terms of values and attitudes. Behind this definition is a picture of a brawling, noisy, often chaotic convocation which develops its own set of customs for the purpose of coming together in terms of rich experiences rather than merely being "correct" and, in the process, achieves movement in terms of its own views of its arrangements and ways of operating. Such an intimate family network would be neither stagnant nor polite, but would involve an extension of the boundaries of the intimate family.[21]

In Stoller's version of the cluster family, the participating families need not live together, although they should live near each other to facilitate frequent meetings. The intimate network creates what Stoller sees as a kind of "family workshop" atmosphere in which sensitivity training and similar techniques are used to deepen the encounters.

Wanda Burgess advocates a similar structure, although for somewhat different objectives. She suggests that if a group of about twelve couples were to purchase their own land and build their separate residences upon it, their cooperative efforts could result in a considerable economy of time, exposure to new ideas, and other practical benefits. She envisions the physical aspects of her cooperative as follows:

A group of twelve families will jointly purchase land, each family building the house they desire, with all members helping to build the houses and a community center. The latter will include a workshop, a children's play area, a kitchen and storage pantry and freezer, a swimming pool and tennis courts. There will also be a large organic garden and some livestock.

It is hoped that we will garner ecological as well as economic benefits. We are investigating methods of composting all household and sewage wastes for use as fertilizer and of recycling waste water in the garden. There will no longer be the necessity of each family having two cars. Probably, each family will have one, or less; we will try to work up carpools and hookups with public transportation

[21]Frederick Stoller, "The Intimate Network of Families in a New Structure," p. 152, in Herbert A. Otto, *The Family in Search of a Future: Alternative Models for Moderns* © 1970. Reprinted by permission of Prentice-Hall, Inc., Englewood Cliffs, N.J.

where possible, and then we will have three or four cars for those who remain at home.[22]

Burgess feels that such a "cooperative housing group" will be an excellent environment in which to bring up children. As she sees it, the cluster family is neither a religious community nor a community motivated toward growth via group techniques. It is simply a voluntary association in which much more cooperation takes place than is customary in contemporary middle-class settings. Burgess does not specify in any detail what will be expected of persons in such a cooperative community. She does, however, point out that most communities fail because the members are not in agreement on what should be expected of them, and for this reason she advocates spending a great deal of time together thinking through the implications of cooperative living before building the cooperative. The successful group marriage described in Chapter 16 required almost one year of intensive preparation before the experiment began, and undoubtedly a successful cluster family would need at least the same amount of careful planning.

THE FUTURE OF MULTIPLE MARRIAGE

There has been widespread speculation on the future of various kinds of multiple marriages. In an examination of one particularly interesting ramification of this subject, Victor Kassel discusses the possibilities of polygyny for persons over sixty.[23] Because there are many more widows than widowers over sixty, polygyny seems to offer considerable promise as a way of combatting the loneliness of old age. One man married to several women could create a home in which many needs could be met. He sees the advantages of such an arrangement as follows:

1. It would meet the companionship needs of the excessive number of women who live alone in our society.

2. It would provide a *family* constellation within which people can overcome their isolation.

3. The diet of the elderly would improve because eating would once again take place in a social setting and appetites would undoubtedly improve.

4. The income that individually would be inadequate to provide a decent standard of living in many instances could provide a very comfortable living if pooled.

[22]Wanda Burgess, "Learning to Cooperate: A Middle Class Experiment," in Louise Kapp Howe, ed., *The Future of the Family* (New York: Simon & Schuster, 1972), pp. 293–94.
[23]Victor Kassel, "Polygamy After Sixty," in Otto, *The Family in Search of a Future.*

5. Living together can provide a nursing community wherein the elderly can be cared for in the privacy of their own homes without having to go to a nursing home or hospital.

6. The opportunity to express their sexual desires would be open to many women who otherwise would repress their sexuality in a continent widowhood.

7. For men, impotency might be overcome in many instances as a result of the greater variety of interesting sexual companionship.

8. In such a household individuals would be encouraged to be neat and attractive in their appearance rather than letting themselves "go to pot" as is often the case when the elderly live alone.

9. In such an environment, depression and loneliness would be less evident; what is more, the intimate association of the members of the household should provide them with a base from which to relate to other people outside the marriage.

10. Health insurance could be modified to consider the group marriage within the definition of a "family," so that the aggregate charge would be less than the sum of each individual's payments if they were living alone.

Thus, Kassel sees polygyny after sixty as a way of meeting a number of the social problems of the elderly even though he realizes that its introduction would mean a radical redefinition of marriage.[24] George S. Rosenberg summarizes the extent of this radical redefinition in terms of present expectations about marriage:

> . . . it seems fair to state that although polygynous marriage in principle may provide an alternative to the status of monogamous spouse, it is neither regarded as significant nor rewarded by the predominantly conjugal values which are retained from earlier socialization to, and experience in, monogamy. The ideological stress on egalitarianism in the conjugal relations, the emphasis on woman's right to choose a husband and the romantic love pattern which assumes that because a husband loves his wife, she has a certain degree of influence over him, would all appear to militate against polygynous marriage for the aged.[25]

Rosenberg's argument that polygyny is not a viable alternative for the elderly because it conflicts with the dominant ideology of the conjugal family overlooks the fact that a considerable amount of anti-conjugal experimentation is going on among the young today. Thus, when this younger generation becomes elderly in the future they may not find it

[24]Kassel, "Polygamy After Sixty," p. 14.
[25]George S. Rosenberg, "Implications of New Models of the Family for the Aging Population, p. 178, in Herbert A. Otto, *The Family in Search of a Future: Alternative Models for Moderns* © 1970. Reprinted by permission of Prentice-Hall, Inc., Englewood Cliffs, N.J.

difficult at all to live in polygynous families. Rosenberg's negative prediction also overlooks the fantastic rate at which our society is changing. Finally, it overlooks our increasing capacity to change our institutions deliberately in order to meet our needs. Thus it does not seem that we can realistically rule out such an option for the elderly at this time. At any rate, the practical benefits of multiple marriage for the elderly seem to be many and obvious, in spite of the largely ideological difficulties associated with redefining marriage.

Those who are studying group or multilateral marriage among the non-elderly predict that it probably will continue into the future for a minority of persons as a viable life style. As Larry and Joan Constantine write:

The most probable coexistent structures of the future all have well delineated roots today. Serial polygyny will be legitimized though probably less statistically prominent than today. Trial or individual marriage will have legal recognition. Group marriages will be a significant minority, socially if not legally condoned. Homosexual marriages and the production of children by unmarried individuals are likely to be peripheral benefactors of liberalization.[26]

The Future of the Commune

Rosabeth Kanter, speculating on the future of the commune movement, points out that a portion of this movement does not value permanence in their settlements and sees change as an inevitable—and highly desirable—aspect of life, even in the area of interpersonal relationships.[27] Thus the high failure rate of particular settlements may not be an adequate indicator of the success or failure rate of the commune movement as a whole. The movement may be thriving even though the individual settlements that are its component parts break up with great regularity, for new communes are constantly being formed to replace them.

Nevertheless, considerable numbers of persons now living in communes are seeking permanent and stable alternative life styles that they hope will persist into the future. Kanter concludes that the communes most likely to survived are the ones that

. . . develop common purposes, an integrating philosophy, a structure for leadership and decision-making, criteria for membership and entrance procedures, that organize work and property communally, that affirm their bonds through ritual, and that work out interpersonal difficulties through regular open confrontation. . . . They will be building commitment and also satisfying their members by creating a strong family-like group.[28]

[26]Larry Constantine and Joan Constantine, "Where Is Marriage Going," *The Futurist* (April 1970), p. 45. Published by the World Future Society, PO Box 30369 (Bethesda), Washington, D.C. 20014.
[27]Rosabeth Moss Kanter, "Getting It All Together: Communes Past, Present and Future," in Howe, *The Future of the Family.*
[28]Kanter, "Getting It All Together," p. 325. Copyright 1972, American Orthopsychiatric Association, Inc. Reproduced by permission.

In a paper presented to the American Sociological Association in New Orleans in 1972, Benjamin Zablocki expressed a less positive prospect for the future of the commune movement. It is his conviction that the commune movement has already reached its peak in terms of the number of persons involved and is likely to decline to a much smaller number in the future.[29]

SOME MORE RADICAL ALTERNATIVES

Strangely enough, the most radical suggestions about the future course of marriage do not focus upon changing the structure of marriage. They assume that the basic contract will remain monogamous in most instances. The commitment to monogamy, however, will no longer be on a lifelong basis and will be supplemented by various kinds of contractual relationships.

Future Shock

The "fractured family" foreseen by Alvin Toffler in his *Future Shock* does not differ *in form* from contemporary marriage.[30] Toffler's assumption that marriage is, should be, and will continue to be a temporary relationship sees the institution of marriage in a radically new light. In the future, Toffler contends, people will become increasingly able to plug themselves into, and take themselves out of, numerous social structures. On the job they will increasingly participate as associate members of task forces designed to solve particular problems. When any one specific task is completed, the task force will be disbanded—a practice which already is common today in the aerospace industry. In their home lives people will practice serial monogamy (or serial polygyny). They will acknowledge the fact that two partners change, grow, and develop at different rates and in different directions, so that two people who may have been suited for each other at the age of twenty may not be appropriate partners at thirty, or even twenty-five. Both husband and wife will readily change partners, just as they will become increasingly detached from things and places in the increasingly mobile society toward which we are headed.

The fractured family of the future will have many options in regard to raising children. Toffler conjectures, for example, that a woman who wants children and wants to experience pregnancy may be able to pre-select a certified embryo and have it inserted in her womb for her to gestate the normal nine months. If she does not prefer to experience pregnancy she can have the embryo raised in a test tube. A woman—

[29]Benjamin Zablocki, "Some Models of Commune Integration and Disintegration," paper presented to the American Sociological Association in New Orleans, August 1972.

[30]Alvin Toffler, *Future Shock* (New York: Bantam Books, Inc., 1972).

Ken Kay

and her husband if she is married—also will have the option of having the infant raised by a "professional" family for a specified number of years. In this connection Toffler fantasizes about the advertisement that may someday appear in the *New York Times* as a result of such practice:

Why let parenthood tie you down? Let us raise your infant into a responsible, successful adult. Class A Pro family offers father, age 39, mother, 36, grandmother, 67. Uncle and aunt, age 30, live in, hold part time local employment. Four child unit has opening for one, age 6–8. Regulated diet exceeds government standards. All adults certified in child development and mangement. Bio-parents permitted frequent visits. Telephone contact allowed. Child may spend summer vacation with bio-parents. Religion, art, music encouraged by special arrangement. Five year contract, minimum. Write for further details.[31]

It is interesting to note that the qualities described in the advertisement are very traditional qualities despite the fact that the way of realizing the desired objectives is very unorthodox by contemporary standards. Moreover, it should not be forgotten that this is but one of the many conceivable choices that Toffler speculates bio-parents of the future may be able to make. Thus Toffler also acknowledges the viability

[31]Alvin Toffler, *Future Shock* (New York: Bantam Books, 1972), p. 244. Copyright © 1970 Random House, Inc.

of multiple marriages and communes as realistic marriage options for the future. Indeed, his whole approach to the future is based on the assumption that we will have more choices about the form of our marriage contract in the decades ahead, not fewer.

Because our contemporary mores emphasize the desirability of permanent partnerships, most people tend to find the idea of temporary contracts somewhat frightening. Today we tend to assume that qualities such as honesty, trust, commitment, identity, integrity, and even love itself can be measured in partnerships simply by the sheer persistence of the union. We know that the partners in one marriage must love each other because they have chosen to stay married for twenty-two years; we know, too, that the partners in another marriage did not love each other or were not honest with each other or were not committed to each other because they stayed married only six years. Indeed, when we define the qualities we look for in a successful partnership, we do so with a built-in assumption that the terms have meaning only (or largely) in relationships of some duration. But is it possible that an increasing number of contracts of brief duration with many persons will produce the same growth that we now look for as a result of prolonged contact with one person, or at most a few? Today we assume that the answer must be in the negative. We assume that temporary relationships with many people are necessarily superficial. But perhaps it is possible—or will become possible—to improve our capacity to communicate "information-rich" messages to one another so that even temporary relationships could have the "depth" now associated with more lasting ones.

We do not know the answer to the questions posed by these suggestions. Toffler himself assumes that there are limits to our capacity to handle the new, the transient, and the different. Just what these limits may be is a question only the future can answer, but what seems clear already is that a new and different world is rapidly coming upon us, regardless of whether or not we have the capacity to deal with it.

The Temporary Society

Approaching the problems raised by increased mobility and the shift from a society based on permanent systems to a society based on temporary systems from an analytical perspective, Philip Slater attributes two primary consequences to these changes: (1) There will be an increase in individuation—that is, there will be a greater separation of the individual from the groups that support his or her sense of identity by confirming his or her values and traits. (2) Concomitantly, people will experience a greater sense of alienation, anomie, and meaninglessness. When an individual loses contact with his or her permanent reference group, "he [or she] becomes a part in search of a whole, feeling neither enough like others to avoid a sense of being alone and lost, nor sufficiently included in a stable pattern of differentiation to have a sense of himself [or herself] as a distinguishable entity."[32] Slater summarizes the situation as follows:

It will be increasingly necessary to take people as one finds them—to relate immediately, intensely and without traditional social props, rituals and distancing mechanisms. Distance will be provided by transience, and the old patterns of gamesmanship, of extended gradual and incomplete unmasking will become inappropriate. By the time the individual reaches his "here-is-the-real-me" flourish, he will find himself alone again. It seems clear that one of the unintended functions of sensitivity training or "basic encounter" groups is anticipating a world of temporary systems, since these groups emphasize openness, feedback, immediacy, communication at a feeling level, the here-and-now more awareness of and ability to express deeper feelings and so on. Members of such groups often express surprise and chagrin at their capacity to respond with warmth and intensity to individuals they would in other situations have regarded with indifference, fear or contempt.[33]

In addition to these two primary consequences of temporary transient systems—increased individuation and increased alienation—Slater also predicts an increase in interchangeability. Each individual will be expected to fit into the system like the interchangeable parts of a machine. As temporary systems come to be dominant, traditional types of relationship based on territoriality and kinship will be further limited and "what we might call the principle of temporary relevance" will obtain, Slater writes.[34] Of course, total interchangeability will never be achieved, for even temporary systems must assume a degree of specialization.

What is more, the rise of temporary systems, in Slater's view, will result in an *intensification* of the marital relationship. Slater points out that in the past, whenever stable systems have begun to break down, husbands and wives have drawn closer together. If this pattern continues it means that much more will be expected of marriage in the future, with the result that marital relations will suffer much greater stresses and strains. "The future of marriage in a society of temporary systems remains uncertain," Slater concludes, because as the intensity of the relationship increases, its stability will in all probability decrease.[35] Like Toffler, he too predicts that serial monogamy will be a probable result.

In trying to predict the effect of the rise of temporary systems upon marriage and the family, Slater realizes that the period of transition between traditional family forms and forms more suited to the temporary society of the future is likely to be quite painful, producing a host of "deviant life styles" in the interim:

[32]Bennis and Slater, *The Temporary Society*, p. 81.
[33]*The Temporary Society*, pp. 86–87.
[34]*The Temporary Society*, p. 85.
[35]*The Temporary Society*, p. 90.

There will be more nostalgia, more revivals, more clinging to real and imagined pasts. There will be more world-rejecting fantasies of static, loving, bucolic, utopian communities, many of which will be carried into action.[36]

Slater does not pretend to be able to weigh the various factors that are shaping our future in order to predict a single outcome. His intention is simply to indicate the general tendency and its likely consequences, and in doing so he has produced a provocative picture of an emerging social order, about which all we can say with certainty is that the society of the near future will be one of increasing stress and strain.

On a more personal plane, Larry and Joan Constantine see that the marriage styles of the future will be the product of the conflict, already emerging in contemporary society, between conventional and innovative attitudes toward the institution of marriage:

A confrontation between society and the participants in and advocates of new forms of marriage is almost inevitable. What the future holds will largely depend upon when the open and direct confrontation takes place. If it comes forcefully and soon, amid rising conservative xenophobia, group marriage and other creative marital structures may never fructify and may be destroyed, as was polygamy in the last century. If the confrontation is spread out and prior discussion is systematic and appropriate, the story may be more like trial marriage, which is not a possibility for the future but a fait accompli.[37]

[36]*The Temporary Society*, p. 95.
[37]Constantine and Constantine, "Where Is Marriage Going," *The Futurist* (April 1970), p. 44. Published by the World Future Society, PO Box 30369 (Bethesda), Washington, D.C. 20014.

SUMMARY

It seems fair to say that most people are somewhat reluctant to look at the future because they are already uneasy about the changes they see around them and even more uneasy about the prospect of even greater changes to come. Yet the technological engine that is fueled by our own curiosity and technological drivenness is gathering speed, and it is not only the aged who are being left behind. If there is yet time, now is the time to begin to look and examine and to take what charge we can. Not all change is desirable. Not all change is inevitable. The quality of the life of the future lies in our hands to a greater extent than it has in any previous generation. How can we begin to evaluate? What, in fact, is desirable in partnerships such as marriage? These are not easy questions to answer, but perhaps Suzanne Keller's statement, from an article entitled "Does the Family Have a Future?" can help by reminding us how to go about answering them:

Ultimately all social change involves moral doubt and moral reassessment. If we refuse to consider change while there is still time, time will pass us by. Only by examining and taking stock of what is can we hope to affect what will be. This is our chance to invent and thus to humanize the future.[38]

[38]Suzanne Keller, "Does the Family Have a Future?" *Journal of Comparative Family Studies* (Spring 1971), p. 14.

SELECTED BIBLIOGRAPHY

1. Introduction

Cuber, John F., and Peggy B. Harroff. *Sex and the Significant Americans: A Study of Sexual Behavior Among the Affluent.* New York: Appleton-Century-Crofts, 1965.

Gallup, George. "Is There Really a Sexual Revolution?" *The Critic.* New York: The Thomas Moore Association, 1972.

Henry, Jules. *Culture Against Man.* New York: Random House, 1963.

Kinsey, Alfred C., et al. *Sexual Behavior in the Human Female.* Philadelphia: W. B. Saunders Co., 1963.

LeMasters, E. E. *Parents in Modern America.* rev. ed. Homewood, Ill.: The Dorsey Press, 1974.

Linton, Ralph. *The Study of Man.* New York: Appleton-Century-Crofts, 1936.

Maslow, Abraham H. *Toward a Psychology of Being.* 2d ed. New York: Van Nostrand Reinhold Company, 1968.

Masters, William H., and Virginia E. Johnson. *Human Sexual Inadequacy.* Boston: Little, Brown and Company, 1970.

Stephens, William N. *The Family in Cross-Cultural Perspective.* New York: Holt, Rinehart & Winston, Inc., 1963.

2. On Partnerships

Back, Kurt W. *Beyond Words: The Story of Sensitivity Training and the Encounter Group Movement.* New York: Russell Sage Foundation, 1972.

Freud, Sigmund. *An Outline of Psychoanalysis.* New York: W. W. Norton & Company, Inc., 1949.

Josephson, Eric, and Mary Josephson. *Man Alone.* New York: Dell Publishing Company, Inc., 1962.

Jung, Carl G. *Modern Man in Search of a Soul.* New York: Harcourt Brace Jovanovich, Inc., 1933.

Maslow, Abraham H. *The Farthest Reaches of Human Nature.* New York: The Viking Press, Inc., 1971.

Slater, Philip E. *The Pursuit of Loneliness: American Culture at the Breaking Point.* Boston: Beacon Press, 1970.

Toffler, Alvin. *Future Shock.* New York: Bantam Books, Inc., 1970.

3. Confirmation and Communication

Altman, Irwin, and Dalmas A. Taylor. *Social Penetration: The Development of Interpersonal Relations.* New York: Holt, Rinehart & Winston, Inc., 1973.

Buber, Martin. *I and Thou.* 2d ed. New York: Charles Scribner's Sons, 1958.
————. *Between Man and Man.* Boston: Beacon Press, 1955.

Burton, Arthur, ed. *Encounter.* San Francisco: Jossey-Bass, Inc., 1969.

Clinebell, Howard J. *The People Dynamic: Changing Self and Society Through Growth Groups.* New York: Harper & Row, Publishers, 1972.

Glidewell, John C. *Choice Points: Essays on the Emotional Problems of Living with People.* Cambridge: The MIT Press, 1970.

Laing, R. D., and A. Esterson. "Sanity, Madness and the Family," *Family of Schizophrenics.* Vol. I. New York: Basic Books, Inc., 1965.

Zunin, Leonard. *Contact: The First Four Minutes.* Los Angeles: Nash Publishing Company, 1972.

4. Conflict in Intimate Partnerships

Bach, George R., and Peter Wyden. *The Intimate Enemy: How to Fight Fair in Love and Marriage.* New York: William Morrow & Co., Inc., 1969.

Charney, Israel W. *Marital Love and Hate: The Need for a Revised Marriage Contract and a More Honest Offer by the Marriage Counselor to Teach Couples to Love and Hate, Honor and Dishonor, Obey and Disobey.* New York: The Macmillan Company, 1972.

Fairfield, Richard. *Communes U.S.A.: A Personal Tour.* Baltimore, Md.: Penguin Books Inc., 1972.

Klemer, Richard H. *Marriage and Family Relationships.* New York: Harper & Row, Publishers, 1970.

Pavenstedt, Eleanor, and Viola W. Bernard. *Crisis of Family Disorganization: Programs to Soften Their Impact on Children.* New York: Behavioral Publications, Inc., 1971.

Saxton, Lloyd. *The Individual, Marriage, and the Family.* 2d ed. Belmont, Calif.: Wadsworth Publishing Co., Inc., 1972.

Southand, Samuel, *Anger in Love.* Philadelphia: The Westminster Press, 1973.

Steinmetz, Suzanne K., and Murray A. Strauss. *Violence in the Family.* New York: Dodd, Mead & Co., 1974.

Stephens, William N. *The Family in Cross-Cultural Perspective.* New York: Holt, Rinehart & Winston, Inc., 1963.

Strauss, Murray A. "Leveling, Civility, and Violence in the Family," *Journal of Marriage and the Family* 36 (February 1974).

Wood, John. *How Do You Feel?* Englewood Cliffs, N.J.: Prentice-Hall, Inc., 1974.

Wynne, Lynn C., et al. "Pseudo-Mutuality in The Family Relations of Schizophrenics," *Psychiatry* 2 (May 1958).

5. Developing Partnerships

Besancency, Paul H. *Interfaith Marriages: Who and Why.* New Haven: College & University Press, 1970.

Blumensteil, Alex. "The Sociology of Good Times," in George Pathas, ed., *Phenomenological Society: Issues and Applications.* New York: John Wiley & Sons, Inc., 1973.

Broderick, Carl B., and Jessie Bernard, eds. *The Individual, Sex, and Society.* Baltimore: The Johns Hopkins Press, 1969.

Bruce, James D., and Hyman Rodman. "Black-White Marriages in the United States: A Review of the Empirical Literature," in Irving R. Stuart and Lawrence E. Abt, eds., *Interracial Marriage: Expectations and Realities.* New York: Grossman Publishers, 1973.

Glick, Paul C. "Intermarriage and Fertility Patterns Among Persons in Major Religious Groups," *Eugenics Quarterly* 1 (1960).

Kirkendall, Lester A., and Rodger W. Libby. "Interpersonal Relationships—Crux of the Sexual Renaissance," *Journal of Social Issues* 2 (April 1966).

Libby, Rodger, and Robert Whitehurst, eds. *Renovating Marriage.* Danville, Calif.: Consensus Publishers, Inc., 1973.

Lyness, Judith, Milton E. Lipety, and Keith E. Davis. "Living Together: An Alternative to Marriage," *Journal of Marriage and the Family* 34 (May 1972.

Mace, David, and Vera Mace. *Marriage East and West.* Garden City, N.Y.: Doubleday & Company, Inc., 1960.

Mead, Margaret. "The Life Cycle and Its Variations: The Division of Roles," in Daniel Bell, ed., *Toward the Year 2000: Work in Progress.* Boston: Beacon Press, 1969.

Murstein, Bernard. "Stimulus-Value-Role: A Theory of Marital Choice," *Journal of Marriage and the Family* 32 (1970).

O'Reilly, Jane. "Notes on the New Paralysis," *New York Magazine* (October 1970).

Reiss, Ira L. "Premarital Sexuality: Past, Present and Future," in Ira L. Reiss, ed., *Readings on the Family System.* New York: Holt, Rinehart & Winston, Inc., 1972.

The School of Social Work. *Families of Sand: A Report Concerning the Flight of Adolescents from Their Families.* Columbus, Ohio: The Ohio State University, 1974.

Skolnick, Arlene, and Jerome Skolnick, eds. *Intimacy, Family and Society.* Boston: Little, Brown and Company, 1974.

6. The Biology of Sex and Reproduction

Boston Women's Health Book Collective. *Our Bodies, Ourselves.* New York: Simon & Schuster, Inc., 1973.

Crawley, Lawrence, et al. *Reproduction, Sex, and Preparation for Marriage.* 2d ed. Englewood Cliffs, N.J.: Prentice-Hall, Inc., 1973.

Fisher, Seymour. *The Female Orgasm: Psychology, Physiology, Fantasy*. New York: Basic Books, Inc., 1973.

Ford, Clellan S., and Frank A. Beach. *Patterns of Sexual Behavior*. New York: Harper & Row, 1970.

Francouer, Robert. *Utopian Motherhood: New Trends in Human Reproduction*. Cranbury, N.J.: A. S. Barnes & Co., Inc., 1970.

Katchadourian, Herant A., and Donald T. Lunde. *Fundamentals of Human Sexuality*. New York: Holt, Rinehart & Winston, Inc., 1972.

McCary, James L. *Human Sexuality: A Brief Edition*. New York: Van Nostrand Reinhold Company, 1973.

————. *Sexual Myths and Fallacies*. New York: Van Nostrand Reinhold Company, 1971.

Masters, William H., and Virginia E. Johnson. *Human Sexual Response*. Boston: Little, Brown and Company, 1966.

Rosenfeld, Albert. *The Second Genesis: The Coming Control of Life*. Englewood Cliffs, N.J.: Prentice-Hall, Inc., 1969.

Rubin, Isadore. *Sexual Life After Sixty*. New York: Basic Books, 1965.

7. On Birth Control

Blake, Judith. "Population Policy for Americans: Is the Government Being Misled?" *Science* 164 (May 2, 1968).

Calderone, Mary S., Ed. *Manual of Family Planning and Contraceptive Practice*. 2d ed. Baltimore: The Williams and Wilkins Co. 1970.

Chastean, Edgar R. *The Case for Compulsory Birth Control*. Englewood Cliffs, N.J.: Prentice-Hall, Inc., 1971.

Crawley Lawrence, et al. *Reproduction, Sex, and Preparation for Marriage*. 2d ed. Englewood Cliffs, N.J.: Prentice-Hall, Inc., 1973.

David, Hugh J. *Intrauterine Devices for Contraception: The IUD*. Baltimore: The Williams and Wilkins Co., 1971.

Hardin, Garret. *Birth Control*. New York: Pegasus, 1970.

Osofsky, Howard, and Joy Osofsky, eds. *The Abortion Experience: Psychological and Medical Impact*. New York: Harper & Row, 1973.

Rosen, Harold. *Abortion in America*. Boston: Beacon Press, 1967.

Rosenbury, Theodor. *Microbes and Morals: The Strange Story of Venereal Disease*. New York: The Viking Press, 1971.

Tietze, C. "Oral and Intrauterine Contraception: Effectiveness and Safety," *International Journal of Fertility* 13 (October-December 1968).

Tunnadine, L. P. D. *Contraception and Sexual Life: A Therapeutic Approach*. Philadelphia: J. B. Lippincott Co., 1970.

8. The Art of Lovemaking

Allen, Gina, and Clement Martin. *Intimacy: Sensitivity, Sex and The Art of Love*. Chicago: Cowles Book Co., Inc., 1971.

Comfort, Alex. *The Joy of Sex.* New York: Crown Publishers, Inc., 1972.

Downing, George. *The Massage Book.* New York: Random House, Inc., 1972.

Fromm, Eric. *The Art of Loving.* New York: Bantam Books, Inc., 1970.

Goldstein, Martin, et al. *The Sex Book: A Modern Pictorial Encyclopedia.* New York: The Seabury Press, Inc., 1974.

Gunther, Bernard. *Sense Relaxation: Below the Mind.* New York: Collier Books, 1968.

Herrigan, Jackie, and Jeff Herrigan. *Loving Free.* New York: Grossett & Dunlap, Inc., 1973.

McCary, James L. *Human Sexuality: A Brief Edition.* New York: Van Nostrand Reinhold Company, 1973.

Malinowski, Bronislaw. *The Sexual Life of Savages.* New York: Harcourt Brace Jovanovich, Inc., 1929.

Marshall, Donald S., and Robert C. Suggs. *Human Sexual Behavior.* New York: Basic Books, Inc., 1971.

Masters, William H., and Virginia E. Johnson. *Human Sexual Inadequacy.* Boston: Little, Brown and Company, 1970.

Rubin, Isadore. *Sexual Life After Sixty.* New York: Basic Books, 1965.

Schulz, William. *Joy: Expanding Human Awareness.* New York: Grove Press, 1967.

9. Sex Roles and Social Interaction

Broderick, Carlfred, and Jessie Bernard, eds. *The Individual, Sex, and Society.* Baltimore: The Johns Hopkins Press, 1969.

Bullock, Vern L. *The Subordinate Sex: A History of Attitudes Toward Women.* Baltimore: Penguin Books Inc., 1974.

Grummon, Donald L., and Andrew M. Barclay, eds. *Sexuality: A Search for Perspective.* New York: Van Nostrand Reinhold Company, 1971.

Mead, Margaret. *Sex and Temperament.* New York: Mentor Books, 1952.

————. *Male and Female.* New York: Mentor Books, 1955.

Money, John, and Anke A. Ehrhardt. *Man and Woman: Boy and Girl.* Baltimore: The Johns Hopkins Press, 1972.

Rossi, Alice, ed. *The Feminist Papers.* New York: Bantam Books, Inc., 1974.

Roy, Rustum, and Della Roy. *Honest Sex.* New York: The New American Library, Inc., 1968.

Rozak, Betty, and Theodore Rozak, eds. *Masculine and Feminine.* New York: Harper & Row, 1969.

Seaman, Barbara. *Free and Female.* New York: Coward, McCann & Geoghegan, Inc., 1972.

10. Marriage in Historical and Cultural Perspective

Blanchard, Paul. "Christianity and Sex: An Indictment of Orthodox Theology," *The Humanist* (March/April 1974).

Francouer, Robert, and Anna Francouer. *Eve's New Rib: Twenty Faces of Sex, Marriage and Family.* New York: Dell Publishing Co., Inc., 1972.

Hastings, Adrian. *Christian Marriage in Africa.* London: SPCK, 1973.

Hunt, Morton. *The Natural History of Love.* New York: Alfred A. Knopf, Inc., 1959.

James, E. O. *Marriage Customs Through the Ages.* New York: Collier Books, 1965.

Mair, Lucy. *Marriage.* Baltimore: Penguin Books Inc., 1971.

Stephens, William N., ed. *Reflections on Marriage.* New York: Thomas Y. Crowell Company, 1968.

Watts, Alan. *Nature, Man and Woman.* New York: Pantheon Books, Inc., 1958.

Wynn, John Charles, ed. *Sexual Ethics and Christian Responsibility.* New York: Association Press, 1970.

11. Husbands and Wives

Allen, Gina, and Martin G. Clement. *Intimacy: Sensitivity, Sex and the Art of Love.* Chicago: Cowles Book Co., Inc., 1971.

Cuber, John F., and Peggy B. Harroff. *Sex and the Significant Americans: A Study of Sexual Behavior Among the Affluent.* New York: Appleton-Century-Crofts, 1965.

Davis, Murray S. *Intimate Relations.* New York: The Free Press, 1973.

Mazur, Ronald. *The New Intimacy: Open-Ended Marriage and Alternative Life Styles.* Boston: Beacon Press, 1973.

O'Neill, George, and Nena O'Neill. *Open Marriage: A New Life Style for Couples.* New York: M. Evans & Co., Inc., 1972.

————. *Shifting Gears: Finding Security in a Changing World.* New York: M. Evans & Co., Inc., 1974.

Otto, Herbert A., ed. *Love Today: A New Exploration.* New York: Association Press, 1972.

Rimmer, Robert, ed. *Adventures in Loving.* New York: Signet Books, 1973.

Rogers, Carl. *Becoming Partners.* New York: Delacorte Press, 1972.

Winter, Gibson. *Love and Conflict: New Patterns in Family Life.* Garden City, N.Y.: Doubleday & Company, Inc., 1958.

12. Parents and Children

Collins, Boyd, and Harold Feldman. "Marital Satisfaction Over the Family Life Cycle," *Journal of Marriage and the Family* (February 1970).

Howe, Louise Kapp, ed. *The Future of the Family: Mothers, Fathers and Children, Sex Roles and Work, Communities and Child Care, Redefining Marriage and Parenthood.* New York: Simon and Schuster, 1972.

LeMasters, E. E. *Parenthood in America.* 2d ed. Homewood, Ill.: The Dorsey Press, 1974.

Lindsey, Judge Ben B., and Wainwright Evans. *The Companionate Marriage.* Garden City, N.Y.: Garden City Publishing Company, Inc., 1929.

Lopata, Helen Z. *Occupation Housewife.* New York: Oxford University Press, Inc., 1971.

Nye, F. Ivan, and Felix M. Bernardo. *The Family: Its Structure and Interaction* New York: The Macmillan Company, 1973.

Russell, Lord Bertrand. *Marriage and Morals.* New York: Bantam Books, 1968.

13. The Developing Family

Benson, Leonard. *The Family Bond: Marriage, Love, and Sex in America.* New York: Random House, Inc., 1971.

Bott, Elizabeth. *Family and Social Networks: Roles, Norms and Extended Relation in Orderly Families.* London: Tavistock Publications, 1957.

Duvall, Evelyn. *Family Development.* 4th ed. Philadelphia: J. B. Lippincott Co., 1972.

Erikson, Erik H. *Childhood and Society.* New York: W. W. Norton & Company, Inc., 1963.

Marcus, Peggy. "In-law Relationships in Couples Married Two or Eleven Years," *Journal of Home Economics* (January 1951).

Rodgers, Roy H. *Family Interaction and Transaction: The Developmental Approach.* Englewood Cliffs, N.J.: Prentice-Hall, Inc., 1973.

Schulz, David A. *The Changing Family: Its Function and Future.* Englewood Cliffs, N.J.: Prentice-Hall, Inc., 1972.

Seligman, Ben B. *Poverty as a Public Issue.* New York: The Free Press, 1967.

Slater, Philip. "Social Limitations on Libidinal Withdrawal," *American Sociological Review* 25 (June 1963).

Udry, J. Richard. *The Social Context of Marriage.* 2d ed. Philadelphia: J. B. Lippincott Co., 1971.

14. Disorganization and Divorce

Bohannan, Paul. *Divorce and After.* Garden City, N.Y.: Doubleday & Company, Inc., 1970.

Fisher, Esther. "Guide to Divorce Counseling," *The Family Coordinator* 22 (January 1973).

Glick, Paul, and Arthur Norton. "Frequency, Duration and Probability of Marriage and Divorce," *Journal of Marriage and the Family* 33 (May 1971).

Goode, William J. *After Divorce.* New York: The Free Press, 1956.

Hart C. W., and Arnold R. Pilling. *The Tiwi of North Australia.* New York: Holt, Rinehart & Winston, Inc., 1962.

Kargman, Marie. "The Revolution in Divorce Law," *The Family Coordinator* 22 (April 1973).

Krishnan, P. "Divorce Tables for Females in the United States," *Journal of Marriage and the Family* 33 (May 1971).

Lasswell, Marcia E., and Thomas E. Lasswell. *Love, Marriage, Family: A Developmental Approach.* Glenview, Ill.: Scott, Foresman and Company, 1973.

Litwick, Eugene. "Divorce Law as Social Control," *Social Forces* (March 1956).

15. Developing Styles for Singles

Pettigrew, Thomas F. *Profile of the Negro America.* Princeton, N.J.: D. Van Nostrand Company, Inc., 1964.

Schulz, David A. *Coming Up Black: Patterns of Ghetto Socialization.* Englewood Cliffs, N.J.: Prentice-Hall, Inc., 1968.

————, **and Robert A. Wilson,** eds. *Readings on the Changing Family.* Englewood Cliffs, N.J.: Prentice-Hall, Inc., 1973.

Stergis, Stanley G. "Understanding Grief," *Mennenger Perspective* (April/ May 1970).

Westman, Jack, and David W. Kline. "Divorce Is a Family Affair," *Family Law Quarterly* 5 (March 1971).

16. Communes and Multiple Marriages

Bettelheim, Bruno. *Children of the Dream.* New York: The Macmillan Company, 1969.

Constantine, Larry, and Joan Constantine. "Where Is Marriage Going?" *The Futurist* (April 1970).

Ellis, Havelock. *Studies in the Psychology of Sex.* Vol. VI: *Sex in Relation to Society.* Philadelphia: F. A. Davis Co., 1961.

Fairfield, Richard. *Communes, U.S.A.: A Personal Tour.* Baltimore: Penguin Books Inc., 1971.

Kinkade, Kathleen. *A Walden Two Experiment: The First Five Years of Twin Oaks Community.* New York: William Morrow & Co., Inc., 1972.

Leon, Dan. *The Kibbutz: A New Way of Life.* New York: Pergamon Press, Inc., 1970.

Lockwood, Maren Carden. *Oneida: From Community to Corporation.* Baltimore: The Johns Hopkins Press, 1971.

Otto, Herbert A., ed. *The Family in Search of a Future.* New York: Appleton-Century-Crofts, 1970.

Rimmer, Robert. *Adventures in Loving.* New York: The New American Library Inc., 1973.

Skinner, B. F. *Walden Two.* New York: The Macmillan Company, 1948.

Spiro, Melford. *The Children of the Kibbutz.* Cambridge: Harvard Univerisity Press, 1958.

Talmon, Yonina. *Kibbutz and Community.* Cambridge: Harvard University Press, 1972.

Zablocki, Benjamin. *The Joyful Community.* Baltimore: Penguin Books Inc., 1971.

17. Fantasies, Forecasts and Trends

Bennis, Warren, and Philip Slater. *The Temporary Society.* New York: Harper & Row, 1969.

Benson, Leonard. *Fatherhood: A Sociological Perspective.* New York: Random House, Inc., 1970.

Cooper, David. *The Death of the Family.* New York: Vintage Books, A Division of Random House, Inc., 1971.

Faber, Bernard. *Family: Organization and Interaction.* San Francisco: Chandler Publishing Co., 1964.

Heiss, Jerold. *Family Roles and Interaction.* Chicago: Rand McNally & Co., 1968.

Hill, Reuben. "The American Family of the Future," *Journal of Marriage and the Family* 26 (1964).

O'Neill, George, and Nena O'Neill. *Open Marriage: A New Life Style for Couples.* New York: M. Evans & Co., Inc., 1972.

Rogers, Carl. *Becoming Partners: Marriage and Its Alternatives.* New York: Delacorte Press, 1972.

Tarus, Carol, and Toby Jayaratne. "What 120,000 Young Women Can Tell You About Sex, Motherhood, Menstruation, Housework—and Men," *Redbook* (January 1973).

INDEX

Intrauterine device (*cont.*)
  choice of, 159
  side effects of, 154

J

Jealousy:
  coping with, 257–59
  in in-law conflicts, 60
  love-sex relations, at Twin
    Oaks, 359
Jesus Christ, 217, 218
Job market, and women, 231
John the Baptist, 350
Joint Account System, The
    (Duvall & Hill), for income
    spending, 295
Jourard, Sidney M., 373
  on physical contact, touching,
    42–43
Judeo-Christian tradition, modern
    society, influence on, 25–26

K

Kanter, Rosabeth, on communes,
    future of, 386
Kargman, Marie, on divorce,
    access to, 317
Kassel, Victor, polygamy, for
    persons over sixty, 384
Katchadourian, Herant, 130, 159
  on oral-genital sex, 181
  on post partum blues, 138
  on sex drives, 206
  on sexual organs, 113
  on sexual pleasure, 186
Kibbutz, Israeli, 353
Kierkegaard, Soren, on loss of
    self, 249
Kinkade, Kathleen:
  on jealousy at Twin Oaks, 359
  on labor system, Twin Oaks,
    356
  on sexual relations, Twin Oaks,
    358–59
Kinsey, Alfred, 175
  on homosexuality, 191
Kinsey studies, on extramarital
    sexual relationships, 11
Kinship:
  socioeconomic differences in,
    298
  system, American, 298
Kirkendall, Lester, on sexual
    morality, 81
Kissing:
  erotic, 181
  genital, 181
Klemer, Richard, 58
  on family income spending, 296
Krishman, P., on women, divorces
    among, 315

L

Labia majora, anatomy of, 117,
    118
Labia minora, anatomy of, 117,
    118
Labor:
  division of, in marriage, 243–45
  in childbirth, 135–37
Labor-credit system, Twin Oaks,
    356
Ladner, Joyce, on lower-class
    sexual behavior, 93
Laing, R. D., 51–52
Lamaze, Bernard, 137
Lamaze Method (childbirth), 137
Landis, Judson T., on dating
    sequence, 85–86
Landis, Mary G., on dating
    sequence, 85–86
Language, as communication,
    40–41
Laparoscope, 162
Laparoscopic sterilization, 161–62
Lawrence, Raymond, on sexual
    contacts outside marriage,
    256–57
LeClair, Linda, 100
Leveling, between partners, 75–76
Limelighters, The, 360
Lippes Loop, 154
Litwack, Eugene, on divorce laws,
    316
Living together, costs and benefits,
    100–105 (*See also*
    Cohabitation)
Lockwood, Maren, on "complex
    marriage," 352
Lollards, 350
Lama Foundation, The, 354
Lord of the Files (Golding), 27
Love:
  agapetic, 217, 218, 222
  as basic human need, 19–20,
    21–23
  Christian concept of, 217–18
  erotic, 222
  as intimate disclosure, 3
  and jealousy, 257–58
  nature of, 4
  and romance, 28–29
  romantic type, 91–92
  and sexual desire, 216
  and sexuality, cross-cultural
    perspective, 224–25
  and sexuality, in West,
    historical perspective, 216–24
Lovemaking, 175, 180–86
  roles, 186
  setting for, 177–78
Lunde, Donald T.:
  on sex drive, 206
  on sexual organs, 113
Luther, Martin, on marriage, 221

M

Male:
  anatomy of, 114
  contraceptive research, 160–61
  divorced, life style of, 332
  dominance, in dating system,
    90–91
  infertility, tests for, 141
  labor, division of in marriage,
    243
  sexual response of, 121–24
  venereal disease, symptoms, 168
  as widowers, statistics, 336
Malinowski, Bronislaw, on sex, 195
Mallus Malefarum, 223–24
Marijuana, sex drives, effect on,
    206
Marriage:
  in America today, 4–12, 225–36
  career pattern, 244
  childless, social criticism of,
    271–72
  companionship pattern, 243–44
  conflict, from routine, 300
  contemporary changes in, 8–9,
    231–36
  costs and benefits of
    traditional, 99–105
  defined, 225–26
  dissolution of, 311–12, 322
  expectations of, 61, 247–48
  experimentation, 379–84
  failure rates, 11–12
  family-plus-partial-career
    pattern, 244–45
  first, general age for, 375–76
  group-, in communes, 354
  income management, 292–95
  and infertility, 140–42
  legal rights in, 227
  mate selection, 97
  maternity-homemaking pattern,
    243
  in Middle Ages, 223
  middle years period of, 300–302
  monogamous, 227
  open, future of, 382
  and parenthood, 269–70
  for procreation, 229–30
  role segregation pattern, 245
  roles, reversal of, 381
  romantic love complex in, 6–8
  outside sexual contacts, 256–57
  trial, and parenthood
    preparation, 277–78
  varieties of, 230–31
  vows, 241
Marriage contract, 241
  of Harriett Mary Cody and
    Harvey Joseph Sadis, 260–65
  nominative definition of, 29
  specially written, 259–66